Security and Conflict in East Asia

This volume has been prompted by the high tensions on the Korean peninsula and between the People's Republic of China and Japan in recent years. In the context of increasingly tense China-US strategic rivalry, the ever present potential for conflict on the Korean peninsula and over Taiwan, the absence of effective regional institutions and regimes to deal with regional disputes, the emerging arms race in the region, the rise in nationalism, and the absence of crisis management mechanisms, there are many good reasons why the strong potential exists for miscalculation and misperception sparking a regional conflict. Given the presence of nuclear-armed powers in East Asia, namely China, North Korea and the USA, it is also possible that any regional conflict could escalate into a nuclear conflict involving the world's three largest economies: the USA, China and Japan. The security of, and any conflict in, East Asia thus has tremendous implications for global security.

The handbook is divided into four parts:

- The introductory section includes chapters which set the context, explain the history of international relations in East Asia, and examine the phenomenon of the regional arms race.
- A series of chapters focusing on China, examining China's military modernization, its relationship with the USA, and the various territorial disputes in which it has been involved.
- A section on Japan and North and South Korea, looking at the security challenges facing Japan and the Korean peninsula.
- A concluding section that examines the future role of China and the USA in East Asia, as well as the prospects for managing security in the region.

The contributing authors are all experts in their respective fields, and all share an abiding concern about developments in East Asia. Their contributions aim to assist in a better understanding of the issues, to suggest possible solutions, and draw attention to the need for diplomacy, confidence-building measures, crisis management mechanisms and other measures to prevent conflict.

Andrew T. H. Tan is Associate Professor, University of New South Wales, Australia.

Security and Conflict in East Asia

Edited by
Andrew T. H. Tan

LONDON AND NEW YORK

First published 2015
by Routledge

2 Park Square, Milton Park, Abingdon, Oxfordshire OX14 4RN
52 Vanderbilt Avenue, New York, NY 10017

Routledge is an imprint of the Taylor & Francis Group, an informa business

First issued in paperback 2018

Copyright © 2015 Taylor & Francis

The right of the editor to be identified as the author of the editorial material, and of the authors for their individual chapters, has been asserted in accordance with sections 77 and 78 of the Copyright, Designs and Patents Act 1988.

All rights reserved. No part of this book may be reprinted or reproduced or utilised in any form or by any electronic, mechanical, or other means, now known or hereafter invented, including photocopying and recording, or in any information storage or retrieval system, without permission in writing from the publishers.

Notice:
Product or corporate names may be trademarks or registered trademarks, and are used only for identification and explanation without intent to infringe.

Library of Congress Cataloging in Publication Data
A catalog record for this book has been requested

ISBN: 978-1-85743-717-1 (hbk)
ISBN: 978-1-857-43977-9 (pbk)

Typeset in Bembo
by Taylor & Francis Books

Contents

List of tables		vii
Foreword		viii
The editors and contributors		ix

PART I
Introduction   1

1   The prospects for conflict in East Asia   3
ANDREW T. H. TAN

2   The international relations of East Asia from a historical perspective   15
ANDREA BENVENUTI

3   Arms racing in East Asia   24
ANDREW T. H. TAN

PART II
China   35

4   China's naval modernization and its impact on Asian Security   37
NAN LI

5   China's East Asia policy since 2009   51
NICHOLAS KHOO

6   US–China strategic rivalry in East Asia: trouble ahead?   60
ROBERT SUTTER

7   The pivot and Peking: the US response to China in East Asia   71
RICHARD A. BITZINGER

8   Stuck over the barren rocks: the Diaoyu/Senkaku Islands dispute and Sino–Japanese relations   81
JINGDONG YUAN

9   China's fluid assertiveness in the South China Sea dispute   91
MINGJIANG LI AND LOH MING HUI DYLAN

10	China and the Strait of Malacca JUSTIN V. HASTINGS	102
11	China's strategy towards Taiwan SHERYN LEE	111
12	Taiwan's defence options BENJAMIN SCHREER	121

PART 3
Japan, North Korea and South Korea 131

13	Japan's decline and the consequences for East Asian conflict and cooperation CHRISTOPHER W. HUGHES	133
14	Nationalism and revisionism: hijacking Japan's security and defence policy agenda? AXEL BERKOFSKY	142
15	Japan's defence: Challenges and future directions BRAD WILLIAMS	153
16	Prospects of conflict in Korea: the threat of North Korea's continuing WMD programme and unreformed economy NOLAN THEISEN	164
17	The paradoxes of vulnerability: managing North Korea's threat to regional security ANDREW O'NEIL	172
18	Park Geun-hye, foreign policy innovation and risk on the Korean peninsula JOHN SWENSON-WRIGHT	181
19	North Korea endgame TERENCE ROEHRIG	190

PART 4
Conclusions 201

20	China's future role in East Asia RICHARD WEIXING HU	203
21	The future role of the USA in East Asia PAUL J. SMITH	214
22	Preventing the next war in East Asia ANDREW T. H. TAN	224

Index 233

List of tables

3.1 Selected Major Weapons Systems in East Asia (1990)   30
3.2 Selected Major Weapons Systems in East Asia (2013)   30

Foreword

This volume has been prompted by the high tensions in Korea and between China and Japan. In the context of increasingly tense China–US strategic rivalry, the ever present potential for conflict on the Korean peninsula and over Taiwan, the absence of effective regional institutions and regimes to deal with regional disputes, the emerging arms race in the region, the rise in nationalism, and the absence of crisis management mechanisms, there are many good reasons why the potential for miscalculation and misperception sparking a regional conflict is strong. Given the presence of nuclear-armed powers in East Asia, namely China, North Korea and the USA, it is also possible that any regional conflict could escalate into a nuclear conflict involving the world's three largest economies – the USA, China and Japan.

The contributing authors are all experts in their respective fields, and all share an abiding concern about recent developments in East Asia. The contributors hope to offer a better understanding of the issues, suggest possible solutions, and draw attention to the need for diplomacy, confidence-building measures, crisis management mechanisms and other measures to prevent a slide into open conflict.

This volume has been fully refereed, with the original project proposal and the final manuscript evaluated by two separate referees. The editor is grateful to the two referees for their careful and useful comments, and also to Cathy Hartley, Europa Commissioning Editor at Routledge, who has strongly supported this project. The editor also wishes to thank Professor Peter Shearman (Webster University) for his suggestions and advice, which have improved the quality of this volume.

Andrew T. H. Tan
University of New South Wales
January 2015

The editors and contributors

Andrew T. H. Tan is Associate Professor in the School of Social Sciences, University of New South Wales, Australia. Educated at Sydney University, Cambridge University and the National University of Singapore, Professor Tan is consulted by various governments and think tanks on security, defence and international relations issues. He was formerly Senior Lecturer, Defence Studies, at King's College London, based at the Joint Services Command and Staff College, Watchfield. To date, he has written many articles on various security issues, and is also the author, editor or co-editor of 15 books, including *The Arms Race in Asia* (Routledge, 2014), *East and South-East Asia: International Relations and Security Perspectives* (Routledge, 2013), *Security Strategies in the Asia-Pacific: The United States' 'Second Front' in Southeast Asia* (Palgrave Macmillan, 2011 – nominated for the Asia Society Bernard Schwartz Book Award), *US Strategy Against Global Terrorism* (Palgrave Macmillan, 2009), *The Global Arms Trade* (Routledge, 2010), *A Handbook of Terrorism and Insurgency in Southeast Asia* (Edward Elgar, 2007), and others. *A Handbook of US–China Relations* (Edward Elgar) is forthcoming in 2016.

Andrea Benvenuti is a senior lecturer in European Studies and International Relations at the School of Social Sciences, Faculty of Arts and Social Sciences, University of New South Wales, Australia. His research interests lie in the field of post-1945 international history with a strong focus on Cold War diplomacy. He is currently working on two projects: the first focuses on Australia's responses to the end of British rule in Malaya and Singapore between 1955 and 1963. The second project charts the development of Australia's political, strategic and economic links with South-East Asia in the early 1970s.

Axel Berkofsky is a professor at the University of Pavia, Italy and Senior Associate Research Fellow at the Milan-based Istituto per gli Studi di Politica Internazionale. Previously, Dr Berkofsky was Senior Policy Analyst and Associate Policy Analyst at the Brussels-based European Policy Centre, and Research Fellow at the Brussels-based European Institute for Asian Studies. Dr Berkofsky has published more than 200 papers, articles and essays in journals, newspapers and magazines and has lectured and taught at numerous think tanks, research institutes and universities in Europe and Asia. He is also a board member of the Executive Committee at the Stockholm-based European Japan Advanced Research Network and a senior advisor at the Brussels-based EU-Asia Centre. He was previously a freelance journalist for the Tokyo-based *Asahi Evening News* and is a regular contributor to the *Asia Times*, the Zurich-based International Security Network and others. His research interests include Japanese and Chinese foreign and security policies, Asian security, EU-Asia relations.

The editors and contributors

Richard A. Bitzinger is a senior fellow and coordinator of the Military Transformations Program at the S. Rajaratnam School of International Studies, Singapore, where his work focuses on security and defence issues relating to the Asia-Pacific region, including military modernization and force transformation, regional defence industries and local armaments production, and weapons proliferation. He has written several monographs and book chapters, and his articles have appeared in such journals as *International Security*, the *Journal of Strategic Studies, Orbis, China Quarterly*, and *Survival*. He is the author of *Towards a Brave New Arms Industry?* (Oxford University Press, 2003), 'Come the Revolution: Transforming the Asia-Pacific's Militaries', *Naval War College Review* (Fall 2005), and 'Military Modernization in the Asia-Pacific: Assessing New Capabilities', *Asia's Rising Power* (NBR, 2010). He is also the editor of *The Modern Defense Industry: Political, Economic and Technological Issues* (Praeger, 2009). Bitzinger was previously an associate professor at the Asia-Pacific Center for Security Studies, Honolulu, Hawaii, and has also worked for the RAND Corporation, the Center for Strategic and Budgetary Affairs, and the US Government. In 1999–2000 he was a senior fellow at the US Atlantic Council. He holds a master's degree from the Monterey Institute of International Affairs, USA and has pursued additional postgraduate studies at the University of California, USA.

Justin V. Hastings is a senior lecturer in International Relations and Comparative Politics in the Department of Government and International Relations at the University of Sydney, Australia. From 2008 to 2010 he was an assistant professor at Georgia Tech's Sam Nunn School of International Affairs. His research focuses on the structure and behaviour of clandestine organizations, including terrorist groups, maritime piracy syndicates, organized crime rings, insurgent movements, black and grey markets, and nuclear proliferation networks, primarily in East Asia. His book, *No Man's Land: Globalization, Territory and Clandestine Groups in Southeast Asia*, was published by Cornell University Press in 2010. Dr Hastings received an AB in Public and International Affairs from Princeton University, USA and a PhD in political science from the University of California, USA.

Richard Weixing Hu is a professor in the Department of Politics and Public Administration, University of Hong Kong. He received a BL in international politics from Peking University, an MA from the School of Advanced International Studies, Johns Hopkins University, and a PhD in political science from the University of Maryland, College Park. He was a John M. Olin fellow in national security studies at Harvard University and an IGCC postdoctoral fellow at the University of California, USA. He held teaching and research positions in the USA at the Monterey Institute of International Studies, the University of Detroit, University of Georgia, and Uppsala University, Sweden. He was a CNAPS visiting fellow at the Brookings Institution, USA, in 2007–08. He has published widely on East Asian international relations, China's foreign relations, Asian regionalism and institution building, and cross-Strait relations.

Christopher W. Hughes is Professor of International Politics and Japanese Studies, and Chair of the Department of Politics and International Studies, University of Warwick, UK. He was formerly a research associate at the University of Hiroshima; Asahi Shimbun Visiting Professor of Mass Media and Politics, University of Tokyo, Japan; and Edwin O. Reischauer Visiting Professor of Japanese Studies, Department of Government, Harvard University. His most recent publications include *Japan's Remilitarisation* (Routledge, 2009) and *Japan's Re-emergence as a 'Normal' Military Power* (Oxford University Press, 2004). His articles have appeared in journals such as *Survival, Journal of Japanese Studies, International*

Affairs, Orbis, Security Dialogue, Pacific Affairs, Asian Survey, Review of International Political Economy, and *Journal of Strategic Studies.* He is currently President of the British Association of Japanese Studies, and Joint Editor of *The Pacific Review.*

Nicholas Khoo (PhD Columbia University, MA Johns Hopkins University, BA University of California) is Senior Lecturer in the Department of Politics at the University of Otago, New Zealand. His research interests cover Chinese foreign policy, the international relations of Asia, international relations theory, and security studies. Dr Khoo's most recent publication is *Collateral Damage: Sino-Soviet Rivalry and the Termination of the Sino–Vietnamese Alliance* (New York: Columbia University Press, 2011).

Sheryn Lee is currently a PhD candidate in strategic studies at the Strategic and Defence Studies Centre, the Australian National University, and a WSD-Handa Non-Resident Fellow at CSIS Pacific Forum, USA. She was previously a Benjamin Franklin fellow at the University of Pennsylvania, USA, where she holds an AM in political science. She is additionally the project officer for the Australian Research Council linkage project, 'The Languages of Security in the Asia-Pacific'. In 2011 she was the inaugural Robert O'Neill scholar at the International Institute for Strategic Studies in Singapore and in 2010 she was a T.B. Millar scholar at the Australian National University.

Nan Li is an associate professor in the Strategic Research Department of the US Naval War College and a member of its China Maritime Studies Institute. He was a John M. Olin fellow at Harvard University, and a senior fellow at the US Institute of Peace, at the S. Rajaratnam School of International Studies, and at the East Asian Institute of National University of Singapore. He has published numerous journal articles and book chapters and several monographs and edited volumes on Chinese security and military policy. Professor Li received a PhD in political science from the Johns Hopkins University, USA.

Mingjiang Li is an associate professor at the S. Rajaratnam School of International Studies (RSIS) at the Nanyang Technological University, Singapore. He is also the coordinator of the China programme and the coordinator of the MSc in Asian Studies programme at the RSIS. He received his PhD in political science from Boston University, USA. His main research interests include China's diplomatic history, Sino-US relations, Asia–Pacific security, and domestic sources of China's foreign policy. He is the author (and editor and co-editor) of nine books. His recent books are *Mao's China and the Sino-Soviet Split* (Routledge, 2012) and *Soft Power: China's Emerging Strategy in International Politics* (Rowman & Littlefield, 2009). He has published papers in various peer-reviewed journals including *Global Governance, Cold War History, Journal of Contemporary China,* the *Chinese Journal of International Politics, China: An International Journal, China Security, Security Challenges,* and the *International Spectator.*

Loh Ming Hui Dylan is a research analyst in the Dean's office at the S. Rajaratnam School of International Studies (RSIS), Singapore. His research interests include ASEAN-China relations; dramaturgical international relations; norms in ASEAN; and new media and governance. Prior to joining the RSIS, Loh Ming Hui Dylan founded and ran an internet marketing and consulting firm.

Andrew O'Neil is head of the School of Government and International Relations at Griffith University, Australia. He is the author of *Asia, the US and Extended Nuclear Deterrence: Atomic Umbrellas in the Twenty-First Century* (Routledge, 2013) and co-editor (with Bruce Gilley) of *Middle Powers and the Rise of China* (Georgetown University Press, 2014).

The editors and contributors

Terence Roehrig is a professor in national security affairs and Director of the Asia-Pacific Studies Group at the US Naval War College. He is also a research fellow at the Kennedy School at Harvard University, USA in the International Security Program and the project on Managing the Atom. He is the author of two forthcoming books: *Japan, South Korea, and the U.S. Nuclear Umbrella: Extended Deterrence and Nuclear Weapons* (Columbia University Press) and *South Korea's Rise: Power, Economic Development and Foreign Policy* (Cambridge University Press) and co-authored with Uk Heo. He has published articles and book chapters on North Korea's nuclear weapons programme, Korean and East Asian security issues, the US–South Korea alliance, the Northern Limit Line, the South Korean Navy, human rights, and transitional justice. Dr Roehrig received his PhD in political science from the University of Wisconsin-Madison, USA, and is a past president of the Association of Korean Political Studies.

Benjamin Schreer is a senior analyst specializing in defence strategy at the Australian Strategic Policy Institute. Previously, Dr Schreer was the deputy head of the Strategic and Defence Studies Centre at the Australian National University where he taught strategy at graduate level, including in the Military Studies Program at the Australian Command and Staff College. He has held positions as deputy director of the Aspen Institute in Berlin, leader of a research group at Konstanz University, and deputy head of research unit at the German Institute for International and Security Affairs (Stiftung Wissenschaft und Politik) in Berlin. He holds a PhD in political science from Kiel University, Germany. His current research interests are Asian strategic and defence trends as well as Australia's defence policy.

Paul J. Smith is a professor of national security affairs at the US Naval War College. His research focuses primarily on Chinese foreign policy and non-traditional security issues related to Asia. His articles have appeared in *Asian Affairs: An American Review, Contemporary Southeast Asia, Dynamics of Asymmetric Conflict, Fletcher Forum of World Affairs, Harvard Asia-Pacific Review, Jane's Intelligence Review, Journal of Conflict, Security and Development, Journal of Third World Studies, Orbis, Parameters, Studies in Conflict and Terrorism, Survival, Naval War College Review* and *Comparative Strategy*. His edited books include *Human Smuggling: Chinese Migrant Trafficking and the Challenge to America's Immigration Tradition* (Center for Strategic and International Studies, 1997) and *Terrorism and Violence in Southeast Asia: Transnational Challenges to States and Regional Stability* (M.E. Sharpe, 2004). He is the author of *The Terrorism Ahead: Confronting Transnational Violence in the 21st Century* (M. E. Sharpe, 2007). Dr Smith frequently provides commentary for national and international news organizations, including the *International Herald Tribune, Christian Science Monitor, Defense News, Japan Times,* and *World Politics Review,* among others. He obtained his Bachelor of Arts from Washington and Lee University, USA, his Master of Arts from the University of London, UK (School of Oriental and African Studies) and his Juris Doctorate (law) and PhD (political science) from the University of Hawaii, USA.

Robert Sutter is Professor of Practice of International Affairs at the Elliott School of George Washington University, USA. His previous full-time position was Visiting Professor of Asian Studies at the School of Foreign Service, Georgetown University (2001–11). A PhD graduate in history and East Asian languages from Harvard University, Professor Sutter taught part-time for 40 years at Georgetown, George Washington, Johns Hopkins Universities, or the University of Virginia. He has published 19 books, over 200 articles and several hundred government reports dealing with contemporary East Asian and Pacific countries and their relations with the USA. His most recent book is *U.S.-Chinese Relations: Perilous Past, Pragmatic Present* (Rowman and Littlefield, 2010). The third edition of his award-winning survey *Chinese Foreign Relations: Power and Policy since the Cold War* (Rowman & Littlefield) was published in early 2012. Professor Sutter's government career (1968–2001) involved work on Asian and Pacific affairs and US foreign policy. He was the Senior Specialist and Director of the Foreign Affairs and National Defense Division of the Congressional Research Service. He also served as the National Intelligence Officer for East Asia and the Pacific at the US Government's National Intelligence Council, and as the China Division Director at the Department of State's Bureau of Intelligence and Research.

John Swenson-Wright is Senior University Lecturer in Modern Japanese Studies and fellow of Darwin College, Cambridge, UK. He has a BA from Christ Church, Oxford, an MA from SAIS, Johns Hopkins, USA, and a DPhil from St Antony's, Oxford, UK. His publications include *Unequal Allies? United States Security and Alliance Policy Towards Japan, 1945–1960* (Stanford, 2005), *The Best Course Available: A Personal Account of the Secret U.S.–Japan Okinawa Reversion Negotiations* (Hawaii, 2002), (with Ruediger Frank) *Security Issues for Northeast Asia: Korea and East Asia: The Stony Road to Collective Security* (Brill, 2013), and (with Chung-in Moon) *Crisis of Peace and New Leadership in Korea: Lessons of Kim Dae-jung's Legacies* (Yonsei University Press, 2014). He is also Senior Consulting Fellow at Chatham House, responsible for the Japan and Korea programmes, and is a member of the World Economic Forum's Global Agenda Council on Korea.

Nolan Theisen is currently under fellowship at the Regional Centre for Energy Policy Research in Budapest. Prior to this, he worked as a project-based research assistant for the KDI School and was a program associate with The Asia Foundation's Korea office in Seoul. In 2011 he graduated from the School of International Relations and Pacific Studies at the University of California, USA, where he studied international political economy and energy policy. Taking a year's leave of absence, he spent the summer in Washington, DC at the Korea Economic Institute, the autumn in Vienna at the Organization for Security and Co-operation in Europe, and the spring at Yonsei University's GSIS programme. He also attended the Azerbaijan Diplomatic Academy's Baku Summer Energy Program in the summer of 2010.

Brad Williams teaches comparative politics and international relations at the City University of Hong Kong. He is the author of *Resolving the Russo-Japanese Territorial Dispute: Hokkaido-Sakhalin Relations* (Routledge, 2007), and the co-editor of *Japan, Australia and Asia-Pacific Security* (Routledge, 2006) and *Japan in Decline: Fact or Fiction?* (Global Oriental/Brill, 2011). Brad has also published in several internationally refereed journals such as the *Japanese Journal of Political Science*, *Japan Forum*, *Journal of Asian Studies*, *The Pacific Review*, *Journal of East Asian Studies* and *Pacific Affairs*.

Jingdong Yuan is Associate Professor at the Centre for International Security Studies at the University of Sydney. Professor Yuan specializes in Asia-Pacific security, Chinese defence and foreign policy, Sino-Indian relations, and global and regional arms control and nonproliferation issues. Prior to his current appointment, he was Director of the East Asia Nonproliferation Program, James Martin Center for Nonproliferation Studies, Monterey Institute of International Studies. Professor Yuan has also held visiting appointments at the East-West Center, the National University of Singapore and the University of Macau. He is co-editor of *Australia and China at 40* and co-author of *China and India: Cooperation or*

The editors and contributors

Conflict? His work has appeared in *Asian Survey, Asian Perspective, Far Eastern Economic Review, Contemporary Security Policy, International Herald Tribune, International Journal, International Politics, Jane's Intelligence Review, Journal of Contemporary China, Journal of International Affairs, Los Angeles Times, Moscow Times, Nonproliferation Review,* the *Washington Quarterly,* and many edited volumes.

Part I
Introduction

1
The prospects for conflict in East Asia

Andrew T. H. Tan

High tensions in East Asia

The high tensions in East Asia, the highest since the end of the Second World War, have led to fears of open conflict involving the states in the region as well as extra-regional powers, in particular the USA. By early 2013 tensions between North Korea on the one hand, and South Korea, the USA and Japan, on the other, had deteriorated to their worst level since the end of the Korean War in 1953, sparking fears of an accidental war due to North Korea's brinkmanship and political miscalculation (ICG 2013a). Tensions between the People's Republic of China and Japan were also at their highest since the end of the Second World War, due to their dispute over the Diaoyu/Senkaku Islands (Hughes 2013). More seriously, China, the USA and North Korea possess nuclear weapons, and Japan has always been regarded as a threshold nuclear power, as it possesses plutonium stocks generated through its power industry, ballistic missile capability and the technology to rapidly transform itself into a significant nuclear weapons power should it choose to do so (Rublee 2010: 62–63). South Korea could also be forced to develop its own nuclear weapons if the threat from a hostile, aggressive and unpredictable North Korea continues to grow as it develops its nuclear, chemical and biological weapons capabilities, and uses them to coerce South Korea (*New York Times* 2013).

The impact of any regional conflict in East Asia will be significant and global. Any conflict in this region would involve not only states in the region and US allies from further afield, but also quickly escalate into a nuclear conflict, given the superiority that the USA enjoys in terms of conventional warfare capabilities over North Korea, and to a diminishing degree, China, thus forcing them to resort to non-conventional means, such as nuclear weapons, in any major conflict. Indeed, the US strategy of Air-Sea Battle, which involves attacking China's surveillance, intelligence and command systems, are likely to be interpreted by China as attempts to disarm its nuclear strike capability and could thus lead to a quick and unwanted escalation into a nuclear conflict (Schreer 2013).

Moreover, today the centre of the global economy no longer resides in Europe or North America but in Asia, in particular, East Asia. Indeed, three of the key actors in the region, namely the USA, China and Japan, are also the three largest economies in the world, with

South Korea ranked 15th in global terms, according to the World Bank. Any conflict in East Asia will therefore have a profound, global economic impact. Furthermore, the fact that any conflict could escalate into a major war, including nuclear war, means that conflict in East Asia will have global implications as well as uncertain consequences for the international system.

The China–US strategic rivalry

China's economic rise has led to it overtaking Japan in 2010 to become the world's second largest economy (Bloomberg 2010). According to the Organisation for Economic Co-operation and Development, China will overtake the USA as early as 2016 after accounting for price differences (*Financial Times* 2013). This has enabled China to challenge the dominant position of the USA globally as well as in Asia, particularly in China's own strategic backyard, East Asia. Current developments therefore point to fundamental changes in the US-led and Western-dominated international system since the end of the Second World War in 1945. However, as Organski famously observed, the rise of a new great power almost always leads to conflict with the prevailing hegemon, which will not voluntarily or easily yield its dominant position (Organski 1968).

The growing clash of interests was epitomized by a serious confrontation in March 2009, when Chinese ships surrounded a US Navy surveillance vessel, the *Impeccable*, in the South China Sea, which is claimed by China. While China asserted that the vessel had violated Chinese waters, the USA took the position that the South China Sea constitutes international waters and that it had the right to the freedom of navigation within such waters (US Department of State 2012). The USA then sent a naval destroyer to accompany the vessel (*Washington Post* 2009).

China has since taken additional steps to assert its claims to the entire South China Sea, which may have significant offshore oil and gas deposits, and which China perceives as vital for its strategic interests due to the fact that its sea lines of communications traverse these waters. In 2012 China issued new passports depicting disputed territory such as the South China Sea as China's territory, established a new administrative unit in Sansha in the disputed Paracel Islands and announced that Hainan maritime authorities would now board and search ships entering disputed maritime areas (Chongkittavon 2012). In March 2013 a People's Liberation Army (PLA) Navy amphibious task force of four vessels were deployed to the southernmost tip of China's claimed territory in the South China Sea in an unprecedented show of force designed to demonstrate China's determination to enforce its sovereignty over the disputed area. The task force visited James Shoal, which is 1,800 km from China but only 80 km from Malaysia (*South China Morning Post* 2013).

Aaron Friedberg expressed the fears of many in the USA when he asserted in 2011 that should current trends continue, the USA would lose the geopolitical contest with China. He argued that 'if through inadvertence, error or deliberate decision we permit China as presently constituted to dominate Asia, our prosperity, security and hopes of promoting the further spread of freedom will be seriously impaired'. Furthermore, according to Friedberg, should the USA fail to halt China and allow it to dominate Asia, China would be able to bring Taiwan to terms as well as be freed from having to defend its maritime periphery. This would enable China to advance its interests in the rest of the world, thus challenging US global dominance (2011: 7–8).

The mistrust and suspicion of China is reflected in the annual reports to the US Congress emanating from the Office of the Secretary of Defense concerning military and security developments in China. These reports, submitted since 2000, have steadily become more alarmist in the Office's assessment of the threat from China. Its 2013 report, for instance, accused China's government and military of cyber-spying. According to the report, 'China is using its computer network exploitation capability to support intelligence collection against the U.S. diplomatic, economic and industrial base sectors that support U.S. national defense programs' (2013: 36). Furthermore, China has also allegedly been active in industrial espionage, utilizing its intelligence services and 'employed other illicit approaches that involve violations of U.S. law and export controls' (ibid.: 12).

The USA has also noted with concern that 'China's anti-access/area-denial focus appears oriented toward restricting or controlling access to China's periphery, including the western Pacific', as such anti-access capabilities would restrict the ability of US forces to intervene in regional flashpoints in Asia (US Office of the Secretary of Defense 2010: 29). These include Korea, Taiwan, the Senkaku Islands and the South China Sea. This has been described by a US analyst, employing Cold War analogy, as 'broadly analogous to the sea-denial force that the Soviet Union developed during the Cold War to deny U.S. use of the sea or counter U.S. forces participating in a NATO-Warsaw Pact conflict' (O'Rourke 2012: 4–5).

On the part of China, its own rapid economic rise, military modernization, and increasing nationalism have led to mirror images of a hostile and threatening USA. This is reflected in works by PLA officers, such as Colonel Liu Mingfu, whose popular book, *China Dream*, speculated on how China could displace US leadership following the Global Financial Crisis in 2008 (Liu 2010). In 1996 a group of Chinese writers co-authored a nationalist best-seller with the self-explanatory title of *China Can Say No*, in which they were critical of the unfair treatment which they perceived was meted out to China by the USA (Zhang *et al*. 1996). In 2009 another popular book was released entitled *China Is Unhappy*, which took a strident nationalist tone in attacking the West, particularly the USA, for attempting to encroach on Chinese territory such as in the South China Sea (Song *et al*. 2009). In 2012, following high tensions between China and Japan over the disputed Senkaku Islands, a PLA colonel, Dai Xu, openly called for a swift and decisive war between China and Japan, one which would enable China to retrieve territory which it claims to own (Richardson 2013).

For its part, the USA has taken steps to contain China, epitomized by the idea of a concert of democracies in Asia, led by the USA. This emerged in the form of the Trilateral Security Dialogue which began between the USA, Japan and Australia in 2002 (Tow 2008: 3). The conclusion of a strategic partnership agreement between India and the USA in 2006 appeared to complete the process by bringing the world's largest democracy, namely India, into the fold (Carter 2007). Apart from strengthening its alliances in Asia, the USA has in recent years also attempted to neutralize China's growing influence throughout the region. Thus, following his re-election in 2012, President Obama's first foreign visits were to three Asian countries with close ties with China, namely Myanmar, Thailand and Cambodia (*Strategic Comments* 2012).

The USA is also taking steps to increase its military presence and visibility throughout East and South-East Asia. Following President Obama's seminal 'Asia Pivot' speech in Australia in 2011, in which he acknowledged that the Asia-Pacific is now the USA's top strategic priority, it was announced that US troops would be stationed in Australia's Northern Territory (*Daily Telegraph* 2012). This was followed up by the deployment of the USA's newest warships, namely its littoral combat ships, in Singapore (*Straits Times* 2013). In 2012, in an impressive show of force, the USA held the largest ever Rim of the Pacific (RIMPAC) naval exercise in the Western Pacific, involving 42 warships, six submarines, 200 aircraft and

25,000 personnel from 12 countries, including allies such as Australia, Japan and Singapore (*Honolulu Star-Advertiser* 2012).

Recognizing the central strategic and economic importance of East Asia, the USA has maintained the bulk of its military assets in Asia in two countries, namely Japan and South Korea. US forces in Japan totalled 50,000 in 2013, with two key naval bases at Sasebo and Yokosuka, where an aircraft carrier and nine other principal surface combatants are based, as well as one Marine division. US forces in South Korea totalled 28,000 in 2013. Located nearby in the western Pacific is the USA Pacific Command in Hawaii, where five aircraft carriers are based (IISS 2014: 55–56). The USA has pledged that it would deploy its latest weapons systems in the Asia-Pacific as part of its strategic shift to the region. These would include P-8 anti-submarine warfare aircraft, Virginia-class nuclear-powered submarines, littoral combat ships, and F-35 joint strike fighters (*Defense News* 2012). Accompanying the more forceful military presence in East Asia and the Western Pacific, the US Air Force and Navy is also developing a joint warfighting doctrine known as Air-Sea Battle. This new strategy appears to be aimed at countering China's anti-access capabilities and to ensure that US forces would continue to retain freedom of movement in the Western Pacific (Von Tol *et al.* 2010: 95).

For its part, China's growing military capabilities have given it much greater confidence in asserting China's claims to disputed maritime territory throughout East and South-East Asia. In 2013 China deployed 2.33m. troops and over 15,000 tanks and armoured personnel carriers, the largest armed forces in the world. Its air force, including naval aviation, had over 2,400 combat aircraft, including Russian-built Su-30MKK and Su-27 combat aircraft as well as locally built J-10 (regarded as being similar to the US F-16 Fighting Falcon) and J-11 (China's imitation of the Su-27) combat aircraft (IISS 2014: 235–236). The rapid development of its military capabilities was demonstrated by the revelation in 2010 of its advanced development of the J-20 stealth combat aircraft, which is similar to the next-generation US joint strike fighter (*DefenceTalk* 2011). The navy's development, however, has been even more impressive. In 2013 China deployed 70 principal surface combatants, including Russian-made Sovremenny-class destroyers and locally developed Type 054 Jiangkai-class stealth frigates. Its asymmetric anti-access capabilities included 70 submarines and large numbers of mine-warfare ships and missile boats armed with the deadly C-803 anti-ship missile (IISS 2014: 233–234). In 2012 it commissioned its first aircraft carrier, the former Russian *Varyag*, and this was likely to be followed by its own locally built aircraft carriers. It also carried out landing exercises with its new J-15 combat aircraft, which it developed for carrier operations (*Huffington Post* 2012). It has also reportedly developed a range of cruise missiles, including the DF-21D, which has been dubbed the 'carrier-killer' as it is capable of striking US aircraft carriers (*The Australian* 2013). In addition, with the development of five nuclear-powered ballistic missile submarines, each capable of launching 12 ballistic missiles with a range of 7,400 km, China has also secured an effective second-strike nuclear capability (Reuters 2012).

Thus, China increasingly has the capability of challenging the dominant position of the USA in East Asia. Its anti-access and nuclear strike capabilities could, in time, effectively keep the US forces at bay should conflict break out over Taiwan, with Japan, or on the Korean peninsula. Would the USA risk a nuclear exchange to defend its allies in East Asia? China could well calculate, or miscalculate, that it would not do so.

The threat from North Korea

Over the years, North Korea has frequently used brinkmanship as part of its foreign policy. Its modus operandi has been to carry out provocative acts accompanied by threats, and then use this to pressure the USA, South Korea and the international community for concessions and aid. The relief, however, would be short-lived, as North Korea would then cause another crisis in order to obtain more concessions. Over the years, North Korea has carried out a number of attacks and provocations, such as the bombing of a South Korean civilian airliner in 1987 which killed 115 people (*Korea Times* 2009). More recently, in 2010 a South Korean naval corvette, the *Choenan*, was sunk by a torpedo fired from a North Korean midget submarine, killing 46 sailors (CNN 2010a). This was followed by artillery shelling of Yeonpyeong, an island in South Korea close to the maritime border (Reuters 2010).

The unpredictable and dangerous behaviour of the North Korean regime has become a fact of life on the Korean peninsula, but the death of Kim Jong-il in December 2011 raised apprehensions over possible instability as he was succeeded by his young and inexperienced son, Kim Jong-un, who needed to demonstrate his leadership credentials and stamp his authority over a near-totalitarian state. Still, no one expected the young Kim to push brinkmanship to dangerous levels in 2012–13.

In April 2012 North Korea carried out a ballistic missile test, which it described as a satellite launch. The test, which failed, was condemned by the international community as the United Nations (UN) had banned the country from carrying out such tests after its second nuclear test in 2009 (*The Guardian* 2013). The failed test was, however, followed by a successful one in December 2012, demonstrating North Korea's steady but relentless development of ballistic missile capabilities (BBC 2012a). After this success, North Korea carried out its third nuclear test in February 2013. Following international condemnation and a fresh round of UN sanctions against it, North Korea unilaterally abrogated the armistice that had ended the Korean War in 1953, thus returning the Korean peninsula to a state of war (Bloomberg 2013).

Currently, however, the USA and South Korea are less inclined towards an easy reconciliation. As each crisis developed and then receded, North Korea has gained the time and space to develop its nuclear weapons as well as ballistic missile capabilities. Every succeeding crisis has thus become more dangerous, as North Korea has exhibited increasingly aggressive and provocative behaviour. Thus, President Obama warned in 2012, in response to the *Choenan* and Yeonpyeong incidents, that 'the old pattern of provocation that then gets attention and somehow insists on the world purchasing good behaviour from them – that pattern is broken' (BBC 2012b). In March 2013 the USA and South Korea carried out large-scale military exercises designed to enhance deterrence against North Korea, leading to more bellicose threats of retaliation. South Korea's President Park Geun-hye also declared that if North Korea carried out an attack similar to the Yeonpyeong incident, South Korea 'would make them pay' (Salon 2013).

These developments have raised the possibility of conflict. Therefore, the International Crisis Group warned in March 2013 that the risk of open conflict on the Korean peninsula had risen dramatically, due to possible miscalculation leading to inadvertent escalation (ICG 2013a). Despite its failed economy and military technology that lags far behind that of South Korea, the USA and Japan, North Korea does possess a range of deadly asymmetric capabilities. For instance, it has some 21,000 pieces of artillery, the bulk of which are aimed at Seoul, the capital of South Korea, located just 40 km from the border between the two countries. This massed artillery capability would enable North Korea to destroy Seoul in the initial phase of a conflict, inflicting a huge number of casualties. North Korea also has a large fleet of 72 submarines, including 50 midget submarines, which are effective anti-access weapons systems as they are hard to detect and can prove deadly to large warships, as demonstrated by the *Choenan* incident (IISS 2014: 255). Apart from nuclear weapons, North Korea is believed to have developed a range of biological and chemical weapons (Han 2010: 100). North Korea has also developed ballistic missiles, including the Taepodong-2 missile which has a maximum range of 6,000 km, putting South Korea, Japan and any US military facilities in the West Pacific within reach. It is also developing longer-range ballistic missiles that could eventually reach Hawaii and the US West Coast (Foxnews 2009).

Even if war does not immediately break out, North Korea's provocative actions, coupled with its development of nuclear weapons and long-range ballistic missiles, are destabilizing, as they undermine US powers of deterrence on behalf of its allies in East Asia. Once the US homeland can be attacked using nuclear missiles, the USA could be deterred from intervening to support its allies, namely South Korea and Japan. To prevent nuclear blackmail and coercion by North Korea, a plausible outcome could be the development and acquisition of nuclear weapons by both South Korea and Japan in order to shore up their deterrent capabilities. Such a scenario would be a repeat of Europe during the Cold War, when both Britain and France developed their own independent nuclear deterrent capabilities owing to doubts about whether the USA would really risk the destruction of the US homeland in order to save Western Europe from an invasion by the Soviet Union and Warsaw Pact countries. The emergence of a nuclear-armed East Asia, however, would be very destabilizing, particularly given the presence of historical and territorial grievances as well as the absence of institutional and normative constraints.

Japan and China tensions

Since the signing of the Mutual Security Treaty in 1951 after the conclusion of the Second World War, Japan has emerged as the principal ally of the USA in Asia, and the lynchpin of the US position in East Asia. Recent tensions between Japan and China, however, have raised the possibility of real armed conflict, which would probably involve the USA, as it is treaty-bound to defend Japan if it was attacked. Indeed, by early 2013 relations deteriorated to such an extent that Christopher Hughes described it as 'the most serious for Sino–Japanese relations in the post-war period in terms of the risk of militarised conflict' (Hughes 2013). The high tensions between Japan and China revolve around the dispute over the Senkaku/Diaoyutai Islands. Japan, which currently administers the islands, has argued that the islands used to be uninhabited and were therefore incorporated into Japan in 1895 (Japanese Ministry of Foreign Affairs 2013). China has asserted that historically the islands formed part of the Chinese territory, and were administered by Taiwan.

The emerging potential of oil and gas resources in the East China Sea has raised the stakes of the dispute. Moreover, the islands are close to strategically important shipping lanes and the seas around them offer rich fishing grounds. In recent years there have been a number of increasingly serious incidents over the islands. In September 2010 collisions between a Chinese fishing vessel and two Japanese coastguard vessels near the Senkaku Islands led to the detention of the crew of the fishing vessel by Japan. China cut off ministerial contacts, thousands of Chinese tourists cancelled their trips to Japan and a concert by a popular Japanese band in Shanghai was cancelled. Under pressure from China, Japan soon released the vessel's crew and captain without charge (BBC 2010). However, Japan and the USA responded by holding joint military exercises which simulated the retaking of an island by enemy force. These exercises, known as Keen Sword, have been held annually since 2010, with the one taking place in November 2012 involving 44,000 troops from both countries, in a clear message of deterrence to China (*IHT Rendezvous* 2013).

In September 2012 the Japanese government purchased the disputed islands from its private Japanese owners, an action which led to a wave of emotive anti-Japanese protests in China, the temporary closure of many Japanese-owned factories and businesses as Chinese boycotted Japanese-made goods such as motor vehicles, and the cancellation by Chinese tourists of holidays in Japan (ABC News 2012). These developments not only demonstrated the strength of popular nationalist sentiment in China, but also the fact that China's rising nationalism is strongly tinged with anti-Japanese sentiment. This is not surprising given the vigour with which China's education, propaganda and media organizations have promoted anti-Japanese sentiment, with a constant bombardment of documentaries and movies reminding the Chinese population about wartime Japanese atrocities and promoting the perception that Japan remains a dangerous, war-mongering power with imperialist designs on China and the rest of Asia (Nasr 2013).

China's anti-Japanese nationalism and assertive behaviour have led to a growing desire by Japan not to be humiliated by China or South Korea, or to be threatened by North Korea. This has underpinned the steady rightward drift in Japanese domestic politics, leading to the ascension of Shinzo Abe as Prime Minister of Japan in December 2012. Abe has argued that in order to prevent China from imposing its dominance in East and South-East Asia, Japan would have to augment its military capabilities, as well as deepen security alliances with other democracies. Abe described his Cold War-style containment alliance strategy as a 'Democratic Security Diamond', echoing calls in conservative circles in the USA for a concert of democracies in the Asia-Pacific to deal with a rising China (Abe 2012).

For its part, China has become increasingly confident that the balance of power, particularly in East Asia, is shifting in its favour and that it could now assert its claims in the East China Sea more forcefully (ICG 2013b). In recent years China has carried out a number of air and sea incursions in the disputed area around the Senkaku Islands, using fishing, maritime patrol boats, naval vessels and its air force, leading to dangerous confrontations with Japan's military forces. China's air and sea intrusions have led, for instance, to the frequent scrambling of Japan's F-15 combat aircraft to intercept Chinese maritime patrol aircraft which have overflown what Japan regards as its territory (NBC News 2013).

In September 2012 the USA assembled two carrier battle groups as well as a Marine Corps task force in the Western Pacific, as the dispute over the Senkaku Islands escalated (*Time* 2012). In January 2013 Chinese warships locked their fire-control radars onto a Japanese destroyer, a provocative act that could have led to open war had the Japanese destroyer responded by firing first (*Japan Times* 2013). By early 2013 it had become obvious that tensions were at their highest level since the end of the Second World War, as the danger of accidental war due to miscalculation had greatly increased. In late 2013 China unilaterally declared an 'air-defence identification zone' around the Senkaku Islands, prompting the USA to warn China that such actions increased the danger of military conflict and that the US–Japan Mutual Defense Treaty applied to the islands (Gertz 2013). Indeed, the USA flew B-52 bombers over the islands in response to this provocation and further declared that it would stand by Japan if it was attacked. Japan has responded to China's assertiveness by developing a new national security strategy involving a military build-up, including the development of amphibious warfare capabilities (*The Economist* 2013). In response, China accused Japan of posing a serious risk to global peace by reviving the militaristic spirit that provoked the Second World War (*The Telegraph* 2014). Thus, the International Crisis Group has warned that 'despite expressions by both governments that they wish to avoid a war, potential for escalation has increased and there is deepening pessimism on both sides over the prospects of a peaceful settlement' (ICG 2013b).

The Taiwan problem

The Taiwan problem is a legacy of China's civil war after 1945 and the subsequent Cold War, which led to the USA intervening to prevent the reunification of Taiwan with China when it signed the Mutual Defence Treaty with Taiwan in 1954. The Taiwan issue remained dormant as China focused on economic modernization after 1978, but it was bound to resurface as China grew stronger economically and militarily. For China, Taiwan is an emotive nationalist cause, as it is regarded as territory which was 'lost' due to foreign imperialism. As Zhu Bangzao, a senior Chinese Foreign Ministry official stated, 'no force can stand in the way' of eventual reunification between Taiwan and China, and further asserted that any declaration of independence by Taiwan would be regarded as a declaration of war (Zhu 2001).

Tensions in the Taiwan Strait worsened following the tenure of the pro-independence Democratic Progressive Party (DPP) led by President Chen Shui-bian from 2000 to 2008, as Chen appeared to be making moves towards independence. China responded by passing the Anti-Secession Law in 2005, which threatened the use of force should Taiwan declare independence. Indeed, Article 4 also stated that 'accomplishing the great task of reunifying the motherland is the sacred duty of all Chinese people, the Taiwan compatriots included' (*People's Online Daily* 2005). However, tensions abated after the Kuomintang (KMT), led by Ma Ying-jeou, won the presidential elections in 2008 and 2012. Ma tapped into popular concerns by Taiwanese over rising tensions with China by offering a clear alternative to the DPP. His policy was to reduce tensions by engaging China based on the 'One China' principle which the KMT and Chinese Communist Party (CCP) both share. Taiwan thus resumed cross-Strait dialogue with China and also signed a free trade agreement in 2010, which has paved the way for further economic integration between the two economies (CNN 2010b).

While tensions eased, the currently stable status quo is deceptive. Taiwan's high economic dependence on China has sparked fears of economic coercion by China should China wish to push more forcefully for reunification. More seriously, there has appeared a growing military imbalance in the Taiwan Strait. This has been due partly to Taiwan's international isolation, which has meant that it has not been able to procure advanced weapons systems or military technology from abroad except from the USA. For its part, the USA has, however, been increasingly reluctant to unduly provoke China by providing advanced weapons systems to Taiwan. The USA no longer has compelling strategic interests in Taiwan and moreover has already recognized that Taiwan is part of China, following the Shanghai Communique in 1972 that paved the way for the normalization of relations between the USA and China. Thus, while the USA has continued to sell defensive arms to Taiwan, such as helicopters, Patriot anti-aircraft missiles and mine-hunting ships in 2010, it rejected Taiwan's request for 66 new F-16C/D Fighting Falcon combat aircraft in 2011, offering instead to upgrade Taiwan's current fleet of ageing F-16A/B combat aircraft (*Washington Post* 2011).

Taiwan's defence capabilities have therefore been eroded on account of its ageing weapons systems, compared to the rapid modernization of China's armed forces and its deployment of ever more sophisticated weapons systems. In 2013 Taiwan's armed forces totalled 290,000, and it possessed about 1,400 tanks and 1,200 armoured personnel carriers, 485 combat aircraft, 26 principle surface warships, 43 missile gunboats, four submarines and 12 principal landing ships. However, the equipment, such as M60A3 main battle tanks and M-113 armoured personnel carriers, are clearly obsolete given that they were first developed in the 1960s. The air force's combat aircraft, comprising Mirage 2000, F-5E Tiger, F-16A/B and the locally developed Ching Kuo, possess the technology of the 1980s. The navy's principal surface warships are also all outdated, the largest of which are four refurbished ex-US Kidd-class destroyers. Taiwan's four submarines consist of two Guppy-class submarines dating back to the Second World War, and two Zwaardvis-class submarines procured from the Netherlands in the 1980s (IISS 2014: 280–282). Furthermore, Taiwan's military manpower will decrease in the coming years as the Ma government has pursued the populist policy of dismantling compulsory military service in favour of an all-volunteer force (*Financial Times* 2012).

China's military capabilities far outclass those of Taiwan, with the gap growing as China has been steadily improving its military technology. This has upset the balance of power in the Taiwan Strait, and has increasingly given China a viable military option with which to coerce Taiwan in the pursuit of reunification. More seriously, Taiwan is hostage to China's domestic politics, given the rise of nationalism in China and the fact that Taiwan is a ready-made nationalist rallying call. Indeed, China has repeatedly made it clear that it will use force if necessary because reunification is considered to be non-negotiable. These are no empty threats, as the very legitimacy of the CCP depends on its ability to complete the nationalist task of recovering all Chinese territories 'lost' to imperialist invasions.

Conclusion

The increasingly tense China–US strategic rivalry, high tensions between China and Japan, tensions in the Korean peninsula and the potential conflict over Taiwan, coupled with the absence of effective regional institutions and regimes in dealing with regional disputes, have complicated the strategic picture. Any one of these tensions could escalate in an unpredictable manner, due to uncontrolled nationalism, brinkmanship and sheer miscalculation into a regional conflict involving Japan, the USA, China, Taiwan as well as US allies from further afield. Given the presence of nuclear-armed powers in East Asia, namely China, North Korea and the USA, it is also possible that any regional conflict would quickly escalate into a nuclear conflict, as the conventional superiority of the USA and its allies could force North Korea and China into resorting to weapons of mass destruction. Unfortunately, the absence of crisis management mechanisms and the presence of misperceptions mean that an accidental war which no state actually wants could occur a result of sheer miscalculation. Such a conflict would cause massive casualties in East Asia, and would also have a devastating global impact as the world's three largest economies, namely the USA, China and Japan would be involved. Preventing conflict emanating from East Asia must now be a primary objective.

Bibliography

ABC News, 'Anti-Japan Protests Spread Across China', *ABC News*, 19 September 2012, www.abc.net.au/news/2012-09-18/anti-japan-protests-spread-across-china/4268494.

Abe, Shinzo, 'Asia's Democratic Security Diamond', *Project Syndicate*, 27 December 2012, www.project-syndicate.org/commentary/a-strategic-alliance-for-japan-and-india-by-shinzo-abe.

British Broadcasting Corporation (BBC), 'Japan Frees Chinese Boat Captain Amid Diplomatic Row', *BBC News*, 24 September 2010, www.bbc.co.uk/news/world-11403241.

British Broadcasting Corporation (BBC), 'North Korea Defies Warning in Rocket Launch Success', *BBC News*, 12 December 2012a, www.bbc.co.uk/news/world-asia-20690338.

British Broadcasting Corporation (BBC), 'North Korea's Provocations Must End, Warn US and Japan', *BBC News*, 30 April 2012b, www.bbc.co.uk/news/world-asia-17903463.

Bloomberg, 'China Overtakes Japan as World's Second Biggest Economy', *Bloomberg*, 16 August 2010, www.bloomberg.com/news/2010-08-16/china-economy-passes-japan-s-in-second-quarter-capping-three-decade-rise.html.

Bloomberg, 'North Korea Fuels Regional Tensions by Quitting Armistice', *Bloomberg*, 9 March 2013, www.bloomberg.com/news/2013-03-08/north-korea-fuels-region-s-tensions-by-quitting-armistice.html.

Carter, Ashton B., 'How Washington Learned to Stop Worrying and Love India's Bomb', *Foreign Affairs*, 10 January 2007, www.foreignaffairs.com/articles/64243/ashton-b-carter/how-washington-learned-to-stop-worrying-and-love-indias-bomb?page=show.

Chongkittavon, Kavi, 'ASEAN-China Conflict on South China Sea Widens', *Mizzima*, 3 December 2012, www.mizzima.com/edop/commentary/8491-asean-china-conflict-on-south-china-sea-widens.html.

CNN, 'Taiwan, China Sign Historic Trade Deal', *CNN*, 29 June 2010a, http://articles.cnn.com/2010-06-29/world/china.taiwan.deal_1_taiwan-strait-china-and-taiwan-chen-yunlin?_s=PM:WORLD.

CNN, 'U.S. Official: N. Korea Torpedo Likely Sunk S. Korean Warship', *CNN*, 26 April 2010b, http://news.blogs.cnn.com/2010/04/26/u-s-official-n-korea-torpedo-likely-sunk-s-korean-warship/.

Daily Telegraph, 'US to Station Troops in Northern Australia as Fears of China's Pacific Presence Grow', 2 February 2012, www.telegraph.co.uk/news/worldnews/australiaandthepacific/8883558/US-to-station-troops-in-northern-Australia-as-fears-of-Chinas-Pacific-presence-grow.html.

DefenceTalk, 'China Reveals New Stealth J20 Jet', 5 January 2011, www.defencetalk.com/china-reveals-new-stealth-j-20-fighter-aircraft-31046/.

Defense News, 'U.S. To Deploy Newest Weapons to Asia-Pacific', 19 December 2012, www.defensenews.com/article/20121219/DEFREG02/312190009/U-S-Deploy-Newest-Weapons-Asia-Pacific.

Financial Times, 'Taiwan Prepares for End of Conscription', 21 November 2012, www.ft.com/intl/cms/s/0/489ed4c4-1eaa-11e2-bebc-00144feabdc0.html#axzz2MvA4XHSE.

Financial Times, 'China Forecast to Overtake U.S. by 2016', 22 March 2013, www.ft.com/intl/cms/s/0/0a3f5794-92b3-11e2-9593-00144feabdc0.html#axzz2Xr3QjahD.

Fox News, 'Fast Facts: A Glance at North Korea's Nuclear Arsenal', *Fox News*, 26 March 2009, www.foxnews.com/story/0,2933,510757,00.html.

Friedberg, Aaron, *A Contest for Supremacy: China, America and the Struggle for Mastery in Asia*, New York: W. W. Norton, 2011.

Gertz, Bill, 'PRC Air Defense Zone Risks Conflict Over Disputed Islands', *Washington Free Beacon*, 25 November 2013.

Han, Yong-sup, 'Arming North Korea', in Andrew T. H. Tan (ed.), *The Global Arms Trade*, London: Routledge, 2010.

Honolulu Star-Advertiser, 'Hawaii Bracing for Largest-Ever RIMPAC Exercise', 23 June 2012.

Huffington Post, 'Liaoning, China's First Aircraft Carrier, Begins Flight Training', 15 October 2012, www.huffingtonpost.com/2012/10/15/liaoning-china-aircraft-carrier_n_1966958.html.

Hughes, Christopher, 'Viewpoints: How Serious are China-Japan Tensions?' *BBC News*, 8 February 2013, www.bbc.co.uk/news/world-asia-21290349.

International Crisis Group (ICG), 'The Korean Peninsula: Flirting With Conflict', 13 March 2013a, www.crisisgroup.org/en/publication-type/alerts/2013/north-korea-the-korean-peninsula-flirting-with-conflict.aspx.

International Crisis Group (ICG), 'Dangerous Waters: China-Japan Relations on the Rocks', Asia Report No. 245, 8 April 2013b, www.crisisgroup.org/en/regions/asia/north-east-asia/china/245-dangerous-waters-china-japan-relations-on-the-rocks.aspx.

International Herald Tribune Rendezvous (IHT Rendezvous), 'Despite Tensions, U.S. and Japan Begin a New Set of War Games', 4 November 2013, http://rendezvous.blogs.nytimes.com/2012/11/04/despite-tensions-u-s-and-japan-begin-a-new-set-of-war-games/.

International Institute for Strategic Studies (IISS), *The Military Balance 2014*, London: IISS, 2014.

Japanese Ministry of Foreign Affairs, 'The Basic View on the Sovereignty Over the Senkaku Islands', 2013 www.mofa.go.jp/region/asia-paci/senkaku/senkaku.html.

Japan Times, 'Chinese Target-Locked MSDF Ship, Chopper', 6 February 2013, www.japantimes.co.jp/news/2013/02/06/national/japan-says-chinese-warships-locked-weapons-radar-on-msdf/#.UZHAw9evPIU.

Korea Times, 'Ex-Spy Reaffirms Plane Bombing in 1987', 3 November 2009, www.koreatimes.co.kr/www/news/nation/2009/07/113_41097.html.

Liu, Mingfu, *China Dream: The Great Power Thinking and Strategic Positioning of China in the Post-American Age* (Zhongguo meng: hou meiguo shidai de daguo siwei zhanlue dingwei), Beijing: Zhongguo youyi chuban gongsi, 2010.

Nasr, Alexander, 'Former China State TV Director Bemoans Anti-Japanese Propaganda: Where's the Creativity?' *Tea Leaf Nation*, 23 January 2013, www.tealeafnation.com/2013/01/former-china-state-tv-director-bemoans-anti-japanese-propaganda-wheres-the-creativity/.

NBC News, 'Japan Likely to Increase Spending Due to Isle Row: Media', *NBC News*, 1 April 2013, www.nbcnews.com/id/50370198/ns/world_news-asia_pacific/t/japan-likely-increase-defense-spending-due-isles-row-media/.

New York Times, 'Towards a Nuclear Deal with South Korea', 18 April 2013, www.nytimes.com/2013/04/19/opinion/south-koreas-nuclear-ambitions.html.

O'Rourke, Ronald, 'China Naval Modernization: Implications for U.S. Navy Capabilities – Background and Issues for Congress', CRS Report for Congress, RL33153, 17 October 2012, https://opencrs.com/document/RL33153/.

Organski, A. F. K., *World Politics*, New York: Knopf, 1968.

People's Online Daily, 'Full Text of Anti-Secession Law', 14 March 2005, http://english.peopledaily.com.cn/200503/14/eng20050314_176746.html.

Reuters, 'North Korea Shells South in Fiercest Attack in Decades', *Reuters*, 23 November 2010, www.reuters.com/article/2010/11/23/us-korea-north-artillery-idUSTRE6AM0YS20101123.

Reuters, 'China Submarines to Soon Carry Nukes, Draft U.S. Report Says', *Reuters*, 8 November 2012, www.reuters.com/article/2012/11/08/us-china-usa-military-idUSBRE8A705720121108.

Richardson, Michael, 'Troubling Signs of the Rise of Chinese Ultra-Nationalists', *Canberra Times*, 13 February 2013, www.canberratimes.com.au/opinion/troubling-signs-of-the-rise-of-chinese-ultranationalists-20130212-2ebf8.html.

Rublee, Maria Rost, 'The Nuclear Threshold States: Challenges and Opportunities Posed by Brazil and Japan', *Nonproliferation Review*, Vol. 17, No. 1, March 2010.

Salon, 'North Korea Threatens U.S., South Korea Over Joint Naval Drills', *Salon*, 7 May 2013, www.salon.com/2013/05/07/north_korea_threatens_u_s_south_korea_over_joint_naval_drills_ap/.

Schreer, Benjamin, *Planning the Unthinkable War: AirSea Battle and its Implications for Australia*, Canberra: Australian Security Policy Institute, 2013, www.aspi.org.au/htmlver/ASPI_planning_the_unthinkable_war/index.html.

Song, Qiang. Huang Jisu, Song Xiaojun, Wang Xiaodong and Liu Yang, *China is Unhappy: The Great Time, Grand Vision and Our Challenges*, Beijing: Kong Hong Book Company, 2009.

South China Morning Post, 'PLA Navy Amphibious Task Force Reaches Malaysia to Defend South China Sea', 27 March 2013, www.scmp.com/news/asia/article/1200564/pla-navy-amphibious-task-force-reaches-james-shoal-near-malaysia.

Straits Times, 'First U.S. Navy Littoral Combat Ship, USS Freedom, Arrives in Singapore', 18 April 2013, www.straitstimes.com/breaking-news/singapore/story/first-us-littoral-combat-ship-uss-freedom-arrives-singapore-20130418.

Strategic Comments, 'U.S. Rebalance: Potential and Limits in Southeast Asia', Vol. 18, Comment 49, December 2012.

The Australian, 'Beijing Tests "Killer" Missile', 25 March 2013, www.theaustralian.com.au/news/world/beijing-tests-killer-missile/story-fnb64oi6-1226604545906.

The Economist, 'Japan and National Security', 16 December 2013.

The Guardian, 'North Korea's Rocket Launch Fails as World Condemns Action', 13 April 2013, www.guardian.co.uk/world/2012/apr/13/north-korea-rocket-launch-fails.

The Telegraph, 'Japan Risks Threat to Global Peace by Rekindling Militaristic Spirit of Second World War, Senior Chinese Officials Warns', 1 January 2014.

Time, 'Big U.S. Fleet Nears Disputed Islands, But What For?' 30 September 2012, http://nation.time.com/2012/09/30/big-u-s-fleet-nears-disputed-islands-but-what-for/.

Tow, William, 'The Trilateral Security Dialogue: Facilitating Security-building or Revisiting Containment?' in *Assessing the Trilateral Security Dialogue*, National Bureau of Asian Research Special Report, December 2008.

US Department of State, 'South China Sea', Press Statement, 3 August 2012, www.state.gov/r/pa/prs/ps/2012/08/196022.htm.

US Department of Treasury, *Gross External Debt Position*, www.treasury.gov/resource-center/data-chart-center/tic/Documents/debta2012q4.html (accessed 7 May 2013).

US Office of the Secretary of Defense, *Annual Report to Congress: Military and Security Developments Involving the People's Republic of China 2010*.

US Office of the Secretary of Defense, *Annual Report to Congress: Military and Security Developments Involving the People's Republic of China 2013*.

Von Tol, Jan, Mark Gunzinger, Andrew F. Krepinevich and Jim Thomas, *AirSea Battle: A Point-of-Departure Operational Concept*, Washington, DC: Center for Strategic and Budgetary Assessment, 2010.

Washington Post, 'Destroyer to Protect Ship Near China', 13 March 2009, www.washingtonpost.com/wp-dyn/content/article/2009/03/12/AR2009031203264.html.

Washington Post, 'Obama Agrees to Sell Arms to Taiwan', 15 September 2011. www.washingtontimes.com/news/2011/sep/15/obama-rules-out-new-f-16s-for-taiwan/?page=all.

World Bank, *GDP (Current US$)*, http://data.worldbank.org/indicator/NY.GDP.MKTP.CD?order=wbapi_data_value_2011+wbapi_data_value+wbapi_data_value-last&sort=asc.

Yang, Jian, 'Japan's Decline Relative to China: Scenarios and Implications for East Asia', *Political Science*, Vol. 62, No. 2, 2010, http://pnz.sagepub.com/content/62/2/146.abstract.

Zhang, Zang Zang, Tang Zhengyu, Song Qiang, Qiao Bian and Gu Qingsheng, *China Can Say No: Political and Emotional Choices in the Post-Cold War Age*, Beijing: China Industry and Commerce Joint Publishing House, 1996.

Zhu, Bangzao, *Frontline*, Autumn 2001, www.pbs.org/wgbh/pages/frontline/shows/china/interviews/bangzao.html.

2
The international relations of East Asia from a historical perspective

Andrea Benvenuti

Introduction

During the second half of the 19th century a new and assertive power emerged in the heart of Europe – Germany. Some 30 independent states were brought together under the King of Prussia, Wilhelm I, who was proclaimed the Emperor of Germany. The unification of Germany in 1871 was a watershed in the international relations of the time: the redrawing of the map of Europe brought about a major structural change in what was then a quintessentially Euro-centric international system. Significantly, British Prime Minister Benjamin Disraeli rated the emergence of a united Germany as 'a greater political event than the French Revolution' (Disraeli cited in Steinberg 2011: 312). He was right. Over the next 70 years, accommodating Germany within the existing international structure would turn out to be a major diplomatic headache. Unsurprisingly, Europe went to war twice to contain German power.

During the past few years, various commentators have drawn intriguing, if not disturbing, parallels between Germany's power trajectory in the pre-1945 international system and China's current ascent to great power status. Predictably, they have tended to view such a rise as a sign of what might happen if the economic and military power of the People's Republic of China continues to grow, and Beijing becomes more assertive on both the East Asian and international scenes (Kissinger 2011: 514). Although during the past 20 years successive Chinese leaders have gone to great lengths to reassure the world that China's intentions are peaceful and that its rise, therefore, should not be perceived as destabilizing, nonetheless the fact remains that these reassurances notwithstanding, China's neighbours and the USA may not view its growing power and influence with equanimity. Germany's neighbours certainly did not do so over a century or so ago (Macmillan 2013). Most of China's neighbours will no doubt be likely to 'fear the consequences of a region dominated by a single power' (Kissinger 2011: 526), especially if the USA were to disengage from the region.

Whether China will become a destabilizing factor (as Germany once was) and present a major threat to regional (and global) stability remains to be seen. Yet it is undeniable that the question of China's place and role in international affairs is hardly a new one, having been in fact one of the most recurrent (and central) themes in the international relations of East Asia since the end of the Second World War. Intimately related to it, of course, has also been the question of how key regional players such as the USA and Japan have responded to China's rising profile and influence. In this context, the role of the USA, the 20th-century's pre-eminent power, is highly significant – so much so that, as Michael Yahuda has rightly argued, future regional dynamics are likely to be dependent upon the character of Sino–US relations (Yahuda 2011: xv). How, for instance, China's neighbours will react to its growing power and assertiveness in the context of the USA's possibly diminishing influence in the region is one of the most challenging (and fascinating) questions confronting contemporary scholars and policymakers. In this chapter, however, I will confine myself to examining these dynamics in a historical context, focusing principally on the interactions between the USA and China since 1949.

The Cold War in East Asia (1949–89)

While in Europe Cold War tensions developed rapidly after the end of the Second World War, bipolar confrontation in Asia took somewhat longer to emerge. The two superpowers remained predominantly focused on Europe, with the Soviet Union (USSR) intent on strengthening its hold on its Eastern European backyard and the USA gradually stepping up its politico-military commitment to the defence of Western Europe. As a result, during the early post-war years East Asia did not loom large in either US or Soviet strategic thinking. The emergence, for instance, of a Vietnamese nationalist-communist movement, the Viet-minh, under the leadership of Ho Chi Minh, did not incite the two superpowers to reassess this region's importance in their foreign policy calculations. The USA initially treated unrest in Vietnam as a quintessentially French colonial problem while the USSR showed no desire to invest significant resources in such a peripheral theatre given Stalin's misgivings about Ho and his chances of beating the French (Gayduk 2011: 66–67; Logevall 2012: 222). Similarly, the two superpowers maintained a fairly cautious approach to the Chinese Civil War despite Stalin's growing support for the Chinese Communist Party (Westad 2005: 64–64; Niu 2010: 226–231; Pechatnov 2010: 108). Not even the communist revolts that erupted across South-East Asia in 1948 (Burma, Malaya, the Dutch East Indies and the Philippines) drew any significant reaction from Washington or Moscow. Despite Western concerns that the USSR might lie behind these revolts, the USA was not yet ready to ramp up its politico-military presence in East Asia. As for the USSR, despite its revolutionary rhetoric, it had no intention of further damaging its relations with the West and, as recent research has shown, Moscow played no role in fomenting these uprisings (Gayduk 2011: 66; Efimova 2009: 449–469). Far from being part of a grand Soviet expansionist design, these revolts were the product of the social dislocation and economic misery brought by the Second World War.

The outbreak of the Korean War in June 1950, however, was to turn this hitherto secondary theatre of great power rivalry into a major – if not the major – cockpit of Cold War tensions (Chen 2001: 3). It had far-reaching consequences on the region's political configuration as it made the division of the Korean peninsula and the inclusion of Taiwan in the Western alliance system two of the most enduring and destabilizing legacies of the Cold War in East Asia. More significantly, it witnessed the emergence of China not only as a major regional power which regarded itself as being at the forefront of a revolutionary process in Asia, but also one determined to model the world in its own image and thus to reclaim its rightful place in the pantheon of great powers following the long 'Century of Shame'. Over the next 30 years, therefore, East Asia would experience significant political instability and two major conflicts (Korea and Vietnam) – quite in contrast to Europe where the two superpowers and their respective blocs remained essentially locked in an uneasy but bloodless stalemate. Finally, but no less importantly, the Korean War also had a profound impact on US foreign policy and Washington's regional role in East Asia.

From the USA's perspective, North Korea's invasion of South Korea was not simply a massive shock. It was also a veritable 'game-changer' as it obliged the Truman administration (and successive ones for that matter) to pay considerably greater attention to East Asian affairs. Coming hot on the heels of Mao Zedong's successful revolution in October 1949, the Korean War clearly reinforced American fears of communism. From it US policymakers drew a number of important conclusions: first, that both the USSR and China shared a common, and 'virtually irresistible', desire to create compatible regimes in East Asia (and around the world); second, that the USSR was able effectively to direct bloc policies; third, that once a power vacuum was created, it would be hard for the two major communist powers to resist the temptation to fill it; finally, that China was a revolutionary force to be reckoned with and a power with both the determination and ability to use its military capabilities beyond its borders. Unsurprisingly, the American response was forceful. In an impressive crescendo that would have been unthinkable only a few years earlier, the USA stepped up its regional engagement: it gave a security guarantee to Taiwan, negotiated a defence treaty with Australia and New Zealand (the so-called ANZUS), and increased military aid to the beleaguered French in Vietnam. More importantly, it sought to rehabilitate Japan which quickly transformed from despised enemy into one of Washington's most reliable allies and the linchpin of the USA's military position in East Asia. From the US perspective, Japan's rehabilitation had a two-fold objective: to create a bulwark against perceived Sino–Soviet expansionism and to anchor the country solidly to the West. For the Japanese (not unlike the situations of the Germans in Europe), it was a timely opportunity to regain the country's full sovereignty and respectability following the trauma of the Second World War.

China's involvement in the Korean War was to inject a crucial political factor into the emerging Cold War dynamics in East Asia and it is, therefore, hardly surprising that during the early phase of the Cold War the USA became increasingly concerned about China's role in regional affairs. The Korean conflict effectively placed China 'in the forefront of the Cold War in Asia as the main target for American isolation and containment' (Yahuda 2011: 143). Beijing's willingness to use conventional military force in Korea, and its ability to repel and then hold in check US-led UN forces made a strong impression on US policymakers (Fenton 2012). China was now thought capable of mounting conventional military operations abroad. Combat experience gained in Korea and a rapid programme of modernization aided by the USSR made China a military power to be reckoned with. Also crucial in American eyes was the fact that China's defence capabilities dwarfed those of its non-communist neighbours (ibid.). China's rising military power, coupled with its strident Marxist-Leninist revolutionary and anti-status quo rhetoric, worried the USA further. It was no doubt this growing American concern that prompted the Eisenhower administration (1953–61) to envisage the possible use of US nuclear weapons to deter Chinese regional expansion (Jones 2010: 453). By the early 1950s Moscow and Beijing had worked out an informal 'division of labour' between them, with China assuming a primary role in the promotion of communist revolutions across East Asia (Chen 2001: 3; Gayduk 2011: 72–73). With China playing a key part in the two offshore island crises (1954 and 1958) (Yahuda 2011: 145–146) and in support of Ho's Vietminh (Qiang 2000), 'the strategic attention of the United States, following the assumption that China was a more daring enemy than the Soviet Union, became increasingly fixed on East Asia' (Chen 2001: 3).

To be sure, Mao's radicalism and revolutionary zeal were tempered by the fact that China was still an underdeveloped nation 'without the military capacity to impose its own preferences on a world that vastly outmatched it in resources and, above all, technology' (Kissinger 2011: 98). According to Kissinger (ibid.), Mao's 'world revolution was a slogan, perhaps a long-range objective'; he and his comrades were 'sufficiently realistic to recognise that they lacked the means to challenge the prevailing international order except by ideological means'. Yet the revolutionary statements made by Beijing were far from being mere rhetoric for internal consumption or overblown reaffirmations of Marxist-Leninist orthodoxy in a calculated effort to strengthen China's claim to the leadership of the communist movement in Asia. They were indeed a genuine reaffirmation of Beijing's commitment to advancing the cause of Communism if not globally, at least regionally (Moyar 2006: 138). As cautiously as China might have acted at times – Chinese backing of anti-government communist rebels in Malaya never went much beyond the rhetorical stage and its support for Burmese and Filipino insurgents remained very modest as well (McMahon 1999: 47) – both China's intervention in Korea and its involvement in Indochina in support of North Vietnam were a clear enough indication that Mao took seriously China's role as the vanguard of the communist movement in Asia. Mao 'strongly believed that history was on his side' and, as any good Marxist-Leninist, he was confident that Communism would one day prevail over its capitalist nemesis (Qiang 2000: 220; Chen 2001: 7). The 'correlation of forces' might not have been in China's favour, especially in the light of the USA's robust adoption of containment in East Asia, yet the 'revolutionary momentum' needed to be kept up whenever possible and wherever feasible.[1]

China's assistance to North Vietnam was a case in point. By 1950 Beijing had begun to provide logistical support, military equipment and tactical advice to the Vietminh. That support proved crucial to the Vietnamese guerrillas' ability to survive French offensives in 1950–51 and to the military gains that they began to achieve soon after. Throughout the course of the first Indochina War, the Chinese supplied 110,000 guns and 4,500 cannons while equipping approximately five infantry divisions, one engineering and artillery division, one aircraft regiment and one guard regiment (McMahon 1999: 46). It is no wonder then, that similarly to the USA, non-communist states across East Asia viewed Chinese actions with concern even during the mid-1950s when Beijing temporarily toned down its revolutionary zeal and fleetingly embraced the Bandung conference's rhetoric of peaceful co-existence (see Shu 2007: 509–528).

Strong concerns about China's role in regional affairs resurfaced again in the 1960s in connection with the deepening political and ideological rift between the USSR and China, and the launch of the Cultural Revolution in China. Mao's criticism of Khrushchev's de-Stalinisation and his rejection of the latter's embracing of peaceful co-existence marked the end of Beijing's post-Bandung 'charm offensive' and signalled a return to revolutionary radicalism, which, in turn, inevitably helped to revive fears of Chinese subversion across East Asia. The USA's deepening involvement in Indochina in the 1960s was no doubt related to Washington's increasing concerns about the radical development in Chinese foreign policy (Moyar 2006: 375–379). Although in the end Beijing's actual actions did not always match its revolutionary rhetoric, its reaffirmations of revolutionary zeal were, on the other hand, no mere pronouncements. Between 1965 and 1969 Beijing dispatched 320,000 engineering and anti-aircraft forces to North Vietnam (Ruane 2000: 158). In the 1960s it also 'provided military and other support to Communist rebels in countries such as Burma, Malaya (Malaysia), and Thailand' (Chen 2012: 187). Hence, while the Johnson administration (1963–69) carefully avoided any direct confrontation with China by refusing to attack North

Vietnam, Washington's desire to contain the spread of Chinese influence in East Asia remained undiminished. Once again, Cold War dynamics highlighted not only the inherently unstable nature of the East Asian regional system, but also the latter's own peculiarities. While Europe witnessed the structuring of the Cold War around two rigid blocs, the situation in East Asia was more fluid. The 'bamboo curtain' was less rigidly and more clearly demarcated than the 'iron curtain' in Central Europe. The risk of instability and conflict always seemed higher in East Asia than in Europe. This state of affairs appeared to be further vindicated – and the potential for instability was further reinforced – in 1969 when the growing tensions between the USSR and China erupted in military clashes along the common border.

If in the short term Sino–Soviet enmity no doubt heightened the risk of conflict in East Asia, in the longer term it was instrumental in influencing China to break away from its Cultural Revolution-induced isolation and move towards a more accommodating stance towards both its non-communist neighbours and the USA. By seeking better relations with Washington, Beijing endeavoured not only to gain US support against what it now regarded as Soviet 'hegemony', but also to isolate the USSR. For its part, by 'opening to China', the Nixon administration (1969–74) sought to exploit Sino–Soviet tensions not only to end the Vietnamese conflict, but also to negotiate a detente with the USSR and to split the communist camp further (Hanhimäki 2004: 57–61). In due course, the emerging *entente cordiale* between Washington and Beijing led to a normalization in Sino–US relations, and to greater political and economic cooperation between China and the West. Significantly, from being the focus of American containment efforts in East Asia, China became a de facto partner of the USA (Yahuda 2011: 66). China's tilt towards the USA also resulted in Beijing gradually abandoning its militant rhetoric and support for regional revolutions, which had done so much to antagonize China's neighbours. Under Mao's successor, Deng Xiaoping, China moved decisively to further normalize China's regional relations. In addition, given China's centrality in the East Asian regional system, the political, security and economic consequences of such a development in Chinese foreign policy were 'both immediate and far reaching' (ibid.).

One of the most glaring changes brought about by such a development was the normalization of relations between China and Japan. Despite Chinese attempts during the 1950s and 1960s to court Japan (Yahuda 2004: 167, 172), it was only after Nixon's visit to China in 1972 that relations between the two East Asian neighbours improved markedly (Chen 2012: 192). Now, far from considering Tokyo's alliance with Washington to be detrimental to its interests, Beijing viewed it as a positive factor not only in terms of containing the USSR and keeping a resurgent Japan in check, but also in securing much needed investment and technology – so vital for Deng's modernizing drive. Deng's 'charm offensive', however, would take time to bear fruit as 30 years of revolutionary rhetoric were not easily forgotten throughout the region. While, for instance, Malaysia, Thailand and the Philippines promptly recognized China in the mid-1970s, Indonesia refused to do so, with Singapore making its recognition conditional upon Jakarta's (Yahuda 2011: 151). As the Prime Minister of Singapore, Lee Kuan Yew, pointedly reminded Deng during the latter's tour of East Asia in late 1978, 'China wanted Southeast Asian countries to unite with it to isolate the "Russian bear"; the fact was that our neighbour wanted us to unite and isolate the "Chinese dragon". There were no "overseas Russians" in Southeast Asia leading communist insurgencies supported by the Soviet Union, as there were "overseas Chinese" encouraged and supported by the Chinese Communist Party and government' (Lee cited in Kissinger 2011: 359). While unease about Chinese regional intentions never fully dissipated – after all, China's neighbours were only too aware of its historical claims of superiority (Yahuda 2011: 15, 157) – the last phase of the Cold War in Asia not only witnessed China's growing engagement with the region, but it also registered a growing acceptance among its neighbours of China's regional role.

East Asia and the end of the Cold War

The end of the Cold War marked a significant change in the political dynamics of East Asia. The rapid unravelling of the Soviet bloc in 1989–90 and the sudden collapse of the USSR in 1991 not only removed a major cause of instability in post-1945 international relations, but also discredited communism both as an ideology and a system of economic relations. In East Asia, the USA and China were the main beneficiaries of such dramatic change. Expectations that Japan would rise to great power status remained unfulfilled. Although during the Cold War it had managed to achieve high rates of economic growth under the reassuring security umbrella provided by a robust US military presence, Japan failed to step up to the role of leading regional power that many analysts were ready to thrust upon it during the 1980s (Yahuda 2011: 314–315). The country's inability to reform its dysfunctional political system and its difficulty in dealing with the effects of the 1992 economic crisis were significant factors in preventing Japan from realizing its ambitions. However, if the post-Cold War era did not quite work out for Japan as predicted, it certainly worked wonders for the USA. The end of the Cold War propelled the USA to a position of unprecedented pre-eminence in modern international affairs. Its improved geopolitical position, coupled with its world-leading technology and sizable economic capabilities, made American power appear so overwhelming that at the end of the 1990s French Minister of Foreign Affairs Hubert Vedrine spoke of the USA as an emerging 'hyper-power' (Herring 2008: 916). As for China, Beijing, too, benefited significantly from the collapse of the old bipolar order. The emergence of a much weaker Russian Federation along its northern borders put China on a stronger geopolitical footing, thus markedly reducing its strategic concerns. In stark contrast to the experiences of the USSR, the demise of international communism as a historical phenomenon did not bring China to its knees. On the contrary, the triumph of the principles of the market economy and the concomitant acceleration in the process of economic globalization provided China's leadership with an opportunity to consolidate Deng's economic reforms and to take advantage of China's rapid transition to a market economy. Over the next two decades China would experience unprecedented rates of economic growth, making it not only the world's leading manufacturer, but also a significant global player (Yahuda 2011: 181). It is in this context that regional concerns over growing Chinese power and influence emerged strongly once again.

The way in which these trends affected regional dynamics were not always entirely straightforward. For one thing, the USA, despite its unrivalled pre-eminence, was slow to adjust to the changed realities of the post-Cold War era (Herring 2008: 922). Throughout the 1990s successive US administrations seemed to oscillate between the desire to provide continued global leadership and the somewhat neo-isolationist temptation to reduce America's global commitments. Yet these oscillations notwithstanding, the USA, in the end, did not skirt around the challenges of the post-Cold War era. In East Asia, the USA, for all its calls upon allies to agree to greater burden-sharing, remained strongly engaged in regional affairs, by playing the role of regional balancer or security guarantor (or both), and by 'facilitating the success of the export-led growth strategies of US allies in Asia' through its open-door import policies (Yahuda 2011: 226). In this context, the USA sought to achieve two principle aims, namely preventing the emergence of a regional hegemon able to dictate the pace of change in Asia, and protecting its economic and trade interests (Yahuda 2011: 228). Although the pursuit of these aims also remained a key feature of Washington's regional policy in the new century, US regional engagement seemed to weaken somewhat as a result of the attacks on the USA in September 2001 (known as 9/11). Following 9/11, Washington became increasingly distracted by its 'war on terror' and its demanding military campaigns in Iraq and Afghanistan. More recently, despite President Barack Obama's declared commitment to a major US politico-military presence in East Asia, the USA's regional role has been somewhat weakened by the global financial crisis which hit it particularly hard.

For its part, China has focused on building up its economic power, taking advantage of the stabilizing role played by the USA in East Asia and the opportunities provided by globalization. Over the past two decades China has increasingly engaged with the region, and has joined regional institutions and organizations. In contrast to the Cold War, it has sought to use its participation in multilateral fora to reassure its neighbours, and to secure political stability and economic prosperity. It has also sought to play up the rhetoric of China's peaceful rise to further dispel regional concerns about its future role in East Asia. China's attempts in this respect have met with mixed results. While its neighbours have increasingly sought to engage economically with China, they have also tried to safeguard themselves against the threat of an increasingly assertive China by encouraging the USA to remain firmly engaged in regional affairs. Regional concerns about China's future regional role have become stronger recently as a result of China's ham-fisted tactics in the quarrel with Japan over the ownership of the Senkaku/Diaoyu Islands in the East China Sea. The uncertainty over President Obama's 'pivot to Asia' and the lingering doubts about America's enduring commitment to regional security have further compounded these concerns. Finally, the fact that the Chinese leadership increasingly has come to rely on nationalism as a unifying ideology as well as a means of compensating for its loss of legitimacy following the collapse of communism (Yahuda 2011: 307) has raised further doubts about the sincerity of Chinese intentions.

Conclusion

In 1910 British journalist Normal Angell argued in a book entitled *The Great Illusion* that economic self-interest would prevent the European powers from going to war. The interdependent nature of finance and trade, he wrote, had so profoundly altered the international politics of the day that military power had become pointless (Best *et al.* 2004: 2, 16). Angell's views reflected a belief prevalent at the time that Europe had entered an era of unprecedented prosperity and progress. Almost as a magic wand, economic interdependence appeared to have provided a solution to the German problem and to the full incorporation of this dynamic and assertive power into the prevailing international system. And yet, with the benefit of hindsight, it is difficult for us today to understand this sense of optimism. Only a few years later, Europe would plunge into a tragic world war, soon to be followed by 20 years of political and economic upheaval and a second global conflict. While historical analogies ought always to be treated with a healthy dose of scepticism, it would not, however, be unreasonable to conclude that, in a manner not so dissimilar to pre-1914 Europe, growing economic and financial interdependence in East Asia might not be enough to ensure the peaceful development of regional relations in the years to come (nor might, for that matter, the complex web of multilateral institutions that have materialized within the region during the past three decades). As was the case in pre-1945 Europe, the 'taming' of China, therefore, might prove to be every inch as difficult as that of Germany. To a great extent, it will be up to China itself to determine whether the post-Cold War regional system, from which Beijing has gained so much in terms of economic prosperity and external stability, is worth undermining for the sake of pursuing greater regional influence and power (Fingar 2012: 195–204).

Note

1 Correlation of forces refers to the idea that in dealing with capitalist states, communist leaders should take into account the balance of political, economic and military advantages and disadvantages. For its part, revolutionary momentum relates to the principle that revolutionary progress was crucial to the success of international communism. For those concepts see Miller 1991: 13–14.

Bibliography

Best, Antony, Jussi M. Hanhimäki, Joseph A. Maiolo and Kirsten E. Schulze, *International History of the Twentieth Century*, New York: Routledge, 2004.

Chen, Jian, *Mao's China and the Cold War*, Chapel Hill, NC: University of North Carolina Press, 2001.

Chen, Jian, 'China and the Cold War after Mao', in Melvyn P. Leffler and Odd Arne Westad (eds), *The Cambridge History of the Cold War. Vol. 1: Crises and Détente*, Cambridge: Cambridge University Press, 2012.

Efimova, Larisa, 'Did the Soviet Union Instruct Southeast Asian Communists to Revolt? New Russian Evidence on the Calcutta Youth Conference of February 1948', *Journal of Southeast Asian Studies*, Vol. 40, No. 3, 2009.

Fenton, Damien, *To Cage the Red Dragon: SEATO and the Defence of Southeast Asia, 1955–1965*, Singapore: NUS Press, 2012.

Fingar, Thomas, 'China's Rise: Contingency, Constraints and Concerns', *Survival*, Vol. 54, No. 1, 2012.

Gayduk, Ilya V., 'The Second Front of the Soviet Cold War: Asia in the System of Moscow's Foreign Policy Priorities, 1945–1956', in Tsuyoshi Hasegawa (ed.), *Cold War in East Asia 1945–1991*, Washington, DC: Woodrow Wilson Center Press, 2011.

Hanhimäki, Jussi M., *The Flawed Architect: Henry Kissinger and American Foreign Policy*, New York: Oxford University Press, 2004.

Herring, George C., *From Colony to Superpower: U.S. Foreign Relations since 1776*, Oxford: Oxford University Press, 2008.

Jones, Matthew, *After Hiroshima: The United States, Race, and Nuclear Weapons in Asia, 1945–1965*, Cambridge: Cambridge University Press, 2010.

Keylor, William, *The Twentieth Century World and Beyond: An International History since 1900*, Oxford: Oxford University Press, 2006.

Kissinger, Henry, *On China*, New York: Penguin Press, 2011.

Logevall, Frederik, *Embers of War: The Fall of an Empire and the Making of America's Vietnam*, New York: Random House, 2012.

McMahon, Robert J., *The Limits of Empire: The United States and Southeast Asia Since World War II*, New York: Columbia University Press, 1999.

Macmillan, Margaret, *The War That Ended Peace: The Road to 1914*, New York: Random House, 2013.

Miller, Robert, *Soviet Foreign Policy Today*, Sydney: Allen & Unwin, 1991.

Moyar, Mark, *Triumph Forsaken: The Vietnam War, 1954–65*, Cambridge: Cambridge University Press, 2006.

Niu, Jun, 'The Birth of the People's Republic of China and the Road to the Korean War', in Melvyn P. Leffler and Odd Arne Westad (eds), *The Cambridge History of the Cold War. Vol. 1: The Origins*, Cambridge: Cambridge University Press, 2010.

Pechatnov, Vladimir O., 'The Soviet Union and the World, 1944–1953', in Melvyn P. Leffler and Odd Arne Westad (eds), *The Cambridge History of the Cold War. Vol. 1: The Origins*, Cambridge: Cambridge University Press, 2010.

Ruane, Kevin, *The Vietnam Wars*, Manchester: Manchester University Press, 2000.

Shu, Guan Zhang, 'Constructing "Peaceful Coexistence": China's Diplomacy toward the Geneva and Bandung Conferences, 1954–1955', *Cold War History*, Vol. 7, No. 4, 2007.
Steinberg, Jonathan, *Bismarck: A Life*, Oxford, Oxford University Press, 2011.
Westad, Odd Arne, *The Global Cold War: Third World Interventions and the Making of Our Time*, Cambridge: Cambridge University Press, 2005.
Yahuda, Michael, *The International Politics of the Asia Pacific*, 2nd edn, London: RoutledgeCurzon, 2004.
Yahuda, Michael, *The International Politics of the Asia Pacific*, 3rd edn, Hoboken, NJ: Taylor & Francis, 2011.

3
Arms racing in East Asia

Andrew T. H. Tan

An arms race in East Asia

Since the end of the Vietnam War in 1975, Asia has engaged in a steady process of arms modernization and expansion. This process accelerated following the end of the Cold War in 1989. By around 2000 Asia's arms build-up, particularly in East Asia, began to draw the attention of regional analysts. In 2001, for instance, Sam Bateman, a former commander of the Australian navy, asserted that a naval arms race had already begun in East Asia (Bateman 2001: 1). In 2010 Australia's leading strategic analyst, Desmond Ball, noted the dramatic increases in the defence budgets of both China and the USA (a key player in Asia), the increased defence capabilities in the region, and evidence of an 'action-reaction' dynamic in some sub-regions, and thus warned that the region was now on the verge of a full-blown arms race. In addition, the lack of regional institutional and normative constraints to contain escalation and promote crisis stability had also increased the possibility of interstate conflict (Ball 2010: 30–51).

In 2012 one of the world's leading strategic studies institutes, Britain's International Institute for Strategic Studies (IISS) reported that Asia's total defence spending had, for the first time, exceeded that of Europe (IISS 2013: 33). The IISS asserted that the escalation in military spending and improvements in defence capabilities were the result of 'increasing uncertainty about the future distribution of power in the region and widespread suspicions, in some cases increasing tension, among the regional armed forces'. While these efforts are meant for deterrent purposes, the IISS concluded that 'there is (also) substantial evidence of action-reaction dynamics taking hold and influencing regional states' military programmes' (ibid.: 245). The IISS also attributed the increase in defence spending in recent years to the region's strong economic growth. Asian economies grew by 9.51 per cent in 2010, and by 7.76 per cent in 2011. This allowed overall defence spending in Asia to rise by 3.76 per cent in 2011 and by 4.94 per cent in 2012 (ibid.: 247–249).

More significantly, East Asia dominated Asian defence spending, making up about two-thirds of total defence spending in 2012. A large proportion of the increase is due to China's expanding defence budget, which exceeded US $100,000m. for the first time in 2012. Both Taiwan and South Korea also increased their defence spending in 2012 (IISS 2013: 250). In 2012 the election of the right-wing Shinzo Abe to government led to a reversal of Japan's decline in defence spending. Alarmed by China's increasing aggressiveness in asserting its claims over disputed maritime territory in the East China Sea, and the brinkmanship practiced by North Korea which included ballistic missile and nuclear tests, the Abe government approved a modest increase in defence spending for 2013, the first increase since 2002. The increase was to be used to fund the acquisition of unmanned aerial vehicles (UAVs) for reconnaissance purposes, new helicopters and anti-aircraft missiles and the upgrading of part of its fleet of F-15 combat aircraft (*The Australian* 2013).

As it has become fashionable to describe recent defence modernization and expansion in Asia, particularly in East Asia, as an arms race, it is necessary clearly to define what exactly constitutes an arms race. A useful conceptual framework was offered by Colin Gray in 1972. According to Gray, there are three criteria for evaluating whether an arms race is taking place. First, there must be two or more parties, each of whom is conscious of their antagonism. Second, these parties must also structure their armed forces by paying attention to the probable effectiveness of their forces in combat with, or as a deterrent to, the other arms race participants. In other words, there must be a competitive action-reaction dynamic in the arms build-up. Finally, the parties must compete in terms of quantity and quality, with evidence of a rapid increase in quantity as well as improvement in the quality of armaments (Gray 1972).

The following examines the evidence for an arms race using Gray's three criteria. If an arms race is indeed taking place, then it must be asked, what are the implications?

Inter-state antagonisms

The first criterion, namely the presence of two or more parties who are conscious of their antagonism, is easily met in East Asia. China and Japan have maintained historical animosities dating back to Japan's imperialist predations since the Meiji Restoration in 1868 and its subsequent rise as a great power. In 1895, following the end of the first Sino-Japanese War, the Treaty of Shimonoseki imposed on China huge indemnities, China's recognition of Korea's independence (subsequently annexed by Japan in 1910), and the ceding of Taiwan and Liaotung (today part of Liaoning province) to Japan (Treaty of Shimonoseki 1895).

Strong anti-Japanese sentiment continues to exist in China today as a result of historical memories of Japan's aggression during the second Sino-Japanese War from 1937 to 1945. This period was marked by various atrocities committed by Japanese troops, such as the Nanjing massacre of some 200,000 civilians in 1937 (see Gendercide.org). While relations were normalized in 1972, and both countries have important trading relations, the ruling Chinese Communist Party's emphasis on promoting nationalism as a means of shoring up its legitimacy has involved evoking and promoting historical memories of Japanese atrocities. Through China's education system and mass media, ordinary Chinese people have been bombarded with nationalistic, anti-Japanese propaganda. This has sustained the presence of deep and widespread anti-Japanese sentiment in China (Jacques 2009: 310).

For its part, Japan's collective amnesia regarding the events of the Second World War has been reflected in its politicians being guilty of attempting to justify the country's role in that war as well as the whitewashing of a number of historical events which still resonate negatively in China and South Korea, such as the use of women as sex slaves. The ascendency of Shinzo Abe to power has been accompanied by attempts to rewrite history as part of Japan's revival. Inevitably, these undignified attempts have stoked tensions with Japan's neighbours, namely China and South Korea. Indeed, A Pew survey in 2013 revealed that 90 per cent of the Chinese have an unfavourable opinion of Japan, which is 17 per cent higher than in 2006 (Pew 2013).

It is this context which partly explains the deterioration in bilateral relations between China and Japan from late 2012 to its worst level since 1945. The issue that has brought the two countries to the brink of open conflict is the territorial dispute over the Senkaku/Daioyu

Islands. Japan nationalized the islands in late 2012, which led to violent anti-Japanese riots in major Chinese cities. This forced many Japanese businesses in China to close temporarily. Patriotic Chinese cancelled orders for Japanese-made products (such as cars) and cancelled their holidays in Japan (ABC News 2012). Regular incursions into Japanese territory by China's warplanes and ships led to the frequent scrambling of Japan's F-15 combat aircraft to intercept the intruders. In early 2013 Chinese warships near the Senkaku Islands also locked their fire-control radars onto a Japanese military helicopter and a Japanese warship, dangerous actions which could have caused an accidental outbreak of full-scale war (VOA News 2013).

Apart from Sino–Japanese relations, relations between South Korea and Japan have also been affected by historical animosities as well as territorial disputes. South Korea suffered decades of brutal colonial rule under Japan from 1910 to 1945. A major issue left unaddressed since that period has been the status of the disputed Dokdo Island (known as Takeshima in Japan). Indeed, this proved such an emotive issue that it prevented the normalization of relations between the two US allies until 1965. However, the issue has not gone away. In August 2012 South Korea's President Lee Myung-bak visited Dokdo Island, which he emotionally proclaimed to be 'truly our territory, and ... worth defending with our lives' (*New York Times* 2012). A Pew survey in 2013 also revealed that some 77 per cent of South Koreans have an unfavourable view of Japan, which is 25 per cent higher than it was in 2008 (Pew 2013).

Another set of interstate antagonisms are found on the Korean peninsula. Since the division of Korea into a communist North and a non-communist South following the end of the Second World War, the two sides have lived in antagonism, with tensions never far from the surface. The Korean War (1950–1953) only served to harden the ideological divide between the two sides. Since then, North Korea has frequently resorted to provocative brinkmanship to force the South and its ally, the USA, to bargain with it. Raked by famine and economic collapse, and with a new and insecure young leader, Kim Jong-un, who came to power following the illness and subsequent death of his father, Kim Jong-il, North Korea has in recent years resorted to previously unseen levels of brinkmanship. In 2010 a North Korean submarine sunk a South Korean naval corvette, the *Choenan*, killing 46 sailors (CNN 2010). This was followed by the artillery shelling of an island in South Korea close to the maritime border, during which two people were killed (Reuters 2010). In late 2012 North Korea carried out a successful ballistic missile test and followed this up with a nuclear test in February 2013. North Korea then reacted to fresh UN sanctions by abrogating the armistice that had ended the Korean War in 1953, thus returning the Korean peninsula to a state of war (Bloomberg 2013). These events raised tensions on the Korean peninsula to their highest level since 1953, and increased the possibility of accidental war due to miscalculation.

Finally, there remains the Taiwan problem. This was created during the onset of the Cold War when the USA extended its protection to the Kuomintang regime that had fled to Taiwan following the end of the Chinese civil war from 1945–1949. The normalization of US–Sino relations in the 1970s led to the growing worldwide acceptance of the 'One China' principle that states that Taiwan is part of China. Thus, Taiwan's very existence as a state has been in question. The threat of forceful reunification by China, where this issue arouses particularly strong emotive and nationalistic feelings, has meant that some kind of military parity in the Taiwan Strait would be needed if China is to be deterred and stability maintained (Lee 2013: 85).

Competitive action-reaction dynamic

The second criterion for an arms race is that the parties involved must structure their armed forces according to the probable effectiveness of their forces in combat with, or as a deterrent to, each other. As Ball and the IISS have indicated, there is evidence that there is a competitive and interactive action–reaction dynamic at work.

An evaluation of some of the new capabilities being acquired by East Asian states supports the notion of an interactive process leading states to procure similar types of weapons systems in order to maintain a military balance and to prevent other states from gaining a conventional edge. The caveat concerns North Korea, which has opted for asymmetric warfare and anti-access capabilities as it does not have access to the latest military technology, nor does it have the resources to do so given the dire state of its economy. Instead, it has opted to develop nuclear weapons, ballistic missiles, the world's largest commando forces, large numbers of midget submarines, and massed artillery in order to threaten the South Korean capital, Seoul.

An evaluation of Airborne Early Warning and Control (AEW & C) aircraft, which are technologically sophisticated and expensive to procure and maintain, gives an indication of the interactive nature of the arms race in East Asia. Such aircraft are a significant force multiplier as they provide early warning and allow large areas of air and maritime space to be controlled. US allies in East Asia have access to US AEW & C technology. Thus, Taiwan operates six Hawkeye early warning aircraft to detect any surprise attack from China (IISS 2014: 282). Japan has a large force of early warning aircraft, comprising 17 Hawkeye and four Boeing 767 aircraft; the latter has a range of 10,370 km and is equipped with sophisticated AN/APY-2 radar system that can detect maritime and air targets up to 320 km away (see *Airforce-Technology.com*). South Korea deploys four B-737 Peace Eye early warning aircraft which were delivered from the USA in 2012 (Boeing 2012). China, on the other hand, has developed its own very efficient early warning aircraft that is reportedly technologically ahead of US systems. It currently operates four KJ-200 early warning aircraft which deploy a system similar to the Swedish-made Irieye system, and large KJ-2000 early warning aircraft based on the latest active phased array radar (Kopp 2010).

The acquisition of similar advanced multi-role combat aircraft is also evident in the air forces of China, Japan and South Korea. Taiwan has not been able to compete in this area due to the reluctance by many countries of offending China by selling it advanced combat aircraft. Its air force thus deploys increasingly outdated combat aircraft, such as the F-5E Tiger, F-16A/B, French Mirage 2000, and the locally developed Ching Kuo, all of which were procured in the 1980s or 1990s (IISS 2014: 282). Taiwan's request for F-16C/D combat aircraft has so far been rejected by the USA, which has instead offered to upgrade its 146 F-16A/B combat aircraft with the retrofitting of the latest active electronically scanned array (AESA) radar, structural upgrades and improved avionics and electronic warfare capabilities (*Flightglobal* 2012).

China has led the way in recent combat aircraft development. Its large and capable air force deployed over 2,400 combat aircraft in 2013, including the Russian-made Su-30MKK Flanker, currently regarded as one of the best combat aircraft in the world; the Russian-made air-superiority Su-27 and its local imitations, the J-11; and the locally made J-10 combat aircraft, which is regarded as the equivalent of the US F-16 (IISS 2014: 235–236). China is also currently developing the new J-20 stealth combat aircraft. Separately, it is developing carrier-borne combat aircraft, namely the J-15 (based on the Su-27) and the J-31 stealth combat aircraft (*The Telegraph* 2012). In 2013 Japan's air force had 201 of the proven US-made F-15J Eagle combat aircraft as its mainstay, with an additional 76 of the locally built F-2 (a longer-range equivalent of the F-16) and 63 obsolete F-4 Phantom combat aircraft (IISS 2014: 253). After failing in its bid to acquire the fifth-generation F-22 stealth combat aircraft from the USA, it turned its attention to the stealth F-35 joint strike fighter (JSF) in order to counter China's development of similar aircraft. Thus, in 2011 Japan announced that it would buy 42 of the US-made F-35s (*The National* 2011). Similarly, South Korea has in recent years also moved to upgrade its air force, procuring 60 of the latest versions of the F-15. Currently, it has over 500 combat aircraft, including 164 modern F-16C/D combat aircraft (IISS 2014: 259). In 2013 South Korea was evaluating the procurement of 60 new combat aircraft, and the F-35 JSF was a key contender (*Defense News* 2013).

Another area of arms competition has been in UAVs. In East Asia, China has led the way in terms of development and deployment, which is reflected in the large number of UAV projects undertaken since the 1980s. They comprise three main classes: mini-drones with a range of up to 70 km (the AW, Z and W series); tactical medium-range drones with a range of 150–200 km (the ASN 200 series); and strategic medium-altitude long-endurance (MALE) drones with a range of up to 2,400 km (Hsu 2013: 6). As demonstrated in various recent air shows, China has a number of new UAVs in development, including the CH-4 MALE UAV, a multi-purpose drone capable of reconnaissance, electronic warfare and ground-strike missions, and the Xianglong/Soar Dragon high-altitude long-endurance (HALE) UAV which resembles the US RQ-4 Global Hawk (ibid.: 10–11). China has also developed the Lijian stealth drone similar to the US X-74B being developed for its aircraft carriers, which was reportedly completing trials in May 2013 (*News China* 2013).

In response, Japan has expressed an interest in acquiring UAVs of its own, such as the US Global Hawk UAV (*The Guardian* 2013). It is also developing a missile-detecting drone to bolster its ballistic missile defence system (AFP 2012). South Korea has developed its own UAV projects in its bid to become a leading UAV operator, such as the KUS-7 and KUS-9 tactical UAVs, a new MALE UAV similar to the US Predator drone to be deployed after 2016, and a Smart UAV which can land and take off vertically (*Airforce-Technology.com* 2010). South Korea has also requested to buy four new US-made Global Hawk HALE UAVs (Bloomberg 2012). Taiwan has responded to China's massive UAV programme by developing its own UAV which is similar to the US Predator drone, as well as an advanced stealth combat drone similar to the US X-47B (*Flightglobal* 2011).

Finally, a naval arms race appears to be taking place in East Asia (Ball 2010: 42). China and South Korea have emerged as major naval powers, while Japan's navy remains one of the largest and most sophisticated in Asia.

In 2013 China's navy deployed 70 principal surface combat vessels, the most prominent of which are its new conventional aircraft carrier, the *Liaoning* (the former Russian *Varyag*), and four modern Russian-made Sovremenny-class air warfare destroyers. In addition, China has developed new stealth multi-role frigates similar to the French Lafayette-class, namely the Type 054A Jiangkai-class frigate (IISS 2014: 233–234). China is also seeking to deploy an increasing number of conventional aircraft carriers, as it has begun to develop the aircraft to be used for them, such as the J-15 and the J-31. Japan deployed 47 principal surface combat vessels in 2012, including two Hyuga-class helicopter carriers that can accomodate up to 10 helicopters (ibid.: 251). It has also commenced the construction of a new and larger class of carriers which can deploy 14 helicopters, the first of which are expected to enter service in 2015 (*Chosun Ilbo* 2013). These carriers are useful for amphibious warfare and anti-submarine purposes, but they could also eventually embark the F-35B JSF capable of taking off and landing vertically that is being developed by the USA. Japan's six Atago- and Kongo-class destroyers are also equipped with the sophisticated US Aegis combat system which facilitates extensive sea, air and ballistic missile defence.

Similarly to China and Japan, South Korea has a expanding navy comprising carriers, destroyers, frigates and corvettes. In 2013 it had 22 principal surface combat warships, with an additional 30 missile corvettes. Its principal warships are six KDX-2 and three KDX-3 air warfare destroyers, with the latter equipped with the Aegis combat system (IISS 2014: 258). In 2007 South Korea also took delivery of its sole helicopter carrier (officially classified as an amphibious assault ship), the *Dokdo*, and another two are planned (*Military-Today* 2013: 255). In 2013 Taiwan had, on paper, 26 principal surface combat vessels. However, the most modern warships in Taiwan's navy are four modernized former US navy Kidd-class destroyers, albeit armed with Harpoon anti-ship and SM-2 anti-aircraft missiles (IISS 2014: 281).

Significantly, China, Japan, North Korea and South Korea all deploy large submarine fleets, which suggests that a submarine arms race among them exists. In 2013 China had 70 submarines, including nine nuclear-powered submarines, some of which carry nuclear ballistic missiles. Japan had 18 conventional submarines including the new Soryu-class equipped with air independent propulsion (AIP) which provides greater endurance, while South Korea deployed 23 vessels, including new Son Won-ill-class AIP-equipped submarines. North Korea had 72 submarines, including 52 midget submarines (IISS 2014). Taiwan is the exception in that it has failed to procure modern submarines from abroad, and therefore was continuing to deploy four obsolete submarines in 2012 (ibid.: 281).

In sum, the arms race in East Asia is characterized by sophistication as it employs the latest military technology, as well as scale given the number of weapons systems involved, thus substantially improving the offensive capabilities of the states in the region. The military build-ups are clearly aimed at each other, given the interactive, competitive element that has resulted in similar weapons systems being procured.

Rapid increase in quantity and quality of armaments

Another indicator of the emergence of an arms race is the rapid increase in quantity and quality of armaments. A comparison of the number of major weapons systems developed between 1990 (after the ending of the Cold War) and 2013 provides an indication of the ongoing military expansion (see Table 3.1 and Table 3.2). However, these figures merely provide an approximate and inaccurate guide when compared with a more in-depth qualitative analysis. This is because in some states the number of weapons systems in certain categories have actually decreased, although this has been more than made up for by the increase in the quality of armaments.

China increased its armoured forces between 1990 and 2013, including the introduction of new Type 98 and Type 99 main battle tanks. It introduced AEW & C aircraft, an important force multiplier for its air force. While its combat aircraft force decreased sharply, it has been more than made up for by the increase in the quality of armaments, in the form of Su-30 MKK, Su-27/J11, J10 combat aircraft and the impending deployment of the stealth J-20. It has acquired its first conventional aircraft carrier, and has expanded the number and increased the quality of its principal surface combat fleet. China has also developed nuclear submarines and has expanded and improved its amphibious landing capabilities. In sum, China has vastly increased its defensive and offensive military capabilities in all major areas.

Fundamentally, Japan maintained its capabilities during the period 1990–2013, though it has clearly lost ground in comparison to China's rapid military development. While the number of principal surface combat vessels fell from 68 to 47, the acquisition of six Aegis destroyers has improved its military quality and capabilities. It also procured more efficient Boeing 767 AEW & C aircraft and two helicopter carriers, and more are to be constructed. Japan has also recently decided to acquire the new stealth F-35 JSFs.

Table 3.1 Selected Major Weapons Systems in East Asia (1990)

	Main Battle Tanks	Armoured Personnel Carriers	AEW & C	Combat Aircraft	Aircraft / Helicopter Carriers	Principal Surface Warships	Submarines	Major Landing Ships
China	8,000	2,800	0	5,070	0	55	93	58
Japan	1,222	550	10	473	0	68	15	6
South Korea	1,550	2,140	0	493	0	34	3	15
Taiwan	309	265	0	504	0	34	4	26
North Korea	3,500	4,200	0	716	0	3	24	0

Source: IISS 1990.

Table 3.2 Selected Major Weapons Systems in East Asia (2013)

	Main Battle Tanks	Armoured Personnel Carriers	AEW & C	Combat Aircraft	Aircraft / Helicopter Carriers	Principal Surface Warships	Submarines	Major Landing Ships
China	6,840	7,952	8	2,525	1	70	70 (9 nuclear)	85
Japan	777	871	17	630	2	47	18	4
South Korea	2,514	3,030	4	568	1	22 (plus 30 corvettes)	23	4
Taiwan	565	1,247	6	485	0	26	4	12
North Korea	3,500	2,500	0	603	0	3	72	10

Source: IISS 2014.

South Korea's military development during the same period has been impressive, with both numbers and quality increasing for all major weapons systems. South Korea introduced a number of new capabilities, such as an amphibious helicopter carrier, Aegis destroyers, and Boeing 737 AEW & C aircraft. It also improved its existing capabilities, such as introducing the locally developed K1 main battle tank and substantially expanding its fleet of submarines. Its adversary, North Korea, impressively has maintained large conventional forces but its weapons systems are obsolete and North Korea does not possess sophisticated military technology. However, it does have asymmetric and anti-access capabilities in the form of nuclear weapons, ballistic missiles and a large force of submarines. Finally, Taiwan appears, on paper at least, to have only slightly reduced its air and naval capabilities while improving its land capabilities during this period. In reality, in 2013 Taiwan fielded increasingly obsolete weapons systems. For instance, its combat aircraft represent the technology of the 1980s, while its navy boasts just two former US Guppy-class submarines of Second World War vintage, and two Zwaardvis-class submarines procured from Holland in the late 1980s.

Overall, however, the picture is clear: significant interstate antagonisms exist, there is evidence of a competitive action-reaction dynamic at work, and finally, there has been a rapid increase in both the quantity and quality of armaments. In short, there is evidence of an arms race in East Asia.

Conclusion: implications of the arms race in East Asia

East Asia's arms race leads to the classic problem of the security dilemma, in which a state that is perceived as becoming too powerful leads to counter-acquisitions by other states. This results in misperceptions, conflict spirals, heightened tensions and ultimately open conflict, thereby destroying the very security that arms are supposed to guarantee (Jervis 1976). East Asia's sustained economic rise since the end of the Korean War in 1953 and the lack of any major conflict since has lulled many into believing that growing economic interdependence will make war unlikely in that region (Khoo 2013: 47–48). However, this is a false premise as significant historical antagonisms have remained. Japan's imperialism prior to 1945 and its failure adequately to account for its past continues to stir up strong nationalist emotions in China and South Korea. In addition, the divisions between North Korea and South Korea are as strong and intractable as ever, leading to an arms race on the Korean peninsula.

The situation is compounded by the weakness or absence of regional institutions, regimes and laws that could regulate interstate relations, build trust and confidence, and otherwise put a stop to the arms race. None of the distinctive confidence- and security-building measures which were in place in Europe during the Cold War and helped to calm tensions as well as contain the arms race exist in Asia. Within East Asia itself, the Six-Party Talks have focused only on the Korean issue and have not managed to stem North Korea's open brinkmanship that in early 2013 almost brought the Korean peninsula to war again.

The arms race in East Asia is dangerous owing to the increased risk of miscalculation as a result of misperception. Chinese policymakers appear to be convinced that Japan is dominated by right-wing conservatives bent on reviving militarism (Glosserman 2012). At the same time, there is also a perception within China that given its growing strength, it should now aggressively assert what it perceives to be its legitimate claims in the East and South China Seas. Thus, China's nationalist discourse perceives that the problems about disputed territory emanate from other powers, not China (Sutter 2012). The consequences of conflict between China and Japan, on the Korean peninsula or over Taiwan, however, will not stay regional. As a key player in East Asia, the USA, which has security commitments to Japan and South Korea, residual commitments to Taiwan, and troops on the ground in East Asia and in the Western Pacific, will be drawn in. The problem is that any conflict in East Asia is not likely to remain conventional for long. In fact, it is likely that it would rapidly escalate into a nuclear war because three of the key players, namely China, North Korea and the USA, possess nuclear weapons.

Bibliography

ABC News, 'Anti-Japan Protests Spread Across China', *ABC News*, 19 September 2012, www.abc.net.au/news/2012-09-18/anti-japan-protests-spread-across-china/4268494.

AFP, 'Japan to Develop Missile Detecting Drone: Report', *DefenseNews*, 3 November 2012, www.defensenews.com/article/20121104/DEFREG03/311040003/Report-Japan-Develop-Missile-Detecting-Drone.

Airforce-Technology.com, 'South Korea's Push for the UAV', 28 April 2010, www.airforce-technology.com/features/feature83412.

Airforce-Technology.com, 'Boeing 767 AWACS Airborne Warning and Control Aircraft, Japan', www.airforce-technology.com/projects/767awacs/ (accessed 26 July 2013).

Ball, Desmond, 'Arms Modernization in Asia: An Emerging Complex Arms Race', in Andrew T. H. Tan (ed.), *The Global Arms Trade*, London: Routledge, 2010.

Bateman, Sam, 'Regional and International Frameworks for Maritime Security Cooperation', Paper delivered at the Maritime Security in South and Southeast Asia Conference, Institute for International Policy Studies (IIPS), Tokyo, 11 December 2001, www.iips.org/Bateman_paper.pdf.

Bloomberg, 'North Korea Fuels Regional Tensions by Quitting Armistice', *Bloomberg*, 9 March 2013, www.bloomberg.com/news/2013-03-08/north-korea-fuels-region-s-tensions-by-quitting-armistice.html.

Bloomberg, 'South Korea to Buy $1.2 Billion in Drones Under U.S. Plan', *Bloomberg*, 25 December 2012, www.bloomberg.com/news/2012-12-24/south-korea-to-buy-1-2-billion-in-drones-under-u-s-plan.html.

Boeing Media, 'Boeing Delivers Final Peace Eye AEW & C Aircraft to Republic of Korea Air Force', *Boeing Media*, 31 October 2012, www.boeing.mediaroom.com/index.php?s=43&item=2477.

Chosun Ilbo, 'Japan to Build New Helicopter Carrier', 26 July 2013, www.english.chosun.com/site/data/html_dir/2011/09/15/2011091501272.html.

CNN, 'Taiwan, China Sign Historic Trade Deal', *CNN*, 29 June 2010.

DefenseNews, 'South Korea's $7.3B Fighter Contest Enters Final Phase', 22 June 2013, www.defensenews.com/article/20130622/DEFREG03/306220008/S-Korea-s-7-3B-Fighter-Contest-Enters-Final-Phase.

Flightglobal, 'Taiwan Looks to Develop Advanced Unmanned Systems', 12 August 2011, www.flightglobal.com/news/articles/taiwan-looks-to-develop-advanced-unmanned-systems-360628/.

Flightglobal, 'U.S. and Taiwan in $3.8bn F-16 Upgrade Deal', 23 July 2012, www.flightglobal.com/news/articles/us-and-taiwan-in-38bn-f-16-upgrade-deal-374601/.

Gendercide, 'Case Study: The Nanjing Massacre, 1937–1938', www.gendercide.org/case_nanking.html.

Glosserman, Brad, 'A Problem Bigger Than the Senkakus', PacNet #62A, 9 October 2012, Washington, DC: CSIS, www.csis.org/publication/pacnet-62a-problem-bigger-senkakus.

Gray, Colin S., 'The Arms Race Phenomenon', *World Politics*, Vol. 24, No. 1, 1972.

Hsu, Kimberly, 'China's Military Unmanned Aerial Vehicle Industry', *U.S.-China Economic and Security Review Commission*, 13 June 2013, www.uscc.gov/sites/default/files/Research/China%27s%20Military%20UAV%20Industry_14%20June%202013.pdf.

International Institute for Strategic Studies (IISS), *The Military Balance 1990–91*, London, IISS, 1990, www.iiss.org/publications/military-balance/the-military-balance-2012/press-statement/.

International Institute for Strategic Studies (IISS), *The Military Balance 2012 – Press Statement*, London, IISS, 2012, www.iiss.org/publications/military-balance/the-military-balance-2012/press-statement/.

International Institute for Strategic Studies (IISS), *The Military Balance 2013*, London: IISS, 2013, www.iiss.org/en/about%20us/press%20room/press%20releases/press%20releases/archive/2013-61eb/march-c5a4/military-balance-2013-press-statement-61a2.

International Institute for Strategic Studies (IISS), *The Military Balance 2014*, London: IISS, 2014.

Jacques, Martin, *When China Rules the World: The Rise of the Middle Kingdom and the End of the Western World*, London: Allen Lane, 2009.

Jervis, Robert, *Perception and Misperception in International Politics*, Princeton, NJ: Princeton University Press, 1976.

Khoo, Nicholas, 'The False Promise of Economic Interdependence: Chinese Foreign Policy in Northeast Asia', in Andrew T. H. Tan (ed.), *East and South-East Asia International Relations and Security Perspectives*, London: Routledge, 2013: 47–55.

Kopp, Carlo, 'China's Eyes in the Sky', *The Diplomat*, 11 August 2010, www.thediplomat.com/2010/08/11/china%E2%80%99s-eyes-in-the-skies/?all=true.

Lee, Sheryn, 'China and Taiwan Relations: Challenges and Prospects', in Andrew T. H. Tan (ed.), *East and Southeast Asia: International Relations and Security Perspectives*, London: Routledge, 2013.

Military-Today, 'Dokdo-class Amphibious Assault Ship', www.military-today.com/navy/dokdo_class.htm.

News China Magazine, 'China to Fly First Stealth UCAV', July 2013, www.newschinamag.com/magazine/china-to-fly-first-stealth-ucav.

New York Times, 'South Korean's Visit to Disputed Islets Angers Japan', 10 August 2012.

Pew Research, Global Attitudes Project, 'Japanese Public's Mood Rebounding, Abe Highly Popular; China and South Korea Very Negative Toward Japan', 11 July 2013.

Reuters, 'North Korea Shells South in Fiercest Attack in Decades', 23 November 2010, www.reuters.com/article/2010/11/23/us-korea-north-artillery-idUSTRE6AM0YS20101123.

Sutter, Robert, 'China's Self-Absorbed Nationalism – It's Worse Than It Looks', *PacNet*, No. 53, 23 August 2012, Washington, DC: CSIS, www.csis.org/publication/pacnet-53-chinas-self-absorbed-nationalism-its-worse-it-looks.

The Australian, 'Sea Row Spurs $2bn Shinzo Abe Defence Spend', 10 January 2013.

The Guardian, 'Japan and China Step Up Drone Race as Tension Builds Over Disputed Islands', 9 January 2013, www.guardian.co.uk/world/2013/jan/08/china-japan-drone-race.

The National, 'Japan Signs Deal for 42 Lockheed Martin F-35 Stealth Fighter Jets', 21 December 2011, www.thenational.ae/news/world/asia-pacific/japan-signs-deal-for-42-lockheed-martin-f-35-stealth-fighter-jets.

The Telegraph, 'China Makes First Test Flight of New Stealth Fighter Jet', 1 November 2012, www.telegraph.co.uk/news/worldnews/asia/china/9647722/China-makes-first-test-flight-of-new-stealth-fighter-jet.html.

Treaty of Shimonoseki, 1895, www.taiwandocuments.org/shimonoseki01.htm.

VOA News, 'Japan Protests Chinese Ship's Alleged Use of Radar to Guide Missiles', 5 February 2013, www.voanews.com/content/chinese-warship-locked-prefiring-radar-on-japanese-navy-tokyo/1597325.html.

Part II
China

4
China's naval modernization and its impact on Asian Security

Nan Li

Introduction

China's military modernization began as early as 1985, when China's then paramount leader Deng Xiaoping ordered the People's Liberation Army (PLA) to make the 'strategic transition' from preparing for an 'early, total and nuclear war' against a Soviet invasion to 'peacetime army construction', resulting in the downsizing of the PLA by 1m. troops (AMS-CDSO 1992). This was accompanied by an intra-PLA debate on what type of war the PLA should be prepared to fight, leading to a 1988 Central Military Commission (CMC) decision that the PLA should make preparations to fight 'local wars', or those concerning sovereignty-based territorial disputes on the margins of China (Hu and Xiao 1989: 173–180; Li 1997; Liu 2010: 15). In 1993 China's new leader Jiang Zemin modified the 'local war' concept to 'local war under high-tech conditions', translating into a 1995 policy to transform the PLA from a manpower-intensive force to a technology-based one. He then introduced the notion of 'leapfrogging development' in 1997 in order to shift the emphasis of military modernization from mechanization (i.e. adding new hardware platforms) to informatization (developing information technology-based network and software) to narrow the technological gap with the more advanced militaries. This concept resulted in a 2002 CMC policy of 'dual construction' (referring to mechanization and informatization) (Army Construction Institute of the NDU 2002: 56, 232–244). These technology-based policies led to decisions to downsize the PLA by 500,000 troops in 1997 and by another 200,000 in 2002. By June 2004 Jiang had for the first time called on the PLA to prepare for fighting 'local war under informatized conditions' (CDSO 2010: 628).

Hu Jintao succeeded Jiang as the CMC chairman in September 2004, and held that position until 2012. This study examines Hu's major contributions to China's military modernization. However, this study focuses on one aspect, namely China's naval modernization, rather than the general issue of military modernization. This aspect deserves special attention mainly because it is most likely to have a significant impact on Asian security. China's military analysts, for instance, believe that China's biggest security challenges and threats in the future may come from the sea.

According to these analysts, China has resolved its territorial disputes with most of its land neighbours by signing treaties to delineate the land boundaries, but has not resolved these disputes with its maritime neighbours. Nor has reunification of Taiwan with the mainland been accomplished, and possible US military intervention may complicate the issue. Moreover, the integration of the Chinese economy with the world economy leads to more resources, imports and traded goods being shipped through vital sea lanes and to more overseas investment, as well as an increasingly prosperous coastal region. As a result, the analysts argue that naval modernization is crucial in order to guarantee the security of these newly emerging Chinese interests in the near and far seas (Li 2009b: 161–162).[1] Finally, the PLA posesses other services that are more capable of power projection such as the PLA Air Force (PLAAF) and these regard China's maritime security as their mission priorities (Ma 2014). Therefore, an analysis of China's naval modernization can shed light on the intentions and direction of China's military modernization in general.

This study, which examines naval modernization, refers to naval strategy and naval capabilities. It attempts to answer two sets of questions. The first refers to China's evolving naval strategy. What conceptual contribution has Hu Jintao made to China's naval strategy since becoming the chairman of the CMC? What are the specific missions which the PLAN is expected to fulfil in terms of its near and far seas operations? What are the different priorities for the near and far seas missions, and why? Finally, how might the PLAN conduct its operations? The second set of questions concerns changing naval capabilities. Which new capabilities have been developed in recent years, and what are the reasons for these new developments?

This study has three sections. While the first section attempts to answer questions related to naval strategy, the second section addresses the issue of capabilities. The concluding section summarizes the findings and discusses their impact on Asian security.

Evolving naval strategy

Hu's contributions to naval strategy

Hu has made two major conceptual contributions to China's naval strategy, one at the strategic level, and the other at the operational level. These contributions become apparent if Hu's priorities are compared with those of his predecessor, Jiang Zemin.

At the strategic level, both Hu and Jiang have promoted naval modernization, but with very different priorities. For Jiang, the top strategic priority, particularly after the 1996 Taiwan Strait crisis, was to deter Taiwan from declaring formal independence. As a result, he promoted the PLAN by acquiring Sovremenny-class destroyers and Kilo submarines from Russia, and by commissioning a handful of indigenously developed major surface and subsurface combatants. As air superiority in any military conflict over Taiwan can be gained by shore-based combat aircraft, Jiang did not endorse the aircraft carrier programme for which Admiral Liu Huaqing had actively lobbied, to provide air cover for naval operations over the more distant Spratly Islands in the South China Sea (Liu 2004: 477–481). Instead, Jiang pursued diplomacy with South-East Asian countries under his 'new security concept', leading to China's signing of the Treaty of Amity and Cooperation with the Association of Southeast Asian Nations (ASEAN) and of the Declaration of Code of Conduct with ASEAN with regard to the South China Sea (Li 2004).

Jiang made the Taiwan issue a priority, and particularly sought to emphasize that the PLAN should 'at present continue to implement the strategic thought of near-seas defense … to realistically appropriate the comprehensive operations capabilities of conducting maritime campaigns in the near seas'. Even though Jiang is the first Chinese leader to endorse the concept of 'far seas operations', he regards the development of such capabilities largely as a secondary, long-term objective (Tang and Wu 2007: 93).

By the time Hu succeeded Jiang as China's leader, the naval capabilities thought necessary to deter Taiwan independence were largely in place. The election of the anti-independence candidate Ma Ying-jeou as Taiwan's new president also rendered the Taiwan issue less urgent. While Hu also wants the PLA to deter flash points such as the Taiwan issue from escalating into a military conflict, so that China can leverage the 20-year window of strategic opportunity (2001–20) to develop its economy, Hu has other strategic priorities on his mind. Among the 'new historical missions' that Hu assigned to the PLA, for instance, he highlighted the need for the PLA to safeguard China's newly emerging interests in maritime, outer, and electromagnetic space (Li 2010: 17–18).

With respect to China's newly emerging maritime interests, Hu was particularly concerned about the issue of energy security stemming from China's increasing dependence on oil imports. As early as November 2003, during the Central Economic Work Conference, Hu, as the new CCP general secretary, stressed the need to develop a new energy development strategy from a 'strategic overall height' to achieve national energy security (Qu 2009). Following the rapid expansion of the Chinese economy and its integration with the global economy, Hu later stated that 'issues of national development security such as energy security, strategic (sea) lanes security, overseas market security, overseas investment and personnel security have become more outstanding day by day' (GPD 2010: 435).

According to Hu, naval modernization has become indispensable for the projection of power to safeguard these newly emerging Chinese interests in the far seas or overseas. While continuing to 'enhance its inner and near-seas comprehensive operations capabilities', Hu particularly stressed that the PLAN should 'make the transformation to far-seas protection step by step, and enhance far-seas mobile operations capabilities' (Tang and Wu 2007: 93). For Jiang, the development of far seas capabilities is a long-term objective. However, for Hu the development of these capabilities has become a near-term objective.

At the operational level, Hu endorsed the new concept of 'information systems-based system of systems operations' at an 'important army conference' in December 2005 (Ren 2010: 26). This concept offers a new framework for thinking about how the PLAN should conduct operations, which also impacts on how the PLAN should develop its operational capabilities. As discussed in detail below, this concept aims to mitigate the unintended but negative consequences of implementing the service-centered 'informatization' policy that was previously endorsed by Jiang Zemin. These consequences include developing lapsed capabilities, and lacking collateral information systems-based integration of various services and systems. In line with Hu's 'scientific development' theory, this concept clearly intends to enhance the overall cost-effectiveness for conducting operations and developing capabilities.

PLAN missions in the near and far seas

Based on the general guidance offered by leaders such as Jiang and Hu, PLA analysts divide the PLAN missions into two major categories: near seas and far seas. In the near seas, besides deterring Taiwanese independence and securing traditional territorial waters, a relatively new mission is 'safeguarding maritime rights and interests' (NDWP 2013). This mission is clearly associated with China's disputes with other countries about jurisdictions over continental shelves and exclusive economic zones (EEZ), and about sovereignty over islands and reefs in the near seas and the territorial and jurisdictional waters they may generate.

However, rather than standing on the front line in such disputes, the PLAN is primarily required to support the forwardly deployed civilian law enforcement fleet and other civilian maritime activities. According to the Defense White Paper, for instance, in order to safeguard maritime rights and interests, 'the navy combines daily war-preparation with offering security support for state maritime law enforcement, fishery production, and oil exploration activities; establishes coordinating and concerting mechanisms respectively with law enforcement departments such as China Maritime Surveillance and China Fishery Law Enforcement Command; and establishes and perfects the military-police-civilian joint defense mechanisms'. Furthermore, the PLAN 'coordinates with related civilian departments to conduct maritime survey and mapping and scientific research; constructs maritime weather monitoring, satellite navigation, radio navigation and navigation-assisting signs systems; publishes timely information on weather and shipping; and establishes and perfects navigation safety support systems within the jurisdictional seas' (NDWP 2013).

Far seas missions, on the other hand, refer to those that safeguard the security of expanding Chinese overseas interests, including the 'security of overseas energy and resources, strategic sea lanes, and overseas (Chinese) citizens and legal entities', as well as those that provide humanitarian assistance (NDWP 2013). The PLAN, for instance, briefly deployed a naval frigate to the Mediterranean in February 2011, to support the evacuation of 35,860 Chinese nationals during the Libyan crisis. However, more importantly, since December 2008 the PLAN has deployed naval escort groups to Gulf of Aden for continuous patrol to keep the sea lanes open against piracy. Finally, the PLAN's dedicated hospital ship *Peace Ark* travelled to five countries in Western Asia and Eastern Africa, and four countries in Latin America during 2010–11, to provide medical assistance to over 50,000 people living in these countries (ibid.).

Near seas missions as a priority

Integrating the notion of far seas operations into China's naval strategy requires the PLAN to develop capabilities to operate in the seas beyond the near seas. However, China's naval strategists argue that the more imminent maritime security challenges to China are largely concentrated in the near seas.

These challenges include reunification with Taiwan, foreign military threats and pressures, and disputes with neighbouring countries about jurisdictions over continental shelves and EEZ, and about sovereignty over islands and reefs in the near seas. Nontraditional security issues in the near seas include smuggling, human trafficking, transnational crimes, and maritime environmental pollution. As a result, 'at present and in a long time to come, safeguarding near-seas security should be the primary goal of China's maritime security strategy'. Also, 'better near-seas security creates favorable conditions for marching to the far seas to meet not only the need for deepening and widening the defense space against foreign threats, but also the needs to enhance security of sea lanes and China's newly emerging overseas economic interests, to promote international cooperation, and to raise China's international status'. Moreover, 'marching to the far seas with clear and selective objectives offers forceful support and coordination for resolving near-seas security issues' (Feng *et al.* 2010: 300–301).

Furthermore, there are major vulnerabilities and limits that may impede the PLAN's far seas operations. For instance, China has neither overseas naval bases nor regularized access points in the far seas of the Indian Ocean. A limited number of at-sea replenishment ships and occasional port visits for re-supply and crew rest may help in terms of logistics support, but not in combat support such as reloading missiles to sustain high-intensity conventional naval battles. The PLAN is also quite weak in its anti-submarine warfare (ASW) capabilities, which leaves Chinese warships exposed to submarine attacks in the far seas. Such attacks may partly explain why China's naval escort groups in the Gulf of Aden comprise only two combat ships supported by one large replenishment ship, and their missions are confined to dealing with low-intensity, non-traditional security issues such as piracy.

Some Chinese naval strategists argue that China should develop overseas naval bases in the Indian Ocean (CRNA 2009). However, this argument has not translated into any change in Chinese policy (*The Hindu* 2012). One of the main reasons for this is that China's non-alignment foreign policy forbids China to develop military alliances with other countries. This makes it difficult for China to establish overseas military bases because they are usually located in close allies' territories. Also, because overseas bases are associated with the legacy of colonialism and a lack of sensitivity towards national sovereignty, China may pay an image cost if it acquires any such bases. In addition, the acquisition of overseas bases might not serve China's national interests well because it could entangle China in regional and domestic disputes and conflicts (Huang, Y. 2009). All these factors reflect the fact that near seas missions will become the PLAN's priority in the near future.

How might the PLAN conduct operations?

There are two different conceptual models that may help to explain how the PLA in general and the PLAN in particular might conduct operations. The first is the concept of 'information systems-based system of systems operations (ISSSO)', and the other is the traditional active defence strategy (TADS).

Information systems-based system of systems operations

As mentioned above, the concept of ISSSO was first endorsed by Hu Jintao in 2005. However, it was not fully articulated and operationalized by PLA analysts until after early 2010, when several unintended but serious consequences stemming from the policy of 'informatization' (previously endorsed by Jiang Zemin) had become apparent.

One such consequence, according to PLA analysts, relates to inter-service integration. As 'informatization' is 'service-centred' but not 'system-centred', what has happened is that as each service becomes more informatized, more powerful stove-pipes or 'isolated information islands' emerge through the lack of collateral information networking across the services. Also, each service tends to be 'self-serving' under the pretext of enhancing joint operations, concentrating on constructing 'all-round service' (referring to ground forces expanding air, shore-defence and ship capabilities, the navy expanding air and land capabilities, and the air force expanding land capabilities). Not only does this result in unnecessary redundancy and wasted resources, but more importantly the erosion of services' comparative advantages. Moreover, service-centred 'informatization' leads to a lack of common information standards and results in information monopolies by each service, which may not only contribute to inter-service tension, but lead to a loss of initiative in times of war (Lin 2011: 19–21; Zhang and Yu 2010: 12).

PLA analysts believe that the concept of ISSSO may help to resolve this inter-service issue. This is because ISSSO requires fostering the awareness that war can be fought and won by the PLA system of systems, but not by individual services. As a result, the emphasis of military modernization should shift from 'forging all-round services to constructing all-round system of systems'. This means that services should transfer ownership rights and command and control of their operational elements and resources to the PLA system, while retaining the usage right of these resources. Services should also become open and transparent to one another and 'share the usage right' of each other's and the PLA system's resources, because services constitute and are the builders of PLA system of systems. 'Transferring communications band width and satellites to the system, for instance, can give full play to the utility of these elements'. In return, services benefit from the system by retaining the usage right of all the resources offered by the system (Lin 2011: 20–21).

Generally speaking, future 'integrated operations' would 'reinforce services' functions for constructing and managing forces, but weaken their role to command operations. … Services will supply functional units and essential elements to integrated operations command according to operational needs'. To optimize the use of these units and elements, the integrated operations command would rely on information systems such as the all-army, unified command and control network, early warning and reconnaissance network, communications grid network, weapons control network and comprehensive support network (Lin 2011: 22).

Besides the relationship between system and services or systems, according to PLA analysts, ISSSO also necessitates the 'construction of collateral, integrated system of systems operations capabilities centered on integrated networks across all services'. This 'network-centred' approach leverages information technologies and networks to permeate, fuse, and connect all forces, units and essential elements deployed in different distances and spatial domains to achieve inter-connectedness, inter-communications, inter-operability and mutual complements, particularly in terms of early warning and reconnaissance, command and control, communications, weapons control, and combat support. This inter-connectivity facilitates synchronized joint action, thus enhancing the precision, coordination, efficiency and orderliness of action and strikes (Lin 2011: 22; Ren 2010: 27–29; Jiang 2010: 27–28).

How then might the concept of ISSSO enhance military operations? First, such a system of systems-based synergy is not only what an individual service, unit, or weapons platform is incapable of achieving, it also helps to reduce its vulnerabilities as an individual service, unit, or platform. For instance, 'employing information systems to permeate, fuse and connect weapons systems can accomplish operational effectiveness that far exceeds what a single weapons system such as an aircraft carrier can accomplish. At the same time, this integration can reduce the risks of an aircraft carrier' (Lin 2011: 22).

Moreover, according to PLA analysts, information systems-based integration leads to real-time and battlefield clarity, reduces reaction time and enables more precise strikes, thus creating conditions for dispersed as well as pointed force deployment, but concentrated firepower. This deployment also stretches from land, sea and air to new domains such as outer, electromagnetic and cyber space, in effect a trend towards 'comprehensive spatial domains'. These deployment patterns involving various distances, altitudes and visibilities may enhance not only force survivability but also battlefield versatility (Ping *et al.* 2010: 41).

Traditionally, quantity superiority in manpower, weapons and materiel may translate into battlefield effect superiority. However, information systems-based integration makes it possible to achieve information superiority, which may translate into decision and action superiority, and as a result quality superiority on the battlefield. What this means, according to PLA analysts, is that the side that can best exploit networked information systems to 'coordinate the dispersed deployment of operational units, but concentration of information and fire power on the decisive targets at the decisive location and decisive time', would gain the battlefield initiative (Ren 2010: 27).

PLA analysts generally believe that information systems integration can optimize the PLA system of systems, and enable real-time, synchronized target acquisition, decision, mobility, strikes, and control. In turn, this shortens decision cycles and increases operational tempo, making it possible to conduct parallel operations and achieve 'all-domains superiority' on the battlefield. It is noted, however, that the PLA may develop similar vulnerabilities to those developed by more advanced militaries as it becomes more integrated through the use of information systems. Therefore, the PLA should prepare for situations during which its own information systems are semi- or completely paralyzed, and 'traditional fighting methods should not be abandoned' (Luo 2010: 56).

ISSSO prescribes approximately what Western analysts term the PLA's so-called anti-access and area denial strategy, particularly in the event of a US intervention in a Taiwan conflict. Based on the premise that information systems-based integration may help to achieve some sort of battlefield parity or even superiority over an opponent, the PLA could wage a direct, frontal assault on the spearhead or comparative strength of a US offensive such as its aircraft carrier strike group and well-protected information systems. A continuous assault based on layered, multi-domain deployment of PLA forces would make it increasingly difficult for the intervening forces to advance as they close in on China's shores.

Some analysts suggest that this type of PLA assault is largely based on its comparative advantage: anti-ship missiles. However, shore, ship, and air-based anti-ship missiles are an extension of traditional anti-ship guns and bombs, and the PLA's opponent is well armed with similar missiles and other weapons systems to counter an attack. What could make a difference appears to be the detection range, shooting range, and precision of these missiles and weapons systems. In all these aspects, however, the PLA does not seem to have an obvious comparative advantage over its opponent. Finally, the possible time and place of such a frontal, force-on-force engagement are quite predictable. It is precisely the possible lack of the PLA comparative advantage or superiority in such a frontal engagement that concerns some PLA analysts. They argue that ISSSO may help the PLA to develop comparative battlefield advantages in the long term. However, in the short term the PLA, being the inferior side, should employ the traditional active defence strategy when engaging a much more superior opponent.

Traditional active defence strategy

The central premise of the TADS is that the PLA is the inferior relative to its opponent. This means that the PLA would adopt a posture of strategic defence, which, however, involves many tactical-level offensive battles. However, rather than a direct, frontal assault on the opponent's comparative advantage, these battles usually require constant manoeuvres to concentrate the PLA's comparative strength on the opponent's vulnerabilities, thus guaranteeing low-cost gains.

In explaining the near seas active defence strategy, for instance, the former PLAN commander, Liu Huaqing, stressed that the PLAN is likely to be the inferior side relative to its potential opponent. As a result, in the general context of strategic interior-line defence, it is necessary for the PLAN to concentrate vital forces through mobile operations at the tactical level in order to develop temporary and local force superiority. This makes it possible to 'resolutely attack the enemy to achieve a victory at one stroke', followed by dispersion and diversion and search for new fighting opportunities, while maintaining the freedom for force movement. As he explained further:

> This is the effective fighting method for the small to win over the large at the strategic and for the numerically superior to win over the inferior at the tactical level. In general,

the enemy is the superior side waging the strategic exterior-line offensive, and we are in a strategic interior-line defensive position. But because the enemy's maritime offensive line is long and its forces are dispersed, it necessarily has vulnerabilities that give us the opportunities to exploit on the vast maritime battlefield. Although we are the inferior side, we concentrate superior forces in each campaign and battle, to conduct exterior-line quick and offensive operations, to strike one (enemy) unit and strive for its total annihilation. To this part, we are the superior and can fight and win. This fighting method, however, requires forces to move quickly and concentrate suddenly, to fight and withdraw quickly but not to get entangled with the enemy and not to engage in competitive attrition with the enemy, to eat the enemy bite by bite, thus achieving the objective of accumulating small victories into big victories.

(Liu 1986)

More importantly, the TADS recently has been employed by some PLA analysts to show the fallacies of the ISSSO. For instance, they identified two new PLA strategies that were developed in order to engage the opponent in the future. One is system of systems operations, and the other is the 'assassin's mace' approach. For system of systems operations, the analysts argue that 'it is impossible to engage in a system-on-system confrontation with the powerful opponent. Under the condition of obvious asymmetry of comprehensive power (in favour of the opponent), such a confrontation may repeat the historical mistake of engaging the powerful opponent in a 'state-on-state, force-on-force combat' (Dan and Ning 2010: 67). For the 'assassin's mace' approach, they argue that 'it is technically infeasible to employ assassin's mace weapons to wage sabotage-and-strike-warfare against the opponent's highly informatized system of systems' (ibid.).

For these PLA analysts, the most effective strategy to fight a powerful, superior opponent is by following the TADS. Fundamentally, they believe that there is no absolute inferiority and superiority, 'as long as the PLA does not engage the opponent in a system-on-system combat, there are ways to make the opponent lose initiative and superiority'. Furthermore, they argue that the PLA should turn parallel operations into sequential operations. The superior side, according to these analysts, prefers parallel operations, i.e. to simultaneously strike all the high-value targets in order to impose effective control of the PLA and to reduce its own casualties. The PLA, however, should turn this first engagement into its first battle, followed by a sequence of other battles. Similarly, 'the superior opponent prefers quick, decisive operations by employing superior informatized arms in order to realize its objectives, without protraction and rallying massive forces'. The PLA, however, should 'strive for protracted decisive operations to shake the opponent's will to fight, to regain control of the style and pace of war, and to force the opponent to yield to our wishes and demands' (Dan and Ning 2010: 68).

Furthermore, these analysts propose that the PLA should follow the TADS principle of 'concentrating vital forces to annihilate the enemy piece by piece'. However, rather than using manpower, the PLA now can concentrate its firepower to strike the opponent's 'strategic and campaign-level weak links that may have a decisive impact on the will of opponent to fight'. Finally, to reduce the opponent's comparative superiority and to gain the initiative, the PLA should force the opponent to fight in locations and times of the PLA's choice, rather than the other way round (ibid.).

The ISSSO and the TADS offer two different models to explain how the PLA in general and PLAN in particular might conduct operations. In the short term, the TADS is likely to be the dominant model that guides PLA operations. Whether the ISSSO gains dominant influence in the long term, however, might depend on how successful information systems integration proceeds, and whether the asymmetry in favor of the 'superior and powerful opponent' could be narrowed by this integration.

Evolving naval capabilities

Since the late 1990s submarine capabilities appear to be a top priority for China's naval modernization. The PLAN, for instance, has acquired a total of 12 Kilo diesel-electric submarines from Russia. It has also built and commissioned 13 Type 039G diesel-electric submarines, and added two Type 093 nuclear attack submarines and three Type 094 nuclear ballistic missile submarines to its fleet. Moreover, eight Type 041 diesel-electric submarines that are probably more efficient than the Russian Kilos, are either under construction, or have been launched or commissioned, and more are planned (*China Defense*).

To achieve a more balanced development, however, the PLAN's surface fleet has become a new development priority since the mid-2000s. This section seeks to examine and account for the new surface capabilities that have been developed in recent years. These new capabilities are divided into two categories: far seas and near seas. While far seas capabilities refer to major naval combatants that can operate in both the far and near seas, near seas capabilities refer to ships that cannot operate in the far seas owing to their limited operational radius and sustainability.

Far seas capabilities

I predicted that following the integration of the concept of far seas operations into China's naval strategy, China would acquire aircraft carrier capabilities (Li 2009b). This prediction was confirmed by the commissioning of the Type 001 aircraft carrier which was purchased from Ukraine and refitted on 25 September 2012 (*China Defense*).

This particular aircraft carrier is categorized as a 'scientific research and training ship'. Scientific research is likely to refer to obtaining technical and operational parameters and data for the construction of further aircraft carriers. Training, on the other hand, apparently refers to training officers and crew on all the functional, technical and operational specializations, and their coordination and integration associated with ship, ship-aircraft, and eventually battle group operations. While scientific research and training may take years to complete, the commissioning of the ship shows the PLAN's serious commitment to big deck aircraft carriers for fixed-wing aviation.

In the short term, it is possible that China could construct an aircraft carrier that is more or less based on the Type 001 configuration, which may feature a ski jump ramp, third-generation combat aircraft, and airborne early warning (AEW) helicopters. In the long term, however, China could develop nuclear-powered aircraft carriers with electromagnetic catapults and fourth-generation low-observable combat aircraft (China.com.cn 2013; Guancha.cn 2014). For one thing, the PLAN needs fixed-wing AEW aircraft, which are too heavy to be launched by the ski jump ramp of the current Type 001 platform, but can be launched by catapult. In comparison with the AEW helicopters to be deployed on the Type 001 carrier, fixed-wing AEW aircraft have much more powerful information, surveillance and reconnaissance capabilities, and therefore are indispensable for the PLAN's maritime 'information systems-based system of systems operations' (Li and Weuve 2010).

A primary reason for the PLAN to acquire aircraft carriers is to form a 'maritime operations system of systems', a requirement of ISSSO. A fleet without aircraft carriers, for instance, is an incomplete system of systems because it cannot reach all spatial domains, particularly the air domain in the far seas. It can deploy major surface ships such as destroyers and frigates to the far seas, but such ships are exposed and vulnerable to air, missile, and submarine attacks. Aircraft carrier capabilities, however, should reduce this vulnerability. This is because a carrier can provide air capabilities that can compete for air superiority and provide air cover for surface operations in the far seas. These air capabilities can also be deployed against the opponent's air-based ASW capabilities, thus protecting China's submarines operating in the far seas. Furthermore, a carrier's air-based ASW capabilities can be deployed against an opponent's submarines, thus providing protection for Chinese surface ships and submarines operating in the far seas. Finally, given the lack of overseas naval bases, carriers could serve as sea bases to sustain the PLAN's system of systems operations in the far seas.

As discussed earlier, an information systems-based system of systems may become a force multiplier, not only because it can accomplish what an individual weapons platform cannot accomplish otherwise, but also because it can reduce the vulnerabilities of that individual weapons platform. PLA analysts believe that a carrier battle group is an ideal 'maritime operations system of systems'. With escorts such as destroyers, frigates, nuclear attack submarines and ocean-going replenishment ships, this system of systems is capable of air operations, strikes, submarine and ASW warfare, air and missile defence, and electronic warfare, thus possessing the so-called integrated five operations capabilities. If integrated well by the information systems, it represents the 'versatilely functional and optimally combined' system of systems, whereby all individual weapons platforms together not only can constitute operational synergy against an opponent, but also offer support and protection to reduce each other's vulnerabilities, particularly those of the carrier itself. On the other hand, it is also recognized that such a battle group is too massive to conceal, and is easy to detect and attack under certain conditions (*Liberation Army Daily* 2012).

In addition to the commissioning of China's first aircraft carrier, another new development in PLAN capabilities is the mass production of 6,000-metric ton Type 052C destroyers and 4,000-ton Type 054A frigates, and the construction of 6,000-ton Type 052D destroyers. Following the launch of the first two 052Cs in 2003 an interval of seven years elapsed during which no new 052Cs were constructed, leading some analysts to conclude that the PLAN had ceased to acquire major surface combatants. However, construction resumed in late 2010, so that by 2013 it appeared that China had four hulls under commission or construction. In 2006–13 18 Type 054A frigates were commissioned, launched or under construction, with as many as four hulls in 2011, and more are reportedly planned.

Finally, by late 2012 and early 2013 photos showing two Type-052D destroyers under construction, an upgraded variant of the Type 052C, began to emerge from the Chinese military websites. This new-type destroyer features a larger active phased-array radar system in comparison with that on the Type 052C. Rather than 48 surface-to-air missiles (SAM) imbedded in eight revolver-type six-cell vertical launching systems (VLS), as per the Type 052C, the Type 052D has two canister-type 32-cell missile VLSs. It has been reported that the total of 62 missiles includes SAMs, anti-ship cruise missiles (ASCMs), anti-submarine missiles, and land attack cruise missiles. If this is true, the Type 052D may be China's first dedicated multi-purpose destroyer.

Chinese naval ship acquisition is traditionally based on an incremental approach whereby a small number of hulls are deployed for tests and sea trials, followed by the construction of a further small number that incorporate remedies to the defects identified during tests and trials. Given that the Type 052C destroyers and Type 054A frigates, being the workhorses of the counter-piracy missions in the Gulf of Aden, were fully tested and trialled, their mass production indicates that the PLAN may be satisfied with their performance in the far seas. The maturity of Chinese shipbuilding techniques such as modular assembling of large ships, together with a substantial increase in the defence budget owing to rapid economic expansion, may also account for this new development. The need to replace a large number of non-modernized Type 051 destroyers and Type 053H series frigates may be another reason. The seven-year interlude during the construction of Type 052C frigates, on the other hand, can be accounted for by the time-consuming relocation of the Jiangnan Shipyard to the Changxin Island outside Shanghai, but not to a PLAN decision not to acquire major surface ships. As the first two 052Cs were constructed by Jiangnan, the interlude might imply that other shipyards did not have the technological capacity to build these high-end ships during this period. Finally, the consideration for organizing aircraft carrier battle groups, or the need to develop 'maritime operations system of systems', may be a major impetus for the surge in the production of these ships, including particularly the Type 052Ds, from the late 2010s on.

Near seas capabilities

One remarkable development for the PLAN's near seas capabilities is the deployment of more than 60 Type 022 fast attack craft (FAC) since 2004. Featuring a wave-piercing catamaran hull, the 220-ton craft reportedly travels at a maximum speed of 36 knots, and has an operational range of 300 nautical miles. It has also adopted stealth features that reduce radar, visual, acoustic, infrared and electronic emissions signatures. Moreover, it is armed with eight 120-km-range YJ83 ASCMs, and a data-link antenna that can receive off-board sensors for over-the-horizon targeting information (Li 2009a).

Acquisition of a large number of Type 022s can clearly be accounted for by the PLA's traditional active defence strategy. The craft, for instance, reflects the original institutional identity of the PLAN as an inferior, small craft navy, which was capable of effective tactical engagement against a superior opponent through mobility and stealth, particularly in the 1950s, 1960s and 1970s. The high speed, small profile and stealth features make it possible for the craft to approach a major target from multiple directions quickly, but with a low probability of detection. The operational range combined with missile range and volume, together with data-link antennae, on the other hand, enables the Type 022s to cover most of the sea areas near China's shores. Both enhance the opportunity for the craft effectively to engage and raise the cost of a superior opponent in the near seas.

As the Type 022 is designed to sortie out in times of war and given its small size and singular role, the craft does not have the level of sustainability and versatility for conducting routine patrols to act as a naval presence in the near seas, particularly during times of peace and crisis. As a result, the PLAN has endorsed Type 056 light frigates to fill this gap. During 2011–13, for instance, ten Type 056 light frigates were either being commissioned, launched or under construction, and more are reportedly planned. The 1,400-ton ship features a 'deep V' hull, sloped surface and reduced superstructure clutters, a 150-km-range air and sea search radar, and a helipad at the stern. It is armed with a 76-mm gun, two two-cell YJ83 ASCM launchers, one eight-cell FL-3000N short-range SAM system, and two three-cell anti-submarine torpedo tubes (Wang 2012; Feng 2012).

These features are clearly designed to enhance the speed, stealth, and versatility of the ship. The relatively simple and conventional weapons systems and sensors may also serve to reduce the production cost so that a large number can be acquired. It is generally believed that the Type 056 is to support the routine patrol of disputed areas in the near seas by China's civilian maritime law enforcement ships, either in managing escalation or engaging in small-scale maritime conflicts if management fails. The ship can also serve to protect Chinese ports and the PLAN's bases, and fulfil non-traditional security missions such as countering piracy and terrorism in the near seas.

Furthermore, the need to replace a large number of non-modernized Type 037 corvettes is clearly another reason for the mass production of the Type 056. That 10 hulls were constructed almost simultaneously in shipyards such as Hudong Zhonghua of Shanghai, Huangpu of Guangzhou, Wuchang of Wuhan, and Liaonan of Dalian, is another example of the way in which the modular construction techniques used by China's shipbuilding industry have matured. Finally, the versatility of a system of systems is not only reflected in the fact that systems can be deployed to different distances and different spatial domains, but also in that they can be deployed to suit different times of need. To the extent that Type 022 and Type 056 can be deployed to similar distances and at times of peace, crisis, and war, they have clearly made an important contribution in the construction of the PLAN's system of systems in the near seas.

Conclusion

This study shows that Hu Jintao has made two conceptual contributions to China's evolving naval strategy. At the strategic level, Hu requires the PLA to enhance the security of China's newly emerging development interests, including the security of energy supplies, strategic sea lanes, overseas markets, and overseas Chinese investment and personnel. At the operational level, Hu endorsed the concept of the ISSSO. These conceptual contributions have had a critical influence on the specific missions for the PLAN to fulfil in both the near and far seas, and on the way in which the PLA in general and the PLAN in particular may conduct their operations.

This study also shows that PLAN analysts believe that near seas missions have a greater priority than far seas missions. This is because near seas missions serve issues of critical importance to China's physical security, whereas PLAN far seas capabilities are still quite vulnerable given the lack of overseas naval bases and robust ASW capabilities. For the ISSSO, some PLA strategists argue that its implicit premise that the PLA can achieve superiority through information systems integration, which warrants a direct, frontal engagement of a powerful opponent, is flawed. Instead, they propose that PLA operations should still be guided by its traditional active defence strategy, which is premised on the 'inferior fighting the superior'.

For evolving capabilities, this study demonstrates that PLAN's acquisition of new far seas capabilities such as an aircraft carrier, destroyers and frigates is primarily driven by the need to construct 'maritime operations system of systems', a requirement of the ISSSO. Factors such as availability of new shipbuilding infrastructures and technologies and funding, and the need to replace obsolete ships have also contributed to the surge in such capabilities. Acquisition of new near seas capabilities such as FACs and light frigates, on the other hand, can be explained by PLA's traditional active defence strategy as well as system of systems considerations. Other contributing factors include the availability of new shipbuilding technologies and the need to replace obsolete ships.

What then is the impact of China's ongoing naval modernization on Asian security? This study considers this impact to be three-fold. On the positive side, owing to the integration of the Chinese economy with other Asian economies, the PLAN, with its increased capabilities, can work with other Asian navies to enhance sea lane security, a public good that is vital for the normal functioning of the regional economy against piracy and terrorism. These capabilities can also be employed for humanitarian assistance and disaster relief (e.g. the despatch of the PLAN hospital ship to the typhoon-ravaged Philippines in 2013), as well as for search and rescue operations (e.g. the involvement of PLAN ships in the international efforts to find the missing Malaysian Airlines flight MH370).

However, China's naval modernization poses two major challenges to Asian security. First, these new capabilities could increase the likelihood that China might attempt to resolve disputes with its maritime neighbours over the sovereignty of islands and reefs through coercive means. This could exacerbate regional tensions and trigger a regional arms race, mainly because other claimants might counteract either by amassing their own military capabilities, or by working with other major powers to organize a countervailing alliance against China.

Second, as more Chinese naval ships are deployed more frequently and engage in naval manoeuvres, it is inevitable and generally considered normal that they could be monitored by naval ships or aircraft belonging to other countries. Chinese ships and aircraft, however, might perceive such scrutiny as hostile and could attempt to respond as witnessed during the USS *Cowpens* incident in December 2013 and the close encounter between a Chinese fighter jet and Japanese surveillance aircraft in early 2014. Such dangerous behaviour may risk unintended military escalation between countries.

Finding ways to mitigate these challenges to avoid military conflict could prove to be a daunting but worthwhile project for policymakers in the years to come.

Note

1 The term 'near seas' refers to the three seas near China, i.e., the South China Sea, the East China Sea and the Yellow Sea. 'Far seas' refers to the seas beyond the near seas, or those in the western Pacific Ocean and Indian Ocean.

Bibliography

Academy of Military Science and Chinese Communist Party Central Documents Studies Office (AMS-CDSO), *Deng Xiaoping on National Defense and Army Construction*, Beijing: Military Science Press, 1992.

Army Construction Studies Institute of the National Defense University (China) (NDU), *A Reader for Studying Jiang Zemin's Thought on National Defense and Army Construction,* Beijing: CCP History Press, 2002.

China.com.cn, 'Research Project on Key Technologies of Nuclear-powered Ships Is Endorsed', 12 May 2013, www.china.com.cn.

China Defense, www.china-defense.com/smf/.

China Review News Agency (CRNA), 'Military Expert: China Should Consider Establishing Land-based Support Center in Eastern Africa', 21 May 2009.

Chinese Communist Party Central Documents Studies Office (CDSO), *A Chronological Compilation of Jiang Zemin Thought 1989–2008,* Beijing: Central Documents Press, 2010.

Dan, Xiufa and Ning Jun, 'Re-study of Mao Zedong's Theory of Inferior Defeating Superior', *China Military Science*, No. 3, 2010.

Feng, 'Type 056 Class, China Air and Naval Power', *China Air and Naval Power*, 12 August 2012, http://china-pla.blogspot.com.au/2012/08/type-056-class.html.

Feng, Liang, Gao Zichuan, and Duan Tingzhi, *China's Peaceful Development and Maritime Security Environment*, Beijing: World Knowledge Press, 2010.

General Political Department (GPD), *Theoretical Studies Reader for Army's High and Middle-Ranking Cadres, Book Two*, Beijing: Liberation Army Press, 2010.

Guancha.cn, 'Academician Ma Weiming Reveals Chinese Electromagnetic Catapult Research Has Achieved Success', 25 January 2014, www.guancha.cn/military-affairs/2014_01_25_202230_s.shtml.

Hu, Guangzheng and Xiao Xianshe, *Contentions Affecting the 21st Century*, Beijing: Liberation Army Press, 1989.

Huang, Binbin, '"Sea Snipers" from a Military Port of Eastern Shandong Manifest Divine Awe', *Liberation Army Daily*, 28 August 2009.

Huang, Yingxu, 'What Kind of Military Force Does Future China Need?', *Study Times*, 27 April 2009.

Jiang, Lei, 'Reflections on Enhancing Information Systems-based Maritime System of Systems Operations Capabilities', *China Military Science*, No. 5, 2010.

Jiang, Yu, 'The History of Aircraft Catapult and Its Development Prospect for China's Navy', *Ship-borne Weapons*, 8 August 2012.

Li, Nan, 'China's Navy Develops Fast Attack Craft', *Jane's Intelligence Review*, September 2009a.

Li, Nan, 'The Evolution of China's Naval Strategy and Capabilities: From "Near Coast" and "Near Seas" to "Far Seas"', *Asian Security*, Vol. 5, No. 2, 2009b.

Li, Nan, 'The Evolving Chinese Conception of Security and Security Approaches', in See Seng Tan and Amitav Acharya (eds), *Asia-Pacific Security Cooperation: National Interests and Regional Order*, New York: M. E. Sharpe, 2004.

Li, Nan, 'The PLA's Evolving War-fighting Doctrine, Strategy and Tactics, 1985–95', *China Quarterly*, No. 146, June 1997.

Li, Nan, *Chinese Civil-Military Relations in the Post-Deng Era: Implications for Crisis Management and Naval Modernization*, Newport, RI: Naval War College Press, China Maritime Studies No. 4, 2010.

Li, Nan and Chris Weuve, 'China's Aircraft Ambitions: An Update', *U.S. Naval War College Review*, Vol. 63, No. 1, Winter 2010.

Liberation Army Daily, 'China's Aircraft Carrier, from Today to the Future', 26 September 2012.

Lin, Dong, 'Development Concepts on Information Systems-based Military Force System of Systems', *China Military Science*, No. 1, 2011.

Liu, Fang,'On Innovation and Development of the Party's Military Guidance Theory in the New Period', *Military History Research*, No. 2, 2010.

Liu, Huaqing, *Liu Huaqing's Memoirs*, Beijing: Liberation Army Press, 2004 .

Liu, Huaqing, 'Naval Strategy and Future Maritime Operations' (29 April 1986), in *Selected Military Works of Liu Huaqing, Book One*, Beijing: Liberation Army Press, 2008.

Liu, Huaqing, 'Situations Require Us to Do Well the Research on Naval Development Strategy' (January 1987), in *Selected Military Works of Liu Huaqing, Book One*, Beijing: Liberation Army Press, 2008.

Luo, Xiangde, 'Several Reflections on Operational Guidance for Information Systems-based System of Systems Operations', *China Military Science*, No. 4, 2010.

Ma, Xiaotian, 'Arduously Raise the Capabilities of the Air Force to Fight and Win War', *Liberation Army Daily*, 2 April 2014.

National Defense White Paper (NDWP), 'Diversified Employment of China's Armed Forces', *Xinhua News Agency*, 16 April 2013.

Ping, Zhiwei, Zeng Xiaoxiao and Zhang Xuehui, 'A Study of Mechanisms for Information Systems-based System of Systems Operations', *China Military Science*, No. 4, 2010.

Qu, Jianwen, 'Sino–Burmese Oil and Gas Pipelines Are Favored by the People of Both Countries', *China Youth Reference*, 1 July 2009.

Ren, Liansheng, 'A Preliminary Understanding Regarding Information Systems-based Systems of Systems Operations Capabilities', *China Military Science*, No. 4, 2010.

Tang, Fuquan and Wu Yi, 'A Study of China's Sea Defense Strategy', *China Military Science*, No. 5, 2007.

The Hindu, 'China Has No Plan for Indian Ocean Military Bases, An Exclusive Interview with Chinese Defense Minister General Liang Guanglie', 4 September 2012.

Wang, Jin, 'New Missions in the New Period, China's Type 056 Light Frigate', *Ship-borne Weapons*, 8 August 2012.

Zhang, Hong and Yu Zhao, 'Forge New-Type Operational Force System of Systems Based on Information Systems', *China Military Science*, No. 5, 2010.

5
China's East Asia policy since 2009

Nicholas Khoo

Until very recently, to the extent that a consensus view existed in the scholarly literature on Chinese foreign policy, it has stressed China's role as a status quo actor, practising proactive, skillful and successful diplomacy (Medeiros and Taylor 2003; Kang 2007; Shambaugh 2004/05; Storey 2011). If this consensus was ever completely true, it no longer is today. It is now apparent that Beijing is a more complex actor, and that China's foreign policy presents particularly acute challenges to the East Asian region and the USA. in particular. This chapter assesses China's policy towards East Asia since 2009. Three prominent issues in China's regional policy are examined. These pertain to the South China Sea issue; the North Korean nuclear issue; and Sino–Japanese relations. In analysing these issues, it should be noted that there is a strong element of strategic interaction at work, and China is not the only actor to have contributed to regional instability. That said, our focus in this chapter is on Chinese policy.

China and the South China Sea issue

China's diplomacy towards South-East Asia has been one of the success stories of its overall foreign policy since the mid-1990s. Yet during the post-2009 period China's relationship with its smaller South-East Asian neighbours has deteriorated markedly. The People's Republic of China has a long-standing claim to the territories in the South China Sea, dating back to August 1951. In the post-Cold War era the issue has taken on a new twist as China became a net importer of petroleum in 1993, emerging as the second largest importer in 2009 (behind the USA). The possibility of untapped oil in the seabed of the South China Sea has raised the stakes. A variety of actors ranging from Brunei, Malaysia, the Philippines, Taiwan and Vietnam have maintained conflicting claims with China, adding to the intractability of the issue. Against this backdrop, the Association of Southeast Asian Nations (ASEAN) has sought to deal with the issue via multilateral dialogue and socialization practices. For a while, the much celebrated, but widely misunderstood ASEAN Way appeared to have succeeded, if not in completely resolving the issue, then at least in taking the sting out of it (Acharya 2009).

Alas, following a period of relative calm after the signing of the 2002 Declaration of Conduct on the South China Sea, the maritime disputes have emerged as an even more serious regional security issue (Delisle 2012). For the purposes of this analysis we shall focus on developments since 2009. In May 2009 China submitted an expansive claim to the

United Nations Commission on the Limits of the Continental Shelf (UNCLCS), reflected in a U-shaped nine-dashed line which cuts deeply into the exclusive economic zones (EEZs) of several littoral states. The regional reaction was decidedly negative, and came to a head at a July 2010 ASEAN Regional Forum in Hanoi. At the meeting, US Secretary of State Hillary Clinton called for the peaceful settlement of maritime disputes based on the United Nations' Convention on the Law of the Sea (UNCLOS). Speaking last after the ASEAN and US response, Chinese Minister of Foreign Affairs Yang Jiechi responded with what one US official described as 'a twenty-five minute stem-winder that shook the meeting' (Bader 2012: 105). Yang countered that Secretary Clinton's comments were 'in effect, an attack on China' (ibid.). He also pointed out that ASEAN meetings were not an appropriate forum to resolve China's territorial disputes, which should be dealt with bilaterally between China and the states concerned (ibid.). Yang, whom the US official observed was 'staring directly at Secretary Clinton for much of the time', declared that 'China is a big country. Bigger than any other countries here' (ibid.). This robust Chinese stance has continued. In June 2011 China's Vice Minister of Foreign Affairs Cui Tiankai warned regional states on this issue, even cautioning the USA against involving itself (Wong 2011).

Since then, China's disputes with two rival claimants, Vietnam and the Philippines, have intensified. In reaction to the passing by Vietnam of a maritime law declaring sovereignty over the Paracel and Spratly Islands in June 2012, China unilaterally established a municipality called Sansha (which means 'three sandbanks' in Chinese) in the South China Sea, with Yongxing (or Woody) Island serving as the administrative hub. According to the official Chinese Xinhua news agency, Sansha's jurisdiction extends over 13 sq km of land *and* 2m. sq km of surrounding water, effectively establishing Chinese control over much of the South China Sea (ICG 2012a). In a direct challenge to Vietnam, China invited foreign bids for oil exploration inside Hanoi's EEZ. China also out-manoeuvred the Philippines over the Reed Bank incident in 2011 and the Scarborough Shoal dispute in June 2012 (ICG 2012b). With a typhoon approaching, both sides agreed to withdraw their naval vessels from the area. The Chinese, however, quickly returned to occupy the shoal, claiming ownership without firing a shot.

China has been adept at driving a wedge between the ASEAN states, forestalling a unified regional response to its South China Sea policy. At the mid-2012 ASEAN Ministerial Meeting (AMM) in Phnom Penh, the host nation Cambodia exercised its right as Chair not to issue a final communiqué which would have noted ASEAN's position on the issue. This was the first time such a development had occurred since ASEAN's formation in 1967. Intra-ASEAN recriminations ensued, with several states holding Cambodia responsible for the turn of events. Many member states see the not so hidden hand of China behind Cambodia's steely posture towards its counterparts, part of a Chinese divide and rule strategy. They note the burgeoning economic relationship between Beijing and Phnom Penh, and a recurring pattern of high-level visits by senior Chinese officials to Cambodia before major ASEAN summits.[1] Indeed, President Hu Jintao had visited Phnom Penh in April, a few weeks prior to the ASEAN meeting.

One Filipino official contended that Cambodia had used its Chair position to exercise a de facto veto over proceedings (Ghosh 2012). Singaporean Minister of Foreign Affairs Kasiviswanathan Shanmugam went further. Reflecting on the damage inflicted on ASEAN's credibility by Cambodia and by implication China, he pointedly observed: 'To put it bluntly, it is a severe dent on ASEAN's credibility … There's no point papering over it' (Jones and Khoo 2013: 28). The Cambodian ambassador to Manila subsequently accused the Philippines and Vietnam of playing 'dirty politics' in pushing the South China Sea issue on the ASEAN meeting's agenda (*The Economist* 2012).

At the November 2012 East Asian Summit, also held in Phnom Penh, the host, Cambodia, unilaterally announced that ASEAN had agreed with China not to 'internationalize the South China Sea from now on', and focus instead on 'the existing ASEAN-China mechanisms' (Bland 2012a). Chinese Premier Wen Jiabao clarified his state's position at a closed-door session, asserting that the islands in the South China Sea belong to China and that 'there is no question over its sovereignty' (Qin 2012). The President of the Philippines, President Benigno Aquino, repudiated both his Cambodian hosts as well as China. Aquino observed ominously, 'that the ASEAN route is not the only route for us. As a sovereign state it is our right to defend our national interests' (Bland 2012b).

If anything, China is digging in for a long fight, suggesting a determination to pursue its interests even at the risk of disrupting the regional status quo. Following the summit, Beijing announced that all new Chinese passports would include a map outlining China's regional maritime claims. That these claims are difficult to reconcile with UNCLOS does not appear to faze the Chinese, who continue to press their claims in the South China Sea (Williams 2014). Indeed, the situation has continued to deteriorate in large part because the Chinese have been confronted by a divided ASEAN, torn between the imperative of economic benefits and the strategic costs of countering Chinese assertiveness.

The Aquino administration in Manila is having to face this conundrum in particularly stark terms. China is the Philippines' third largest trading partner and number one strategic concern.[2] In January 2013 Minister of Foreign Affairs Rosario informed the Chinese Ambassador, Ma Keqing, that Manila would take the conflict to UNCLOS for resolution. China, while a signatory to UNCLOS, has consistently declined to participate in the institution's voluntary dispute resolution mechanism. Manila has demonstrated its lack of faith in international institutions and moved to balance China via a different mechanism. Rosario articulated the view that the Philippines' stance that it is 'looking for balancing factors … and Japan could be a significant balancing factor' (Landing et al. 2012). Significantly, Manila is also deepening the once frazzled US–Philippines military relationship. Both countries commenced negotiations in July 2013 on the establishment of a rotational air and naval agreement that allows for an increased US military presence (Whaley 2013). The foregoing suggests that at least in the short run, China's policy on this issue has been successful in dividing ASEAN, causing ASEAN states to look to external actors for succour. Regional tensions have correspondingly increased.

China and the North Korea nuclear issue

The discussion above highlighted developments suggesting an erosion of Beijing's commitment to regional stability, with some distinct success in dividing the ASEAN. China's relationship with North Korea underscores a rather different dimension in its foreign policy. With respect to North Korea, China is so committed to stability that its policy has often been distinctly reactive and less than skilful. Admittedly, the Chinese position on North Korea has to balance delicate competing interests. On the one hand North Korea provides China with a valuable buffer zone against a long-standing US presence in mainland Asia via the US–South Korean alliance. However, precisely because North Korea knows that China highly values this particular aspect of the status quo, the regime has a qualified liberty to engage in provocations that serve Pyongyang's interests, but threaten regional stability, thus challenging China's interests. In this respect, one clearly stated and long-standing Chinese interest has been that North Korea should not develop a nuclear capability.

Early in the first Obama administration, in April 2009, North Korea quit the Six-Party talks that were first convened in 2003 to deal with North Korea's nuclear weapons programme. This was followed by the detonation of a North Korean nuclear device on 25 May 2009, which caught the Chinese by surprise. Beijing publicly criticized North Korea and agreed to sanctions imposed by the United Nations' Security Council (UNSC) under Resolution 1874. Then, during a visit to Pyongyang in early April 2012 Madam Fu Ying, China's Vice Minister for Foreign Affairs, was reported to have warned North Korean leader Kim Jong-un against testing a ballistic missile that could be fitted with a nuclear warhead. The North Koreans went ahead and tested the missile on 12 April. The missile was in flight for only a few minutes before entering the sea west of the Korean peninsula. In December Pyongyang again conducted a ballistic missile test, successfully putting a satellite into space via a three-stage rocket launch. Significantly, China responded by voting in favour of UNSC Resolution 2087 which called for a tightening of sanctions against Pyongyang. In April 2013 North Korea staged its third nuclear test.[3] This prompted China's leader, Xi Jinping, to comment forcefully during a speech at the Boao Forum for Asia in 2013 that 'no one should be allowed to throw a region, and even the whole world, into chaos for selfish gains' (Hatton 2013). The passage of time has only reinforced Chinese scepticism of North Korea. This is illustrated by Beijing's September 2013 decision to initiate a ban on the export of a 236-page list of items that could be used by North Korea to develop its nuclear weapons programme (Perlez 2013a).

WikiLeaks documents suggest that there is reason to believe that there are genuine tensions in Sino–North Korean relations. In a cable dated 28 August 2009, former North Korean leader Kim Jong-il reportedly made a comment, without elaboration, of 'not trusting' China (Agence France Presse 2011). Over a lunch discussion with US diplomats on 26 October 2009, China's Vice Foreign Minister He Yafei is quoted as stating that while China 'may not like them', it was nevertheless forced to deal with the North Koreans because 'they are a neighbour'.[4] Nor is it clear that the Chinese are necessarily more knowledgeable about aspects of North Korea's internal politics which impacts on the nuclear issue. According to the cables, in February 2010 Chinese experts suggested the implausibility, due to youth and inexperience, of Kim Jong-un emerging as the successor-in-waiting to his father Kim Jong-il. Yet in June a Chinese diplomat cited precisely these factors as helping the young leader to consolidate his position (Sanger 2010). Occasionally, Chinese policy on North Korea's nuclear programme appears to be in disarray. North Korea's programme has long been known to be plutonium-based. Suspicions have lingered among specialists in the West that the North Koreans have also been running a parallel uranium-based nuclear weapons programme. In June 2009 WikiLeaks documents contained assertions by senior Chinese Foreign Ministry officials that uranium 'enrichment was only in its initial phases' (ibid.). Yet just over a year later, in November 2010, Pyongyang exposed the limitations of these claims by revealing an industrial-scale uranium enrichment plant to the world. It is therefore no surprise that the Chinese were, by all accounts, surprised by the dismissal and execution in late 2013 of North Korea's second highest-ranking leader Jang Song-thaek. Peking University Professor Zhu Feng characterized Jang as 'the man China counted on to move the economy in North Korea', and his execution as 'a very ominous signal' (Choe and Perlez 2013). As Kim Jung-un consolidates his regime, China is very much an onlooker.

Sino–Japanese relations

There are a variety of generalizations that one can make about China's Japan diplomacy since 2009. However, neither skilfulness nor support for the status quo could be numbered among them. To be absolutely clear, Japan has played an important role in the escalation of tensions since 2009. In particular, the Japanese decision (see below) to purchase a number of the Senkaku/Diaoyu Islands in 2012 significantly exacerbated underlying tensions. Nor has the Abe government shown much restraint in its actions, even going against US advice to de-escalate tensions with China. That said, our focus is on China's role. Here, in recent years, China has on numerous occasions played a prominent role in escalating conflict with Japan. Moreover, while Beijing has shown an ability to actively regulate the level of domestic anti-Japanese protest, shutting down protests when it wishes, its behaviour in respect to Japan has been marked by a distinctly retaliatory quality, undermining favourable regional perceptions that China has worked hard to develop in the pre-2009 period.

The first episode of intense Sino–Japanese conflict during the period of our analysis occurred in late 2010. On 8 September 2010 a collision between a Chinese trawler and a Japanese coastguard vessel near disputed islands in the East China Sea led to the imprisonment of the trawler's Chinese fishermen for 20 days. Beijing subsequently cancelled scheduled talks on the joint exploration of a gasfield in the East China Sea, summoned the Japanese ambassador on repeated occasions, and demanded an apology. As tensions flared, China reportedly blocked the shipment of rare earths to Japan, which are critical components in the production of high technology products. On the Chinese side, anti-Japanese protests persisted, both on the internet, and on the ground, even after the Chinese authorities attempted to quell them. At one point, an estimated 30,000 people took part in protests in Chengdu in south-west China.

During August–September 2012 Sino–Japanese tensions escalated again over the Senkaku/Diaoyu Islands. This flare-up has its origins in an attempt by former Tokyo mayor Shintaro Ishihara to purchase three of the islands, which are owned by a Japanese family. Seeking to forestall this development, which would have severely destabilized Sino–Japanese relations, the Japanese government stepped in and nationalized the islands. This was taken as a severe affront to Chinese sovereignty, and a catalyst for anti-Japanese protests throughout China. During this period, Japanese-themed shops, restaurants and Japanese consulates in China were subject to vandalism. When the Chinese authorities eventually clamped down on the protests, Chinese premier Wen Jiabao delivered a speech asserting that China 'will never budge, even half an inch, over the sovereignty and territorial issue' (Harlan 2012). Subsequently, patrol ships from the China Marine Surveillance fleet were dispatched to the vicinity of the disputed islands. The escalation of the situation was sufficiently severe and extended that US Secretary of Defense Leon Panetta took the unusual step of expressing concern that the accidental use of force could occur. Just as the events in the region were beginning to calm down, Minister of Foreign Affairs Yang Jiechi raised the issue at the United Nations in late September, eliciting a vigorous response from Japan's deputy ambassador Kazuo Komada. Chinese ambassador to the United Nations Li Badong intervened, accusing Japan of having an 'obsolete colonial mentality' (Associated Press 2012).

In December 2012 the situation escalated further. During that month, eight Japanese F-15 fighters scrambled to intercept a Chinese marine surveillance aircraft, which was flying over the disputed Senkaku/Diaoyu Islands. This occurred again on 11 January 2013, when the Japanese Air Self-Defence Forces responded to Chinese air force J-10 fighters operating near the islands. On 19 and 30 January 2013 the Japanese Ministry of Defence claimed that a Chinese navy vessel had activated its missile guidance system and 'painted' a Japanese Maritime Self-Defence Forces vessel with its radar system. Japanese Minister of Defence Itsunori Onodera made it clear that he considered this action as tantamount to threatening to use force.

The situation intensified further when China released a White Paper on 16 April 2013 which identified Japan as bearing sole responsibility for the spike in tensions over the East

China Sea.[5] The next day, a People's Liberation Army Type-052 Lanzhou missile destroyer and Type-054A Hengshui missile frigate entered waters near the contested islands. This occasioned an escalating process of action-reaction. On 21 April members of Japanese Prime Minister Shinzo Abe's cabinet visited the Yasukuni Shrine which contains the remains of Japanese war criminals executed in 1945. Meanwhile, on 23 April 170 members of the Japanese Diet, and a small flotilla carrying 80 Japanese nationalists visited waters off the Senkaku/Diaoyu Islands, thus further intensifying an already volatile situation. Reacting to this provocation, on 26 April a Chinese Ministry of Foreign Affairs spokesman allegedly asserted that 'The Diaoyu (Senkaku) Islands are about sovereignty and territorial integrity. Of course, it's China's core interest' (Kyodo Press 2013). The official transcript of the conference was subsequently revised to affirm that 'China would resolutely safeguard the country's core interests, including the national sovereignty, national security and territorial integrity. The Diaoyu Islands involve China's territorial sovereignty' (Swaine 2014b: 3).

While doubtless working furiously behind the scenes, the USA has been very much limited in its public response to this unfolding drama. At a two-day informal meeting in California in June 2013, President Barack Obama urged his counterpart President Xi Jinping to 'de-escalate' the conflict with Japan (Reuters 2013). However, neither China nor Japan has demonstrated much interest in following Obama's counsel. In a sign of increasing Japanese frustration, the Japanese Ministry of Defence's annual White Paper, released in July, proposed an increasingly hard-line stance towards China. This led the Chinese Ministry of Defence to contend that Japan was compromising regional stability (Perlez 2013b). On 8 August 2013 the Japanese government summoned the acting Chinese ambassador to Japan to account for repeated Chinese maritime incursions into Japan's territorial waters. At the United Nations in late September Japanese Prime Minister Shinzo Abe rejected Chinese Foreign Minister Wang Yi's recommendation, offered in a talk at the Brookings Institution in Washington, DC, that the Japanese should accept the existence of a territorial dispute, since this implies a question over Japanese sovereignty of the islands. Interestingly, the scope of the Senkaku/Diaoyu conflict now involves the use of unmanned aerial vehicles on the Chinese side, which reportedly occurred on the first anniversary of the Japanese purchase of the three islands in early September.

China's declaration of an air defence identification zone (ADIZ) over the East China Sea on 23 November 2013 represents a further phase in the escalation process. There is a 50 per cent overlap between China's ADIZ and Japan's. The USA challenged this declaration by flying two B-52 bombers through the ADIZ without notifying Beijing (Barnes and Page 2013). Seoul and Tokyo followed suit with their own sorties. On 6 December the lower house of the Japanese parliament passed a resolution urging China to abolish the ADIZ, eliciting a predictable rebuke from China (Warnock 2013). During a Japan–ASEAN summit in mid-December, Prime Minister Abe criticized Beijing's ADIZ, 'demanding China rescind all measures like this that unjustly violate the general rule [regarding freedom of navigation]' (Hornby 2013). Beijing predictably slammed this idea, characterizing it as 'malicious slander' (ibid.). In any case, Prime Minister Abe went against US advice to de-escalate tensions with China by visiting the Yasukuni Shrine on 26 December 2013 (Tabuchi 2013). This led to a Chinese Foreign Ministry spokesman to take the unusual step of directly criticizing Abe for honouring 'fascists' and the 'Nazis of Asia' (Wong 2013).

Developments in 2014 suggest that the Sino–Japanese conflict will carry on even as the US State Department adopts a largely reactive rather than a proactive stance. The State Department has continued to reject China's ADIZ declaration. This occurred most recently on 5 February 2014 during congressional testimony by Assistant Secretary of State for East Asia

Daniel Russel. At September 2013 the Chinese appeared to be taking steps to revise previous agreements reached in Sino–Japanese relations. This is suggested by the Shanghai Maritime Court's April 2014 decision to seize a Japanese cargo ship in response to alleged unpaid compensation for Chinese ships used by the Japanese in 1936 (BBC 2014). The issue of wartime reparations was previously believed to have been settled in a 1972 agreement (Ming 2006: 83–108).

The critical point in this narrative lies in the larger conclusion that Chinese diplomacy has been as much a part of the problem as it is the solution. In these episodes in Sino–Japanese relations there is little evidence to be found of skilful diplomacy, let alone regional leadership on the part of Beijing. Indeed, as with the Sino-Filipino case, Japan is at once a major Chinese economic partner and the central focus of Chinese nationalism (Reilly 2012). During the last two decades, Japan has consistently been one of China's largest trading partners.[6] Yet this has done little to prevent the episodes of intense anti-Japanese outbursts which we explored above. A critique of the view presented here may be that it is unrealistic to expect the Chinese to resolve their intractable relationship with the Japanese. However, this is precisely the hard test for whether China has the necessary diplomatic inclination and *gravitas* to lead the region. Until then, regional states will continue to look to the USA as a regional stabilizer, however much the Chinese may disagree.

Conclusion

China's policy towards key security issues in East Asia has become increasingly complex during the post-2009 period. While other states are increasingly not averse to taking actions that challenge regional stability, Beijing's commitment to the regional status quo is itself increasingly in question. Should we expect more of the same? Or will China revert to something akin to behaviour seen before 2009? The Chinese leadership's convening of a high-level meeting of ambassadors and officials responsible for China's Asia policy prior to the third plenum of the Eighteenth Party Congress suggests a desire to contribute to regional stability (Swaine 2014a). Nevertheless, it is a poor portent that the fundamental issues at stake in both the East China and South China Sea remain far from being resolved. Moreover, a satisfactory settlement of the North Korean issue continues to elude Beijing. The foregoing suggests a gulf between intent and policy. Moving forward, regional stability will hinge on whether this gulf can be closed (or not).

Notes

1 During President Hu's April 2012 visit to Cambodia both sides pledged to double their bilateral trade from US $2,500m. to $5,000m. by 2017.
2 See the Filipino government's statistics for 2012 at www.census.gov.ph/content/foreign-trade-statistics-philippines-2012 (accessed 23 April 2014).
3 The first nuclear test occurred in 2006; the second in 2009, and the third in 2013.
4 See US embassy document contained in 'US embassy cables: China's "dislike" of North Korean regime', *The Guardian*, 29 November 2010, available at www.guardian.co.uk/world/us-embassy-cables-documents/231221 (accessed 22 July 2012).
5 The White Paper is available at http://news.xinhuanet.com/english/china/2013-04/16/c_132312681.htm (accessed 10 January 2014).
6 See figures from the US–China Business Council available at www.uschina.org/statistics/tradetable.html (accessed 10 January 2014).

Bibliography

Acharya, Amitav, *Constructing a Security Community in Southeast Asia: ASEAN and the Problem of Regional Order*, 2nd edn, London: Routledge, 2009.
Agence France Presse, 'North Korea's Kim Does Not Trust China', 6 September 2011.
Associated Press, 'At UN, China Takes Aim at Japan over Island Dispute', 28 September 2012.
Ba, Alice, 'Who's Socializing Whom? Complex Engagement in Sino-ASEAN Relations', *Pacific Review*, Vol. 19, No. 2, June 2006.
Bader, Jeffrey A., *Obama and China's Rise: An Insider's Account of America's Asia Strategy*, Washington, DC: Brookings Institution Press, 2012.
Barnes, Julian E. and Jeremy Page, 'U.S. Sends B-52s on Mission to Challenge Chinese Claims', *Wall Street Journal*, 27 November 2013.
Bland, Ben, 'ASEAN Curbs US Regional Role', *Financial Times*, 18 November 2012a.
Bland, Ben, 'Regional Tensions Flare at ASEAN Summit', *Financial Times*, 19 November 2012b.
British Broadcasting Corporation (BBC), 'China Seizes Japanese Cargo Ship Over Pre-War Debt', *BBC News*, 21 April 2014.
Choe, Sang-Hun and Jane Perlez, 'Public Ouster in North Korea Unsettles China', *New York Times*, 9 December 2013.
Delisle, Jacques, 'Troubled Waters: China's Claims and The South China Sea', *Orbis*, Vol. 56, No. 4, Fall 2012: 608–642.
Ghosh, Nirmal, 'ASEAN Forum Fails to Reach Accord', *Straits Times*, 14 July 2012.
Harlan, Chico, 'China Sends Patrol Ships to Contested Islands after Japan Buys Them', *Washington Post*, 12 September 2012.
Hatton, Celia, 'Is China Ready to Abandon North Korea?' *BBC News*, 12 April 2013.
Hornby, Lucy, 'China Attacks Abe Air Defence Zone "Slander" at ASEAN', *Financial Times*, 15 December 2013.
Hou, Qiang, 'Announcement of the Aircraft Indentification Rules for the East China Sea Air Defence Identification Zone of the P.R.C.', Xinhua News Agency, 23 November 2013.
International Crisis Group (ICG), *Stirring Up the South China Sea (I)*, Report No. 223, 23 April 2012a.
International Crisis Group (ICG), *Stirring Up the South China Sea (II): Regional Responses*, Report No. 229, 24 July 2012b.
Jones, David Martin and Nicholas Khoo, 'The Delusion of Asian Engagement', *Quadrant Magazine*, Vol. 57, No. 1–2, January–February 2013.
Kang, David, *China Rising: Peace, Power, and Order in East Asia*, New York: Columbia University Press, 2007.
Kyodo Press, 'China Says Senkaku Islands Are Its "Core Interest"', 26 April 2013.
Landing, Roel, David Pilling and Jonathan Soble, 'Philippines Backs Rearming of Japan', *Financial Times*, 9 December 2012.
Medeiros, Evan and Fravel Taylor, 'China's New Diplomacy', *Foreign Affairs*, Vol. 82, No. 6, 2003.
Ming, Wan, *Sino–Japanese Relations: Interaction, Logic, and Transformation*, Stanford, CA: Stanford University Press, 2006.
Perlez, Jane, 'China Ban On Items for Nuclear Use to North Korea May Stall Arms Bid', *New York Times*, 29 September, 2013a.
Perlez, Jane, 'Japan and China Trade Sharp Words Over Islands', *New York Times*, 13 July 2013b.
Qin, Jize, 'China Eelaborates on Regional Situation', *China Daily*, 21 November 2012.
Reilly, James, *Strong Society, Smart State: The Rise of Public Opinion in China's Japan Policy*, New York: Columbia University Press, 2012.
Reuters, 'Obama Urges De-escalation, Dialogue in China-Japan Maritime Row', 8 June 2013.
Sanger, David, 'North Korea Keeps the World Guessing', *New York Times*, 29 November 2010.
Shambaugh, David, 'China Engages Asia: Reshaping the Regional Order', *International Security*, Vol. 29, No. 1, 2004/05.
Storey, Ian, *Southeast Asia and the Rise of China: The Search for Security*, London: Routledge, 2011.

Swaine, Michael D., 'Chinese Views and Commentary On Periphery Diplomacy', *China Leadership Monitor*, No. 44, 2014a.

Swaine, Michael D., 'Chinese Views Regarding the Senkaku/Diaoyu Islands Dispute', *China Leadership Monitor*, No. 41, 2014b.

Tabuchi, Hiroko, 'With Shrine Visit, Leader Asserts Japan's Track From Pacifism', *New York Times*, 26 December 2013.

The Economist, 'ASEAN in Crisis: Divided We Stagger', 18 August 2012.

Warnock, Eleanor, 'Japan Passes Resolution Urging China to Scrap ADIZ', *Wall Street Journal*, 6 December 2013.

Whaley, Floyd, 'U.S. Seeks Expanded Role for Military in Philippines', *New York Times*, 12 July 2013.

Williams, Carol J., 'China Asserts Control Over Vast Sea Area, Angering Neighbours, U.S.', *Los Angeles Times*, 10 January 2014.

Wong, Edward, 'Beijing Warns U.S. About South China Sea Disputes', *New York Times*, 22 June 2011.

Wong, Edward, 'No Meeting With Leader of Japan, Chinese Say', *New York Times*, 30 December 2013.

6
US–China strategic rivalry in East Asia
Trouble ahead?

Robert Sutter

Post-Cold War trends forecast an increasingly developed and capable People's Republic of China continuing to rise while facing major encumbrances in an East Asian order led by the USA. The end of the Soviet Union and the Cold War destroyed the strategic framework for the Sino–US cooperation initiated by US President Richard Nixon and Chinese Chairman Mao Zedong. Occasional dramatic crises since that time have seen policymakers, strategists and scholars in both the USA and China register concern and sometimes alarm over potential conflict. Major turning points include:

- the multi-year virulent American opposition to Chinese leaders responsible for the crackdown against demonstrators in Tiananmen Square in 1989;
- the face-off of US–Chinese forces as a result of the Taiwan Strait crisis of 1995–96;
- the crisis in 1999 prompted by the US bombing of the Chinese embassy in Belgrade and resulting mass demonstrations and destruction of US diplomatic properties in China;
- the crash in 2001 of a Chinese fighter jet and a US reconnaissance plane over international waters near China and resulting crisis over responsibility for the incident and release of the American crew and damaged plane; and
- the explicit and growing US–Chinese competition for influence in East Asia featuring Barack Obama's government's so-called pivot or rebalancing policy to the Asia-Pacific region coinciding with greater Chinese assertiveness in dealing with differences with the USA and its allies and associates over issues of sovereignty and security along China's rim (Sutter 2013a; Shambaugh 2012).

In 2012 the relationship was tested many times. Growing Chinese–US divergence and competition in East Asia headed the list of issues that challenged the ability of Chinese and American leaders to manage their differences, avoid confrontation and pursue positive engagement. Competition for influence along China's rim and in the broader Asia-Pacific region exacerbated an obvious security dilemma featuring China's rising power and the USA's reaction, shown notably in the two sides' respective military build-ups.

Hyperbolic attacks on Chinese economic and security policies were features of the Republican presidential primaries. President Obama also resorted to harsh rhetoric not heard during his presidential campaign in 2008. Calling China an 'adversary', he highlighted his administration's reengagement with countries in the Asia-Pacific region as a means of competing with China in security, economic and other terms (Keyser 2012).

China resorted to extraordinary demonstrations of state power, falling short of direct use of military force, in response to perceived challenges by US allies, the Philippines and Japan, regarding disputed territory in the South China Sea and the East China Sea. Chinese leaders criticized American interference with the disputed claims and also highlighted regional trade arrangements that excluded the USA, seeking to undermine the American-led Trans-Pacific Partnership (TPP) trade pact (Elliott School of International Affairs 2013: 39).

At the start of the year, Kenneth Lieberthal and Wang Jisi highlighted the pervasive and deeply rooted distrust between the two governments (Lieberthal and Wang 2012). At year's end, David Shambaugh concluded that the overall US–China relationship was 'more strained, fraught and distrustful' (Shambaugh 2012).

Unexpectedly, increased competition and tension in Sino–US relations in 2012 was followed by a summit meeting in California in June 2013 and an overall moderation in Sino–US differences. Prevailing trends showed that avoiding serious confrontation and endeavouring to manage differences through a process of constructive engagement remains in the overall interests of both countries.[1] There are three general reasons for this judgement:

- Both administrations benefit from positive engagement.
- Both administrations see that ever growing China–US interdependence means that emphasizing the negatives in their relationship will hurt the other side but also will hurt them.
- Both leaderships are preoccupied with a long list of urgent domestic and foreign priorities; in this situation, one of the last things they would seek is a serious confrontation in relations with one another.

Looking ahead, it is hard to envisage how the Obama government would see its interests well served by a more assertive US stance leading to a major confrontation with China. Given China's recent record of assertive expansion at its neighbours' expense, there is more uncertainty regarding China's future actions and intentions.

Obama's policy and competition with China

Obama and his department directors announced policy initiatives beginning in 2011 under the rubric of a US 'pivot' to the wider Asia-Pacific region. The initiatives covered security, economics and politico-diplomatic efforts. Although China objected strongly, they were generally welcomed in the region. Facing strong criticism from Beijing and advice from regional friends and allies to avoid confrontation with China, the Americans redefined the pivot beginning in the latter part of 2012 by using the less dramatic term 'rebalancing'. The earlier emphasis on controversial US security measures was played down in favour of emphasis on less sensitive economic and diplomatic initiatives. Furthermore, the US leadership strengthened dialogue with China, resulting in the US–China summit in California in June 2013. It well understood that while allies in the Asia-Pacific region favoured strong US regional engagement as a hedge against possible domineering behaviour by a rising China, almost all governments opposed serious confrontation. Such tensions would upset regional stability and undermine development, which together serve as the basis of the political legitimacy of almost all East Asian governments (North Korea being the exception) (Saunders 2012).

Greater Chinese assertiveness towards the USA and especially towards US allies, Japan and the Philippines over China's broad and disputed territorial claims along its rim in the East China Sea and the South China Sea was the driving force to which others reacted. Since the early years of the post-Cold War period, Beijing's emphasis has been on peace, development and cooperation, but in recent years there also has been repeated use of coercion and intimidation in support of broad maritime claims in the South China Sea and the East China Sea. Neighbouring countries and other concerned powers that accept Chinese claims are promised a beneficial relationship of 'win–win' cooperation. Those that do not, the two most prominent examples being the Philippines and Japan, are subjected to threats and heavy coercion, falling short of direct use of military force. The US government endeavours to calm the situation while it engages in wide-ranging improvement of military, economic and political relationships throughout the Asia-Pacific region. In North-East Asia, the situation is complicated by efforts to deal with the North Korean threat as well as multilateral great power competition, but in East Asia, the US approach entails greater competition with China for regional influence on the one hand, and greater constructive engagement with the Chinese leaders on the other.

The pivot was prompted in part by encouragement from regional leaders concerned with Chinese assertiveness amid a perception of declining US interest and disengagement. The shift to a more moderate approach of rebalancing was influenced by their concerns too. Yet as China's actions continued, they complicated US calculations. The USA for a time seemed uncertain about how to deal with assertiveness by China over territorial claims. Beginning in late 2013 it adopted a tougher public stance against Chinese coercive and intimidating tactics against Japan, the Philippines and other concerned powers. It also deepened security and other ties with these allies and other partners, notably during President Obama's four-nation tour of East Asia in April 2014.

China's foreign policy shift on regional territorial disputes is the most important in a decade (Sutter and Huang 2013). Concerned governments have come to recognize that China's 'win–win' formula emphasizing cooperation is premised on the foreign government eschewing actions acutely sensitive to China over Taiwan, Tibet and Xinjiang, and that the scope of acute sensitivity has now been broadened to include the maritime disputes along China's rim. For now, a pattern of varied regional acquiescence, protests and resistance to China's new toughness on maritime claims seems likely. It raises the question about future Chinese assertiveness, challenging neighbouring governments with disputes over Chinese claims and challenging the US leadership in promoting stability and opposing unilateral and coercive means to change the regional status quo.

Constraints on Chinese assertiveness

Forecasts talk of US retreat from domineering China or an inevitable conflict between the USA and China (Friedberg 2011; Nathan 2013). However, enduring circumstances have prevented Chinese leaders from confronting the USA, the regional leader.

Domestic preoccupations

Chinese economic growth and one-party rule require stability. Furthermore, protecting Chinese security and sovereignty remains a top concern. Although China also has regional and global ambitions, domestic concerns get overall priority.

President Xi Jinping is preoccupied with uncertain leadership legitimacy, pervasive corruption, widespread mass protests and unsustainable economic practices. Beijing's reform agenda will require strong leadership for many years (Roach 2013). Under these circumstances, Xi was unusually accommodating in meeting President Obama in California in 2013; he seeks a new kind of major power relationship. Xi also presides over China's greater assertiveness on territorial issues that involve the USA, but thus far Chinese probes have avoided direct confrontation with the superpower.

Mutual interdependence

Growing economic and other US–China interdependence reinforces constructive relations. Respective 'Gulliver strategies' tie down aggressive, assertive or other negative policy tendencies through webs of interdependence in bilateral and multilateral relationships.

China's insecure position in the Asia-Pacific

Nearby Asia is the world area where China has always exerted greatest influence and to which China devotes the lion's share of its foreign policy attention. It contains security and sovereignty issues (e.g. Taiwan) of top importance. It is the main arena of interaction with the USA. The region's economic importance far surpasses the rest of world (China is Africa's biggest trader but it does more trade with South Korea). Stability along the rim of China is essential for China's continued economic growth – the lynchpin of leadership legitimacy and continued communist rule. Against this background, without a secure periphery and facing formidable American presence and influence, China almost certainly calculates that seriously confronting the USA poses grave dangers for the Chinese regime (Sutter 2013b: 1–26, 311–327).

Chinese strengths in the Asia-Pacific region include extensive trade and investment; a growing web of road, rail, river, electric power, pipeline and other linkages with nearby countries; leadership attention and active diplomacy; and expanding military capabilities.

Nevertheless, these strengths are offset by various weaknesses and limitations. First, Chinese practices alienate nearby governments, which broadly favour key aspects of US regional leadership. Leadership involves costly and risky efforts to support common goods involving regional security and development. China avoids such risks and costs unless there is adequate benefit for a narrow win-set of tangible Chinese interests (Sutter 2013b: 315). It 'cheap rides', preserving resources to deal with the long array of domestic challenges confronting China's leaders.

Second, recent Chinese assertiveness towards its neighbours puts nearby governments on guard and weakens Chinese regional influence. It reminds China's neighbours of its long-standing and justified reputation dating from the Cold War as the most disruptive and domineering force in the region (Garver 1993).

Third, China's achievements in advancing its influence in the Asia-Pacific region in the post-Cold War period – a period that now extends almost 25 years – are mediocre. China faces major impediments, many home-grown. Its long-standing practice of promoting an image of consistent and righteous behaviour in foreign affairs is so far from reality that it grossly impedes resolution of disputes with neighbours and the USA. As the Chinese government holds a truly exceptional position among the other major powers of having never acknowledged any of its foreign policy mistakes, when China gets into a dispute with neighbours, the fault never lies with China. If Beijing chooses not to blame the neighbour, its default position is to blame larger forces usually involving the USA. Of course, Chinese elites and public opinion also remain heavily influenced by the prevailing Chinese media emphasis on China's historic victimization at the hands of outside powers like the USA, Japan and others. In sum, they are quick to find offence and are impervious of the need for change and recognition of fault on their part (Rozman 2013).

Measuring China's relationships

We can assess how far China has to go in order to be confident of its position in Asia, and it must be reiterated that without such confidence Beijing would be poorly positioned to confront the USA. Relations with Japan, arguably Asia's richest country and the USA's key ally, have worsened to their lowest point (Przystup 2013). India's interest in accommodation with China has been offset by border frictions and competition for regional influence (Limaye 2014). Russian and Chinese interest in close alignment waxes and wanes and seems to be secondary to their respective relationships with the West (Yu 2014).

The new Taiwanese government that came to office in 2008 changed relations for the better, but the political opposition in Taiwan remains opposed to recent trends and has improved its standing with Taiwanese voters (Bush 2013).

Ever closer economic ties came with the decline in South Korea's opinion of China, notably over China's refusal to condemn North Korea's attacks on South Korea and other provocations. Efforts to improve ties with a new South Korean president have been offset by provocations from North Korea and Chinese advances in disputed territory claimed by South Korea (Snyder 2014).

Disputed claims in the South China Sea seriously complicate often close economic relations with South-East Asian countries. China's remarkable military modernization raises suspicions on the part of a number of China's neighbours, including such middle powers as Australia (Jacobson 2012). They endeavour to build their own military power and work cooperatively with one another and the USA in the face of China's military advances.

The so-called Overseas Chinese communities in South-East Asian countries have often favoured political forces supportive of their home country's good relations with China, but those same communities have a long and often negative history in South-East Asian countries (Sutter 2013b: 319).

China's growing trade in Asia remains heavily interdependent (Yu 2010). Half of Chinese trade is conducted by foreign-invested enterprises in China; the resulting processing trade sees China often add only a small amount to the product; and the finished product often depends on sales to the USA or the European Union. A Singaporean ambassador told Chinese media in August 2013 that 60 per cent of the goods that are exported from China and Association of Southeast Asian Nations (ASEAN) are ultimately manufactures that go to the USA, Europe and Japan. Only 22 per cent of such goods stay in the China–ASEAN region (Pu 2013). Meanwhile, the large Asian and international investment in China did not go to other Asian countries, thus hurting their economic development. Actual Chinese aid (as opposed to financing that will be repaid in money or commodities) to Asia is very small, with the exception of Chinese aid to North Korea.

North Korea looms large and negatively in China's strategic calculus. China has shown no viable way of dealing with the wide array of problems associated with Pyongyang. Overall, it is a major source of insecurity for the Xi Jinping government (Pollack 2014).

China in the shadow of US leadership

US strengths in the Asia–Pacific region involve:

- *Security guarantor.* In most of Asia, governments are viable and make the decisions that determine direction in foreign affairs. In general, governments seek legitimacy through nation building and economic development, which require a stable and secure environment. Unfortunately, Asia is not particularly stable and Asian governments tend to distrust one another. They rely on the United States to maintain regional stability. The US security role is very expensive and involves great risk; neither China nor any other Asian power or coalition of powers is able or willing to undertake even a fraction of these risks and costs.
- *Essential economic partner.* Most Asian governments depend importantly on export-oriented growth. Growing intra-Asian trade relies on the United States Most notably, Asian exports lead to a massive trade surplus with the open US market. China, which consistently runs an overall trade surplus, avoids such costs that nonetheless are very important for Asian governments.
- *Government engagement.* The Bush administration was generally effective in interaction with Asia's powers. The Obama government's emphasis on consultation with international stakeholders before coming to policy decisions has been broadly welcomed. Meanwhile, US military, other security and intelligence organizations have grown uniquely influential, developing wide-ranging military, security and intelligence relationships with almost all regional governments.
- *Non-government engagement.* US longstanding business, religious, educational, media and other non-government interchange is widespread, uniquely influential and strongly reinforces overall US sway. Generally color-blind US immigration policy since 1965 means that millions of Asian migrants call America home and interact with their countries of origin in ways that undergird US interests.
- *Asian hedging.* As power relations change in the region, notably on account of China's rise, Asian governments seek to work positively and pragmatically with rising China, but they also seek the reassurance of close security, intelligence and other ties with the United States, especially amid evidence that rising China is shifting to more assertiveness. The US concern to keep stability while fostering economic growth overlaps constructively with the priorities of the vast majority of regional governments.

(Sutter 2013b: 321–326)

The bottom line is this: the Obama government rebalance seeks stability while fostering economic growth and overlaps constructively with the priorities of the vast majority of regional governments. China seeks advantageous economic interchange, but it remains insecure as its ambitions, coercion, intimidation and gross manipulation are achieved at its neighbours' expense.

Robert Sutter

Future Asian dynamics, the China challenge and the USA

As Chinese capabilities grow, Beijing is likely to take actions that will further challenge the international order supported by the USA (Lawrence 2013). The challenges to the security and stability in East Asia and the broader Asia-Pacific have been clear and seem primed to continue and perhaps advance. China's erosion of international economic norms is largely concealed. China seems to support free trade by the USA and others in its ongoing efforts to exploit this open environment with state-directed means, widespread theft, intimidation and coercion of companies and governments in a wholesale grasp of technology, know-how, capital and competitive advantage in a headlong drive for economic development at the expense of others.

The USA will face continuing impediments from China in dealing with nuclear proliferation by North Korea and Iran; China was of little help in dealing with Syria's use of chemical weapons or Russia's annexation of Crimea and coercion of Ukraine. The Chinese leaders remain determined to support the Leninist one-party system in China that treats human rights selectively and capriciously, with eyes always focused on sustaining the communist state.

Taken together, these issues represent the focus of the China challenge for the USA in the immediate period ahead. They promise numerous headaches and problems for US policymakers; American officials may grow somewhat weary in their efforts to deal with various Chinese probes and machinations. However, the above assessment shows that the China challenge is not a fundamental one, at least not yet. The USA can have some confidence that prevailing circumstances and constraints seem to preclude China seeking confrontation or a power shift in Asia. Some aver that China has adopted a slow and steady pace as it seeks to spread its influence and undermine that of the USA, especially in the all important Asia-Pacific region (Friedberg 2011). Maybe so, but the record of Chinese advances over the past 25 years shows such mediocre results and conflicted approaches that the prospect of Chinese leadership in the Asia-Pacific region seems remote. More likely, China will continue to rise in the shadow of a USA that is increasingly tied to a wide range of independent-minded Asia-Pacific governments which view the USA as critically important to their stability, growth and independence.

Despite regional doubts, the USA seems likely to pursue the kind of engagement policy towards both the Asia-Pacific region and China seen in the Obama government's rebalancing policy initiatives. The reasons are obvious and strong:

- the region is an area of ever greater strategic and economic importance for the USA; and
- the USA remains strongly committed to long-standing US goals of supporting stability and the balance of power; sustaining smooth economic access; and promoting US values in this increasingly important world area.

Future dynamics in Asia are seen as being determined by five sets of factors:

1. the changing power relationships among Asia's leading countries (e.g. the rise of China and India; changes in Japan; rising or reviving middle powers, namely South Korea, Indonesia and Australia);
2. the growing impact of economic globalization and related international information interchange;

3   the ebb and flow of tensions in the Korean peninsula, south-western Asia and the broader US-backed efforts against terrorism and proliferation of weapons of mass destruction;
4   the rise of Asian multilateralism; amd
5   the changing extent of US engagement with and withdrawal from involvement with Asian matters (Sutter 2014)

In addition, a survey of leadership debates about foreign policy among Asia-Pacific leaders (Nau and Ollapally 2012) shows a tendency towards perspectives of realism in International Relations theory in the USA, China, Japan, Russia, India and several middle and smaller powers including Indonesia, Australia, South Korea, Vietnam, Malaysia and Singapore (Sutter 2013a). Such perspectives are important for showing the way in which these leaders view the changing power dynamics and security issues (which are particularly evident in factors 1, 3 and 5).

While vigilant with respect to changing circumstances that could have an impact on their security, sovereignty and other important interests, government leaders also clearly recognize the importance of economic development, the lynchpin of their political legitimacy. Thus, they endeavour to use the liberal international economic order in ways that benefit them and their countries, and in so doing they subscribe in various ways and to varying degrees to aspects of liberalism in International Relations theory.

Asia-Pacific leaders also show support for aspects of the International Relations theory of constructivism. Such support is manifest in their ongoing efforts to build regional and international organizations and to support international norms as effective means to manage interstate tensions and differences and to promote greater interstate cooperation. Domestically, most Asia-Pacific governments also foster a strong identity for their nations as independent actors in regional and global affairs representing the interests and qualities of the peoples of their respective countries. Supporting such an identity is an important element in their continued political legitimacy (Rozman 2013).

A continuation of the type of US engagement policy seen in the Obama government's rebalancing initiatives fits well with most of these regional dynamics. The US strengths look even stronger when compared with China's recent and likely future approaches.

The USA has a proven record of bearing the costs and risks of sustaining regional stability that is essential for the development and nation building sought by the regional government leaders. There is little perceived danger of offensive US military, economic or other policy actions amid repeated stress by American leaders against unilateral change in the status quo. By contrast, China has accompanied its rise in regional prominence with a conflicted message of closer economic cooperation on a mutually beneficial (win-win) basis and often strident Chinese threats and coercive actions backed by civilian and military government power against neighbours that disagree with China, especially on issues of sovereignty and security. The fact that China's stridency on these matters has grown with the expansion of coercive civilian and military power alarms many Asian neighbours who seek reassurance from closer relations with the USA in a variety of forms, thereby deepening and strengthening the American integration with the region.

Meanwhile, Chinese leaders continue to focus on a narrow win-set of Chinese interests. They avoid the kinds of costs and risks borne by the USA in support of perceived American interests in the broader regional order that are well recognized by regional governments, reinforcing the regional governments' support for closer American involvement in regional affairs. Asian leaders watch closely for signs of US military withdrawal or flagging American interest in sustaining regional stability. The Obama government has affirmed its commitment to sustaining the robust American security presence which involves the close military cooperation with the vast majority of Asia-Pacific governments fostered during the post-Cold War period. This builds on the strong engagement efforts of the Clinton and Bush administrations, enjoys bipartisan political support in Congress and seems likely to continue for the reasons noted above.

China's role as a trader, a location for investment and an increasing importance as a foreign investor will continue to grow in regional affairs. Unlike the USA, China has a great deal of money that could be used to the benefit of its neighbours. The governments engage in sometimes protracted talks with Chinese counterparts with a view to finding ways to use the money consistent with China's ubiquitous win-win formula. In general, China will part with its money only if there is assurance that it will be paid back and that the endeavour will support China's narrow win-set. China's location and advancing infrastructure connecting China to its neighbours are major positive attributes supporting closer Chinese relations with neighbouring states.

Of course, much of that trade remains dependent on foreign investment and access to markets in the USA in particular. The USA almost certainly will not quickly reverse the large trade deficit that undergirds the export-oriented economies of the region. Asian leaders are watchful for signs of American protectionism, but the continued US economic recovery reinforces support for enhanced free trade initiatives from the USA.

By contrast, China's commitment to free trade remains selective and narrow. Beijing's tendency to go well beyond international norms in retaliating against others over trade and other issues has grown with the advance of China's economic size and influence. Its cybertheft of trade and economic information and property is enormous. Its currency manipulation and other neo-mercantilist practices are used deliberately to advance China's economy without much consideration of how they disadvantage not only neighbouring economies but also the USA. China's recent extraordinary pressure on Japan regarding its territorial claims risks enormous negative consequences for the regional economic growth. By contrast, the USA will probably see its interests best served in endeavouring to calm the tensions and play the role of stabilizer highly valued by most regional governments.

The growing US security, economic and political relationships with the wide range of Asia-Pacific governments built by the Clinton, Bush and Obama administrations have the effect of strengthening these governments and countries, and reinforcing their independence and identities. While many of these governments continue to disagree with US policies regarding the Middle East peace process, electronic spying and other issues, American interest in preserving a favourable balance of power in the region is supported by the prevalence of such stronger independent actors.

By contrast, China's assertiveness shows its neighbours that Beijing expects them to accommodate a growing range of Chinese concerns, even to the point of sacrificing territory. The range of Chinese demands probably will broaden with the growth of Chinese military, economic and other coercive power. Strengthening those in the region that resist China's pressure is regarded in Beijing as a hostile act. Nevertheless, President Obama's trip to East Asia in April 2014 was the latest demonstration that the USA will counter Chinese pressure with concrete building blocks of closer security, economic and political ties with Japan, the Philippines and other targets of China's ire (VOA News 2014).

It is important to reiterate here that most Asia-Pacific governments likely will expect the US government to carry out its improvement of relations in the region in ways that do not exacerbate China–US tensions and thereby disrupt the Asia-Pacific region. Indeed, Chinese commentators carefully avoided harsh criticism of President Obama's trip. A flexible US stance involving positive and negative incentives to dissuade China from disruptive assertiveness while strengthening the US regional relationships with allies and other partners holds promise for American interests in regional stability and development in accord with internationally accepted norms.

The Obama government has also advanced markedly US relations with the various regional organizations valued by Asian governments as part of their 'constructivist' efforts to create norms and build institutions to ease interstate rivalries and promote cooperative relations. The Obama government seems sincere in pursuing interchange that is respectful of the regional bodies. These initiatives enjoy broad bipartisan support in Congress and are likely to continue to do so. China also depicts close alignment with these groups, though China's more assertive ambitions regarding disputed territories have seen Chinese leaders grossly manipulate these bodies or resort to coercion and intimidation.

Conclusion

Prevailing circumstances suggest a continuation of trends seen in recent years of China's rise in Asia and the broader US leadership role in the Asia-Pacific region as examined above. This author assesses that those circumstances will continue to encumber China and preoccupy Chinese leaders who will probably probe for advantage and aim to cause trouble for US policymakers, but who will also remain cautious and unwilling to engage in serious military confrontation with the USA. The circumstances are also perceived to support a stronger American leadership position that has become increasingly well integrated with regional governments and organizations.

Note

1 The author participated in consultations in Washington, DC, on 8, 15 and 16 November 2012, involving groups of visiting Chinese specialists assessing US–China relations following the US elections and groups of concerned American specialists.

Bibliography

Bush, Richard, *Unchartered Strait*, Washington, DC: Brookings Institution, 2013.
Elliott School of International Affairs, *Balancing Acts*, Washington, DC, 2013, www2.gwu.edu/~sigur/assets/docs/BalancingActs_Compiled1.pdf.
Friedberg, Aaron L., *Contest for Supremacy. China, America and the Struggle for Mastery in Asia*, New York: W. W. Norton and Company, 2011.
Garver, John, *Foreign Relations of the People's Republic of China*, Englewood Cliffs, NJ: Prentice Hall, 1993.
Jacobson, Linda, 'Australia-China Ties: In Search of Political Trust'. *Policy Brief*, Sydney: Lowy Institute, June 2012.
Keyser, Don, 'President Obama's Re-election: Outlook for U.S. China Relations in the Second Term'. China Policy Institute, Nottingham University, UK, 7 November 2012.
Lawrence, Susan, *U.S.-China Relations: An Overview of Policy Issues*, Washington, DC, Congressional Research Service of the Library of Congress, Report R41108, 1 August 2013.
Lieberthal, Kenneth and Wang Jisi, *Addressing U.S.-China Strategic Distrust*, Washington, DC: Brookings Institution, March 2012.
Limaye, Satu, 'India-US Relations', *Comparative Connections*, Vol. 15, No. 3, January 2014.

Nathan, Andrew, 'Hugh White, The China Choice', *Foreign Affairs*, January–February 2013, www.foreignaffairs.com/articles/138661/hugh-white/the-china-choice-why-america-should-share-power.

Nau, Henry and Deepa Ollapally, *World Views of Aspiring Powers*, New York: Oxford University Press, 2012.

Pollack, Jonathan, 'Why Does China Coddle North Korea?', *New York Times*, 12 January 2014, www.nytimes.org.

Przystup, James, 'Japan-China Relations'. *Comparative Connections*, Vol. 14, No. 3, January 2013.

Pu, Zhendong, 'Singapore Supports Strengthened Free-Trade Agreement with Beijing', *China Daily*, 30 August 2013, http://usa.chinadaily.com.cn/epaper/2013-08/30/content_16932418.htm.

Roach, Stephen, 'China's Policy Disharmony', *Project Syndicate*, 31 December 2013, www.project-syndicate.org.

Rozman, Gilbert, *East Asian National Identities: Common Roots and Chinese Exceptionalism*, Stanford, CA: Stanford University Press, 2013.

Saunders, Philip, *The Rebalance to Asia: U.S.-China Relations and Regional Security*, Washington, DC: National Defense University, Institute for National Security Studies, 2012.

Shambaugh, David, 'The Rocky Road Ahead in U.S.–China Relations', *China-U.S. Focus*, 23 October 2012, www.chinausfocus.com/print/?id=20902.

Shambaugh, David (ed.), *Tangled Titans*, Lanham, MD: Rowman & Littlefield, 2013.

Snyder, Scott, 'China-Korea Relations'. *Comparative Connections*, Vol. 15, No. 3, January 2014.

Sutter, Robert, *U.S.–Chinese Relations*, Lanham MD, Rowman & Littlefield, 2013a.

Sutter, Robert, *Foreign Relations of the PRC*, Lanham, MD: Rowman & Littlefield, 2013b.

Sutter, Robert, 'Rebalancing, China and Asian Dynamics – Obama's Good Fit', *Pacnet*, No. 1, 5 January 2014, www.csis.org/pacfor.

Sutter, Robert and Huang Chin-Hao, 'China-Southeast Asia Relations'. *Comparative Connections*, Vol. 15, No. 2, September 2013, www.csis.org/pacfor.

VOA News, 'As Obama Leaves Asia, One Last Swipe at China', 29 April 2014, www.voanews.com/content/as-obama-leaves-asia-one-last-swipe-at-china/1903321.html.

Yu, Bin, 'China-Russia Relations'. *Comparative Connections*, Vol. 15, No. 3, January 2014.

Yu, Yongding, 'A Different Road Forward'. *China Daily*, 23 December 2010.

7
The pivot and Peking
The US response to China in East Asia

Richard A. Bitzinger

China's emergence as an economic, geopolitical and perhaps even cultural great power has been undeniable. Its military rise has been equally indisputable, even if the implications of this military build-up are still open to debate. Beijing has, for at least a decade and a half, invested considerable resources, in terms of both money and human capital, into building up its armed forces – and it is paying off. The People's Liberation Army (PLA) is a much more capable force, compared to its neighbours, than it was 20 years ago. This modernized and revitalized military force is being matched by (or perhaps this modernization process has even enabled) a new assertiveness, obstinacy and obduracy in international affairs; this 'bad behaviour' has been witnessed almost daily in both the East and South China Seas. When coupled with the country's long-standing – and perhaps even growing – sense of 'victimhood' and the need to 'reclaim lost status', the result is a more militarily capable China that may be much less inclined to negotiate and compromise, and instead may be more prone to use force or the threat of force to achieve its goals (Medeiros 2009: 10–11).

Even though there has been little in the way of making of overt or explicit references to a 'China threat', most nations in the Asia-Pacific have met growing Chinese military power – and the aggressiveness that has accompanied it – with a mixture of alarm and dread. Officially, of course, most countries in the Asia-Pacific are reluctant to designate China as an outright threat, preferring instead, as the US Defense Department has put it, oblique allusions to 'matters of concerns' or 'legitimate questions about [China's] future conduct and intentions' (US Department of Defense 2010: 60). In addition, engagement with China, rather than containment, is almost always stressed when dealing with Beijing. Nevertheless, countries in the Asia-Pacific *are* reacting to China's rise as a regional military power with military build-ups of their own. Japan, India and several nations in South-East Asia are beginning at least partially to justify their current military modernization programmes as a hedge against Chinese aggressive behaviour. Consequently, many regional militaries have attempted to match the Chinese build-up, in intensity at least, if not in comparable numbers. Consequently, during the past decade the pace of advanced arms acquisitions has picked up throughout much of the Asia-Pacific (Bitzinger 2012: 35).

In the case of the USA, Washington's response to a rising China can be basically summed up in one phrase: 'the pivot back to Asia'. Within this so-called pivot (also termed 'the rebalancing back to Asia', or 'the return to Asia') is contained most of the elements of an emerging US strategy – one that has economic, security and military implications – regarding the Asia-Pacific. Overall, the pivot constitutes a significant, even consequential, realignment of US global power. After a decade-long preoccupation with fighting ground-based counter-insurgency wars in the Middle East, the US military now seeks to emphasize air- and sea-based operations in an 'arc extending from the Western Pacific and East Asia into the Indian Ocean region and South Asia' (US Department of Defense 2012: 2).

This fundamental shift in US strategic focus was first enunciated in a speech made by President Barack Obama in November 2011, while on a state visit to Australia:

> Our new focus on this region reflects a fundamental truth – the United States has been, and always will be, a Pacific nation ... As President, I have, therefore, made a deliberate and strategic decision – as a Pacific nation, the United States will play a larger and long-term role in shaping this region and its future, by upholding core principles and in close partnership with our allies and friends. Let me tell you what this means. First, we seek security, which is the foundation of peace and prosperity. We stand for an international order in which the rights and responsibilities of all nations and all people are upheld ... [We are also] modernizing America's defense posture across the Asia-Pacific. It will be more broadly distributed maintaining our strong presence in Japan and the Korean peninsula, while enhancing our presence in Southeast Asia. Our posture will be more flexible with new capabilities to ensure that our forces can operate freely. And our posture will be more sustainable, by helping allies and partners build their capacity, with more training and exercises ... At the same time, we'll reengage with our regional organizations ... [W]e're forging the economic partnerships that create opportunity for all.
> (ibid.)

The dual economic and security elements of the 'pivot back to Asia' have been reiterated elsewhere by other US officials. US National Security Advisor Susan Rice has stated that the 'rebalancing toward the Asia-Pacific remains a cornerstone of the Obama administration's foreign policy' (Rice 2013).

At issue, of course, is how much China factors into the pivot. Obama and others in his administration have gone to great lengths to assure Beijing that the 'rebalancing towards the Asia-Pacific' is *not* directed in any antagonistic or belligerent way towards it, and the usual language of inclusiveness has been employed. In Obama's 2011 speech promulgating the pivot, he specifically avowed that 'the United States will continue our effort to build a cooperative relationship with China' (US Department of Defense 2012). Yet it is undeniable that the pivot is directed, in large part, in response to growing Chinese aggression and assertiveness in the Asia-Pacific. There are, quite simply, few other plausible reasons for articulating such a policy, save for China and Chinese aggressive behaviour. In the absence of a 'China threat', whether implicit or explicit, to traditional US primacy in the Asia-Pacific, there would be little motivation for Washington to go to such lengths to reiterate its role in the region. In particular, without China, the military aspect of the pivot would be irrelevant.

This 'counter-China' feature of the US pivot has, if anything, become even more apparent recently. At the 2014 Shangri-la Dialogue in Singapore, for example, US Secretary of Defense Chuck Hagel specifically criticized China for undertaking 'destabilizing, unilateral actions asserting its claims in the South China Sea', singling out China's recent clashes with Vietnam and the Philippines as examples of this destabilizing behaviour (Hagel 2014). He added:

> The United States has been clear and consistent. We take no position on competing territorial claims. But we firmly oppose any nation's use of intimidation, coercion, or the threat of force to assert those claims ... The United States will not look the other way when fundamental principles of the international order are being challenged.
>
> (ibid.)

Consequently, the rebalancing is significant because it symbolizes Washington's renewed focus on China and its growing concern about the growth of Chinese military power in the Asia-Pacific. The strategic pivot is not merely a diplomatic and economic reengagement with Asia – it is a decidedly military effort by the USA to counterbalance Beijing's growing strength and influence in the region. In this regard, therefore, the pivot must be viewed through the lens of the Pentagon's nascent Air-Sea Battle (ASB) concept, an ambitious war-fighting model that anticipates massive counterstrikes against an enemy's home territory, incapacitating the adversary by taking out its military surveillance and communications systems, while also targeting the enemy's missile bases, airfields and naval facilities. In the Asia-Pacific, that perceived adversary is, increasingly, China.

The remainder of this chapter addresses the pivot with regard to the two facets most generally attributed to it. The first part discusses the supposed economic aspects of the pivot, embodied in US efforts to secure the Trans-Pacific Partnership (TPP) free trade deal. The second deals with the rebalancing's military facet, as manifested in the ASB concept and its application to the Asia-Pacific.

The pivot and the Trans-Pacific Partnership

Many have viewed the TPP as the economic component of the US pivot. As Ernest Bower put it:

> For the United States, the TPP represents its primary tactic in implementing a strategy to promote regional peace and prosperity through economic engagement, in effect rebalancing the Asia 'pivot', which was interpreted by many in the region to be dominated initially by security concerns.
>
> (2014: 42–43)

The TPP is a massive free trade agreement that the USA is currently negotiating with 12 other Asia-Pacific nations (Australia, Brunei, Canada, Chile, Japan, South Korea, Malaysia, Mexico, New Zealand, Peru, Singapore and Vietnam). If the TPP can be realized, it will encompass 40 per cent of global gross domestic product and just over a quarter of the world's trade. It would eliminate tariffs on goods and services traded between partnership countries, reduce non-tariff barriers, and harmonize such regulations as intellectual property rights (e.g. copyrights and patents) and investor-state dispute resolution (DePillis 2013).

Former US National Security Advisor Tom Donilon has called the TPP the 'centerpiece of our economic rebalancing', and a 'platform for regional economic integration' (Donilon 2013). To be sure, the TPP is controversial, opposed by organized labour, environmentalists, internet freedom activists and global health advocates; it is also a long way from being realized (DePillis 2013).

According to some, the TPP is also perceived to be an initiative deliberately intended to exclude and even contain China. Beijing has not been invited to participate in TPP negotiations, and many of the agreement's proposals – such as the 'yarn-forward rule' (a provision that yarns used in textiles and clothing must come from other TPP countries) and limits on government support to state-owned enterprises (in order to foster free market competition) – are intentionally construed so as to isolate China (Kelsey 2013; Gordon 2014).

Such criticisms may be exaggerated, or, in any event, soon irrelevant. In the first place, TPP predates the pivot, growing out of a 2005 free trade agreement between Singapore, Chile, New Zealand and Brunei. The USA jumped into the process in 2008, during the George W. Bush administration, which viewed a prospective TPP simply as a way of protecting US exports to Asia; the Obama administration later grafted the language of the pivot onto the TPP (Gordon 2014). Second, the whole argument about the TPP deliberately excluding – and therefore somehow 'containing' – China may be moot. China has reversed its criticism of the TPP and is likely to request membership. More importantly, the Obama administration has openly supported Chinese participation in the TPP. National Security Adviser Rice has stated: 'We welcome any nation that is willing to live up to the high standards of this agreement to join and share in the benefits of the TPP, *and that includes China*' (Rice 2013, emphasis added).

It is perhaps an exaggeration, therefore, to portray the TPP as a US device to counter and contain China, although it does promote some of the economic aspects of the pivot, by buttressing US commercial and trade interests in the Asia-Pacific. It could be argued, of course, that Washington is not being sincere in wishing to include China in the TPP, or that Beijing will find it so difficult to meet the criteria for membership that the prospects are a fool's errand. Even so, the prospects are not inconceivable, and allowing for the possibility of joining makes it difficult to perceive the TPP as an indisputably anti-China contrivance. The TPP may constitute an integral piece of the pivot, but with regard to China, its potential impact is trivial compared to the military component of the rebalancing, as embodied in ASB. It is to this issue that we next turn our attention.

The pivot and Air-Sea Battle

More than anything, the US pivot to Asia has a decisively military tinge to it. In particular, it entails a significant redeployment of US forces from other parts of the world to the Asia-Pacific region. The US Navy, for example, plans to position 60 per cent of its fleet in the Pacific Ocean by 2020, compared to a current 50:50 split between the Pacific and Atlantic. In addition, 2,500 US Marines are to be based in Darwin, Australia, while Singapore has agreed to host up to four of the new US Navy littoral combat ships. Finally, the USA has sought to strengthen security relations with its East Asian allies and partners. During President Obama's April 2014 trip to Asia, for example, he reiterated the US security guarantee to Japan, explicitly including the disputed Senkaku/Daioyu Islands in this commitment. During the same month the USA and the Philippines signed an Enhanced Defense Cooperation Agreement, expanding bilateral security cooperation and giving US armed forces easier access to, and freer use of, forward operating bases in the Philippines (Thayer 2014). In the wake of the worsening South China Sea situation, Vietnam and the USA have also grown closer to each other (Tiezzi 2014).

Of course, much of this supposed redeployment is just old wine in new bottles. The USA never really decoupled that much from the Asia-Pacific, militarily speaking. Six of the US Navy's 11 aircraft carriers are already based in the Pacific, as well as 31 of its 53 nuclear-powered attack submarines. Additionally, there are more than 60,000 US military personnel based in the Western Pacific alone, along with 42,500 uniformed service members in Hawaii and 13,600 more afloat. That said, perhaps the newest and most ominous wrinkle to the military side of the pivot is the US military's embrace of ASB and its likely application of ASB war-fighting concepts to future US strategy in the Asia-Pacific. More than any other feature of the pivot, ASB has the most potentially serious consequences for US–Sino military relations.

In September 2009 the US Navy and Air Force signed a classified memorandum to initiate an inter-service effort to develop a new joint operational concept, dubbed Air-Sea Battle. Emulating intellectual transitions in military doctrine along the lines of the Air-Land Battle (ALB) war-fighting concept developed in the early 1980s to counter advances in Soviet operational art, ASB has been designed, at the strategic level, to preserve stability and to sustain US power projection and freedom of action, and, at the operational level, to offset current and anticipated asymmetric threats through a novel integration of US Air Force and Navy's concepts, assets and capabilities.

Central to the ASB concept is overcoming the purportedly emerging 'anti-access/area denial challenge' that challenges the operational freedom of US military forces. Advocates of ASB frequently emphasize the growing abilities of potential adversaries (e.g. China, Iran and North Korea) to deny US forces the ability to enter or operate in maritime territories adjacent to these countries. A2/AD is seen as especially crucial in deterring or countering third-party interventions – for example, efforts on the part of the US military to come to the aid of Taiwan in the case of a cross-Strait crisis, or Saudi Arabia and neighbouring states in the case of attacks on shipping in the Persian Gulf (Office of the Secretary of Defense 2011: 2). According to the Center for Strategic and Budgetary Affairs (CSBA), 'anti-access (A2) strategies aim to prevent US forces from operating from fixed land bases in a theater of operations', while 'area-denial (AD) operations aim to prevent the freedom of action of maritime forces operating in the theater' (Krepinevich 2010: 9–10). The CSBA defines the A2/AD threat as strikes by ballistic and cruise missiles (both land attack and anti-ship), artillery and rocket barrages, submarine operations, and long-range air strikes. Cyber-attacks, anti-satellite warfare, and even coastal mines are also usually characteristic of A2/AD.

To counter a hypothetical crisis scenario or conflict in which an adversary employs an A2/AD strategy, ASB in turn envisions a pre-emptive, standoff, precision-strike – or 'Networked, Integrated Attack-in-Depth' – initiated and carried out by US forces alone, in three distinct phases: (1) by striking the enemy's intelligence, surveillance and reconnaissance assets from afar through a 'blinding campaign' in order to deny their situational awareness; by reducing the adversary's ability to 'see deep', US aircraft carrier groups would thereby gain access to the battlespace; (2) by carrying out a 'missile suppression campaign' to disrupt the enemy's air-defence networks, using stealthy long-range platforms, and supported by submarine-launched weapons and sensors; through this destruction or degradation of the enemy's critical air-defence assets and the consequent achievement of air superiority, US forces would be able to attack the adversary's land-based missile launchers, surface-to-surface missiles, and their supporting infrastructure; (3) by conducting diverse follow-on operations, such as 'distant blockades', in order to seize the operational initiative and to ensure protracted US freedom of action in the region.

While details surrounding ASB are sketchy, it has significant repercussions for security in the Asia-Pacific, because it is an essential component of Washington's response to the growth of Chinese military power. This is because *China, above all other potential adversaries, is regarded as the most critical potential employer of an A2/AD strategy, and therefore the main object of an ASB-based response*. The PLA's strategic priorities have shifted since the Taiwan Strait crisis of 1996 towards adopting a diverse portfolio of A2/AD capabilities for air, sea and land operations designed to deter, delay and prevent external (i.e. US) entry into specific areas deemed vital to China's 'core interests'. To this end, the PLA has been gradually upgrading its existing weapons systems and platforms, while experimenting with the next generation of design concepts. This can be seen in the comprehensive modernization of China's nuclear and conventional ballistic missiles; integrated air, missile and early warning defence systems;

electronic and cyber-warfare capabilities; submarines; surface combat vessels and the introduction of fourth- and fifth-generation multi-role combat aircraft.

Alongside the qualitative shifts in 'hardware', the PLA has also been revamping its 'software', including its military doctrine, organizational force structure and operational concepts, which are now conceptualized in the context of 'local wars under conditions of informationization' (Information Office of the State Council 2006). In particular, China's military doctrine envisions future conflicts as being short in duration, limited to its coastal periphery or 'near seas' (the Yellow, East and South China Seas), and involving integrated or joint military operations across the air, sea, land, space and cyber-space domains. The shifting character of the future battlefield in turn alters the PLA's operational requirements and compels the Chinese military to adopt innovative concepts and capabilities that would constrain the USA's strategic advantage and freedom of action in the region. These include A2/AD-oriented 'attack and defence' concepts that aim to offset the military effectiveness of US forward-deployed bases, mobile forces and their supporting infrastructure.

In a range of conventional potential crisis scenarios on the Korean peninsula, for example, China could take measures to disrupt the build-up of US combat power in terms of size, location and time frames. Specifically, the PLA could delineate clear air, sea and land buffer zones (conflict limit lines) beyond which US–South Korean forces could not operate. In such a case, the USA would need to construct alternative points of entry for its reinforcements, which could effectively delay its initial and follow-on responses. Similarly, in a scenario involving a Chinese attack on Taiwan, the use of anti-ship cruise and ballistic missiles would impede the use of aircraft carriers around the island. Finally, depending on the modalities of China's A2/AD strategies, the USA could potentially have to adjust the scope of its involvement in the region, limiting its operational conduct and freedom of action, particularly with regard to its naval deployments in the South China Sea.

Interestingly, while ASB appears to be inherently designed to counter China's emerging A2/AD systems and capabilities, its proponents still go out of their way to deny that ASB does not specifically target China. The CSBA, for example, has explicitly stated in a 2010 briefing that 'ASB is NOT about war with China or containment of China' but rather 'part of a larger "offsetting strategy" aimed at preserving a stable military balance and maintaining crisis stability in East Asia'. Nevertheless, the briefing also describes the PLA's acquisition of A2/AD capabilities as the 'most stressful case' for an ASB strategy. It then goes on to describe, in excruciating detail, how ASB would be employed to fight a war against China, including attacks on the Chinese mainland (Van Tol et al. 2010).

Regional responses to Air-Sea Battle

The political and military establishment in the USA emphasizes the growing importance and complexity of East Asia's security challenges, including the strategic and operational consequences of China's ongoing military modernization. US allies in East Asia, however, have not fully embraced the ASB concept or the rationale behind it. Indeed, South Korea, Japan, Australia and other US partners in the region have been relatively quiet about the implications of ASB, largely because they do not possess the full extent of the planned operational details, which remain classified. Such hesitance is also attributable to concerns, from the allied perspective, over the extent to which ASB provides strategic reassurance, as opposed to representing abandonment by the USA. Indeed, the US Department of Defense has not clarified the link between the ASB concept and its 'rebalancing strategy' in the Asia-Pacific region, nor what particular aspects of ASB will be relevant for future allied interoperability requirements and involvement. Moreover, at the operational level, US allies question whether implementing ASB would actually mitigate military effectiveness and the defence of nearby US allied bases in the region (Bitzinger and Raska 2013: 6).

At this point, no US ally or potential military partner in North-East or South-East Asia is anywhere near to being sufficiently equipped to make much of a contribution to US Air-Sea Battle operations. Japan is probably the most concerned about a rising Chinese military threat, as reflected in its 2011 National Defense Program Guidelines and its embrace of a 'dynamic defence force'. This 'dynamic defence' emphasizes high mobility, an expeditionary capacity (to specifically defend off-shore islands), jointness (within the entire Japan Self-Defense Forces – JSDF), and interoperability with US forces (Japanese Ministry of Defense 2010). At the same time, the JSDF remains overwhelmingly a defensively oriented military; its major potential contributions to ASB are in providing secure forward basing to US forces, missile defence, and a small but growing capacity for power projection (e.g. new helicopter carriers, an expanding submarine force, additional sea- and airlift). According to Benjamin Schreer, 'Japan's defense planning has thus started to shift toward complementarity in a possible "Allied Air-Sea Battle" concept. Militarily, it's increasingly well placed to "plug and play" in a future Sino–US conflict' (2013: 25).

On the other hand, Japan remains militarily and strategically hamstrung by an extremely tight defence budget that limits the acquisition of ASB-supporting equipment or infrastructure, and a continuing pacifist streak that runs through the general populace; its ability to make a substantial contribution to ASB operations is still limited, therefore.

For their part, most other countries in the region are even less prepared, either militarily or politically (or both) to support ASB. Most South-East Asian militaries, for instance, possess little in the way of area-denial capabilities – especially sea denial – when it comes to countering China. Even more importantly, it is highly unlikely that South-East Asian countries – even Singapore, a close partner with the US military which possesses the resources to play a 'supporting role in an Air-Sea Battle concept' – are prepared to commit themselves to 'an operational concept that could see [them] involved in a major war with China' (Schreer 2013: 29.) Embracing ASB would also place them too explicitly in the US camp, violating most of these countries' nonalignment strategies and/or balanced approaches towards both US and Chinese relations; this would also likely undermine their priorities to engage Beijing via statecraft and diplomacy in order to extract peaceable concessions from China.

In this context, therefore, US allies and partners in the region may even question whether and to what extent ASB foresees active multinational participation in the envisioned 'deep-strike missions' targeting China's military infrastructure on the mainland. This operational uncertainty in turn translates into broader strategic uncertainty, in which future alliance credibility may be compromised. Consequently, if ASB indeed comes to shape US operational conduct, US allies and partners in the region may feel the need to devise alternative defence strategies, and rethink the pace, direction and character of their military modernization, including their resource allocation and weapons acquisition priorities (Bitzinger and Raska 2013: 6).

Conclusions

Some argue that the pivot is only about China and, furthermore, that it is causing a dangerous deterioration in Sino–US relations:

> Washington's increased activity on China's periphery has led Beijing to conclude that the United States has abandoned strategic engagement, the cornerstone of U.S. policy toward China since the end of the Cold War. In contrast to previous administrations, the Obama administration has dismissed China's legitimate security interests in its border regions, including even those that are not vital to U.S. security. By threatening China and challenging its sovereignty claims over symbolic territories, Washington has encouraged Chinese leaders to believe that only by adopting belligerent policies will a rising China be able to guarantee its security. Herein lies the great irony of the pivot: a strategy that was meant to check a rising China has sparked its combativeness and damaged its faith in cooperation.
>
> (Ross 2012)

Other argue that the pivot is really about addressing not only China but a variety of long-neglected Asia-Pacific security concerns:

> [The pivot] was widely interpreted in the Western media as being all about China, which the administration denies, while in China, the strategy was widely perceived as being one more step in a Washington containment strategy. The truth, of course, is that China is a significant consideration, but it is also true that the rebalance is not all about China, nor is it an attempt to contain China.
>
> (McDevitt 2012: 14)

The truth is probably in the middle, which is still worrisome, nevertheless. Chinese strategic behaviour of late, particularly in the East and South China Seas, clearly warrants a more forceful response on the part of the USA. In this regard, the pivot, as a means of signalling to China that the USA is serious about preserving status quo peace and stability, is not only necessary, but desirous. After this broad enunciation of US hegemony, however, the message behind the pivot wavers. This is due to the continued lack of clarity in promulgating exactly what the pivot means for China. The USA's 'return to Asia' has been only fitfully enunciated, even more so when it comes to the whole issue of ASB. The US military has embraced ASB as a novel approach to warfare intended to counter 21st-century threats. Yet given that so many have made ASB such an essential element of US war-fighting, and considering the high stakes that it supposedly deals with, it is mystifying that so few particulars have been made public about what ASB really entails. Beyond a few banalities, little is still known about how ASB is supposed to work in a real-world situation and, more importantly, why it is necessary.

Owing to this ambiguity, it is not surprising that ASB is increasingly regarded, first and foremost, as a response to perceived growing Chinese military power in Asia. This discernment of a 'counter-China' emphasis has especially been spurred by the many briefings and writings that predominantly identify China as the *raison d'être* behind ASB. These perceptions, even if exaggerated, raise concerns that ASB could paradoxically imperil security and stability in the Asia-Pacific region.

At this point, ASB is either too vague to sufficiently discuss as a conceivable war-fighting construct, or too apparently focused on being simply a 'counter-China' strategy in order to be credible – for instance, would the US really initiate deep strikes on Chinese territory, and, if so, under what conditions? How 'scalable' is ASB as a response, and how believable might ASB be as a deterrent or response to lesser forms of Chinese aggression – for example, China's use of limited military actions (gunboat battles, harassing ships) to press its claims in the South China Sea? In all these cases, the answer is either unclear or the inferred conclusion simply too frightening.

In the final analysis, ambiguity is a challenge not just for the Sino–US strategic relationship; it affects all of the Asia-Pacific region. Many US allies in the region are justifiably wary of ASB, for instance, to a large part because the USA has not clarified the link between ASB and its 'rebalancing strategy' in the Asia-Pacific region, nor what particular aspects of ASB will be relevant for future allied interoperability requirements and involvement. Chinese international behaviour does demand some kind of diplomatic, economic and even military retort from the USA, but it is questionable whether ASB is the proper response.

Bibliography

Bitzinger, Richard A., 'Will the US Pivot Trigger a New Regional Arms Race?' *Global Asia*, Vol. 7, No. 4, Winter 2012.

Bitzinger, Richard A. and Michael Raska, *The AirSea Battle Debate and the Future of Conflict in East Asia*, RSIS Policy Brief, Singapore: S. Rajaratnam School of International Studies, 2013.

Bower, Ernest Z., Matthew Goodman and Scott Miller, 'How Important Is TPP to Our Asia Policy?' in Craig Cohen, Kathleen Hicks and Josiane Gabel, *2014 Global Forecast: US Security Policy at a Crossroads*, Washington, DC: Center for Strategic and International Studies, 2014.

China's National Defense in 2006, Beijing: Information Office of the State Council,2006, www.china.org.cn/english/features/book/194421.htm.

DePillis, Lydia, 'Everything You Need to Know about the Trans-Pacific Partnership', *Washington Post*, 11 December 2013.

Donilon, Tom, *The United States and the Asia-Pacific in 2013*, Washington, DC: The White House, 11 March 2013), www.whitehouse.gov/the-press-office/2013/03/11/remarks-tom-donilon-national-security-advisory-president-united-states-a.

Gordon, Bernard, 'Bring China into TPP', *National Interest*, 11 April 2014, http://nationalinterest.org/commentary/bring-china-tpp-10227.

Information Office of the State Council, People's Republic of China, *Defence White Paper 2013*, 2013, www.sldinfo.com/wp-content/uploads/2013/04/Chinese-Military-White-Paper-April-2013.pdf.

Hagel, Chuck, Speech of the US Secretary of Defense to the IISS Shangri-la Dialogue, Washington, DC: US Department of Defense, 31 May 2014, www.defense.gov/Speeches/Speech.aspx?SpeechID=1857.

Japanese Ministry of Defense, *National Defense Program Guidelines for FY2011 and Beyond*, Tokyo: Ministry of Defense, 17 December 2010, www.mod.go.jp/e/d_act/d_policy/pdf/guidelinesFY2011.pdf.

Kelsey, Jane, 'US–China Relations and the Geopolitics of the Trans-Pacific Partnership Agreement (TPPA)', *Global Research*, 11 November 2013, www.globalresearch.ca/us-china-relations-and-the-geopolitics-of-the-trans-pacific-partnership-agreement-tppa/5357504.

Krepinevich, Andrew F., *Why AirSea Battle?*, Washington, DC: Center for Strategic and Budgetary Assessments, 2010.

McDevitt, Michael, 'America's New Security Strategy and Its Military Dimension', *Global Asia*, Vol. 7, No. 4, Winter 2012.

Medeiros, Evan S. *China's International Behavior: Activism, Opportunism, and Diversification*, Santa Monica, CA: RAND, 2009.

Obama, Barack, Remarks by President Obama to the Australian Parliament, Washington, DC: The White House, 11 November 2011.

Office of the Secretary of Defense, *2011 Report to Congress: Military and Security Developments Involving the People's Republic of China*, Washington, DC: US Department of Defense, August 2011.

Rice, Susan E., *America's Future in Asia*, Washington, DC: The White House, 20 November 2013.

Ross, Robert S., 'The Problem with the Pivot', *Foreign Affairs*, November/December 2012, www.foreignaffairs.com/articles/138211/robert-s-ross/the-problem-with-the-pivot.

Schreer, Benjamin, *Planning the Unthinkable War: 'AirSea Battle' and Its Implications for Australia*, Canberra: Australian Strategic Policy Institute, 15 April 2013.

Thayer, Carl, 'Analyzing the US-Philippines Enhanced Defense Cooperation Agreement', *The Diplomat*, 2 May 2014, http://thediplomat.com/2014/05/analyzing-the-us-philippines-enhanced-defense-cooperation-agreement.

Tiezzi, Shannon, 'Amid South China Sea Tensions, Vietnam Seeks Closer Ties with US', *The Diplomat*, 29 May 2014, http://thediplomat.com/2014/05/amid-south-china-sea-tensions-vietnam-seeks-closer-ties-with-us/.

US Department of Defense, *Quadrennial Defense Review Report 2010*, Washington, DC: US Department of Defense, February 2010.

US Department of Defense, *Sustaining U.S. Global Leadership: Priorities for the 21st Century*, Washington, DC: US Department of Defense, January 2012).

Van Tol, Jan, Mark Gunzinger, Andrew F. Krepinevich and Jim Thomas, *AirSea Battle* (PowerPoint Briefing), Washington, DC: Center for Strategic and Budgetary Assessments, 18 May 2010.

8
Stuck over the barren rocks
The Diaoyu/Senkaku Islands dispute and Sino–Japanese relations

Jingdong Yuan

Sino–Japanese relations have deteriorated to the lowest point since 1972 when the two countries normalized diplomatic relations. At issue are territorial disputes over the uninhabited rocky Diaoyu/Senkaku Islands and the East China Sea, historical grievances, and geostrategic rivalry between Asia's two great powers. Related to these significant developments are the broader geopolitical contexts of China's rise and growing Sino–US competition for regional primacy (Friedberg 2011). Beijing increasingly has displayed a more assertive diplomatic stance in responding to issues it considers to be of core national interest while Washington, in an effort to retain its dominant power position in the Asia-Pacific that it has enjoyed since the end of the Second World War, has adopted a rebalancing strategy to assure allies and partners, and to manage a new type of major power relationship (Lampton 2013).

The simmering dispute between China and Japan over the Diaoyu/Senkaku Islands erupted in early September 2012 when the Japanese government decided to purchase three of the five islands for ¥2,050m. (US $26m.), ostensibly to ward off a similar attempt by the ultra-nationalist Governor of Tokyo, Shintaro Ishihara, who had been campaigning to raise private funds since April. China's response was swift and unequivocal. Beijing denounced Tokyo's action and took specific measures to demonstrate its sovereign claims to the island group, including sending maritime enforcement vessels and submitting to the United Nations (UN) the coordinates table and chart of the base points and baselines of the territorial sea of Diaoyu/Senkaku Islands (Perlez 2012).

Meanwhile, anti-Japanese demonstrations took place in major cities in China, with some turning into angry riots targeting Japanese-owned businesses. Emotions were boiling over as the Japanese move was also close to the 81st anniversary of the Mukden Incident when Imperial Japan invaded Manchuria in 1931, thus marking the beginning of the 14-year aggression against China. While the Chinese government subsequently reined in these demonstrations and bilateral talks were held to address the issue, both sides maintained their positions and no signs of any compromise appeared to be in sight. The standoff over the Diaoyu/Senkaku Islands was a serious setback in bilateral relations, as Asia's two largest economies marked their 40th anniversary of diplomatic relations. The stalemate was continuing in 2014.

Underlying the dispute regarding the barren rocks in the East China Sea there are a series of contentious issues between China and Japan. These range from the different interpretations regarding the ownership of the islands, the potential natural resources, to domestic political pressure and legitimacy, and strategic rivalry. For both countries, any apparent 'concession' in the settlement of the dispute could affect their separate territorial disputes with third parties (Japan with Russia and South Korea, and China with other claimants to the South China Sea disputes) (Pan 2007). The leadership transition in China and Abe's return to power in late 2012 has made it more difficult for both sides to seek any compromise. However, the continuing stalemate and growing tension over the islands could lead to military conflicts, which neither China nor Japan want but which could take place, resulting in significant economic, political and diplomatic damage to both. Given the contentious nature of the dispute and the stakes involved between two powerful countries, existing international law appears anachronistic and incapable of resolving the Diaoyu/Senkaku issue (Harry 2013).

Both countries' maritime enforcement ships are patrolling more frequently in the vicinity of the Senkaku/Diaoyu Islands and at times experience close encounters, and as a result this naval game of chicken runs the risk of leading to further direct confrontation that in theory could drag the USA into the conflict. Clearly, in order to achieve regional peace and stability Beijing and Tokyo need to try to de-escalate the situation and seek diplomatic ways out of this impasse. However, the larger issue is how the major powers in the region respond to and handle ongoing geopolitical transformation at a time of rising nationalism, the growing salience of maritime resources for economic development, historical legacies and domestic political legitimacy, and power transition.

The curse of history

China and Japan both claim sovereignty over the Diaoyu/Senkaku Islands but each has differing historical accounts of how ownership came about. The five small uninhabited islets and three barren rocks are together known as the Diaoyu (in Chinese)/Senkaku (in Japanese) Islands, which lie 230 nautical miles east of the Chinese coast, 120 nautical miles north-east of Taiwan, and 200 nautical miles south-west of Okinawa (Pan 2007: 71). They have been under Japanese administrative control since 1972 but are contested by both China and Taiwan. Chinese records date back almost 600 years ago to the Ming when an imperial envoy was dispatched to the Ryukyu Islands. Official Chinese records suggest that the Diaoyu/Senkaku Islands are not part of the Ryukyu Islands. During the Qing Dynasty, the Diaoyu/Senkaku Islands were described as part of Taiwan. Japan's claim to the islands can be traced to the post-Meiji Restoration period, in the late 19th century, when Tokyo incorporated the Ryukyu Islands into Japanese territory as Okinawa Prefecture, and conducted a survey of the area surrounding the Diaoyu/Senkaku Islands. The Chinese Qin Dynasty lost the 1894–95 war with Japan and was forced to cede Taiwan and the adjacent islands to Japan in addition to huge amounts of reparations. The Diaoyu Islands were annexed in 1895 and subsequently named the Senkaku Islands in 1900. In this case, the timing of the annexation of the Diaoyu/Senkaku Islands remains disputed. Japanese sources suggest that the island group was recognized as part of Okinawa Prefecture in January 1895 while China (and Taiwan) maintain that the islands were ceded to Japan under the 1895 Treaty of Shimonoseki as a result of the defeat of the Qing Dynasty in the first Sino–Japanese War (Gao 2010; Kawashima 2013).

Japanese claims to the island group have always been based on the concept of *terra nullius* (land without an owner), since a survey conducted by Japanese officials in 1885 confirmed that the islands were uninhabited and not under the control of any country (McDevitt 2014:

101). Historical interpretations apart, the islands have always remained uninhabited and Japan, with the exception of 1945–71 when the USA controlled the islands and Okinawa, has exercised administrative control. The 1943 Cairo Declaration stated that 'Japan shall be stripped of … all the territories Japan has stolen from the Chinese, such as Manchuria, Formosa, and the Pescadores, [which] shall be restored to the Republic of China', although Diaoyu/Senkaku was not specifically mentioned (Harry 2013). Japan surrendered in 1945 and Taiwan was returned to the Nationalist government under Chiang Kai-shek. The 1951 San Francisco Peace Treaty placed the administrative control of Okinawa and Diaoyu with the USA, which Beijing regarded at the time as an illegal occupation of Chinese territories. The 1971 Okinawa Reversion Treaty between the USA and Japan led to the return of Okinawa and the administrative control of the Diaoyu/Senkaku Islands to Japan, although Washington stated that it took a neutral position on the competing claims over Diaoyu/Senkaku by China, Japan and Taiwan (Manyin 2013). Neither Beijing nor Taipei recognized the Diaoyu/Senkaku Islands as part of Okinawa.

Another development was a 1968 survey conducted by the UN Economic Commission for Asia and the Far East (ECAFE) that pointed to the possibility of the existence of a wealth of resources beneath the seabed surrounding the Diaoyu/Senkaku Islands. This, in addition to the symbolism of their sovereignty, increased the economic value of the islands. This further cemented Taipei's view that the Republic of China did not approve of the reversion of the islands to Japan (Kawashima 2013). Indeed, Tokyo maintains that Beijing did not raise the Diaoyu/Senkaku issue until the release of the 1968 ECAFE study. In December 1971 the Chinese Ministry of Foreign Affairs released an official statement claiming that the islands were Chinese territories (McDevitt 2014: 101). There was also indication that prior to 1971 both China and Taiwan referred to the islands as Senkaku, and subsequently, they used, respectively, the names Diaoyu and Diaoyutai (Harry 2013; Kawashima 2013). During the negotiations leading to the re-establishment of diplomatic relations between China and Japan in 1972, both sides were aware of the competing claims and the intractable nature of the territorial disputes over Diaoyu/Senkaku. They chose to shelve the issue and to proceed with normalization. This tacit understanding also allowed the two countries to sign the 1978 Sino–Japanese Treaty of Peace and Friendship (Harry 2013). The Chinese leader, Deng Xiaoping, famously quipped that the dispute should be left to future generations of leaders to resolve, while in the mean time the two countries could contemplate jointly developing these valuable resources. The overall geostrategic interests shared by Beijing and Tokyo at the time – concerns with and opposition against Soviet expansionism – allowed them to paper over but not resolve the territorial dispute. Even with the ending of the Cold War, and sporadic frictions between the two countries over intrusions by fishermen and survey ships, the installation of lighthouses on the islets, and occasional landings by protestors, Beijing and Tokyo more or less managed to keep the dispute under control until 2010 (Fravel 2010).

Sino–Japanese territorial disputes extend beyond the Diaoyu/Senkaku Islands to the maritime boundary in the East China Sea. These are largely driven by strong economic incentives given the reported 160,000m. barrels of oil equivalent, including trillions of cubic feet of gas (Valencia 2014: 185). Japan has historically always depended on imports of oil and gas, and China became a net importer of oil in 1993. China, Japan, and South Korea all have overlapping claims to continental shelves, which in turn are used to determine a state's claim to exclusive economic zones (EEZs). For instance, opinions are divided regarding where the dividing lines should be drawn in the Chunxiao oil- and gasfields. China maintains it extends from the continental shelf whereas Japan argues it should be the median line. In June 2008 the two countries negotiated a joint development agreement. However, it quickly fell through because they could not agree where the location of the joint development zone should be. In addition, the agreed development zones triggered protests from South Korea while Chinese citizens accused the Chinese government of 'betraying national interest', humiliating the nation, and forfeiting sovereignty' (Bush 2010: 75–81; Valencia 2014: 192).

Since the late 1990s China has intensified its efforts to assert its sovereign claim to the East China Sea, including the Diaoyu/Senkaku Islands. Tokyo typically reacts strongly to what it considers as serious intrusions into its territorial waters by Chinese maritime survey ships and demands explanations from Beijing. In November 2004 a Chinese submarine reportedly sailed into Japanese waters without identifying itself. Beijing eventually acknowledged that 'technical problems' caused the accidental veering off course (Cody 2004). On the other hand, Beijing has protested against the Japanese government's acquiescence in allowing right-wing Japanese groups (and some politicians) to conduct provocative activities. Offshore developments of oilfields along the continental shelf have caused additional disputes about the exact extent of the EEZ in areas where Chinese and Japanese territorial waters overlap (Fedorova 2005; Hagström 2005). The fact that both countries now depend on oil imports is the reason for fierce rivalry between them over energy sources in Russia and the East China Sea. Beijing claims the entire area in accordance with the continental shelf principle set forth in the 1994 UN Convention on the Law of the Sea while Tokyo insists on dividing the maritime territories by the median line (Harrison 2002).

A turning point in Sino–Japanese territorial disputes was reached in 2008. For the first time, Chinese survey ships reportedly entered Japan-claimed 12-nautical-mile territorial waters near the Diaoyu/Senkaku Islands. Beijing dismissed Tokyo's protests, stating that these waters were Chinese sovereign territory. Chinese naval presence in the East China Sea has also increased, as have Chinese maritime survey activities. In September 2010 a Chinese fishing trawler collided with a Japanese coastguard patrol ship, resulting in the arrest of the Chinese fishermen and the detainment of the vessel's captain. This sparked a wave of violent protests in major Chinese cities and the alleged suspension of Chinese exports of rare earths to Japan. Although the captain of the trawler was subsequently released, bilateral relations have not yet recovered. Instead, tensions have increased yet further following Japan's purchase of three of the Diaoyu/Senkaku Islands in September 2012, and a subsequent increase in Chinese maritime surveillance and patrol ships in the islands' vicinity. In November 2013 Beijing outlined an air defence identification zone, which overlaps with the zones of Japan, South Korea and Taiwan and covers the disputed islands (IISS 2013; ICG 2014: 10–14). Close encounters between the two countries' maritime law enforcement ships as well as close fly-bys in airspace claimed by both countries have been reported. Analysts have pointed out that it is only a matter of time before a major aerial and/or maritime incident takes place, risking serious escalation to military confrontation that could also involve the USA given its security commitments to its ally (McDevitt 2014; Schwartz 2014).

Territorial disputes and the changing bilateral relationship

Sino–Japanese relations developed rapidly after normalization, in particular in the economic sphere. Two-way trade grew from US $1,000m. in 1972 to $340,000m. in 2011, but subsequently decreased to $312,000m. in 2013. China became Japan's largest trading partner in 2007. From the 1980s onwards Japan provided over $30,000m. in official development aid in the form of yen loans, which greatly assisted China's economic development in the areas of infrastructure and environment projects. Japanese investment in China has grown over the years, and major Japanese electronics and automobile makers have opened factories in China.

Despite these positive developments and, from time to time, official commitments from both governments to maintain and promote peaceful and stable bilateral relationship, Beijing and Tokyo have at best only managed to contain, but not to resolve, the territorial disputes over the Diaoyu/Senkaku Islands and the East China Sea (Wiegand 2009). In addition, controversies over historical issues, such as Japanese high school history textbooks, visits by Japanese politicians to the Yasukuni Shrine, where the remains of 14 class-A war criminals are also enshrined, and the Nanking Massacre, continue to cast a shadow over bilateral relations and remain the principal obstacles to genuine Sino–Japanese reconciliation and normalization. Major disruptions have flared up each time historical issues and territorial disputes have been brought to the fore: in 1978, 1984–85, 2005, and 2010. The current standoff is a continuation of this pattern (Bush 2010; He 2007).

Indeed, Sino–Japanese territorial disputes reflect and reinforce deeply seated mutual distrust and growing rivalry and animosity between the two countries. During the Cold War their common interests in opposing the Soviet Union, and efforts by the older generations of Chinese and Japanese leaders in developing and nurturing peaceful and friendly relations, helped to contain or push aside the unresolved historical and territorial issues between the two countries. Indeed, leaderships in both countries tried to keep territorial disputes under control, both out of recognition that these could not be resolved anytime soon and concerns that failure to do could seriously undermine bilateral ties (Kraus et al. 2014).

The ending of the Cold War and the changing geostrategic landscape, coupled with the discovery of valuable resources in the disputed maritime territories in the East China Sea as well as the Diaoyu/Senkaku islands, have contributed to heightened tensions between China and Japan. The common threat that used to glue them together no longer exists. With rising nationalism and a growing appetite for resources to sustain economic development, the contention for disputed territories and maritime resources has become a test of wills. Neither side is willing to compromise, lest it be perceived as weak and selling out the national interests. For Beijing, Tokyo's decision to 'nationalize' the Diaoyu/Senkaku island group the day after the meeting between Chinese President Hu Jintao and the Japanese Prime Minister Noda during which Hu warned Noda not to take any provocative action over a very sensitive issue was a blatantly insulting act that China simply could not tolerate (Moore 2014). It also was regarded by Beijing as violation of what it understands as a long-held tacit agreement over the Diaoyu/Senkaku Islands territorial dispute. The new Abe administration that came to power in 2012 further convinced the Chinese leadership that Tokyo is changing its position on the issue and in fact is using the dispute to justify fundamentally transforming post-war Japanese security policy, including introducing new interpretations of the Constitution, such as the right to collective defence.

The stalemate and confrontation are costing both countries economically and damaging the foundation of Sino–Japanese relations. Japanese businesses in China have sustained sizeable losses and bilateral economic ties have suffered, contrary to the wishful thinking and previous experiences of 'cold politics, hot economics'. Japanese and export investments to China have also decreased in comparison with similar periods in previous years. Meanwhile, the uncertainty and further animosity could also impede the two countries' willingness to cooperate in promoting East Asian regionalism in expanding trade, investment, and currency swaps. The Liberal explanation that economic interdependence fosters cooperation given the mutual gains to be had becomes increasingly unsustainable in the Sino–Japanese case (Koo 2009). Instead, emerging rivalry and reluctance in striving for compromises, coupled with the conviction that countries with the greater power and resources will prevail in the new game of geopolitical and geo-economic competition (Patalano 2014).

Sustaining these disputes are fundamental undercurrents that define future Sino–Japanese relations (Wan 2014). China has overtaken Japan as the world's second largest economic power and, with a 7–8 per cent annual growth rate, has a far more dynamic economy than Japan, which has yet to pull itself out of the economic stagnation that started in the 1990s despite the measures introduced by the Abe administration. China has emerged from the 2008 global financial crisis with growing confidence and diplomatic activism. Beijing seeks to redefine relations between major powers, support new power groupings such as BRICS, and become more vocal in regional and global issues where its interests are affected (Yan 2014).

One important issue that weighs heavily on the minds of Chinese leaders and people is the so-called 100-year humiliation inflicted on China when the country was weak and disunited. Beijing is determined to right the wrong and erase this painful memory. It therefore remains resentful of Japan's lack of true repentance over its past (Wang 2012). Tokyo, on the other hand, is concerned about China's growing military power and its assertiveness in territorial disputes, and seeks reassurance of US commitment under the bilateral security treaty. In recent years, and especially since Abe returned to power in 2012, in accordance with its priorities Japan has undertaken major steps to strengthen its self-defence forces, and to build strategic partnerships with countries in the region that share similar concerns about China's rise (Grønning 2014; Hook 2014). Japanese defence spending has been expanding for three consecutive years, with the Ministry of Defence requesting a budget of US $47,100m. for the upcoming fiscal year starting 1 April 2015, a 2.4 per cent increase over the current year (Sekiguchi 2014).

The leadership transitions in China and Japan in 2012 provided opportunities to negotiate a way out of the impasse, but instead they imposed significant constraints on both capitals. Past experiences suggest Sino–Japanese negotiations on territorial issues are likely to yield some concrete albeit limited results only when certain conditions prevail. First, leaders in both countries are determined to prevent further free fall in bilateral relations after a period of estrangement and serious setback. Second, when the principal goal in the negotiation is to manage rather than solve these disputes, with a view to reaching some consensus on either about maintaining the status quo and/or on joint developments without prejudice to either side's claims on sovereignty, then it is possible that some agreement can be reached. And third, negotiations are conducted away from public scrutiny, with neither party seeking to score political points or to appeal to domestic constituents (Kraus et al. 2014).

It is not clear whether these conditions exist today. The new Chinese leadership under Xi Jinping has completed the transition to power and is apparently in firm control. In Japan, the election of Shinzo Abe to a second term has been met with more conservative and hawkish positions on China and the territorial issues. The Xi administration has clearly adopted a more assertive posture regarding these territorial disputes, for a number of reasons (Takeuchi 2014). First, Xi needs to consolidate his position as a decisive leader and appeals to the People's Liberation Army, a key constituent of his power base. Numerous reports have been circulated that before he was appointed leader of the country, Xi had already been given the responsibility of overseeing an elite small group charged with managing the Diaoyu/Senkaku dispute.

Second, Beijing's non-yielding stance on these territorial disputes may be part of a broader strategy to establish and strengthen its negotiations for any future negotiation on settlement (He and Fung 2013). China's growing economic power and military capabilities now allow much more scope for diplomatic manoeuvring, unlike in the past when a relatively weak China, fearing diplomatic isolation and without adequate naval reach, settled for less in its negotiations with a number of neighbouring countries, including reportedly ceding Chinese territories to its counterparts. Third, China's assertiveness also reflects the mentality of a rising power seeking to establish the ground rules in regional security affairs and recognition of the strategic importance of protecting its maritime rights and interests for economic reasons. The former is clearly demonstrated in Beijing's insistence on bilateral negotiations on resolving the territorial disputes and its rejection of multilateral forums on these matters. On the one hand the latter stance is pragmatic since the dispute exists not just between China and the other claimant states but also among the other contenders themselves, and on the other hand it is defensive in the sense that bilateral negotiations are geared more to precluding US involvement than to gaining the advantage over its weaker counterpart. Meanwhile, given the growing importance of maritime commerce to China's overall gross domestic product and of the critical sea lanes of communication for the country's international trade and importation of oil and raw materials, it has become essential that China demonstrate and exercise maritime superiority over the South China Sea and its key passages.

The US role

Between 1953 and 1971 the USA administered the Okinawa and the Ryukyu chain, which 'defines the boundaries of "Nansei Shoto [the south-western islands] south of 29 degrees north latitude" to include the Senkakus'. During the period of US military administration 'the US Navy established firing ranges on the islets and paid an annual rent of $11,000 to Jinji Koga, the son of the first Japanese settler of the islets' (Manyin 2013: 3–4). The Okinawa Reversion Treaty, signed on 17 June 1971, returned to Japan 'all and any powers of administration, legislation and jurisdiction' over the Ryukyu and Daito islands (ibid.: 4). Since then, Washington has maintained a neutral position on the Diaoyu/Senkaku issue as far as sovereignty claims by China, Japan, and Taiwan are concerned. Secretary of State William Rogers stated at the Senate reversion hearings at the time that 'this treaty does not affect the legal status of those islands at all'. State Department Acting Assistant Legal Adviser Robert Starr expounded:

> The Governments of the Republic of China and Japan are in disagreement as to the sovereignty over the Senkaku Islands. You should know as well that the People's Republic of China has also claimed sovereignty over the islands. The United States believes that a return of administrative rights over those islands to Japan, from which the rights were received, can in no way prejudice any underlying claims. The United States cannot add to the legal rights Japan possessed before it transferred administration of the islands to us, nor can the United States, by giving back what it received, diminish the rights of other claimants. The United States has made no claim to the Senkaku Islands and considers that any conflicting claims to the islands are a matter for resolution by the parties concerned.
>
> (Manyin 2013: 5)

However, the 1960 US–Japan Security Treaty also stipulates (Article 5) that the USA is obliged to protect territories under Japanese administration, which includes Diaoyu/Senkaku. This position was reiterated by Secretary of State Hillary Clinton when she stated in 2010 that 'we have made it very clear that the islands are part of our mutual treaty obligations, and the obligation to defend Japan' (Clinton 2010). Clinton further stated in 2013 that the USA opposes any unilateral actions that seek to undermine Japanese administration of the islands. Continued stalemate and further escalation will only lead to even greater US involvement, including direct military assistance to its alliance partners; a recent US Senate amendment to the 2013 Defense Authorization Act reaffirms US treaty obligations to the defence of Japan, including territories under its administrative control. This treaty obligation has been reaffirmed publicly by high-ranking Obama administration officials several times (Manyin 2013: 6). Indeed, Japan has actively sought this commitment, including changes to the treaty guidelines that would allow the two allies to exercise closer military cooperation in response to scenarios involving Chinese use of force over Diaoyu/Senkaku.

The USA is in a bind here. On the one hand, since the Obama administration announced its Asia pivot in 2011, largely in response to growing Chinese power in the region and partly to reassure its allies and partners, Washington has sought to strengthen its alliances and has publicly advocated multilateral and diplomatic solutions to the multiple territorial disputes in East and South China Seas even though it maintains a neutral position on sovereignty claims. At the same time, administration officials remain non-committal about the extent of US treaty obligations to the Philippines despite Manila's call for such reassurance. In this context, Clinton's remarks become all the more interesting, as are US–Japanese military exercises in the East China Sea.

Washington is unlikely to become embroiled in a military conflict with China over a few barren rocks, given the risks and uncertain outcomes. The Obama administration may angle for broader strategic advantage over China, but will not seek war with it, however critical its alliance with Japan. Indeed, press reports suggest that the Noda government ignored Washington's warnings that the island purchase could result in strong Chinese responses, causing instability in the region and risking drawing the USA into the conflict (Lee 2013). While it is hard to believe that territorial disputes might lead to direct Sino–US military confrontation, the absence of crisis management mechanisms and confidence-building measures in the region are grave concerns in the unlikely event of incidents rapidly spiralling out of control (Lampton 2013).

Ways forward

At August 2014 Sino–Japanese territorial disputes over the Diaoyu/Senkaku Islands and the East China Sea remained deadlocked and it appears unlikely that they will be resolved in the near future. However, continued stalemate and growing escalation, with both sides' maritime and paramilitary (coastguard) enforcements patrolling in close proximity with one another, could potentially result in major incidents. The two Asian powers are also engaged in major military modernization programmes aimed at boosting naval and air capabilities. Given the enormous economic stakes involved, Beijing and Tokyo recognize the sheer stupidity of deliberate provocation. However, the risk of inadvertent clashes remains. Likewise, US involvement due to its alliance commitments and therefore potential military confrontation with China cannot be ruled out.

So long as the prospect of resolving the territorial disputes remains elusive, a number of urgent and pragmatic mechanisms need to be put in place, including rules of engagement, crisis management and de-escalation protocols, and confidence building measures. These would require, at a minimum, that regular contacts between the two militaries and maritime law enforcement agencies and channels of communication be kept open. Broadly accepted norms, such as the non-binding Code for Unplanned Encounters at Sea and multilateral forums such as the Western Pacific Naval Symposium provide guidelines and opportunities for engagement (ICG 2014).

Bilateral diplomatic dialogue, at both the functional and ministerial level, must also be encouraged, held, and maintained. Conditions that have resulted in previous agreements should be studied and restored, with a view to seeking long-term solutions and agreements, including shelving the sovereignty issue but focusing on mutually beneficial joint development projects instead. Most critically, the leaders of both countries should find the courage to face the realities of a changing Asia and chart a course for Asia's largest economies that is stable, durable, and conducive to overall peace and prosperity for the region as a whole. The USA, having significant stakes in the outcome, should and can make a positive contribution.

Bibliography

Auslin, Michael, 'The Asian Cold War', *Foreign Policy*, 4 October 2012.
Bush, Richard C., *The Perils of Proximity: China-Japan Security Relations*, Washington, DC: Brookings Institution Press, 2010.
Clinton, Hillary Rodham, Remarks Following Signing Ceremonies, Hanoi, Vietnam, 30 October 2010.
Cody, Edward, 'Beijing Explains Submarine Activity: Japan Considers Account an Apology', *Washington Post*, 17 November 2004: A22.
Fedorova, Maria, 'The Roots of Sino–Japanese Differences over the Senkaku (Diaoyudao) Islands', *Far Eastern Affairs*, Vol. 33, No. 1, January–March 2005.
Fravel, M. Taylor, 'Explaining Stability in the Senkaku (Diaoyu) Islands Dispute', in Gerald Curtis, Ryosei Kokubun and Wang Jisi (eds), *Getting the Triangle Straight: Managing China–Japan–US Relations*, Tokyo: Japan Center for International Exchange, 2010.
Friedberg, Aaron L., *A Contest for Supremacy: China, America, and the Struggle for Mastery in Asia*, New York: W. W. Norton and Company, 2011.
Gao, Jianjun, 'The Territorial Status of the Diaoyu Islands in 1895: A Crucial Issue for the Dispute of These Islands', *Social Sciences in China*, Vol. 31, No. 4, November 2010.
Grønning, Bjørn Elias Mikalsen, 'Japan's Shifting Military Priorities: Counter-Balancing China's Rise', *Asian Security*, Vol. 10, No. 1, 2014.
Hagström, Linus, 'Quiet Power: Japan's China Policy in Regard to the Pinnacle Islands', *The Pacific Review*, Vol. 18, No. 2, June 2005.
Harrison, Selig S., 'Quiet Struggle in the East China Sea', *Current History*, September 2002.
Harry, R. Jade, 'A Solution Acceptable to All? A Legal Analysis of the Senkaku-Diaoyu Island Dispute', *Cornell International Law Journal*, Vol. 46, 2013.
He, Kai and Huiyun Fung, 'Xi Jinping's Operational Code Beliefs and Chinese Foreign Policy'. *Chinese Journal of International Politics*, Vol. 6, No. 3, Autumn 2013.
He, Yinan, 'History, Chinese Nationalism and the Emerging Sino–Japanese Conflict', *Journal of Contemporary China*, Vol. 16, No. 50, 2007.
Hook, Glenn D., 'Japan's Risky Frontiers: Territorial Sovereignty and Governance of the Senkaku Islands', *Japanese Studies*, Vol. 34, No. 1, 2014.
International Crisis Group (ICG), *Old Scores, New Grudges: Evolving Sino–Japanese Tensions*, Asia Report No. 258, 24 July 2014.
International Institute for Strategic Studies (IISS), 'China's Air Zone Rouses Regional Fears', *Strategic Comments*, Vol. 19, No. 9, December 2013.
International Studies Quarterly, 'Tacit Agreement on Shelving Island Dispute and Policy Change in the Abe Administration', No. 6, 2013 (in Chinese).
Kawashima, Shin, 'The Origins of the Senkaku/Diaoyu Islands Issue: The Period before Normalization of Diplomatic Relations Between Japan and China in 1972', *Asia-Pacific Review*, Vol. 20, No. 2, November 2013.
Koo, Min Gyo, 'The Senkaku/Diaoyu Dispute and Sino–Japanese Political-Economic Relations: Cold Politics and Hot Economics?' *The Pacific Review*, Vol. 22, No. 2, May 2009.
Kraus, Charles, Sergey Radchenko and Yutaka Kanda, 'China and Japan: Always at Odds?' Introduction to CWIHP e-dossier No. 48, Washington, DC: Woodrow Wilson Center for International Scholars, 2014.

Lampton, David M., 'America and China's Dangerous Dance in Asia', *The National Interest Blog*, 5 August 2014.

Lampton, David M., 'A New Type of Major-Power Relationship: Seeking a Durable Foundation for U.S.-China Ties', *Asia Policy*, 16 July 2013.

Lee, Peter, 'Japan Stirs Campbell's US "Pivot" Soup', *Asia Times*, 26 April 2013.

McDevitt, Michael, 'The East China Sea: The Place Where Sino-U.S. Conflict Could Occur', *American Foreign Policy Interests*, Vol. 36, No. 2, May 2014.

Manyin, Mark E., *Senkaku (Diaoyu/Diaoyutai) Islands Dispute: U.S. Treaty Obligations*, No. R42761, Washington, DC: Congressional Research Service, 2013.

Moore, Gregory J., '"In Your Face": Domestic Politics, Nationalism, and "Face" in the Sino–Japanese Island Dispute', *Asian Perspective*, Vol. 38, No. 2, April-June 2014.

Pan, Zhongqi, 'Sino–Japanese Dispute over the Diaoyu/Senkaku Islands: The Pending Controversy from the Chinese Perspective', *Journal of Chinese Political Science*, Vol. 12, No. 1, April 2007.

Patalano, Alessio, 'Seapower and Sino–Japanese Relations in the East China Sea', *Asian Affairs*, Vol. 45, No. 1, 2014.

Perlez, Jane, 'China Accuses Japan of Stealing after Purchase of Group of Disputed Islands', *New York Times*, 11 September 2012.

Schwartz, Laura, *Competition and Confrontation in the East China Sea and the Implications for U.S. Policy: A Roundtable Report*, Seattle, WA: The National Bureau of Asian Research, 2014.

Sekiguchi, Toko 'Japan's Defense Ministry Asks For Budget Increase', *Wall Street Journal*, 30 August 2014, http://online.wsj.com/articles/japans-defense-ministry-asks-for-budget-increase-1409373498.

Takeuchi, Hiroki, 'Sino–Japanese Relations: Power, Interdependence, and Domestic Politics', *International Relations of the Asia-Pacific*, Vol. 14, No. 1, January 2014.

Valencia, Mark J., 'The East China Sea Disputes: History, Status, and Ways Forward', *Asian Perspective*, Vol. 38, No. 2, April–June 2014.

Wan, Ming *Sino–Japanese Relations: Interaction, Logic and Transformation*, Stanford, CA: Stanford University Press, 2006.

Wan, Ming, 'Coevolution and Sino–Japanese Tensions', *Asia-Pacific Review*, Vol. 21, No. 1, May 2014.

Wang, Zhang, *Never Forget National Humiliation: Historical Memory in Chinese Politics and Foreign Relations*, New York: Columbia University Press, 2012.

Wiegand, Krista E., 'China's Strategy in the Senkaku/Diaoyu Islands Dispute: Issue Linkage and Coercive Diplomacy', *Asian Security*, Vol. 5, No. 2, May 2009.

Yan, Xuetong, 'From Keeping a Low Profile to Striving for Achievements', *Chinese Journal of International Politics*, Vol. 7, No. 2, Summer 2014.

9
China's fluid assertiveness in the South China Sea dispute

Mingjiang Li and Loh Ming Hui Dylan

China's claim in the South China Sea is extensive, trenchant, and to a large extent ambiguous. It has disputes with the Philippines, Taiwan, Brunei, Malaysia, Vietnam, and potentially Indonesia. In the past Jakarta has intentionally positioned itself as a non-claimant party in the South China Sea disputes, perhaps wisely so. However, Indonesia now seems to be more prepared to identify itself as a disputant country when it announced on 12 March 2014 that China's nine-dash line map outlining its claims overlaps with the exclusive economic zone (EEZ) of Indonesia's Riau province which includes the Natuna Islands (Murphy 2014). Whether Indonesia does become a disputant country depends on how China clarifies its nine-dash line. It is worth noting that in 1993 the then Chinese Minister of Foreign Affairs reassured Indonesia that Beijing and Jakarta had no dispute in the South China Sea; however, China has failed formally to confirm this position since then (Dillon 2011).

Indonesia's new policy move is perhaps an illustration of growing regional concerns about China's policy in the South China Sea dispute. In recent years China's behaviour in the South China Sea has taken a far more strident undertone compared to previous decades. Chinese assertiveness has been manifested in Beijing's stronger rhetoric, harsher responses to actions taken by other claimant parties, unilateral actions in some cases, and increasing willingness to consolidate China's presence in the South China Sea. It seems that the 'shelving dispute and seeking joint development' approach attributed to Deng Xiaopeng in the 1980s is fast losing traction (Ministry of Foreign Affairs, People's Republic of China).

This chapter attempts to analyse China's policy in the South China Sea over the past few years. It traces the trajectory of recent Chinese behaviour in the South China Sea dispute and argues that China's policy could be characterized as 'fluid assertiveness'. We further argue that domestic socio-political impetuses have helped to shape Chinese action over the South China Sea contestations.

Conceptualizing China's policy regarding the South China Sea

Existing interpretations of Beijing's foreign policy in the South China Sea are generally represented as 'assertiveness' (or 'aggressiveness') or variations of 'assertiveness'. A number of scholars have argued that China's assertiveness is due to the competition between China and the USA for supremacy in the South China Sea especially in light of the 'rebalancing' strategy of the Obama administration (Buszynski 2012). This school of thought places tensions in the South China Sea as the by-product of major power strategic rivalry. The 'US factor' certainly figures in China's strategic calculus. However, it should be noted that the USA has always been a Pacific power; its 'rebalance' was more a case of it trying to play catch-up following a period of neglect under the previous administration. One can perhaps even argue that there are more continuities than changes in Washington's South China Sea policy.

Others have argued that China is practising 'proactive assertiveness' as a deliberate approach whereby its activities in the South China Sea reflect China's intention to use legal, diplomatic and administrative measures to bolster its future diplomatic and legal claims (Zhang 2013). There are a number of variants of the 'assertiveness' argument. One such position characterizes China's policy as 'non-confrontational assertiveness' in which China combines periodic displays of assertiveness and restraint in order to allow it to exercise territoriality without severely damaging ties with its Association of Southeast Asian Nations (ASEAN) counterparts (Li 2012). Another perspective characterizes Chinese behaviour as a 'creeping assertiveness', whereby it makes slow, small, seemingly harmless gains in order to achieve a big win. One of its most significant wins resulting from this creeping assertiveness is the de facto occupation of Mischief Reef (Storey 1999). It is also argued that China has practised a policy of 'reactive assertiveness' in the South China Sea dispute over the past years. When other claimant countries took action Beijing seized the opportunity to respond with much larger and harsher counteractions to expand its presence and protect its perceived interests (Kleine-Ahlbrandt 2012; International Crisis Group 2013; You 2013).

Another school of thought, mainly that of Chinese analysts, sees nothing aggressive or assertive about Chinese activities. They argue that China was merely being defensive, reacting to provocations and simply being protective of its integrity against perceived encroachment (Ratner 2013: 22). Chinese officials and analysts have frequently argued that the USA and regional claimant countries, particularly the Philippines and Vietnam, have ganged up against China. They believe that the USA has always been behind the actions that the Philippines and Vietnam have taken in the South China Sea over the past few years. A more moderate conspiracy theory in China would take the view that Washington's strategic 'rebalance' to the Asia-Pacific has emboldened other claimant parties and encouraged them to challenge China in the dispute.

It is noteworthy that there are also scholars who argue that China's foreign policy action over the South China Sea has been one of 'decreasing assertiveness' when comparing current activities to those carried out in earlier decades – the lack of conflict and the failure to occupy geographical features are illustrated as evidence (Fravel 2011). While that is an important observation, it narrows the definition of 'assertiveness' and neglects the anthology of very real and consequential economic, diplomatic and political levers that China has employed and can employ. Indeed, the tools available to China to assert its territoriality have increased with the concomitant increase in resources.

Beijing's growing fluid assertiveness

In view of the variety of characterizations available, each of which has its own merits, what is one to make of Chinese policy in the South China Sea? An analysis of China's activities in recent years – post-2009 – when most of the debates on China's assertiveness (or otherwise) surfaced, would be particularly instructive. Beijing's actions have undoubtedly become far more assertive in the post-2009 years compared to the 2000s. It is hard to ignore these facts.

The most crucial question is what has caused China's policy change? Has Beijing adopted a brand-new policy and is it determined to pursue an aggressive policy in order to completely subjugate other claimant countries? Or is Beijing simply responding to the changing strategic environment and other claimant parties' actions?

We believe that the policy change occurred due to a combination of several factors, namely Beijing's growing capabilities and confidence, the US policy of strategic rebalance to Asia, regional countries' expanding maritime interests, and the spread of nationalism in many claimant countries. By the end of the 2000s China's economic development, military modernization, and maritime law enforcement capabilities had reached a level that would enable China to take a heavy-handed approach to the dispute. Also, Beijing's relations with South-East Asia and its strategic position in the Asia-Pacific were much stronger compared to a decade previously, largely due to its expanding economic influence in the region. Consequently, Beijing did not need to be overly concerned about the negative consequences of its harsh actions in the South China Sea or its relations with the South-East Asian region as a whole. The growth of Chinese power provided a fairly new context for Beijing's decision making.

The US strategic rebalance played a twofold role. First, from the Chinese perspective, Washington's new strategic move was aimed at constraining, if not containing, China in the region. Beijing paid particular attention to the military and security aspects of the US rebalance policy, believing that Washington intended to strengthen its military presence in the region at the expense of China's security interests. Second, the US strategic rebalance emboldened regional countries, particularly the Philippines and Vietnam, to challenge China's position in the dispute. Hanoi and Manila may have wanted to ride on the USA's 'pivot' strategy to put pressure on China and create a fait accompli in the dispute. The Chinese may have exaggerated the collaboration and collusion between the USA and the regional claimant parties; nevertheless, hardly any Chinese officials or analysts believed that Washington had not played a part in the rising tensions and disputes over the past few years. In this context, Beijing felt that it could not retreat or offer any concessions as otherwise China's interests in the South China Sea would be further encroached upon. Putting up a tough stance was China's strategy for discouraging further US involvement in the dispute.

There has been a notable increase in Chinese nationalism over the past decade. This is partly a result of the popularization of various social media. The Chinese public is now far better informed about international events. They have become more vigilant of any statements made and any actions taken by foreign countries regarding territorial disputes that involve China. Equally, they are watchful of the way in which the Chinese government handles such territorial and maritime disputes. Over the past few years the predominant public opinion in China was that regional claimant countries and the USA have bullied China and that the Chinese government has been too timid and too weak in responding to these challenges, despite the fact that the outside world has been extremely critical of Beijing's behaviour in the dispute. In this kind of domestic socio-political context, decision makers in Beijing probably had very few policy options but cater to popular demand to some extent.

In actual fact, China's policy in the dispute has been characterized by overreactive assertiveness and a degree of unilateral activity, which we describe as fluid assertiveness. China's assertiveness is fluid in the sense that Beijing has not developed an outright strategy of aggression to coerce other claimant parties to surrender their claims. It is fluid also in the sense that much Chinese behaviour is reactive to other countries' actions, although Beijing clearly intends to take advantage of those opportunities to overreact and change the status quo in China's favour. China's fluid assertiveness also means that it must consider other strategic, diplomatic and economic interests when engaging in the South China Sea dispute. Beijing has many other important interests in South-East Asia and the Asia-Pacific region as a whole that require China to exercise restraint in the dispute. Fluid assertiveness also means that Beijing may exercise caution should it decide to take any unilateral action in the South China Sea. Its goals would be limited were it to attempt to take unilateral initiatives. Finally, fluid assertiveness also means that Beijing remains interested in proposing and pushing for cooperation in the South China Sea.

We want to elaborate why fluid assertiveness may be a more useful conceptualization of China's policy in the dispute. First, there is very little convincing evidence to show that Beijing is becoming outrightly aggressive in the South China Sea. Among the ASEAN disputant claimants, it is the Philippines–China and Vietnam–China dynamics that broadly define the level of tensions in the South China Sea (Li 2014). The Chinese themselves have singled out the Philippines and Vietnam in the South China Sea too (Long 2011: 11). If China had a coherent and well-developed strategy to dramatically assert its claims in the South China Sea, it is questionable why it would target only Vietnam and the Philippines, and not the other claimant countries.

Some analysts believe that China's assertive enforcement of the unilateral ban on fishing in the South China Sea contributed to the tensions and disputes of 2009 and 2010 (Huo and Cui 2009; Vietnam Breaking News 2009). This may be partly true. As a matter of fact, China started the 10-week fishing ban policy in the area lying 12 degrees north of latitude in 1999. During much of the 2000s the fishing ban was rarely a major source of contention in the South China Sea. The Chinese authorities effectively prevented Chinese fishing boats from accessing the banned area during that period. It is noteworthy that China did not prohibit Vietnamese fishermen from using the area for fishing activities when the fishing ban period was over. This indicates that the Chinese authorities may indeed be concerned about the depletion of fishing resources in the South China Sea and want to encourage greater sustainable fishing in the region. Of course, the Vietnamese perspective that China's fishing ban policy constituted Beijing's assertion of sovereignty and maritime jurisdiction rights can be easily understood.

More damaging to the stability in the South China Sea were two cable-cutting events. In May 2011 Vietnam reported that three Chinese patrol vessels intentionally cut a submerged cable towed by the *Binh Minh 02* (an oil and gas supply ship) in the South China Sea. China's Ministry of Foreign Affairs laid the blame firmly on Vietnam for the incident, stating that its oil and gas operations 'undermined China's interests and jurisdictional rights' (BBC 2011). That statement, in essence, shows an attempt to justify the cable cutting. An editorial in the *Global Times* argued that China was defending itself against provocative Vietnamese behaviour and would 'answer the provocation with political, economic or even military counterstrikes' (*Global Times* 2011). Later that year, Vietnam and China agreed a set of principles for settling maritime territorial disputes (Chan 2011). However, in December 2012 once again two Chinese vessels cut the cables of the same Vietnamese ship carrying out oil exploration activities in the South China Sea. The Chinese portrayed themselves as the victims and highlighted Vietnamese harassment of Chinese fishermen. Hong Lei, a spokesman for the Ministry of Foreign Affairs, stated, 'What the Vietnamese side said is not in accordance with the facts … Chinese ships conducted routine fishing activity in the waters, but were driven away by Vietnamese military vessels' (CNTV 2012). China may argue that it was only responding to Vietnam's actions, but it is very challenging for China to defend the two cable-cutting incidents. Both events took place some distance from the coast of China or the Paracel and Spratly Islands. For China to justify its cable-cutting actions, if at all, it would have to argue that the location lay within China's nine-dash line and that China has jurisdictional and historical rights to the whole of that area. However, the international community and the other disputant countries in particular would find it difficult to accept such arguments.

Another serious source of contention between China and Vietnam was China's decision in July 2012 to establish a municipal city, Sansha, to administer the three archipelagos in the South China Sea. The move was actually an upgrade of the administrative status of the previous county-level administrative office that had existed on Woody Island, one of the Paracels. As part of the new move, China also announced the establishment of a Sansha military garrison. While the outside world criticized China for taking this unilateral action, Beijing claimed that its move was in response to Vietnam passing the maritime law in 2012 that laid out its formal claims to the Paracel and Spratly Islands. China regarded Vietnam's new maritime law as a major step by Hanoi to strengthen its sovereignty and jurisdictional claims in the South China Sea. The China National Offshore Oil Corporation (CNOOC) invited foreign companies to bid for nine oil blocks in Vietnam's EEZ but also within China's nine-dash line. Beijing's moves, in particular the upgrading of the Sansha administrative body, were clear examples of China's overreactive assertiveness.

Another major incident in the South China Sea contestations that took place in the past few years was the Scarborough standoff between China and the Philippines. On 10 April 2012 crew members of the Philippines' newest and most advanced warship, the *Gregorio del Pilar*, attempted to board and inspect eight Chinese vessels near the Scarborough Shoal claimed by China and the Philippines. Two of the Chinese ships attempted to obstruct them. When the Filipinos eventually boarded the vessels, they found large caches of illegally harvested corals, giant clams and live sharks onboard (Inquirer 2012). The warship attempted to arrest the Chinese fishermen and fishing boats, but Chinese patrol boats rushed to the scene and the two sides engaged in a standoff for several weeks. The Philippines eventually decided to retreat and China took control of the Scarborough Shoal.

During the standoff China's response was swift and potent. A flurry of commentators took turns to variously admonish the Philippines and warned that an armed conflict would break out (Hookway 2012). China also promptly stopped shipments of bananas and fruits from the Philippines, citing 'quality' issues, thus imposing unofficial economic sanctions against the Philippines (*Asia Sentinel* 2012). China also took steps to completely halt tourism tours to the Philippines, thereby damaging the already weak Philippine economy. The Scarborough Shoal incident was a typical example of China's overreactive assertiveness. Chinese authorities took advantage of the opportunity of an apparent mistake by the Philippines in using its military warship to arrest the Chinese fishing boats and responded by using its asymmetrical power against Manila.

Another major conflict between Beijing and Manila involved the Second Thomas Shoal. In 2013 Chinese government patrol vessels attempted to prevent Philippine ships from delivering supplies to the Manila-controlled Second Thomas Shoal. The Chinese eventually relented and allowed the resupply, citing 'humanitarian considerations' (*Qianjing Wanbao* 2013). In March 2014 China again set up a blockade to hinder the Philippines' attempts to deliver vital supplies to the *Sierra Madre*, a Philippine naval vessel that ran aground in the Second Thomas Shoal in 1999 and had been stranded there ever since with only a handful of Filipino marines on board (Castro and Ng 2014). The Philippines eventually managed to evade the blockade by airlifting in the supplies. The Chinese argued that they were blocking the Philippines' supply activities because the Philippines' ships were carrying construction materials that would allow Manila to consolidate its occupation of the Second Thomas Shoal. China also claimed that Manila had promised to withdraw the stranded Philippine ship in the late 1990s and demanded that Manila now fulfil its pledge. China may have wanted to use this on–off blockade to pressurize Manila to relinquish its control of the Shoal. It is possible that the blockade of March 2014 could be linked to China's wish to discourage Manila from submitting its memorandum to the UN Tribunal for the Law of the Sea in support of its legal arbitration case against China.

In November 2012 China decided to print a map showing the nine-dash line on its new e-passport. This decision resulted in strong diplomatic protests from the Philippines and Vietnam and caused concerns in Indonesia (Ririhena and Santosa 2012). At a media briefing a spokesman for the Chinese Ministry of Foreign Affairs, Hong Lei, stated that the map was not targeted at any one country and that the 'picture should not be overinterpreted'. He added that 'China is ready to maintain communication with relevant countries and promote the sound development of personnel exchanges' (Santamaria 2012). The Chinese seemed to have been caught unawares by the vigorous protests over its passport move and subsequently sought to downplay and reassure its maritime neighbours. Chinese analysts suggest that this passport initiative came from the Ministry of Public Security and the decision was not widely discussed with other agencies. Clearly, Beijing realized that it was a mistake and has stopped printing such passports.[1]

In November 2012 the local Hainan Provincial People's Congress passed a revised offshore border defence and security management law, allowing the law enforcement agencies to inspect, board and expel foreign vessels in disputed waters (Blanchard and Mogato 2012; Fravel 2013). Naturally, the move caused unhappiness and concern among the disputant countries in ASEAN. Hong Lei was quoted saying the 'management of the seas according to the law is a sovereign nation's legitimate right' (Blanchard and Mogato 2012). In November 2013 the Hainan local parliament again passed a revised version of fishing regulations in the South China Sea. The new law specifically requires foreigners and foreign vessels entering China's jurisdictional waters to obtain prior approval from the Chinese government. This new law has also caused a huge outcry from other claimant countries and the USA. However, Chinese analysts have suggested that the new regulations contain only minor changes to the original laws and were more symbolic than real. Furthermore, there has been no substantive change to the Chinese law enforcement activities in the South China Sea. The applicability of these laws is seriously hindered by the failure of China to clarify its position over the nine-dash line and to specify the maritime zones that the Spratly Islands may be able to generate. Without clarifying these claims, it remains unclear which waters fall under China's jurisdiction. Although the local Hainan government has not aggressively enforced these laws, there is no doubt that these moves were Chinese unilateral actions that contributed to the growth of tensions in the South China Sea. One can also identify China's recent deployment of the HY 981 oil exploration platform near the Paracels and land reclamation and construction activities at the Johnson South Reef as unilateral actions.

While Beijing has been engaged in such action-reaction moves and diplomatic war of words with other concerned parties, it is important also to recognize that China has also displayed a willingness to generate goodwill and improve ties. For instance, in 2011 China and ASEAN countries concluded the implementation guidelines for the 2002 ASEAN Declaration on the Conduct of the Parties in the South China Sea. In 2012 China unveiled a substantial US $474m. Maritime Cooperation Fund with ASEAN (Fox News 2012). China has hosted several workshops that aimed at finding ways to enhance maritime cooperation among claimant countries in the South China Sea. In July 2013 China agreed to discuss a 'code of conduct' with ASEAN, which was widely perceived as a positive sign of progress (Orendain 2013). Senior officials from China and ASEAN countries have officially started the Code of Conduct process, although it is widely believed that the process will likely be long and complicated. A number of high-level visits were exchanged between Beijing and Hanoi even during the challenging years 2011 and 2012 and the two countries reached significant consensus on their conflict management in the South China Sea. In fact, for much of 2013 Beijing and Hanoi enjoyed fairly stable, if not entirely peaceful, interactions in the South China Sea. In 2014 senior ASEAN and Chinese officials also agreed to push forward the establishment of an ASEAN–China Cooperation Partnership (tapping into the Maritime Cooperation Fund), set up a hotline for search and rescue at sea and to regularize the China–ASEAN Defense Ministers Meeting (InterAksyon 2014). China now is keen to push for the proposal of a new Maritime Silk Road with South-East Asian countries. These are noteworthy and encouraging gestures considering the ongoing maritime spats.

The incidents described above are not meant to be exhaustive, but to present the broad contours and content of China's recent activities in the South China Sea. What is one to make, then, of China's, forward-backward, assertive and sometimes positive manoeuvres? There are three implications arising from an analysis of these events. First, China's range of economic, military, diplomatic, hard and soft power options at its disposal has expanded considerably. It will increasingly seek to leverage on a combination of these options to pursue what would be most advantageous to it in asserting its territoriality. Second, it has adopted bilateral and multilateral policies in affirming its claims over disputed regions. Third, and most importantly, while no one single characterization of Chinese actions in the South China Sea can explain its activities convincingly, China's policy over the South China Sea can be best described as fluid assertiveness.

The domestic rationales of China's activities in the South China Sea

A closer inspection of Chinese foreign policy behaviour in the South China Sea reveals one underlying theme – the domestic element – that explains much of China's fluid movements in the region. This fluidity, we argue, is not entirely the result of a deliberate cost-benefit calculation by China's leaders. Rather, it is the culmination of nationalistic-fuelled assertiveness, a desire to legitimize the rule of the Chinese Communist Party (CCP) and its domestic bureaucratic politics.

There is plenty of evidence to suggest that China is concerned about internal stability and preserving the longevity of the CCP (Scobell 2001; Huang 2011). In 2013 China announced that its budget for internal security would be increased to RMB ¥740,600m. (approximately US $119,000m.). This amount is higher than the ¥769,100m. apportioned to the military (Perlez 2012), leading one analyst to comment that China is more fearful of internal destabilization than outside threats (Blanchard and Ruwitch 2013). One of the key ways that the government can continue to legitimize its rule is to deliver continued economic growth and defend its territory – it must be seen to be visibly defending, protecting and asserting its territoriality.

One phenomenon that parallels China's rise in nationalism is the affiliated rise of the *fenqing* – mostly angry young people who often use the Internet to express their views and anger (Wang 2009). This breed of angry youths have inadvertently helped the CCP to deliver its message as they have not been shy about expressing their nationalistic views online. Allowing netizens to express their nationalistic anger in a non-physical controlled space, re-channelling dissatisfaction away from the government and externalizing an outside threat boosts the government's nationalistic credentials (Yip and Weber 2011). However, the ultimate efficacy in legitimizing the government's rule is unclear and at times has been proven to backfire.

For example, regarding the April 2012 blockade of the Philippine resupply ships, netizens widely viewed China's foreign ministry's response ('China has undisputed sovereign claim to the Ren'ai Jiao [i.e. the Second Thomas Shoal]. No matter what the Philippines says or does, it still cannot change this fact') as a weak response, lacking in bite. One netizen was quoted saying that 'This must be the most patient ministry in history … [Let's say] someone runs into your house and sleeps with your wife. You can say: 'No matter what she says, or does, it still does not change the fact that so-and-so is my wife'.

Many others called the leaders 'impotent' and 'cowardly' (Wertime 2012). It is clear how such nationalistic sentiments can quickly turn on the CCP and threaten its legitimacy (Lovell 2011: 357). These challenges and criticisms of the CCP can fuel it to be more assertive. For example, in an op-ed on the subject of the East China Sea disputes, the *Global Times* stated in 2013 that: 'Chinese society is tired of simple verbal protests toward Japan. The Chinese people hope the country will carry out actions against Japan's provocations. China's sending fighter jets to the islands reflects Chinese public opinion'.

Indeed, the government is treading a difficult line in allowing nationalistic sentiments to propagate while trying to ensure this does not prove uncontrollable. It is a problem that the CCP has not yet managed to resolve. What is clear is that as internal nationalistic sentiments continue to grow (with the CCP's permission and through patriotic education) nationalism-fuelled assertiveness will continue. In addition, the CCP will continue to *externalize threats that will endure* in order continually to justify its role as the defender of China's sovereignty; legitimize Party rule; and deflect domestic unhappiness outwards. The South China Sea disputes (together with the more East China Sea contestations) are such exercises.

Some scholars have also shown that internal politicking is behind many of China's key foreign policy actions. Indeed, in the nine-dash line passport episode, Zha Daojiong, an international relations expert from the Peking University, stated that 'We have different agencies, different individuals. Sometimes people assume it's all very well co-ordinated, but that may not always be the case' (Kaiman 2012). In addition to domestically fuelled nationalism, China's assertiveness is also an aggregation of bargaining and negotiations between different power brokers and agencies in Beijing, local governments, and even state-owned enterprises.

This observation is not lost on President Xi. On 10 March 2013 China unveiled a series of major government restructuring initiatives (Martina 2013). Significantly, maritime enforcement agencies will be consolidated into a single National Oceanic Administration under the Ministry of Land and Resources giving it control over customs, coastguard forces and fisheries enforcement in disputed maritime regions. This can be viewed as an attempt to exercise greater control and discretion over the actions undertaken in disputed maritime territories. Additionally, Xi's rallying calls for realization of the 'Chinese Dream' and a high-profile anti-corruption drive to root out both 'tigers' and 'flies' are also widely perceived as moves to consolidate his power base in order to implement difficult economic, political and diplomatic reforms (Lim and Rajagopalan 2014).

Conclusion

China's policy in the South China Sea dispute is more complex than it appears. On the other hand, despite the ongoing maritime disputes, China has been keen to cultivate ties with

ASEAN members. It has been the largest trading partner of ASEAN since 2009 and was the first dialogue partner of ASEAN to accede to the Treaty of Amity and Cooperation in October 2003. Multiple bilateral and multilateral track 1 and track 2 forums and initiatives, with ASEAN and ASEAN members, have been in place and continue to grow. It is clear that China values its relationship with ASEAN. Regarding the maritime disputes in the South China Sea, in 2014 Chinese Foreign Minister, Wang Yi stated that 'China is sincere about it … the door for dialogue and consultation is always open' (*Global Times* 2014). Certainly, if one looks at the official statements from the foreign ministry, a common theme of 'peace' and 'dialogue' emerges.

It is all too easy to dismiss such overtures as hypocritical and volte-face. Nonetheless, as we have tried to show, these goodwill-generating activities are not just symbolic but have produced substantial results. The best way to characterize China's policy in the South China Sea dispute is 'fluid assertiveness'. 'Fluid assertiveness' shows how the CCP tends to be assertive (and 'aggressive' at times) while still maintaining its goodwill-generating capacities. What we have also demonstrated shows that much of its assertive actions are domestically driven while its positive moves are largely unaffected by domestic pressures. There are two dissimilar but not entirely distinct strands affecting China's policy in the South China Sea. On the one hand, China's assertiveness is powered by domestic socio-political factors while on the other, its positive overtures are largely undisturbed by domestic factors. Both of these strands have their own trajectories and they sometimes intertwine – China's tendency to calm and reassure neighbours when things become too tense is illustrative of this. In addition to the evidence already presented above, China has also moved to reassure its South China Sea neighbours that the Hainan administration rules would be enforced only with 12 nautical miles and that they have no ill intent (Press TV 2014). In addition, they have been quick to refute reports claiming the imminent establishment of an air defence identification zone over the South China Sea (Li 2014). 'Fluid assertiveness', as a conceptual framework, is able to accommodate current existing paradigms in understanding China's activities while simultaneously enabling the recognition of positive moves it has made in the South China Sea. More importantly, it investigates the domestic motivations of Beijing's actions in the South China Sea and how it has shaped and continues to shape its future path.

Note

1 Mingjiang Li's interviews with Chinese analysts at various government-affiliated research institutes in 2013.

Bibliography

Asia Sentinel, 'The China-Philippine Banana War', 6 June 2012, www.asiasentinel.com/society/the-china-philippine-banana-war/.

Blanchard, Ben and Manuel Mogato, 'Chinese Police Plan to Board Vessels in Disputed Seas', *Reuters*, 29 November 2012, www.reuters.com/article/2012/11/30/china-seas-idUSL4N0991Z020121130.

Blanchard, Ben and John Ruwitch, 'China Hikes Defense Budget, To Spend More on Internal Security', 5 March 2013, www.reuters.com/article/2013/03/05/us-china-parliament-defence-idUSBRE92403620130305.

British Broadcasting Corporation (BBC), 'Vietnam Accuses China in Sea Dispute', *BBC News*, 30 May 2011, www.bbc.com/news/world-asia-pacific-13592508.

Buszynski, Leszek, 'China's Naval Strategy, The United States, ASEAN and the South China Sea', *Security Challenges*, Vol. 8, No. 2, 2012.

Castro, De Erik and Roli Ng, 'Philippine Ship Dodges China Blockade to Reach South China Sea Outpost', *Reuters*, 30 March 2014, www.reuters.com/article/2014/03/30/us-philippines-china-reef-idUSBREA2T02K20140330.

Chan, Minnie, 'China, Vietnam Seal Accord Over Maritime Territory', *South China Morning Post*, 13 October 2011.

CNTV (English), 'China Urges Vietnam to Stop Unilateral Oil, Gas Exploration in South China Sea', 6 December 2012, http://english.cntv.cn/program/asiatoday/20121206/107997.shtml.

Dillon, Dana R., 'Countering Beijing in the South China Sea', *Policy Review*, Stanford, CA: Hoover Institution, 1 June 2011, www.hoover.org/research/countering-beijing-south-china-sea.

Fox News, 'China Unveils $474M Maritime Cooperation Fund with ASEAN Amid Territorial Disputes', 5 October 2012, www.foxnews.com/world/2012/10/05/china-unveils-474m-maritime-cooperation-fund-with-asean-amid-territorial/.

Fravel, Taylor M., 'China's Behavior in its Territorial Disputes and Assertiveness in the South China Sea', Centre for Strategic and International Studies, 2011, https://csis.org/files/attachments/111128_Fravel_China_Behavior_Territorial_Disputes.pdf.

Fravel, Taylor M., 'Hainan's New Maritime Regulations: An Update', *The Diplomat*, 3 January 2013, http://thediplomat.com/2013/01/hainans-new-maritime-regulations-an-update/?allpages=yes.

Global Times, 'China Must React to Vietnam's Provocation', 21 June 2011, www.globaltimes.cn/NEWS/tabid/99/articleType/ArticleView/articleId/662453/China-must-react-to-Vietnams-provocation.aspx.

Global Times, 'China Ready for Worst-case Diaoyu Scenario', 11 January 2013, www.globaltimes.cn/content/755170.shtml.

Global Times, 'China Committed to Upholding Regional Peace: Foreign Minister', 14 April 2014, www.globaltimes.cn/content/854526.shtml#.U1jMkFWSxK0.

Hookway, James, 'Philippine Warship in Standoff with China Vessels', *Wall Street Journal*, 11 April 2012, http://online.wsj.com/article/SB10001424052702303815404577336550439399694.html.

Huang, Yukon, 'China's Internal Dilemas', US–China Economic and Security Review Commission, Carnegie Endowment for International Peace, Washington, DC, 2011, http://carnegieendowment.org/files/0225_testimony_huang.pdf.

Huo, Yan and Xiaohuo Cui, 'Patrol Ships Trawl for Disorder in Beibu Gulf', *China Daily*, 28 May 2009, www.chinadaily.com.cn/china/2009-05/28/content_7950753.htm.

Inquirer, 'Scarborough Shoal Standoff: A Timeline', 8 May 2012, http://globalnation.inquirer.net/36003/scarborough-shoal-standoff-a-historicaltimeline.

InterAksyon, 'South China Sea Pact Moving Forward? Chinese, ASEAN Execs Vow to Enhance Maritime Cooperation', 23 April 2014, www.interaksyon.com/article/85287/south-china-sea-pact-moving-forward-chinese-asean-execs-vow-to-enhance-maritime-cooperation.

International Crisis Group, 'Dangerous Waters: China-Japan Relation on the Rocks', *Asia Report*, No. 245, 2013, www.crisisgroup.org/~/media/Files/asia/north-east-asia/245-dangerous-waters-china-japan-relations-on-the-rocks.

Kaiman, Jonathan, 'Chinese Passport Map Causes Diplomatic Dispute', *The Guardian*, 27 November 2012, www.theguardian.com/world/2012/nov/27/chinese-passport-row-diplomatic-dispute.

Kleine-Ahlbrandt, Stephanie, 'Choppy Weather in the China Seas', *Le Monde Diplomatique*, December 2012.

Li, Jianwei, 'Managing Tensions in the South China Sea: Comparing the China-Philippines and the China-Vietnam Approaches', *RSIS Working Paper*, No. 273, Singapore: S. Rajaratnam School of International Studies, Nanyang Technological University.

Li, Ming Jiang, 'China's Non-confrontational Assertiveness in the South China Sea', *East Asia Forum*, 2012, www.eastasiaforum.org/2012/06/14/china-s-non-confrontational-assertiveness-in-the-south-china-sea/.

Li, Xiaokun, 'Beijing Dismisses Report of Planned S. China Sea ADIZ', *China Daily*, 28 February 2014.

Lim, Benjamin and Megha Rajagopalan, 'China's Xi Purging Corrupt Officials to Put own Men in Place: Sources', *Reuters*, 16 April 2014,www.reuters.com/article/2014/04/16/us-china-corruption-xi-insight-idUSBREA3F1UT20140416.

Long, Tao, 'Time to Teach Those around South China Sea a Lesson', *Global Times*, 29 September 2011, www.globaltimes.cn/NEWS/tabid/99/ID/677717/Time-to-teach-those-around-South-China-Sea-a-lesson.aspx.

Lovell, Julia, *The Opium War: Drugs, Dreams and the Making of China*, Sydney: Picador, 2011.

Martina, Michael, 'Factbox: Main Changes in China's Government Restructuring Plan', *Reuters*, 10 March 2013, www.reuters.com/article/2013/03/10/us-china-parliament-ministries-factbox-idUSBRE92903J20130310.

Ministry of Foreign Affairs, People's Republic of China, *Shelving Disputes and Seeking Common Development*, www.mfa.gov.cn/chn//gxh/xsb/wjzs/t8958.htm.

Murphy, Ann Marie, 'Indonesia Enters the Fray with China', *Bangkok Post*, 4 April 2014.

Orendain, Simone, 'China Agrees to Discuss "Code of Conduct" Rules', *VOA News*, 4 July 2013, www.voanews.com/content/asean-south-china-sea-dispute-heads-to-beijing-for-talks/1694932.html.

Perlez, Jane, 'Continuing Buildup, China Boosts Military Spending more than 11 Percent', *New York Times*, 4 March 2012, www.nytimes.com/2012/03/05/world/asia/china-boosts-military-spending-more-than-11-percent.html?_r=0.

Press TV, 'China Explains New Controversial Laws over South China Sea', 24 April 2014, http://presstv.com/detail/2012/12/31/281121/china-explains-new-controversial-laws-over-south-china-sea/

Qianjing Wanbao, 'Chinese Military Expert Say due to Humanitarian Consideration China Allowed the Philippine Navy to Carry Out Supply to its Wrecked Vessel', 21 June 2013, http://mil.news.sina.com.cn/2013-06-21/1121728787.html.

Ratner, Ely, 'Rebalancing to Asia With an Insecure China', *Washington Quarterly*, Vol. 36, No. 2, 2013.

Ririhena, Yohanna and Novan Santosa, 'RI Concerned about Map in New Chinese Passport', *Jakarta Post*, 29 November 2012, www.thejakartapost.com/news/2012/11/29/ri-concerned-about-map-new-chinese-passports.html.

Santamaria, Carlos, 'PH Protest New Chinese Passport Map', *Rappler*, 22 November 2012, www.rappler.com/nation/16601-ph-protests-new-chinese-passport-map.

Scobell, Andrew, 'The Rise of China: Security Implications', *Report on Conference conducted by Strategic Studies Institute*, 2001, http://tiss.sanford.duke.edu/pubs/documents/TheRiseofChina.pdf.

Storey, Ian, 'Creeping Assertiveness: China, the Philippines and the South China Sea Disputes', *Contemporary Southeast Asia*, Vol. 21, No. 1, 1999.

Vietnam Breaking News, 'Fishermen Intimidated and Harassed by Chinese Patrol Boats', 9 June 2009, www.vietnambreakingnews.com/2009/06/fishermen-intimidated-and-harassed-by-chinese-patrol-boats/#.U1df4lWSxK0.

Wang, Linyan, 'Post-80s: The Vexed Generation?', *China Daily*, 27 May 2009.

Wertime, David, 'Chinese Netizens to Government: Don't Back Down from Philippines', *Tea Leaf Nation*, 9 May 2012, www.tealeafnation.com/2012/05/chinese-netizens-to-government-dont-back-down-from-philippines/.

Xinhua, http://news.xinhuanet.com/english/video/2012-12/07/c_132026023.htm.

Yip, Michael and Craig Webber, 'Hacktivism: A Theoretical and Empirical Exploration of China's Cyber Warriors', ACM WebSci '11, Koblenz, Germany, 14–17 June 2011.

You, Ji, 'Deciphering Beijing's Maritime Security Policy and Strategy in Managing Sovereignty Disputes in the China Seas', *RSIS Policy Brief*, October 2013.

Zhang, Jian, 'China's Growing Assertiveness in the South China, A Strategic Shift?', *The South China Sea and Australia's Regional Security Environment*, National Security College Occasional Paper, No. 5, 2013.

10
China and the Strait of Malacca

Justin V. Hastings

Introduction

What role does the Strait of Malacca play in China's strategic thinking? In this chapter I look at the Malacca Strait as both a necessary part of China's dreams of economic development and emergence of a regional and global power, and an issue relevant to a number of problems that China faces in its development. I argue that the Malacca Strait is of great strategic importance to China for a number of reasons. The Strait's geopolitical centrality as a shipping lane makes China dependent on goods that pass through the Strait, and it thus has an incentive to try to ensure that its goods continue to pass through unimpeded. Partly because of this imperative, China's relations with the littoral states of the Malacca Strait are important, but not always easy, and it faces the problem of how to deal with them when the USA is a viable regional competitor, leading to a 'Malacca dilemma' (Chen 2010). The Malacca Strait also serves as the point connecting both the South China Sea, where China has territorial disputes with a number of other countries, and the Indian Ocean, where China is attempting to establish a greater naval presence.

China has attempted to ameliorate the conundrums associated with the Malacca Strait through several strategies. First, it has attempted to bypass the Malacca Strait altogether as a major corridor for essential energy supplies, leading to pipeline projects with a number of neighbouring countries. Second, it has asserted its power in the South China Sea, resulting in a growing unease and outright hostility from South-East Asian countries. This hostility may not ultimately be in China's interest. China thus faces the dilemma that attempts to solve problems related to the Malacca Strait only seem to cause more problems.

Finally, I illustrate the clash between China's strategic interests and its actual behaviour with a discussion of the role that China played in the search for the missing Malaysia Airlines flight MH370, an incident that took place in and around the Malacca Strait and Indian Ocean, and involved both China and littoral states in the Malacca Strait. While the tragedy presented China with a number of opportunities to engage in global public goods provision and improve relations with South-East Asian countries, China arguably squandered those opportunities, and was left rushing to pick up the pieces.

The strategic importance of the Malacca Strait to China

The strategic importance of the Malacca Strait to the world at large is almost entirely due to its role as the primary sea line of communication for ships moving between Europe and the Middle East, and East Asia through the Indian Ocean. As approximately 80 per cent of the world's cargo moves by sea, a large portion of the goods necessary to keep the global economy functioning pour through the Malacca Strait (Chalk 2008: 10). In part due to the just-in-time nature of both manufacturing and shipping, any disruption to marine traffic is likely to have cascading effects out of proportion to the initial disruption. This is due partly to the presence of three major transshipment ports in the Malacca Strait – Singapore, and Port Klang and Tanjung Pelepas in Malaysia – that funnel ships through the Strait to offload and load shipping containers for onward shipment. In the global shipping network the Malacca Strait thus serves as both a link and a very prominent node.

The strategic problem of a heavy volume of ship traffic is exacerbated by the narrowness and shallowness of the Strait at its southern end. Consequently, large cargo ships must reduce speed and pass through designated channels to avoid scraping the bottom of the Strait. The Singapore Strait is so narrow that the northern islands of Indonesia's Riau Archipelago can easily be seen from Singapore's southern beaches, and is congested with ships either transiting or waiting at anchor for entry to Singapore's transshipment terminal. Ships in the southern Malacca Strait have thus historically been at risk from accidents and attacks that block the Strait, or from pirate attacks launched from islands in Indonesia (or less frequently from Malaysia) (Ong 2007; Chalk 2008).

The general strategic importance of the Malacca Strait is magnified for China. The country's supercharged economic growth relies on a steady supply of imports of raw materials for construction, manufacturing, and energy production, much of which pass through the Malacca Strait from the Middle East and Africa, and exports, many of which go through the Malacca Strait to other parts of Asia, the Middle East, and Europe. Essentially, all of the oil and natural gas China gets from the Middle East and Africa comes through the Malacca Strait, and much of the transshipment traffic moving through Singapore, Port Klang, and Tanjung Pelepas is bound or comes from China (Lanteigne 2008). China, in other words, needs the Malacca Strait to be free and clear of disruptions for its economy to grow properly.

The Strait's littoral states themselves – Thailand, Malaysia, Indonesia, and Singapore – are all important to China as trading partners in their own right. The Malacca Strait is also the core of South-East Asia economic production: the littoral states represent the four largest economies (by nominal gross domestic product) in the Association of Southeast Asian Nations (ASEAN) (World Bank 2014). Maintaining good relations with the Malacca Strait states is thus important for China's continued peaceful rise.

While China's relations with the littoral states have generally been good enough not to impede economic development – Singapore has an industrial zone in Suzhou, for example – it has periodically run into problems with both Malaysia and Indonesia. China has an ongoing territorial dispute with Malaysia in the South China Sea, although this has not led to active conflict as it has in China's disputes with Vietnam, and in particular the Philippines. China's post-2009 assertiveness in the South China Sea dispute also eventually spread to Indonesia, which expressed concern in 2014 about encroaching Chinese territorial claims and actions in the Natuna archipelago controlled by Indonesia. Indonesia subsequently announced military movements to the islands designed to buttress its defences (Keck 2014). China also experienced a flare-up in its relations with Malaysia during the search for Malaysia Airlines flight MH370 in 2014 (see below).

Perhaps worryingly for China, the Malacca Strait is also an area with a significant US and more generally Western diplomatic and military presence. Thailand is a treaty ally of the USA, and between military coups, conducts regular exercises with US forces. Singapore has long served as a base for some US Navy support operations and a stopover point for US Navy ships; the US military personnel stationed in Singapore are the largest of any contingent in South-East Asia, and in 2011 Singapore agreed to allow the USA to base littoral combat ships in the country (Yee 2011). Malaysia and Singapore are also aligned with the United Kingdom, Australia, and New Zealand in the Five Powers Defence Arrangement. While the Arrangement at this point entails only a minimal constant commitment of personnel by the outside powers, the Five Powers have long engaged in annual joint military exercises and high-level consultations. The Arrangement thus remains a signal of the closeness of Malaysia and Singapore with Western powers for the purpose of maintaining their security.

South-East Asian nations in general, and the Malacca Strait littoral states in particular, have been careful not to choose between China and the USA, engaging in what can at times be elaborate hedging strategies, and using the institutional prestige of ASEAN (such as it is) to envelop both the USA and China in multilateral groupings that encourage engagement, and that centre on ASEAN, such as the ASEAN Regional Forum, ASEAN Plus Three, and (more recently) the East Asian Summit (Chen and Yang 2013). Thus, while the Malacca Strait littoral states have taken very strong steps to avoid having to choose between the USA and China, they are capable of doing so, and have the infrastructure and relationships in place to hedge with the West against China if it comes to it. As a result, China must be careful to manage its relations with the Malacca Strait littoral states to prevent their balancing with the West against China and to protect its own ability to continue its peaceful rise.

In the Malacca Strait, China also theoretically has an area that is more pacific and has fewer entanglements than other areas on its periphery, such as the South China Sea, the East China Sea, and the Korean peninsula. This suggests that win-win cooperation is a better possibility in the Strait of Malacca than in other areas of Asia. Unlike the South China Sea, the Malacca Strait and the neighbouring Singapore Strait have not been the subject of any territorial disputes that are likely to lead to militarized interstate disputes. The only dispute that even caused any rancour – Malaysia and Singapore's dispute over the island known as Pedra Branca – was essentially resolved in 2008 by an international tribunal decision, largely in Singapore's favour. Rancour over Ambalat, Malaysia and Indonesia's territorial dispute east of Borneo, has largely been confined to that area, and has not spread into the Malacca Strait. While the littoral states are unlikely to fight each other, they are quite prickly about safeguarding their sovereignty and preventing what is perceived as outside interference. At times, this prickliness can have salutary effects, leading the littoral states to engage in public security goods provision as a means of staving off outside intervention. Perhaps most notoriously, in 2004, Malaysia and Indonesia reacted harshly to US suggestions that the US Navy might help with safeguarding the security of the Strait against pirate attacks, and soon initiated a programme of multilateral cooperation (with Singapore, and later Thailand) to combat piracy themselves (see Yeoh 2004).

At the same time, the Malacca Strait poses a strategic problem for China's involvement in the South China Sea territorial dispute. The 'nine-dash line' on official Chinese maps of the country's territory, marking out its claims to virtually the entire South China Sea, implies that China's claimed territory essentially abuts the Singapore Strait and the Malacca Strait. The two straits control the approaches to the South China Sea from the south-west. Being cut off from the Malacca Strait could imperil China's bid to press or administer its claims in the

South China Sea. It also poses something of a dilemma for China. Pressing its rights to send military vessels through the Malacca Strait in the face of hostile or indifferent littoral states puts China at odds with its claims in the South China Sea. There, while China's actions to assert its claims have yet to impede the free passage of foreign naval vessels through the South China Sea, its aggressive behaviour towards Philippine and Vietnamese commercial and naval vessels and its expansive territorial claims have placed some doubt among outside actors such as the USA and Australia about its willingness to continue to honour freedom of navigation in the future (Emmers 2012). It remains an open question whether China's logic of control in the South China Sea will eventually collide with its logic of freedom of navigation in the Malacca Strait.

The Malacca Strait is also at the periphery of one of China's other strategic interests – the Indian Ocean. As China develops a blue-water navy and attempts to operate its first aircraft carrier, it has begun to expand, ever so gingerly, into operating naval vessels and building military bases in the Indian Ocean. The Chinese contribution to international patrols against pirates off the Horn of Africa is one such example, with the People's Liberation Army (PLA) Navy sending warships that have actively pursued pirates and rescued seafarers. Counter-piracy efforts are a win-win for China and others: they give the PLA Navy experience in blue-water combat operations far from their home bases, and they give all navies (including China) experience of engaging in the coordination of multinational security operations without having to deal with sovereignty issues. Pirates are a common enemy that the navy of every state can agree on attacking. Navies, in other words, can engage in combat without going to war. It is not surprising, then, that China jumped on the chance to send the PLA Navy to the Horn of Africa. In 2010 China agreed to an expanded role in joint patrols against pirates, along with the USA, the European Union, and other countries (BBC 2010). Following this initial cooperation, in 2012 China sent more personnel to patrol jointly with Japan and India in the Indian Ocean (Luke 2012).

Yet this expansion also places the PLA Navy on a potential collision course with India and the US Fifth Fleet. While cooperation on anti-piracy patrols is an ideal way to pursue confidence building in an actual operational environment (and this is, in fact, behind much of the impetus for the massive international response to piracy off the coast of Somalia that is out of all proportion to the actual threat posed by pirates to the global economy), the pirates will not be around forever (and indeed, there was not a single successful hijacking off Somalia in 2013, although how much the lack of hijackings was due to the naval patrols rather than the armed guards posted on many ships passing by Somalia is unclear), and there are few other such opportunities on the horizon. India sees a certain strategic importance to the Indian Ocean (given that it is located in the centre of it), and is wary of Chinese movements into 'its' ocean. The USA publicly states that it is open to Chinese operations in the Indian Ocean, but wants to see China step up in terms of responsibility as a global public goods provider (Holmes and Yoshihara 2008). While the Indian Ocean is certainly big enough for all three navies, it will be difficult for China to access the Indian Ocean without access to the Malacca Strait. In a sense, much of any future Chinese multi-ocean blue-water navy strategy depends on access to the Strait.

China's attempts to ameliorate its strategic concerns

While the Malacca Strait represents many opportunities for China – trade in support of economic development, a greater role in providing global public security goods, better relations with other economically dynamic countries – the strategic concerns for China discussed above mean that China has taken steps to ameliorate threats to its growth and security associated with the Malacca Strait (Chen 2010). These steps have not always resulted in optimal strategic outcomes for China.

The current dispute over the South China Sea is a case in point. Whatever the initial reasons behind China's recent assertive behaviour in the South China Sea since 2009, how the interactions between China and South-East Asia have progressed since then is in some sense a classic security dilemma: China engages in self-help to assert its territorial claims against what it perceives as encroachment by other claimants, building up its military forces, establishing concrete markers of sovereignty (moving to incorporate its claims as a city in Hainan in 2012), and approving mineral exploration rigs in disputed waters (as happened in 2014). This self-help then leads to questions by other countries, particularly the Philippines and Vietnam, regarding China's intentions in the South China Sea, leading them also to engage in self-help, behave more provocatively, and cement ties with external actors such as the USA. While China has been able to establish facts on the ground in the South China Sea more to its liking than in the past, this has come at the cost of worse relations with a plurality of ASEAN members, deep suspicion from most of the rest, rhetorical battles with outside powers such as the USA, Australia, and Japan, and the destruction (or at least near death) of the notion of China's 'peaceful rise'.

As the South China Sea dispute has approached the Malacca Strait, the littoral states, all of whom have tried to stay relatively aloof from China's troubles with Vietnam and the Philippines, have grown more concerned. In March 2014, while the Indonesian Ministry of Foreign Affairs denied that there was any dispute at all with China (which is generally what countries do when they have de facto control over disputed territory), Indonesian military officers publicly stated their concern about China's claims to the waters of the Natuna Sea impinging on Indonesia's control of the islands. The Indonesian Air Force subsequently began upgrading Ranai airfield in the Riau Islands, in the north-eastern approach to the Malacca Strait, for transfer of a contingent of fighter jets and attack helicopters to Indonesia's northern waters (Keck 2014). China thus risks its relationships with the littoral states of the Malacca Strait, an otherwise pacific region, as it presses its South China Sea claims with increased vigour and increases certainty about the limits of those claims (and those claims overlap with those of otherwise uninvolved parties).

The geostrategic liabilities posed by the Malacca Strait – the fact that a large portion of world trade passes through a narrow, shallow chokepoint – has not been lost on China. While 80 per cent of China's imported oil and natural gas currently pass through the Malacca Strait, China has attempted to ameliorate the strategic problems associated with the Strait of Malacca as a chokepoint by bypassing the Strait entirely (Noel 2014). The South China Sea dispute is itself perhaps an example of China's attempts to bypass the Strait. Given the potential opportunities for exploiting mineral resources in the South China Sea, establishing firm de facto control over the area and at least deterring other claimant states from pressing their own claims militarily would allow China to reduce its need to transport its oil and natural gas through the Malacca Strait. Indeed, in contrast to the pipelines from Myanmar and Central Asia, it would enable China to exploit natural resources in areas it actually controls.

To this end, it has also sought to expand trade and improve transportation infrastructure links with countries on its land borders (Meidan 2014). In the past decade, for instance, China has built up military and trade ties with Myanmar and Kazakhstan (and more generally Central Asia) in (small) part as a hedge against problems or loss of access in the Strait of Malacca. In 2004, for instance, China and Myanmar began investigating the possibility of oil and gas pipelines stretching from Kyaukphyu in the Bay of Bengal in Myanmar into

Kunming in Yunnan, China. The Myanmar section of the gas pipeline was completed in 2013, with the pipeline coming into full operation in October of that year (Du 2013). China also built a crude oil pipeline with Kazakhstan, with an initial agreement signed in 1997, and the final section of the pipeline completed in 2009 (Savin and Ouyang 2013). China is thus making an effort to render the Malacca Strait less important in its strategic calculus.

Case study: Malaysia Airlines flight MH370

The tragedy of the missing Malaysia Airlines flight MH370, which disappeared on 8 March 2014 while flying from Kuala Lumpur to Beijing, highlights the opportunities and challenges for China in the Strait of Malacca as it pursues economic growth, trade and a peaceful rise that will secure what it believes is its rightful place on the world stage. When the plane went missing, China was presented with both a crisis and an opportunity. Not only was the plane headed to Beijing, but most of the passengers on the plane were Chinese citizens, as were most of the people waiting increasingly anxiously at the airport demanding information. China thus had a duty and an opportunity to look very publicly after the interests of its citizens. At the same time, the anger and confusion of the passengers' families in Beijing forced the Chinese government to be assertive with Malaysia in looking after those interests. China's attacks on Malaysia came with some risk. In the first few days of the search, there was some suspicion that the missing airliner might have been hijacked by Uyghur separatists, given that the airliner went missing so soon after the attack on the railway station in Kunming. While this was extremely unlikely in any case – Uyghur separatists had never previously engaged in anything as sophisticated as an international jetliner hijacking – if it had turned out to be true, it would have been a diplomatic disaster for China.

The result was that China berated Malaysia, with a ferocity that it normally reserved for Japan, over the general incompetence in the way the investigation was handled, namely the changing stories from Malaysian government officials; the delay in providing clarity about what actually happened; the confused and confusing coordination of the search itself. Chinese media outlets began directly attacking the Malaysian government's handling of the matter, and demanding greater transparency in the investigation (Kor 2014). Given the Chinese government's penchant for secrecy, this was nearly an unprecedented opportunity to come down on the side of openness while also defending patriotic sentiment (although Chinese media were given a directive not to interview the grieving relatives of the MH370 passengers without permission, or to report anything besides Xinhua copy) (Rudolph 2014). For some weeks, the Chinese government kept up the pressure, going so far as to allow Chinese protesters to stage a march outside of the Malaysian embassy in Beijing as a means of pressuring Malaysia, much as the Chinese state routinely does with anti-Japanese protesters (Branigan and Farrell 2014). Chinese passengers also shunned Malaysia Airlines, with Chinese passenger traffic on the airline down 60 per cent in March 2014 (Sky News 2014). Yet Malaysia was not Japan; it was not used to over-the-top Chinese rhetoric and, up until the disappearance of the airliner, had enjoyed cordial relations with China. China itself seems to have realized that it had gone too far, and within a month had pulled back on the attacks on Malaysia and had moved to calm tensions and anti-Malaysia sentiment in China.

Besides being able to frame itself to its citizens as an advocate for transparency and competence, the Chinese government also seized on the 'opportunity' of flight MH370's disappearance to demonstrate its emergence on the global scene as a responsible great power with the resources and desire to provide global public goods (such as, in this case, search and rescue). By international convention, Malaysia was in charge of the search and rescue operation. However, China was eager to provide highly visible public support (particularly given its rhetorical attacks on Malaysia's competence) and put naval vessels, aircraft, and satellites at the disposal of the search operation. The search was in essence an opportunity for China to showcase its new military might in South-East Asia without causing undue alarm to other countries (but at same time allowing other countries to see just what its military was capable of) (Wen 2014).

However, there was a downside to China's eagerness to show off its technical prowess: the signal that China had emerged as a great power was significantly weakened by the ineffectiveness of the resources deployed. China claimed to deploy its network of satellites to look for debris from the aircraft, but as of May 2014, every single piece of debris that the satellites found turned out to be unrelated to flight MH370 or failed to be located when surface vessels raced to the area where the debris had been spotted. Chinese search and rescue vessels sent to the southern Indian Ocean used sonar to detect underwater pings (presumably from the aircraft's 'black box') that could then not be located. Other countries began to grumble that the combination of Chinese enthusiasm and ineffectiveness was costing them valuable time and resources pursuing dead ends (Semple and Schmittapril 2014). That said, even after global media attention had begun to subside, China was still willing to invest resources where other countries were not. By the middle of May, when many other countries had withdrawn their resources after more than two months of fruitless searching, it was left to China, Malaysia and Australia jointly to decide how to proceed with a slower, more deliberate, scaled-down search that could take over a year to complete (Rajca 2014).

The MH370 search had ambiguous ramifications for China with regard to the Strait of Malacca, broadly understood. On the one hand, China was presented with both a duty and an opportunity publicly to advocate for its citizens with a littoral state of the Malacca Strait. The presence of so many Chinese passengers on flight MH370 was itself a sign of China's emerging status, as Chinese businesspeople and tourists move to and from South-East Asia in ever greater numbers. At the same time, China's overreaction to Malaysia's incompetent handling of the search arguably sent a signal that, while Chinese foreign policymakers had long articulated the theory of a peaceful rise for China, any downturn in relations with other countries could be met with the same sudden and surprising ferocity in Chinese behaviour to which Japan had long been accustomed. While there was never any danger of actual conflict between Malaysia and China (at least over flight MH370), the speed with which relations with China could take a downturn, despite China's decades-long charm offensive in South-East Asia, was probably not lost on other countries in the region.

Owing to the many false starts and failures of the resources that China deployed to search for the plane it is not clear whether China's role in the search itself actually tarnished China's image or whether it signalled its emergence as a technologically sophisticated, organizationally competent great power ready and willing to provide global public goods such as search and rescue resources. China's friends and competitors alike were treated to the spectacle of a great power that still had significant teething problems when it came to international cooperation and service provision.

Conclusion

What does the future hold for China and the Strait of Malacca? While the Malacca Strait occupies an important place in China's strategic calculations, and thus in China's quest to become a superpower and developed country, China's ability to deal with the Malacca Strait in its overall strategic framework is complicated by several factors. First, the Malacca Strait itself is both central to China's economic growth inasmuch as it is a chokepoint for the trade and energy supplies that power that growth. At the same time, it is geographically peripheral to a number of regions, particularly the South China Sea and the Indian Ocean, where China is attempting to fly the flag and increase its influence. This results in complicated calculations for how China approaches the Malacca Strait. Precisely because China's foothold in the region surrounding the Malacca Strait is not particularly strong, is contested with the USA, and is to a large extent contingent upon its (sometimes problematic) relationships with the Strait's littoral states, China's behaviour and competence when dealing with the Strait and its littoral states is paramount. In this respect it has not necessarily been supremely successful, as evidenced by the search for flight MH370. China's attempts to decrease the importance of the Malacca Strait through alternative trade and energy supply agreements will no doubt provide at least some outside options, but it is unlikely to render the Malacca Strait irrelevant. The result is that the Malacca Strait will continue to be a dilemma for years to come as China seeks to maintain its growth.

Bibliography

Branigan, Tania and Paul Farrell, 'MH370: Relatives of Chinese Passengers Protest at Malaysian Embassy in Beijing', *The Guardian*, 25 March 2014.

British Broadcasting Corporation (BBC), 'China's Anti-Piracy Role Off Somalia Expands' *BBC News*, 29 January 2010.

Chalk, Peter, *The Maritime Dimension of International Security: Terrorism, Piracy, and Challenges for the United States*, Santa Monica, CA: RAND, 2008.

Chen, Ian Tsung-Yen and Alan Hao Yang, 'A Harmonized Southeast Asia? Explanatory Typologies of ASEAN Countries' Strategies to the Rise of China', *The Pacific Review*, Vol. 26, No. 3, 2013.

Chen, Shaofeng, 'China's Self-Extrication From the "Malacca Dilemma" and Implications', *International Journal of China Studies*, Vol. 1, No. 1, 2010.

Du, Juan, 'Myanmar-China Gas Pipeline Completed', *China Daily*, 20 October 2013.

Emmers, Ralf, *The US Rebalancing Strategy: Impact on the South China Sea*, Canberra: National Security College, Australian National University, 2012.

Holmes, James R. and Toshi Yoshihara, 'China and the United States in the Indian Ocean', *Naval War College Review*, Vol. 61, No. 3, Summer 2008.

Keck, Zachary, 'Indonesia Beefs Up Air Force in South China Sea: Indonesia is Deploying Su-27s, Su-30s, and AH-64E Apache Helicopters to a South China Sea Air Base', *The Diplomat*, 7 April 2014.

Kor, Kian Beng, 'Missing Malaysia Airlines Plane: Chinese Media Attack MAS and Malaysia Government Over Handling of MH370', *Straits Times*, 10 March 2014.

Lanteigne, Marc, 'China's Maritime Security and the "Malacca Dilemma"', *Asian Security*, Vol. 4, No. 2, 2008.

Luke, Leighton, 'India, China and Japan Co-ordinate Anti-Piracy Patrols', *Future Directions International*, 8 February 2012.

Meidan, Michal, 'The Implications of China's Energy-Import Boom', *Survival*, Vol. 56, No. 3, 2014.

Noel, Pierre, 'Asia's Energy Supply and Maritime Security', *Survival*, Vol. 56, No. 3, 2014.

Ong, Graham Gerard (ed.), *Piracy, Maritime Terrorism and Securing the Malacca Straits*, Singapore: Institute for Southeast Asian Studies, 2007.

Rajca, Jennifer, 'MH370: Australia, Malaysia and China Discuss Next Phase for Search for Missing Malaysia Airlines Plane', *News.com.au*, 5 May 2014, www.news.com.au/national/mh370-australia-malaysia-and-china-discuss-next-phase-for-search-for-missing-malaysia-airlines-plane/story-fncynjr2-1226905951460.

Rudolph, Josh, 'Minitrue: Malaysia Airlines Flight MH370', *China Digital Times*, 8 March 2014, http://chinadigitaltimes.net/2014/03/minitrue-malaysia-airlines-flight-mh370/.

Savin, Vladislav and Cherng-Shin Ouyang, 'Analysis of Post-Soviet Central Asia's Oil and Gas Pipeline Issues', *Geopolitika.ru*, 25 December 2013, www.geopolitika.ru/en/article/analysis-post-soviet-central-asias-oil-gas-pipeline-issues#.U4UqpJSlm8B.

Semple, Kirk and Eric Schmittapril, 'China's Actions in Hunt for Jet Are Seen as Hurting as Much as Helping', *New York Times*, 14 April 2014

Sky News, 'Missing MH370: Passengers Shun Malaysia Carrier', 15 May 2014.

Wen, Philip, 'China Throws Full Weight Behind Search for Malaysia Airlines Flight MH370', *Sydney Morning Herald*, 23 March 2014.

World Bank, *World Development Indicators*, 2014, Washington, DC: World Bank, 2014.

Yee, Andy, 'U.S. Deployment of Littoral Combat Ships to Singapore', *East Asia Forum*, Canberra: Australian National University, 21 July 2011.

Yeoh, En-Lai, 'Nations Rejecting U.S. Help in Policing Malacca Straits', *Associated Press*, 4 June 2004.

11
China's strategy towards Taiwan

Sheryn Lee

Introduction

The primary purpose of the Chinese Communist Party (CCP) is to ensure regime survival and to maintain political power over the Chinese state. Conversely, the national objective of the Chinese state is to protect the political legitimacy of the CCP by way of upholding its core interests, namely its territorial sovereignty claims. The promotion of the 'one China' policy under the 'one country, two systems' framework demonstrates its belief in the indivisibility of China and is a key driver of its military strategy in the Asia–Pacific – to deny the USA access to the 'first island chain', and the defence of its near seas through anti-access/area denial (A2/AD) and dominating its neighbours (Erickson 2014: 61). A key element in the success of this strategy is maintaining its territorial claim over Taiwan (Republic of China) and achieving (re)unification, if necessary by force. In its 2013 Defence White Paper, the government of the People's Republic of China stated that 'the "Taiwan independence" separatist forces and their activities are still the biggest threat to the peaceful development of cross-Strait relations' (Information Office of the State Council 2013).

Taiwan remains the heart of Beijing's geopolitical concerns for two reasons. First, under its constitution, the democratically elected Taiwanese government does not recognize the legitimacy of the CCP, and second, Taipei rejects Beijing's sovereignty claims to Taiwanese territory (Easton 2013: 4). The CCP thus pursues a two-fold strategy to compel Taiwan's leaders to move towards accommodation with Beijing, namely retaining elements of its economic independence and political autonomy for a prolonged period of time in return for accepting Chinese sovereignty. In order to do so it employs an approach introduced under the leadership of former President Hu Jintao: Beijing provides preferential economic agreements to increase integration between the two sides of the Strait, while at the same time it creates a dominant military balance in China's favour to deter Taiwan from declaring *de jure* independence (Chen 2014: 3).

In recent years, China's increased assertiveness over its maritime claims in the East and South China Seas, and the election of Kuomintang (KMT) President Ma Ying-Jeou, has implied for many observers the greater likelihood of a solution to the Taiwan problem (Li 2014: 119; Wang 2010). However, the success of Beijing's policies remains at the mercy of Taiwan's changing demographics and electoral system – it has de facto sovereignty, a democratic political system, and a populace that increasingly identifies itself as purely

Taiwanese. China's two-fold strategy towards achieving (re)unification under the 'one country, two systems' framework thus could ultimately fail as it has two inherently contradictory pillars. On the one hand it is threatening invasion, and on the other it is promoting friendly political and economic policies.

This chapter first reviews the cross-Strait military balance and whether the People's Liberation Army (PLA) could meet its military objectives to achieve (re)unification. It places this in context of Beijing's broader geostrategic objectives in East Asia, and its military strategy of denying the USA access to the first island chain and the defence of its near seas. Second, it examines the preferential economic agreements between China and Taiwan, and the successes and failures of creating a congenial atmosphere for political (re)unification. Third, it examines the divergent domestic political situations in China and Taiwan – Chinese nationalism is rising, yet on the other side of the Strait Taiwanese people increasingly identify themselves as being purely Taiwanese, and the desire to maintain the status quo is also rising. The chapter concludes with an assessment of China's strategy towards Taiwan, whether (re)unification will be achieved in the near future and what might happen if this is not achieved through peaceful means.

The military balance

China's strategic objectives in East Asia serve to secure the CCP's political legitimacy on territorial issues. Taiwan is critical to these objectives – not only does it serve as a precedent for other regions such as Tibet, Xinjiang and Inner Mongolia, its strategic geography means that China would lose control of its portal to the Western Pacific (Nathan and Scobell 2012: 152). Politically, with the return of Macau and Hong Kong to Chinese control, it would be very hard for Beijing to explain to its citizens why Taiwan should be left out. Any mainland Chinese government could not survive should Taiwan achieve *de jure* independence (Wu 1998: 131). The CCP maintains its policy of (re)unification, by force if necessary, and Beijing insists that the only peaceful solution for the Taiwan dispute is (re)unification under the 'one country, two systems' framework.

Beijing argues that the credible threat of the use of force is essential to maintaining the political conditions for political progress, and preventing Taiwan from making moves towards *de jure* independence (Ministry of National Defense, People's Republic of China 2011: Section 1). Moreover, it claims that it will not use force as long as it believes that (re)unification in the long term remains possible and the cost of conflict outweighs the benefits. Yet China has warned that there are circumstances under which it would use force against Taiwan. These include the formal declaration of Taiwanese independence; undefined moves towards Taiwanese independence; internal unrest in Taiwan; Taiwan's acquisition of nuclear weapons; indefinite delays in the resumption of cross-Strait dialogue on (re)unification; foreign intervention in Taiwan's internal affairs; and foreign forces stationed in Taiwan (US Department of Defense 2013: 53). This is reiterated in Article 8 of the March 2005 Anti-Secession Law which states that China may use 'non-peaceful means [if] secessionist forces … cause the fact of Taiwan's secession from China', 'if major incidents entailing Taiwan's secession occur', and if 'possibilities for peaceful unification are exhausted' (National People's Congress 2005).

To this end, the primary focus of PLA force planning, operational concepts, and military modernization – in particular, naval power – remains on developing options for a Taiwan contingency (IISS 2014: 201). Since the early 2000s the PLA has been developing capabilities to execute its A2/AD strategy, namely the ability to deter a US intervention in a conflict involving Taiwan, or failing that, delay the arrival or reduce the effectiveness of intervening

US naval and air forces (O'Rourke 2013: 1). The 1995/96 Taiwan Strait Crisis was a critical incident in the long-term shift towards this strategy. Not only did it demonstrate Washington's resolve to Beijing – the USA deployed two carrier battle groups to the Strait, the largest deployment to East Asia since the Vietnam War – but also that the PLA's bellicose posture could not contribute to achieving (re)unification objectives (Scobell 2000: 227). China's current A2/AD strategy thus stems from two overlapping objectives: first, to achieve (re)unification without direct confrontation and conflict, and second to tilt the cross-Strait military balance overwhelmingly in the PLA's favour to compel Taiwan to abandon independence, and deter any US support or intervention in the Strait. Moreover, these capabilities are being increasingly oriented towards pursuing broader operational goals in the Asia-Pacific region such as dominating the near seas of the East and South China Seas so as to assert its maritime claims, and protecting its sea lines of communications (US Department of Defense 2013: 27).

The military balance continues to tilt in the PLA's favour, eroding Taiwan's deterrent capabilities and increasing Beijing's options to achieve its objectives in the Taiwan Strait (Lee and Schreer 2013: 56). In March 2014 Beijing announced a 12.2 per cent increase in its military budget to US $132,000m., continuing more than two decades of double-digit increases in annual defence spending (Wong 2014). Significantly, it is very likely that China will have the fiscal strength and political will to support such defence-spending growth at comparable levels, and thus its military modernization, for the foreseeable future (US Department of Defense 2013: 43). In contrast, Taiwan's defence budget fell to an all-time low of approximately 2 per cent of gross domestic product in 2014 – well below Taipei's bipartisan goal of budgeting at 3 per cent (Kan 2014: 1). Moreover, Taiwan's defence expenditure is strained by its dual imperatives of military reform – including the establishment of all-volunteer armed forces by 2017 – and major procurement programmes (Phipps 2013).

In line with its objectives, China's modernization has encompassed a broad range of weapon acquisition programmes, such as anti-ship ballistic missiles, anti-ship and land attack cruise missiles, nuclear submarines, modern surface combatants, and its first aircraft carrier (US Department of Defense 2013: 27). These capabilities are being developed to threaten key US military assets, in particular aircraft carriers and naval battle groups, and to incapacitate critical US information systems (Ball 2012: 3). For instance, China's 'carrier killer', the DF-21D anti-ship ballistic missile, has a range of over 1500 km, is armed with a manoeuvrable warhead, and could enable the PLA to attack large US surface combatants, including aircraft carriers (O'Rourke 2013: 5). This rapid and substantial military modernization has reduced Taiwan's previous military advantages. While the Taiwanese armed forces are well-trained and operate some advanced technology, their relatively small size, lack of combat experience and ageing equipment, such as the F-16A/B fighter jets, has meant that the capacity for such a force to withstand a concerted Chinese offensive is increasingly doubtful (IISS 2014: 280).

Furthermore, Washington's reluctance to supply Taipei with next-generation fighters or the AEGIS combat system – owing to Beijing's objections to such sales, and Washington's desire for Taipei to develop its own defensive capabilities indigenously – is an indication that the military balance will continue to tilt in China's favour. Taiwan's 2013 *National Defense Report* highlighted the impact of the PLA's growing strength on US ability to assist the island should Beijing decide to mount an offensive, with the report stating that by 2020 the PLA could be in a position to invade and occupy Taiwan (Ministry of National Defense, Republic of China 2013b: 66).

Yet despite the PLA's apparent dominance over the Taiwan Strait, it remains questionable whether China could achieve its military objectives of invasion for two key reasons. First, the USA remains superior in advanced technologies, in particular command, control, communications, computers, intelligence, surveillance and reconnaissance (C4ISR) capabilities, and its ingenuity with respect to conceptual innovation is unparalleled. The danger is that Beijing, perhaps persuaded in part by simplistic Western assessments, will underestimate US qualitative strengths to the point of over-confidence in its denial capabilities and initiate a military conflict (Ball 2012: 4). Second, its strategic objectives remain at odds with its economic policies to develop mutual trust. While cross-Strait economic interaction has intensified since the mid-1990s, strategic relations between Beijing and Taipei have remained strained, making political détente elusive. Taiwan's 2013 Quadrennial Defense Review is critical of the relationship, stating that greater economic interaction has not led to mutual trust (Ministry of National Defense, Republic of China 2013a: 31).

Preferential economics

The use of preferential trade and economic agreements as a means of building mutual trust and promote understanding of the 'one country, two systems' framework has resulted in a series of measures. These agreements stem from the belief that economic integration between countries generates spillover effects, in this instance, creating a congenial atmosphere for resolving Taiwan's political status and relaxing tensions across the Strait (Chao 2003: 281). Bilateral trade between China and Taiwan flourished in the 1990s and 2000s, increasing from US $3,800m. in 1987 to $14,500m. in 1992, $30,000m. in 2000, $90,000m. in 2006, $105,000m. in 2008, and $197,000m. in 2013 (Ministry of Commerce, People's Republic of China 2014). This active promotion of cross-Strait commercial expansion as part of an 'embedded reunification strategy' began under the leadership of Deng Xiaoping who emphasized mutual culture and economic gain while utilizing Taiwan's growing economic dependence on the Chinese economy as a liability for Taiwan's security and autonomy (Dent 2005: 400).

Two types of economic agreements characterize Beijing's approach – on the one hand experimental projects with (re)unification, such as the proposed 'joint' development of the Pingtan Comprehensive Experimental Zone; and on the other hand encouraging long-term commercial engagement as a bedrock for political integration, such as the Economic Cooperation Framework Agreement (ECFA). These agreements are intended not only to help to isolate Taiwan on the international stage, but also to increase Taiwan's dependence on China's economy with the prospect that this will lead to political negotiations on (re)unification (Chao 2003: 293).

First, Beijing has often unilaterally implemented measures (which it calls joint ventures) in order to experiment with ways of imposing its 'one country, two systems' framework on Taiwan. Under this framework, Taiwan, similarly to Hong Kong and Macau, would become a special administrative zone subordinate to the central government in Beijing, but its socio-economic system would remain unchanged (Central People's Government of the People's Republic of China 2000). The most recent example is Beijing's plan to develop Pingtan Island – the closest Chinese territory to Taiwan – into a special economic zone of industrial cooperation between China and Taiwan. Under its Five Joint Implementation Regulations, Beijing claims that it will be 'jointly planned, jointly developed, jointly managed and jointly profiting', and it has earmarked US $40,000m. under its 12th Five Year Development Plan to attract Taiwanese talent and investment (Soong 2012). It rolled out numerous policies to encourage Taiwanese citizens to move to the island, including the possibility of serving in the island's local government, driving Taiwan-licenced cars, gaining tax incentives, and the simultaneous circulation of Taiwanese and Chinese currencies (WantChinaTimes 2012).

The project was rejected by Taiwan's Mainland Affairs Council, which stated that the 'Mainland has over-interpreted the concept of "joint planning" which is not the overall policy position of Taiwan' (Mainland Affairs Council 2012). Moreover, since the Pingtan island project has been promoted through the Fujian provincial government, Taiwan's participation would be perceived as cooperation between two local governments and the tacit recognition of China's claim to Taiwan (Chang and Wang 2012). Thus, despite the preferential economic treatment proposed, the project was rejected due to its underlying political motives, namely how to integrate a capitalist economic system into a centralized political state where power is focused in Beijing.

The second type of preferential treatment concerns agreements designed to create long-term economic interdependence to facilitate political integration. A pertinent example of this was the landmark June 2010 signing of the ECFA, which consolidated the previous decade of economic normalization and paved the way for further integration (Rosen and Wang 2010: 2). For Taiwan, the agreement has proved to be the best short-term option for reviving its stagnant economy, while in the long term the ECFA favours China's political intentions (Chiang 2011: 683). For Taiwan's export-driven manufacturing economy, the high exports to China facilitated by the ECFA have meant that Taiwan maintains its trade surplus and increases its foreign exchange reserves (ibid.: 690; Liu and Shih 2013). For China, this has created an asymmetric dependence on Taiwan's investment in the mainland in order to sustain its economic development. Since 2008, while Beijing has allowed Taiwan to participate in more non-government organizations and international forums for which statehood is not a requirement, it continues to restrict Taiwan's international space (Chen 2014: 25). By stifling Taiwan's participation in international organizations – particularly the World Trade Organization – yet simultaneously increasing privileges to encourage the Taiwanese to do business on the mainland, such as the Pingtan economic zone, Beijing's promotion of cross-Strait commercial expansion is a vital component of its 'embedded (re)unification' strategy.

However, China's economic leverage has still not translated into political influence, let alone become sufficient to have an impact on the question of (re)unification. On 18 March 2014, following two days of protests against the successor to the ECFA – the Cross-Strait Services Trade Agreement (CSSTA), which opened up various sectors for investment and preferential treatment including, commerce, telecommunications and health – a group of students from the Black Island Youth Alliance stormed the Legislative Yuan (LY) (Cole 2014). In the ensuing days tens of thousands of activists known as the student Sunflower Movement joined together to stage a sit-in at the legislature buildings, accusing President Ma of intransigence and bypassing democratic procedure, and demanding that the KMT not only commit anew to a full clause-by-clause review at the LY but also establish and institutionalize a legal mechanism to monitor the CSSTA and any future agreements with China (ibid.).

Although there was a practical and economic component to the movement, it was predicated on maintaining democratic processes and a public fear of mainland China. The negotiated end of the sit-in – when President Ma's cabinet approved a bill for monitoring such pacts with China, but still did not agree to enacting it for the CSSTA – was a further sign of Taiwan's consolidated democracy (The Economist 2014). The movement also marked the first time that Taiwan's legislature had been occupied by its citizens, further demonstrating the Taiwanese people's awareness that China's use of economic policies to enforce dependence on the mainland was designed to bring about eventual (re)unification. Despite this, China's attempts to demonstrate the benefits of (re)unification via preferential economics therefore remain not only at the mercy of Taipei's strategic concerns but also Taiwan's democratic electoral cycle and changing demographics.

Domestic constraints

Arguably, the success of China to achieve (re)unification ultimately will depend on Taiwan's socio-political conditions. Not only is it far from clear that the economic and strategic pillars of Beijing's Taiwan policy are effective, but also converting Taiwanese nationalism to Chinese nationalism would be no easy matter due to two conflicting trends. First, China's rising nationalism over its political and economic power is an indication that it will not remain content with the status quo. The CCP's reliance on nationalism to legitimize its current rule – as well as the retrocessions of Macau and Hong Kong – have increased the political stakes of achieving (re)unification (Dittmer 2006: 671). Chinese political and intellectual elites place a high value on (re)unification, more so than the Taiwanese (Pei 2002). In the run-up to the 18th National Congress of the CCP in November 2012, the Taiwan Affairs Office Minister, Wang Yi, in an interview with *Xinhua* newspaper, linked the Taiwan issue to both nationalistic sentiments and China's rising power, stating that (re)unification was a 'major historic mission' for the CCP as it had a 'great bearing on national sovereignty and territorial integrity, as well as the prospects and destiny of the Chinese nation'. He added that the CCP is 'duty-bound to shoulder and fulfil this historic responsibility and should strongly oppose and resist acts of "Taiwanese independence" in all their forms' and that 'the mainland's comprehensive strength and rising international status are sure to have a deep impact on and determine the development of cross-Strait relations' (Deng 2012).

Any Chinese leader who permits the recognition of Taiwan as an independent sovereign state would find it impossible to stay in power, because it would also weaken China's other territorial claims, from Tibet and Xinjiang to the East and South China Seas (Saunders 2005: 978). The promotion of nationalism is a key mechanism used by the CCP to ensure regime survival, and as a result the territorial integrity of China also determines the political survival of individual Chinese leaders. Consequently, the stronger the rise of Chinese nationalism in domestic politics, the less scope its leaders have when confronting perceived hostile actions against the Chinese nation, such as the declaration of Taiwanese independence. The current Chinese leadership under President Xi Jinping has hinted that Beijing will push for a cross-Strait political solution within the next 10 years. In October 2013, ahead of the Asia-Pacific Economic Cooperation summit in Bali, President Xi told the Taiwanese envoy, Vincent Siew, 'looking further ahead, the issue of political disagreements that exist between the two sides must reach a final resolution, step by step, and these issues cannot be passed on from generation to generation' (Dua 2013). Moreover, Beijing's rhetoric under President Xi has shifted from 'economy first, politics next' to 'comprehensive development', thus signalling that the CCP will attempt to take on more political issues (Chen 2012).

However, this is at odds with the second trend that is emerging in Taiwan, namely the increasing tendency for citizens to identify themselves as purely Taiwanese, as well as a rising desire to maintain the current status quo. In polls conducted in 2014 by the Election Study Center, National Chengchi University Taiwan, 59.1 per cent of respondents identified themselves as being purely Taiwanese, compared to a decreasing number who identified themselves as being both Taiwanese and Chinese (35.8 per cent), and those who identified themselves as Chinese (3.8 per cent) (Election Study Center 2014a). On the issue of (re) unification, an increasing number of respondents preferred to maintain the status quo and allow the matter to be resolved at a later date (32.6 per cent), while 26.3 per cent preferred to maintain the status quo indefinitely. By comparison, 17.2 per cent of respondents would like to maintain the status quo but move towards independence, 9.3 per cent would move towards unification, 4.9 per cent would like independence as soon as possible, and 1.9 per cent would like unification as soon as possible (Election Study Center 2014b). The preferences of Taiwanese citizens indicate that the longer the status quo is maintained, the more the proportion of those who identify themselves as being purely Taiwanese will increase, and as Taiwan's democracy continues to consolidate, so will its desire to remain politically independent.

Furthermore, President Ma's approval rating has dropped from a peak of 68 per cent at the beginning of his second term in 2012 to an extreme low of 9 per cent by September 2013 (Era Survey Research Center 2013). This means that the last two years of Ma's final presidential term offer not only a small window of opportunity for Beijing to promote (re)unification and initiate closer ties with a friendly government, but also they limit how much Ma can offer Beijing in enhanced cross-Strait relations due to a now hostile legislature, particularly after the fallout over the CSSTA. The recently formed Sunflower Movement has awakened Taiwanese fears of the mainland as well as affected the reputation of President Ma's administration with most probable negative consequences for the KMT in the 'seven-in-one' local elections in November 2014, and for the presidential and legislative elections in 2016 (Cole 2014). President Ma's decreasing popularity and the increase in public concern about policies perceived to increase Chinese leverage over Taiwan suggest that many Taiwanese people remain suspicious of the mainland despite the preferential treatment that Beijing hopes will woo the hearts and minds of Taiwanese citizens.

Taiwan's domestic politics are a significant structural factor that will influence both the success of China's strategy regarding Taiwan, as well as the future of cross-Strait relations. Compounded to this, Xi Jinping's major preoccupation since taking leadership of the CCP in 2012 has been domestic, mainly the curbing of rampant official corruption and the pursuit of bolder economic reforms and restructuring (Chen 2014: 29). Inevitably, Beijing is caught between a rock and a hard place: the longer it lets the status quo continue, the harder it will be to enforce (re)unification. Not only will it have to deal with an increasingly wary Taiwanese population with a consolidated democracy, but also any unprovoked attack of the island would have enormous ramifications for Beijing's international image, particularly its relations with Washington, and would increase the stakes in the East and South China Seas.

Conclusion

China's strategy of achieving (re)unification with Taiwan through the 'one country, two systems' framework is likely to fail because it is based on two conflicting pillars. On the one hand, since the 2000s the PLA has created a military balance in the Taiwan Strait overwhelmingly in its favour to prevent Taiwan from making moves towards *de jure* independence, as well as to deter any US intervention. On the other hand Beijing uses economic policies as a concerted campaign to attempt to win the hearts and minds of the Taiwanese people through preferential access to its markets. However, the simultaneous development of China's A2/AD capabilities and cross-Strait commercial expansion as part of an 'embedded (re)unification' strategy has only made the Taiwanese public wary of increasing dependence on the mainland which could translate into Beijing's political leverage over Taipei. Only one military course of action guarantees China control of Taiwan: a successful invasion and occupation of the island. However, politically this would come at enormous cost to its international image and converting Taiwanese nationalism to Chinese nationalism after such a move would be no easy matter.

Should the Chinese leadership consider these costs too high, it would be left with only one 'peaceful' course of action: to wait until the political and economic conditions are such that the (re)unification of Taiwan with China would seem to be a natural course of action. However, the longer Beijing waits and the status quo is prolonged, the greater the likelihood that Taiwan's democracy continues to consolidate and its citizens identify themselves as being purely Taiwanese, thereby making (re)unification an increasingly unpopular choice. China's strategy of (re)unification is thus constrained by Taiwan's domestic politics and changing demographics, and inevitably if it cannot bring Taiwan under Chinese sovereignty, it weakens claims from Xinjiang and Tibet to the East and South China Sea. However, given that China's leaders have repeatedly stated that maintaining the cross-Strait status quo is unacceptable this creates a volatile situation. This chapter has demonstrated that economic integration has not been sufficient in promoting political conciliation and the threat of force is increasingly being used to pressure Taipei, thus questioning the CCP's ability to achieve (re)unification through peaceful means.

Bibliography

Ball, Desmond, 'Northeast Asia: Tensions and Action-Reaction Dynamics', Working Paper, International Institute for Strategic Studies-Asia, 25 January 2012.

Central People's Government of the People's Republic of China, *The One-China Principle and the Taiwan Issue*, February 2000, www.gov.cn/misc/2005-10/24/content_82571.htm.

Chang, Rich and Chris Wang, 'Pingtan "Somewhat" Political: Spy Chief', *Taipei Times*, 27 March 2012, www.taipeitimes.com/News/front/archives/2012/03/27/2003528795/1.

Chao, Chien-Min, 'Will Economic Integration Between Mainland China and Taiwan Lead to a Congenial Political Culture', *Asian Survey*, Vol. 43, No. 2, March/April 2003.

Chen, Dean P., 'Constructing Peaceful Development: The Changing Interpretations of "One China" and Beijing's Taiwan Strait Policy', *Asian Security*, Vol. 10, No. 1, March 2014.

Chen, Joan, 'Taiwan Examines Obama's Re-election and China's New Leadership', *Taiwan Insights*, 19 November 2012, www.taiwaninsights.com/2012/11/19/positive-taipei-washington-relations-set-to-continue/.

Chiang, Min-Hua, 'Cross-Strait Economic Integration in the Regional Political Economy', *International Journal of China Studies*, Vol. 2, No. 3, December 2011.

Cole, J. Michael, 'Sunflowers in Springtime: Taiwan's Crisis and the End of an Era in Cross-Strait Cooperation', *China Brief*, The Jamestown Foundation, Vol. 14, No. 7, April 2014, www.jamestown.org/single/?tx_ttnews%5Btt_news%5D=42209&tx_ttnews%5BbackPid%5D=381&cHash=1d998e2d82c86b4c0c3eabadfd34450c#.U1ZkM-aSw00.

Deng, Shasha, 'Mainland Official Voices Determination to Realize National Reunification', *Xinhua*, 23 October 2012, http://news.xinhuanet.com/english/china/2012-10/23/c_131925228.htm.

Dent, Christopher M., 'Taiwan and the New Regional Political Economy of East Asia', *China Quarterly*, Vol. 182, June 2005.

Dittmer, Lowell, 'Taiwan as a Factor in China's Quest for National Identity', *Journal of Contemporary China*, Vol. 15, No. 49, November 2006.

Dua, Nusa, 'China's Xi Says Political Solution for Taiwan Can't Wait Forever', *Reuters*, 6 October 2013, www.reuters.com/article/2013/10/06/us-asia-apec-china-taiwan-idUSBRE99503Q20131006.

Easton, Ian, *China's Military Strategy in the Asia-Pacific: Implications for Regional Stability*, Washington, DC: Project 2049 Institute, 26 September 2013.

Election Study Center, *Trends in Core Political Attitudes Among Taiwanese*, Taipei: National Chengchi University, 12 February 2014a, http://esc.nccu.edu.tw/course/news.php?Sn=167#.

Election Study Center, *Taiwan Independence vs. Unification with the Mainland Trend Distribution in Taiwan*, Taipei: National Chengchi University, 12 February 2014b.

Era Survey Research Center, 'Popular Opinion Poll on whether Wang Jinping Should Be Removed from the Kuomintang Party', Era Survey Research Center, 13–14 September 2013, http://survey.era com.com.tw/item/i24.xml.

Erickson, Andrew S., 'China's Near-Seas Challenge', *National Interest*, Vol. 129, January/February 2014.

Information Office of the State Council, People's Republic of China, *Defence White Paper 2013*, 2013, www.sldinfo.com/wp-content/uploads/2013/04/Chinese-Military-White-Paper-April-2013.pdf.

International Institute for Strategic Studies (IISS), *The Military Balance 2014*, London: IISS and Routledge, 2014.

Kan, Shirley A., *Taiwan: Major U.S. Arms Sales Since 1990*, Washington, DC: Congressional Research Service Report, RL30957, March 2014.

Lee, Sheryn and Benjamin Schreer, 'Taiwan Strait: Still Dangerous', *Survival*, Vol. 55, No. 3, 2013.

Li, Yitan, 'Constructing Peace in the Taiwan Strait: a Constructivist Analysis of the Changing Dynamics of Identities and Nationalisms', *Journal of Contemporary China*, Vol. 23, No. 85, June/July 2014.

Liu, Da-Nien and Shih Hui-Tzu, 'The Transformation of Taiwan's Status Within the Production and Supply Chain in Asia', *Brookings Series: Taiwan-U.S. Quarterly Analysis*, Brookings Institution, No. 13, December 2013, www.brookings.edu/research/opinions/2013/12/04-taiwan-production-supply-chain.

Mainland Affairs Council, 'Mainland Policy and Work: March 15, 2012', *Cross-Strait Exchanges*, Mainland Affairs Council, Republic of China (Taiwan), 2012, www.mac.gov.tw/ct.asp?xItem=102566&ctNode=6607&mp=3.

Ministry of Commerce, People's Republic of China, 'Regional Trade Statistics: Statistics of Mainland-Taiwan Trade and Investment', Beijing, 2014, http://english.mofcom.gov.cn/article/statistic/lanmubb/.

Ministry of National Defense, People's Republic of China, *China's National Defense 2010*, Beijing, 2011, http://eng.mod.gov.cn/Database/WhitePapers/2010.htm.

Ministry of National Defense, People's Republic of China, *The Diversified Employment of China's Armed Forces*, White Paper 2012, http://eng.mod.gov.cn/Database/WhitePapers/2012.htm.

Ministry of National Defense, Republic of China, *2013 Quadrennial Defense Review*, Taipei, March 2013a.

Ministry of National Defense, Republic of China, *National Defense Review 2013*, Taipei, October 2013b.

Nathan, Andrew J. and Andrew Scobell, *China's Search for Security*, New York: Columbia University Press, 2012.

National People's Congress, People's Republic of China, *Anti-Secession Law*, Third Session of the Tenth National People's Congress, Beijing, 14 March 2005, http://english.peopledaily.com.cn/200503/14/eng20050314_176746.html..

O'Rourke, Ronald, *China's Naval Modernization: Implications for U.S. Navy Capabilites – Background and Issues for Congress*, Washington, DC: Congressional Research Service Report, RL33153, 30 September 2013.

Pei, Minxin, 'Domestic Politics and China's Taiwan Policy', paper for the Carnegie Endowment, 9 October 2002, http://carnegieendowment.org/files/pei_paper_100902.pdf.

Phipps, Gavin, 'Taiwan Postpones Plans for All-professional Force', 18 September 2013, www.janes.com/article/27203/taiwan-postpones-plans-for-all-professional-force.

Rapp-Hooper, Mira, 'Strength or Strategy in the Taiwan Strait?', *National Interest*, 26 October 2013, http://nationalinterest.org/commentary/strength-or-strategy-the-taiwan-strait-9310.

Rosen, Daniel H. and Wang Zhi, 'Deepening China-Taiwan Relations Through the Economic Cooperation Framework Agreement', No. PB10-16, Policy Brief, Peterson Institute for International Economics, 2010, www.piie.com/publications/pb/pb10-16.pdf.

Saunders, Phillip, C., 'Long-Term Trends in China-Taiwan Relations: Implications for US Taiwan Policy', *Asian Survey*, Vol. 45, No. 6, November/December 2005.

Scobell, Andrew, 'Show of Force: Chinese Soldiers, Statesmen and the 1995–1996 Taiwan Strait Crisis', *Political Science Quarterly*, Vol. 115, No. 2, Summer 2000.

Soong, Grace, 'Gov't Rules Out Joint Pingtan Development', *China Post*, 16 March 2012, www.chinapost.com.tw/taiwan/china-taiwan-relations/2012/03/16/334800/Govt-rules.htm.

Sutter, Robert, 'China's Good Neighbour Policy and its Implications for Taiwan', *Journal of Contemporary China*, Vol. 13, No. 41, 2004.

The Economist, 'Politics in Taiwan: Sunflower Sutra', 8 April 2014, www.economist.com/blogs/banyan/2014/04/politics-taiwan.

US Department of Defense, *Annual Report to Congress [on] Military and Security Developments Involving the People's Republic of China 2014*, Washington, DC: Office of the Secretary Defense, June 2013.

Wang, Yuan-kuang, 'China's Growing Strength, Taiwan's Diminishing Options', *Brookings Series: Taiwan-U.S. Quarterly Options*, Brookings Institution, No. 4, November 2010, www.brookings.edu/research/papers/2010/11/china-taiwan-wang.

WantChinaTimes, 'Taiwan Should Not Sweep Pingtan Under the Carpet', 23 March 2012, www.wantchinatimes.com/news-subclass-cnt.aspx?id=20120323000013&cid=1701.

Wong, Edward, 'China Announces 12.2% Increase in Military Budget', *New York Times*, 5 March 2014, www.nytimes.com/2014/03/06/world/asia/china-military-budget.html?_r=0.

Wu, Xinbo, 'China: Security Practice of a Modernizing and Ascending Power' in Muthiah Alagappa (ed.), *Asian Security Practice*, Stanford, CA: Stanford University Press, 1998.

12
Taiwan's defence options

Benjamin Schreer

The key goal of Taiwan's (Republic of China) defence policy is to prevent the People's Republic of China – with the support of the USA – from attempting to use military force to enforce unification on Beijing's terms. Should such a strategy of deterrence fail, Taiwan's armed forces would need to be in a position to prevent a Chinese invasion. Previously, Taiwan relied on a number of military factors to deter Chinese aggression. These included the People's Liberation Army's (PLA) inability to project sufficient power across the 100-mile Taiwan Strait; the Taiwanese forces' technological superiority; the inherent geographic advantages of island defence; and the high likelihood of US intervention in the event of an unprovoked Chinese attack, based on the Taiwan Relations Act (TRA) of 1979.

However, Taiwan's geographic location aside, these favourable conditions have been eroding or have become more questionable. Taiwan's Quadrennial Defense Review (QDR) of March 2013 concluded that the PLA was now in a position to 'impose a partial blockade of Taiwan and conduct "A2/AD" operations in certain areas, which can deny US intervention in the Taiwan Strait' (Ministry of National Defense 2013a: 21). Similarly, the 2013 National Defence Report stated that the PLA was 'capable of blockading Taiwan and seizing our offshore islands' (Ministry of National Defense 2013b). These statements point to two interrelated factors that greatly complicate Taiwan's strategic situation, namely the fact that the PLA has changed the cross-Strait military balance, thereby also raising doubts about the US will and ability to come to Taiwan's defence.

To be sure, most of Taiwan's political and military elite have long recognized the need to restructure the Taiwanese armed forces in order to deal with the new external and internal dynamics (Swaine 2005: 135). However, the problems of Taiwan's defence posture are becoming harder to ignore in the face of China's rise. Against this backdrop, this chapter proceeds in three main steps. First, it outlines the internal and external challenges to Taiwan's defence in more detail. The second part discusses Taiwan's defence options, recent developments as well as the remaining obstacles for military modernization. The conclusion provides an assessment of the future of Taiwan's defence policy.

Strategic challenges

Taiwan's current strategic situation is affected by several long-term trends. Externally, China has gradually altered in its favour the military balance across the Taiwan Strait. The days when a numerically smaller Taiwanese defence force enjoyed a qualitative edge over the PLA through a range of offensive and defensive capabilities are over. Moreover, the PLA is steadily increasing the cost of an US intervention in a Taiwan crisis through the development of a sophisticated anti-access/area denial (A2/AD) strategy. Domestically, Taiwan's armed forces face an interrelated set of challenges in the form of declining defence spending, negative demographics, and a relative benign threat perception among large parts of the population.

A changing cross-Strait military balance

China has been working in earnest towards a favourable military balance across the Taiwan Strait since the 1990s. Back then, the PLA's Second Artillery Corps was already starting to deploy conventionally armed ballistic missiles opposite Taiwan. Currently, the US Department of Defense estimates that more than 1,000 short-range ballistic missiles (SRBMs) could target Taiwan. The PLA is also working on new medium-range ballistic missiles (MRBMs) which could strike the island (US Department of Defense 2014: 6). Moreover, the Second Artillery Corps has invested in a large arsenal of ground-launched land attack cruise missiles (LACMs) which would be central to a campaign against Taiwan (Gormley et al. 2014: Chapter 6). These capabilities significantly increase the threat to Taiwan's air combat capability, command and communications centres, as well as airfields. In the event of a Taiwan crisis, they could also be used to target forward deployed US forces.

Other key military areas are also shifting in China's favour. For example, the PLA is estimated to operate about 2,300 combat aircraft capable of large-scale operations; 490 of these aircraft are already based within range of Taiwan. In contrast, the Republic of China Air Force (RoCAF) has only about 410 combat aircraft of which most are ageing (US Department of Defense 2013: 77). As one report has pointed out, 'by 2020, Taiwan's fighters would drop in number by 70% without new [US-made] F-16s, and by 50% with 66 new F-16s' (Kan 2014: 23–24). In other words, in addition to its numerical inferiority the RoCAF has also lost its qualitative advantage over the PLA Air Force (PLAAF).

With regard to China's naval assets, the PLA Navy (PLAN) commands about 75 major surface combatants, 85 missile patrols boats, and at least 60 conventional and nuclear submarines. An increasing proportion of its fleet is being modernized to feature advanced weaponry. In contrast, the Republic of China Navy (RoCN) has only 26 mostly ageing major surface combatants, 45 missile patrol boats and two operational submarines (US Department of Defense 2013: 76). The fleet is largely ill-equipped to conduct effective operations to deny the PLAN control of the waters in the Strait (Holmes and Yoshihara 2010). Finally, the PLAN has also increased its amphibious operations capabilities. While these assets are still insufficient to support a large-scale invasion of Taiwan, they improve its ability to seize and hold Taiwan's offshore islands such as Pratas, Matsu or Kinmen (US Department of Defense 2014: 55).

As a consequence, the US–China Economic and Security Review Commission concluded in 2013 that Taiwan's 'ability to defend [itself] against China's growing military capability is declining' (US–China Economic and Security Review Commission 2013: 338). Taiwan's strategic predicament could even become worse because the PLA's modernization also increases the costs of a third-party, US intervention in the event of a military conflict. While the long-term strategy behind PLA modernization appears to be to contest US primacy across the Western Pacific (Montgomery 2014), its current efforts are predominantly designed to complicate US operations to support Taiwan. The development of ballistic and cruise missiles to target forward deployed US assets, including carrier strike groups, is the most prominent example of China's 'counter-intervention' strategy (Cliff *et al.* 2007; O'Rourke 2014).

In sum, China has not only shifted the cross-Strait military balance vis-à-vis Taiwan in its favour but has also significantly increased the potential costs of intervention for the USA (Shlapak *et al.* 2009). This could erode the political will of the US government to come to the defence of Taiwan. Some voices in the US strategic community already advocate for Washington to abandon its defence commitment to Taiwan (Glaser 2011: 87) and argue that Taiwan is a lost cause (Mearsheimer 2014). While the current US administration of President Barrack Obama has vowed to adhere to US defence commitments under the TRA (Gienger 2012), China's military build-up certainly complicates US defence planning with regard to the Taiwan Strait.

Domestic challenges

Apart from the fact that the cross-Strait military balance is shifting irrevocably in China's favour, the Taiwanese armed forces face a number of domestic hurdles on the path to modernization. One is significant defence budget pressure. The current President, Ma Ying-jeou, has pledged to spend 3 per cent of Taiwan's gross domestic product (GDP) on defence. However, the reality is one of decline. Indeed, since 1994 – when Taiwan spent 3.8 per cent of GDP and 24.3 per cent of the total budget on defence – defence spending is on an almost continuous downward spiral. In 2014 Taipei only invested about 2.0 per cent of GDP (or 16.2 per cent of overall government spending) on its armed forces, thus setting a new record low (Kan 2014: 34). Rhetoric notwithstanding, the Ma administration appears to be content with this spending level and it is unlikely that the trend will be reversed until at least the end of his presidency in 2016. Instead, Ma focuses on improving cross-Strait relations through political rapprochement and closer economic integration, thereby promoting 'soft power' approaches to deterrence by attempting to gain a moral high ground vis-à-vis the Chinese leadership (*Defense News* 2013).

From a purely domestic perspective this approach makes sense as in recent years the public has become less wary of the threat of a Chinese invasion. Moreover, Taiwan's declining economy has led to an even greater emphasis on addressing the issues of social welfare and a dwindling workforce (Murray 2013). However, assigning a low priority to defence modernization, including through decreased spending, disregards the fact that Beijing has not renounced the use of force to bring about reunification on its own terms. In addition, US official reports and public statements have repeatedly warned that lower spending could jeopardize Taiwan's efforts to modernize its forces and to implement its ambitions for an independent defence capability (US Department of Defense 2013: 59). Indeed, Taiwan's armed forces have long faced the problem of high personnel costs which far exceed the operational expenses and money available for defence acquisitions. Since the Taiwanese armed forces traditionally rely on sophisticated but expensive US defence equipment, this situation has not only limited Taiwan's ability to invest in sufficient indigenous or foreign (mostly US) equipment but has also negatively impacted on military training and readiness levels.

In addition to budget pressures, demographic trends pose serious challenges to that modernization. Since the 1980s Taiwan has experienced an almost steady decline in its birth rate. In 2013 the total fertility rate was 1.07, down from 1.27 in 2012 (Su and Low 2014). This development has not only exacerbated the challenge of a rapidly declining and ageing workforce. In terms of defence policy, it has also complicated recruiting, in turn driving up personnel expenditure. On current projections the future outlook for defence recruitment is grim indeed: while in 2000 the population pool of 18-year-old males for military service stood at 209,547, it is predicted to be about 129,537 in 2020, and only 87,213 in 2028 (Cole 2013). If Taiwan's demographic trend is not reversed, by default the country's armed forces will need to be drastically reduced over the coming decades.

Taiwan's efforts, beginning in 2008 under the 'Jingtsui Program', to transform the largely conscripted military on active duty into an all-volunteer force (AVF) exemplify these domestic hurdles hindering defence reform. The QDR 2013 reiterated the goal to complete the transition to an AFV by the end of 2014. This included the reduction of the active duty Taiwanese armed forces from 275,000 to 215,000 personnel. It is planned that 176,000 of this future force will be volunteers. However, the transition has been more expensive than expected and annual recruitment targets have not been met (Enav 2013). As a result, the Ministry of National Defense had to make budget trade-offs to increase the prospects for attracting high-quality volunteers. Consequently, the defence budget share allocated for personnel increased to over 50 per cent in 2013. This came at the expense of the budget for operations which decreased to about to 22.5 per cent, and for acquisition which declined to approximately 25.9 per cent (Murray 2013). In September 2013 Taiwan announced that the final implementation of the AVF had been deferred to at least 2017 because of recruitment difficulties (Wang 2013).

Taiwan's military options

In the face of these external and domestic factors shaping Taiwan's strategic landscape, the Taiwanese armed forces have been obliged to rethink their defence strategy and force posture. Already during the 2000s the strategic debate about how to maintain a credible deterrence strategy vis-à-vis China intensified. Three main points of contention emerged. First, there was an argument about the relative importance of air, naval and ground forces in Taiwan's future force posture. Some opined that Taiwan's armed forces should invest more in capable air and naval forces to defeat the most likely PLA operations against Taiwan such as air and missile attacks, a naval blockade, or an amphibious assault. From this perspective, the ground forces should shrink but become lighter and more mobile to defeat limited PLA operations on Taiwanese soil. This approach was rejected by those who argued for the ongoing need for a sizeable ground force to repel a large invading PLA force (Swaine 2005: 154–155).

Second, the debate about the utility of offensive weapons grew sharper. Some argued that Taiwan needed to acquire offensive conventional counterforce capability against China. This included the development of SRBMs, LACMs, and airborne stand-off attack capabilities to threaten critical military infrastructure on the mainland. From this perspective, shared by a number of US analysts, Taiwanese and US forces should also consider using such forces pre-emptively (Stokes and Schriver 2008). Others argued that such an approach was unrealistic and that Taiwan instead should focus on limited offensive counter-value capabilities to threaten major Chinese cities, including the use of a small number of intermediate-range ballistic missiles or MRBMs.

A third view, also supported by many within the US strategic community, purported that neither offensive capabilities yielded any significant deterrent effect (Swaine 2005: 156). Instead, they argued for a purely defensive strategy and to forego offensive options altogether. For instance, William Murray made the case for a 'porcupine' strategy based on increasing uncertainty in Chinese defence planning through a range of defensive measures, including hardening aircraft shelters, improving runway repair, missile defence systems, and sea mining. In his view, this defensive approach would also put even greater pressure on the USA to come to the defence of Taiwan (Murray 2008). Senior US defence officials also advocated the importance of investing in innovative and asymmetrical capabilities, the development of a smaller, yet more agile force, and to take advantage of Taiwan's geographic island location. In bilateral talks with their Taiwanese counterparts, Pentagon officials also linked future arms sales for the development of such a defence posture (Kan 2014: 4–5).

Towards a Taiwanese A2/AD strategy

From 2009 onwards Taiwanese defence officials and public documents adopted the terms 'innovation' and 'asymmetry' to describe the context of Taiwanese defence modernization. US experts on Taiwan's defence policy pointed out that while it was unlikely that the Taiwanese forces would fully adopt a defensive 'porcupine' strategy they would nevertheless incorporate some of its key elements (Chase 2010: 6–7). This assessment reflects the fact that inter-service rivalries and systemic problems within the Taiwanese defence bureaucracy to make and execute defence policy make a coherent modernization of the armed forces a rather unlikely prospect. Yet, because of the increasing external and internal pressures outlined above, Taiwan's defence strategy partly by design, partly by default had to place greater emphasis on maritime- and air-denial capabilities with the main objective to prevent or delay a PLA amphibious landing while imposing substantial costs on the attacking force. The Taiwanese armed forces have to adopt their own version of an A2/AD strategy against the PLA by exploiting the advantages of defending an island with a small but sophisticated force (Lee and Schreer 2013).

Defence policy documents and a number of procurement decisions taken since 2010 demonstrate that the Taiwanese forces have indeed moved closer to such a strategy by combining elements of a defensive 'porcupine' strategy with limited offensive counterforce capabilities. At the same time, elements of traditional defence thinking prevail. The QDR 2009 is a good case in point. It sets out the ambition to develop 'small but smart' forces based on 'the innovative and asymmetric' concept in order to implement a strategy of 'resolute defense, credible deterrence' (Ministry of National Defense 2009).

The overall operational directive for the Taiwanese forces is to attack 'the enemy at sea'. The key capabilities identified in this context include:

- *Joint Counter Air Capabilities*: the vision is to obtain 'local air superiority in the Taiwan Strait' through (among other things) the acquisition of next-generation combat aircraft, featuring stealth, advanced electronic warfare (EW), and LACMs; long-range missile systems; a robust missile defence capability; enhancement of overall air defence capabilities; as well as enhancing base protection.
- *Joint Sea Control Capabilities*: the aim is to develop 'high quality and efficient, rapid deployment, and long-range strike' capabilities to establish sea control. Apart from enhancing maritime surveillance and early warning capabilities, the QDR formulates the goal to acquire submarines and advanced surface combatants; reinforce airborne anti-submarine (ASW) and mine-warfare; to acquire stand-off precision anti-ship weapons; and to acquire mine hunting vessels.
- *Joint Ground Defense Capabilities*: the goal is to develop a 'three-dimensional, digitized, automated and special operations' ground combat capability to defeat PLA amphibious landing, special operations, and to protect critical infrastructure. Key capabilities include

multiple-launch rocket systems; utility and attack helicopters; beachhead combat capabilities; mobile counterstrike; and a new type of tank.

(Ministry of National Defense 2013a, Chapter 3)

In addition, the QDR 2013 notes the importance of improving joint command, control, communications, computers, intelligence, surveillance and reconnaissance (C4ISR).

The QDR did indeed make progress towards formulating a defensive military strategy based on 'asymmetry' and 'innovation'. This included the announcement that investment would be increased on, for example, mine warfare, ASCMs, mobile rocket launchers, as well as the hardening of bases and improving the speed of runway repairs (Saunders 2014: 4). Some procurement decisions reached since 2010 also support this assessment. US sales of 'defensive weapons' were instrumental in this regard. The administration of US President Barack Obama approved two arms sales packages in 2010 and 2011, worth over US $12,000m. (Hickey 2013: 47). One focus was on strengthening Taiwan's ballistic missile and air-defence systems. The USA agreed to provide the Taiwanese forces with advanced Patriot missiles (PAC-3) which in combination with other missile defence capabilities will significantly enhance the ROC's capability against Chinese ballistic and cruise missiles (Ross 2011).

Washington also sold sophisticated military aircraft optimized for maritime-denial operations to Taiwan. Those included 12 refurbished P-3C Orion maritime patrol aircraft, 30 AH-64E Apache attack helicopter and 60 UH-60M Black Hawk utility helicopter (Minnick 2013b). Furthermore, in addition to three Osprey-class mine hunting ships, the package also comprised Harpoon anti-ship cruise missiles, to be fitted on Taiwan's frigates, combat aircraft and submarines. These systems enhance Taiwan's anti-ship missile capabilities; they also constitute a limited counterforce capability by being able to strike military targets on the Chinese coast (Minnick 2014). The RoCN also took some innovative steps to increase its 'sea denial' capabilities against the PLAN. For instance, it introduced small, indigenously built, twin-hull stealth missile corvettes (Hsun Hai-class) which are equipped with domestically produced Hsuing Feng-2 and Feng-3 supersonic anti-ship cruise missiles. If developed in adequate numbers, this capability could indeed pose serious problems to an advancing Chinese fleet. Taiwan has lost the ability to 'control the seas' and therefore it should focus on 'sea denial' options, including 'dispersing large numbers of small combatants to hardened sites – caves, shelters, fishing ports – around the island's rough coast. Such vessels could sortie to conduct independent operations against enemy shipping. Or, they could mass their firepower in concerted "wolf pack" attacks on major PLAN formations. While Taiwan is no longer mistress of the waters lapping against its shores, "sea denial" lies within its modest means' (Holmes 2012).

Furthermore, Taiwan has invested in a new mobile, land-based, supersonic Hsuing Feng-3 missile which increases its capability to defend against a possible PLA amphibious attack or limited counterforce strikes against military targets on China's coast. It is also reportedly working on a new supersonic offensive surface-to-surface cruise missile with a range of up to 1,200 km, which could be used to strike military targets deeper inside China (Minnick 2013b). Finally, Taiwan's air defence and early warning system has been upgraded under the Po Sheng C4ISR programme. A new, long-range ultra high frequency early warning Surveillance Radar Programme (SRP) located on Loshan Mountain has provided the Taiwanese forces with the capacity to track and monitor ballistic and air-breathing targets inside China, as well as with a limited capability to track Chinese vessels (IISS 2013: 275). However, China

Taiwan's defence options

is reportedly already working on countermeasures to deny Taiwan the ability to use the SRP (Fisher and O'Connor 2014).

Therefore, Taiwan's armed forces have taken steps towards a more asymmetric strategic approach to address the widening capability gap vis-à-vis China. The foundations of a Taiwanese A2/AD capability are emerging. However, obstacles remain for the emergence of a coherent Taiwanese defence strategy which fully embraces and reflects the twin pillars of innovation and asymmetry.

Unresolved challenges

As mentioned above, limited defence spending and the disruptive potential of the AVF for force modernization need to be urgently addressed. Insufficient funding and lack of political commitment could lead to further questions from the USA about Taiwan's seriousness regarding defence reform. In addition, the problems of recruitment and retention are likely to persist, potentially further delaying the arrival of the AVF and 'hollowing out' the force structure. The armed forces would also be unable to invest enough in defence equipment, training and maintenance, with negative implications for readiness levels.

In addition, the military and political leadership need to rectify a conceptual capability gap in Taiwan's defence planning and acquisition. In other words, the armed forces continue to plan some defence capabilities which are either highly unlikely to materialize or which could use up resources for questionable operational rationales. For instance, as mentioned above, the 2013 QDR aims for 'local air superiority' and the acquisition of a 'next-generation' combat aircraft. To be sure, the USA recently agreed to upgrade the RoCAF's ageing F-16s fighters with modern radars (Mehta 2014). The RoCAF also upgraded its Ching-kuo indigenous fighters (IDF/F-CK-1) with a modern standoff air-to-surface missile. However, there is no solution in sight for the future replacement of Taiwan's ageing fleet of combat aircraft. The USA has consistently refused to sell Taiwan a next-generation fighter (such as the F-35 joint strike fighter) or even the modern F-16C/D variant for fear of upsetting its strategic relations with China – a policy which is unlikely to change. However, even if Taiwan was able to acquire a next-generation fighter aircraft this could turn out to be an expensive distraction given that China would very likely be able to overwhelm Taiwan's air combat capability. In other words, Taiwan has to rely critically on US capabilities in an air campaign over the Strait.

The QDR and Taiwanese policymakers also continue to make a case for the acquisition of new submarines given that the RoCN only operates two ageing boats, acquired from the Netherlands in the 1980s (plus two Second World War boats for training purposes). However, while an upgraded diesel-electric submarine capability would make sense in a 'sea denial' strategy, it is difficult to see how this goal could be achieved. Despite having promised the delivery of eight diesel-electric boats in 2001, the USA stopped manufacturing such systems in the 1950s and it is highly unlikely that European suppliers in Germany, France or Sweden will step in. Calls in Taiwan for the indigenous development of a new class of submarines (Phipps 2014) disregards the cost, expertise and time required to build and operate such complex systems – unless the USA finds ways to provide Taiwan with critical support in this area.

It is also noticeable that the 2013 QDR continues to emphasize the operational goal of 'joint sea control' and the acquisition of 'advanced surface combatants'. Recently, the US Congress authorized the sale of four Oliver Hazard Perry-class guided missile frigates; during the 2000s the RoCN also invested in four former US Kidd-class destroyers to strengthen its fleet of major surface combatants. However, as pointed out, 'sea control' seems no longer to be a realistic option and it is not clear in what ways major surface combatants would contribute to a 'sea denial' concept which is still strikingly absent from the 2013 QDR or RoCN doctrine. Finally, the QDR wants a new type of tank for the ground forces, without providing a convincing rationale for such an acquisition (Ministry of National Defense, Republic of China, 2013a).

In sum, a full conceptual shift towards a defensive 'maritime/air denial' strategy has yet to occur across the Taiwanese forces and the broader defence establishment. Instead, the 2013 QDR reflects 'the syndrome where each service needs to get its top acquisition priority included', and fails to address the 'real question [of] how Taiwan should spend its limited defense resources to maximize the effectiveness of its deterrent strategy' (Saunders 2014: 5). Furthermore, while the Taiwanese armed forces have made some progress towards a more asymmetric defence strategy and posture, they are still far from a concerted, joint effort towards greater force integration, improving defence and operational planning, and a systematic strengthening of active and passive defence capabilities. The preoccupation of Taiwan's military with expensive high-end US defence equipment further reduces the available funding for smaller, but nevertheless innovative defence projects. As a consequence, there are serious imbalances in Taiwan's force structure and these may well persist into the future.

Conclusion and outlook

Despite a shifting balance of military power in the Taiwan Strait, Taiwan's defence policy still lacks coherence and sufficient political support. As a result, its defence policy is in limbo. Given the widening capability gap vis-à-vis the PLA, the Taiwanese armed forces cannot hope to achieve the declared goal of an independent defence capability. Instead, if needs be, Taiwan will depend critically on US military support. However, President Ma publicly has ruled out US military deployments to assist Taiwan's self-defence, arguing that his country 'will never ask the Americans to fight for Taiwan' (Kan 2014: 29). While such statements are mostly for the benefit of the public, they could complicate a joint US–Taiwanese military response to PLA action against Taiwan. Given that the PLA's emerging A2/AD capabilities will raise the cost of a US intervention in a Taiwan contingency the Pentagon is likely to expect Taiwan's political and military leadership to invest more systematically in capabilities that can either credibly deter PLA operations or lengthen the US military's response time. Otherwise, the US government could question the seriousness of Taiwan's defence modernization efforts. Worse, the Chinese leadership could feel emboldened by a perceived lack of political will and military capability on the part of Taiwan. If Taiwan's aim is to avoid giving in to future Chinese military coercion it needs to fully address the internal obstacles to military modernization while remaining close to its US strategic partner.

Bibliography

Chase, Michael S., 'The Role of U.S. Arms Sales in Taiwan's Defense Transformation', *China Brief*, Vol. X, March 2010.

Cliff, Roger, Mark Burles, Michael S. Chase, Derek Eaton and Kevin L. Pollpeter, *Entering the Dragon's Lair: Chinese Antiaccess Strategies and Their Implications for the United States*, Santa Monica, CA: RAND, 2007.

Cole, Michael J., 'Taiwan's "All-Volunteer" Military: Vision or Nightmare?', *The Diplomat*, 9 July 2013, http://thediplomat.com/2013/07/taiwans-all-volunteer-military-vision-or-nightmare/1/.

DefenseNews, 'Analyst Urges Dramatic Rethink of Taiwanese Defense Force', 25 January 2013.

Enav, Peter, 'Taiwan Runs Short of Volunteers in Military Shift', *Associated Press*, 13 May 2013, www.apnewsarchive.com/2013/Taiwan_runs_short_of_volunteers_in_military_shift/id-2a8fedd824f9430ebdd30bfc45c4d98d.

Fisher, Richard D. and Sean O'Connor, 'New Chinese Radar May Have Jammed Taiwan's SRP', *Jane's Defence Weekly*, 5 June 2014.

Gienger, Viola, 'Taiwan Weighed for U.S. Jet Sale at Risk of Riling China', *Bloomberg*, 28 April 2012, www.bloomberg.com/news/2012-04-27/u-s-to-consider-sales-of-new-f-16s-to-taiwan-white-house-says.html.

Glaser, Charles, 'Will China's Rise Lead to War? Why Realism Does Not Mean Pessimism', *Foreign Affairs*, Vol. 90, No. 2, March/April 2011.

Gormley, Dennis M., Andrew S. Erickson, and Yuan Jingdong, *A Low-Visibility Force Multiplier: Assessing China's Cruise Missile Ambitions*, Washington, DC: National Defense University Press, 2014.

Hickey, Dennis V., 'Dilemmas for US Strategy: Imbalance in the Taiwan Strait', *Parameters*, Vol. 43, No. 3, Autumn 2013.

Holmes, James, 'Taiwan's Navy Gets Stealthy', *The Diplomat*, 30 April 2012.

Holmes, James and Toshi Yoshihara, 'Taiwan's Navy: Able to Deny Command of the Sea?' *China Brief*, Vol. 10, No. 8, 2010.

International Institute for Strategic Studies (IISS), *The Military Balance 2013*, London: International Institute for Strategic Studies, 2013.

Kan, Shirley A., *Taiwan: Major US Arms Sales Since 1990*, Washington, DC, Congressional Research Service, 3 March 2014, www.fas.org/sgp/crs/weapons/RL30957.pdf.

Lee, Sheryn and Benjamin Schreer, 'The Taiwan Strait: Still Dangerous', *Survival*, Vol. 55, No. 3, June/July 2013.

Mearsheimer, John J., 'Say Goodbye to Taiwan', *National Interest*, March/April 2014.

Mehta, Aaron, 'USAF: Taiwan Will Still Receive F-16 Radar Upgrade', *DefenseNews*, 19 March 2014.

Ministry of National Defense, *Quadrennial Defense Review 2009*, March 2009, www.us-taiwan.org/reports/taiwan_2009_qdr.pdf

Ministry of National Defense, *Quadrennial Defense Review 2013*, March 2013a, http://qdr.mnd.gov.tw/file/2013QDR-en.pdf.

Ministry of National Defense, *2013 National Defence Report*, October 2013b, www.mnd.gov.tw/English/Publish.aspx?cnid=39&p=723.

Minnick, Wendell, 'Taiwan Working on New "Cloud Peak" Missile', *DefenseNews*, 18 January 2013a.

Minnick, Wendell, 'Taiwan to Receive New Aircraft to Repel China', *DefenseNews*, 20 February 2013b.

Minnick, Wendell, 'Taiwan's Sub-launched Harpoons Pose New Challenge to China's Invasion Plans', *DefenseNews*, 6 January 2014.

Montgomery, Evan Braden, 'Contested Primacy in the Western Pacific: China's Rise and the Future of U.S. Power Projection', *International Security*, Vol. 38, No. 4, Spring 2014.

Murray, Craig, 'Taiwan's Declining Defense Spending Could Jeopardize Military Preparedness', US–China Economic and Security Review Commission, Staff Research Backgrounder, Washington, DC, 11 June 2013.

Murray, William S., 'Revisiting Taiwan's Defense Strategy', *Naval War College Review*, Vol. 61, No. 3, Summer 2008.

O'Rourke, Ronald, *China Naval Modernization: Implications for U.S. Navy Capabilities – Background and Issues for Congress*, Washington, DC: Congressional Research Service, 10 April 2014, www.fas.org/sgp/crs/row/RL33153.pdf.

Phipps, Gavin, 'Taiwanese Opposition Party Calls for Submarine Procurement', *Jane's Defence Weekly*, 5 March 2014.

Ross, Ed, 'Taiwan's Ballistic Missile Deterrence and Defense Capabilities', *China Brief*, Vol. 11, No. 3, February 2011.

Saunders, Phillip, 'Defending Taiwan: The QDR and Beyond', *Defense Security Brief*, Vol. 4, No. 1, January 2014.

Shlapak, David A., David T. Orletsky, Toy I. Reid, Murray Scot Tanner and Barry Wilson, *A Question of Balance: Political Context and Military Aspects of the China-Taiwan Dispute*, Santa Monica, CA: RAND, 2009, www.rand.org/content/dam/rand/pubs/monographs/2009/RAND_MG888.pdf.

Stokes, Mark and Randall Schriver, *Evolving Capabilities of the People's Liberation Army: Consequences of Coercive Aerospace Power for United States Conventional Deterrence*, Washington, DC, Project 2049 Institute Report, August 2008.

Su, Justin and Y. F. Low, 'Taiwan's Birth Rate Down 13% in 2013', *Focus Taiwan*, 9 January 2014, http://focustaiwan.tw/news/asoc/201401090009.aspx.

Swaine, Michael D., 'Taiwan's Defense Reform and Military Modernization Program: Objectives, Achievements, and Obstacles', in Nancy Bernkopf Tucker (ed.), *Dangerous Strait: The U.S.-Taiwan-China Crisis*, New York, Columbia University Press, 2005.

US Department of Defense, *Annual Report to Congress: Military and Security Developments Involving the People's Republic of China 2013*, Washington, DC, 2013.

US Department of Defense, *Annual Report to Congress: Military and Security Developments Involving the People's Republic of China 2014*, Washington, DC, 2014.

US–China Economic and Security Review Commission, *2013 Annual Report to Congress*, Washington, DC, November 2013, www.uscc.gov/Annual_Reports/2013-annual-report-congress.

Wang, Chris, 'Date for All-Volunteer Military Delayed', *Taipei Times*, 13 September 2013, www.taipeitimes.com/News/front/archives/2013/09/13/2003572014.

Part 3
Japan, North Korea and South Korea

13
Japan's decline and the consequences for East Asian conflict and cooperation

Christopher W. Hughes

Japan's fortunes in its rise and decline as a great power have always been intimately bound up with the fortunes of conflict and cooperation in the East Asia region. In the late 19th and early 20th centuries, Japan's economic and military rise vis-à-vis China and the imperial Western powers became perhaps the major source of inter-state conflict (Welfield 1988: 1–20; Koshiro 2013: 7–10). During the post-war period Japan's experience of defeat and decline, followed by its rapid rise under the aegis of the USA to become the number two economy in the world and a 'civilian power', were largely a source of stability and helped to restart regional economic cooperation (Maull 1990–91). As the 21st century has progressed, Japanese decline and its ramifications for the East Asia region have again become a source of intense debate domestically and throughout the region.

Japanese policymakers and analysts, and more widely the Japanese public, have shown considerable interest in various 'declinist' theses and the implications for their country's international standing and relations in East Asia. Prior to the 1990s there was considerable Japanese triumphalism about the potential for catching up with the USA economically and there was talk of Japan as the world number one (Vogel 1979; Ishihara 1991), which was followed by concern about the possible effect of the USA's relative decline upon international stability (Akaha 1990). Since the early 2000s and the bursting of the 'bubble' economy this has given way to anxieties about Japan's own relative decline. Japanese concerns have been compounded not only by the fact that Japan has now experienced relative decline compared to the USA, but most importantly because the USA and Japan have both experienced relative decline vis-à-vis China's rise, economically and militarily. Japan's displacement by China as the global number two economic power has been a major blow to national confidence, and this relative power shift has been accompanied by significant bilateral tensions about economic and security ties, and most particularly rival territorial claims in the East China Sea and maritime security competition (Wan 2006: 11–79; Bush 2010). Meanwhile, policymakers and analysts outside Japan in the region and beyond have also speculated about the consequences of Japanese decline, including, inter alia, the impact on the surety of the US security presence in the region, emboldening China's assertion of influence, and the economic integration of South-East Asia and the wider East Asia and Asia-Pacific regions.

Japan's relative decline, therefore, whether real, perceived, or at times a mixture of both, is replete with potential ramifications for regional cooperation and conflict. The objective of this chapter is to assess in more depth the likely impact of Japan's decline by considering a range of changing dimensions of Japanese influence and power, and the mechanics of how these might feed through into opportunities for conflict or cooperation. Specifically, the chapter tests propositions about Japanese decline against the three main International Relations paradigms and perspectives of neo-realism, neo-liberalism and constructivism. These theoretical approaches, even if applied with less than strict orthodoxy and a degree of overlap, do arguably provide insights for judging how decline may be capable of generating possibilities for cooperation or alternatively conflict. Through the use of these approaches it is possible not only to outline different scenarios involving the potential impact of decline, but also to assess the most likely outcomes.

The chapter then moves towards a set of conclusions that partly support a view of Japanese decline as not necessarily tending towards conflict because this may lead to a repurposing of Japan's power for new forms of cooperative relations resulting from domestic institutions that are more predisposed for cooperation, enhanced economic interdependency, and the exercising of 'soft power'. Hence, there is much to be said for the sanguine view of a gentle Japanese decline, and for pointing out that such decline is indeed relative, and that Japan still remains a highly prosperous society capable of functioning as a source of stability for the region. On the other hand, the chapter proposes strong evidence to suggest that conflict is also highly possible, given contentions over the balance of power, economic asymmetries, suboptimal functioning multilateral institutions, and domestic regime legitimacy and instability. Consequently, the chapter tests the more dramatic view of Japan's decline that if left un-arrested it will at the very least lead to renewed Japanese isolation and deprive the region of a key stabilizing democratic and economic influence, and at the very worst pressurize Japan into formulating more erratic and conflicting foreign policies as it seeks to recover its deteriorating economic and security position in the face of a rising China.

Japan's decline, realism and power transitions

The issue of Japan's decline and the potential implications for regional cooperation and conflict are the very substance of realist theorizing. Much of neo-realism analysis is, of course, fundamentally concerned with the issue of power transition in the international system whether this involves hegemonic, great, or major powers (Levy 1987; Väyrynen 1983). Neo-realism's preoccupation with the distribution of capabilities in the international system, and the belief that state interests and security are focused on the desire for relative gains, means that any uneven growth of power among states, including relative rises and declines, is the very driving force of inter-state relations. Neo-realism, and most particularly offensive neo-realism, argue that perceived or real declines in state power can become the trigger for inter-state war, either as states pre-emptively attempt to unseat a dominant power on the wane, or as the dominant state strengthens its alliances to constrain, or even initiate preventive war, to halt the rise of a challenger state (Mearsheimer 2001).

From the perspective of neo-realism, Japan might be a prime candidate for becoming embroiled in a power transition conflict given the evidence of significant declines in its relative power. Japan's own 'comprehensive national power' measured in various metrics compared to that of China appears to be very much on the wane. Japan's gross domestic product (GDP) in 2000 was approximately US $4,700,000m., whereas China's was approximately $1,200,000m.. By 2010 China's GDP had risen to $5,900,000m., surpassing Japan's at $5,500,000m., and thus Japan was relegated to number two economically in the world (Yahuda 2014: 39). Japan's declining economic position is further indicated by problems in its traditionally most globally competitive industries such as consumer electronics, and its perceived slowness to restructure many protected industries such as finance and agriculture. Japan demographic trends, with the population expected to decrease by approximately 1m. per annum due to a falling birth rate and almost zero net immigration, compound the decline of economic scale and dynamism. Japan's public debt now stands at over 200 per cent of GDP, the highest among the Group of Eight major industrialized nations, severely constraining the government's ability to stimulate the domestic economy, and to project national power due to the halving of the Official Development Assistance budget from ¥11,000,000m. in 1997 to ¥6,000,000m. in 2011 (Ministry of Foreign Affairs 2011). Meanwhile, Japan's economic outlook was badly affected by the severe earthquake and tsunami that struck and heavily damaged the Fukushima Daiichi nuclear power plant in March 2011 (the event is also known as 3/11) (Samuels 2013). The catastrophe highlighted Japan's energy vulnerabilities, pushed Japan into rare trade deficits necessitated by increases in imports of fossil fuels, and further undermined Japan's image of technological and economic competence.

Moreover, in another crucial measure of national power – military might – Japan has remained largely constrained. In comparison to China's double-digit defence expenditure increases over the past decade, Japan has maintained its defence spending within its self-imposed limit of 1 per cent of gross national product which has resulted in a largely static budget. In turn, Japanese and international policymakers and analysts have become concerned that the military balance of power has begun to swing away from Japan, thus complicating its efforts to defend its own territory from Chinese incursions, in particular the disputed Senkaku/Diaoyutai Islands, and to maintain freedom of the vital sea lines of communication. China is thought to be gaining the military edge in terms of its procurement of fifth-generation fighter aircraft; blue water naval capabilities, including aircraft carriers; and new destroyers, submarines, and ballistic missiles (Hughes 2012a: 203–205).

Japan's concerns about the erosion of its security position are exacerbated by signs of the decline of its US ally's national power. Although the USA has entered into recovery since the financial crisis of the late 2000s, it is still perceived to have moved backwards in terms of economic influence in the region, to be heavily constrained in its military budget, and to be increasingly wary of the cost of intervening in regional conflicts due to China's growing access denial military capabilities. As a result, the genuine effectiveness of the US 'rebalance' to the region appears questionable (Hughes 2012a: 217–225). As a result, Japanese policymakers fret that the USA, a global superpower with interests that supersede those directed towards Japan, and with a limited ability to manage China's rise other than through diplomacy, may neither fulfil security commitments regarding the Senkaku Islands nor more generally counter China's rising military presence in the region.

Thus, from the perspective of neo-realism, the shifting balance of power in the region sets up a range of scenarios for Japan's response, and has implications for regional security. Japan's prime impulse is clearly to support the US 'rebalance', to reinforce the existing status quo of US hegemony, and Japan's place within this US-led international system. In part this means for Japan to restore its own economy and also to harness its economic efforts more closely with those of the USA in the Trans-Pacific Partnership (TPP) initiative. Even more importantly, from the neo-realist perspective Japan will need to consider military balancing efforts. This will involve the augmentation of Japan's national military capabilities for an element of 'internal balancing' to demonstrate a robust national territorial defence stance, as well as facilitating a broader contribution to the US–Japan military relationship.

Indeed, for the past decade or more, a constant theme of all Japanese administrations, be that the Liberal Democratic Party (LDP) or the Democratic Party of Japan (DPJ), has been to bolster national military capabilities in order to boost bilateral military cooperation (Hughes 2012b). The current LDP administration of Prime Minister Abe Shinzō has emphasized a stronger Japanese Self-Defence Forces (JSDF) posture through the revision of the National Defence Programme Guidelines (NDPG) to establish a Joint Dynamic Defence Force (JDDF) to facilitate a more proactive response to military contingencies in and around Japan's national territory. The NDPG has continued to procure fifth-generation fighter planes, sought to increase Japan's destroyer and submarine fleets, and to create the JSDF's first amphibious force for the defence of outlying islands (Ministry of Defence 2013). The Abe administration has also begun to increase Japan's defence budget for the first time in more than a decade, although with still modest increases of one per cent and 2.6 per cent in 2013 and 2014, respectively. In turn, Abe's government has sought to boost US–Japan bilateral defence ties through projects such as ballistic missile defence and cyber-security; the revision of the US–Japan Defence Guidelines, which outline Japanese logistical and information support for the USA in regional contingences; support for US base realignments in Okinawa Prefecture, mainland Japan, and the wider region; and even Japan's breaching of its self-imposed ban on the exercising of collective self-defence to assist in defensive combat actions in support of the USA.

Japan's efforts to bolster alliance ties may help to restore the balance of power in the region and effectively deter China from potential territorial and maritime provocations that might spark a conflict. Japan's stance arguably remains one of 'defensive realism' whereby it still enjoys the advantages of its geographical island location that presents a defensive barrier, and of incremental increases in defensive weaponry that can still effectively ensure national security (Midford 2011). Nevertheless, neo-realism points to the fact that Japan's efforts to recover its declining power position relative to China are still not without considerable risk of security tensions.

First, Japan and the USA need to be extremely careful to calibrate their security stance vis-à-vis China. If they are seen to 'over-balance' against China and to undermine its basic national ambitions and interests, this may only exacerbate security dilemmas among the three powers. Second, Japan and the USA need to maintain their strong alliance as any potential detachment of respective bilateral interests may enhance concerns about Japanese abandonment. In that case, Japan may find itself having to operate as an autonomous security actor in dealing with the rise of China. This may lead to deeper security dilemmas and the further strengthening of Japan's military capabilities, including turning defensive weaponry to offensive uses, and even the consideration of the need for the acquisition of a nuclear deterrent. The outcome could be a rapidly escalating Sino–Japanese arms race. This might lead to a new equilibrium in security stances and help to stabilize the region, but it could also prove to be highly unpredictable and destabilizing, especially because Japan and China's security interactions are heavily influenced by nationalist sentiment (see below).

Although at present this scenario appears less probable than attempts to restore a stable balance of power, the dynamics that might trigger this situation are not entirely unfeasible given the ongoing shifts in the relative distribution of capabilities between Japan, China and the USA. In addition, the Abe administration, while clearly keen to balance China's

The consequences of Japan's decline

influence through the US–Japan alliance, appears to be hedging its options by strengthening the JSDF's overall capabilities and building common diplomatic and incipient military linkages with other powers in the region such as Australia and the Association of Southeast Asian Nation (ASEAN) states.

Japan's decline and the neo-liberal perspective

Set against neo-realism's tendency to view Japanese decline as posing incipient risks for regional security, neo-liberal institutionalism's assumptions lean towards the sense that power shifts may not be inherently conflictual and might be accompanied by opportunities for enhanced cooperation (Keohane and Nye 1977).

The decline in Japan's power, especially economic decline, vis-à-vis China is occurring without accompanying interactions, which means that this process could not generate absolute gains to improve cooperation rather than just concerns over relative gains. Hence, even as Japan's economy has diminished in size compared to that of China, both states have benefited from increasing bilateral trade and investment relations. Japan's largest overall trading partner since 2007 has been China, and Japan is China's second largest individual national trade partner after the USA. China is second to the USA as the largest national destination for Japanese foreign direct investment (FDI). Japan and China have thus built a considerable relationship of economic interdependency, and the continuous efforts in the past of both sides to avoid bilateral political tensions spilling over to impact on economic ties works in favour of the argument that economic interdependency trumps political issues and can eventually constrain conflictual behaviour.

Similarly, Sino–Japanese economic dynamism and the beneficial impact of driving forward wider regional economic integration is seen as fostering East Asian economic and political institutions that can build cooperation. Japan and China have been key players in promoting the ASEAN Plus Three (APT) and East Asia Summit (EAS), as well as the China–Japan–South Korea Trilateral Cooperation Dialogue (Hook *et al.* 2012: 211–214). Japan's enhanced multilateral interaction and building of confidence with East Asian regional neighbours, even as it slips somewhat economically in standing, should be reinforced by Japan's status as an advanced industrial democracy. Japan's democratic credentials provide surety that it will not easily be provoked into conflict with neighbours due to domestic constituencies' wariness of the costs involved and a general impetus to respect the rule of domestic institutions and international law in conducting foreign relations.

Hence, even as Japan declines economically it may be possible to consider that a 'small' Japan can actually become a more effective regional and cooperative player. Previously, Japan was considered to be a great or even a superpower, but now might be perceived to be a 'middle power', adept at using various forms of 'soft power', and negotiating and promoting a more rules-based multilateral order to enhance regional cooperation, which China might be drawn into (Soeya 2011).

Conversely though, the logic of neo-liberal institutionalism may not argue for an entirely cooperative outlook following Japan's decline. The relative disparities emerging in Sino–Japanese economic relations may give rise to an asymmetric form of interdependence. The consequence is that Japanese policymakers and citizens may feel a new vulnerability in economic ties by being exposed to potential Chinese economic pressure. This type of scenario appeared very real in the aftermath of the 2010 Sino–Japanese dispute over the detention of a Chinese vessel by the Japanese authorities that had made an incursion into the waters surrounding the Senkaku Islands, resulting in China seemingly in protest embargoing the export of rare earths to Japan. Meanwhile, other elements of growing economic interdependence have generated tensions such as Japanese concerns about the lack of Chinese safeguards for intellectual property rights of Japanese technology and safety in food exports. As a result of concerns about possible overdependence on the Chinese market Japan has attempted to diversify its economic ties by reducing FDI in China and seeking alternative investment opportunities in ASEAN member states.

In addition, Japan's interactions with regional multilateral institutions and networks may not promote cooperation. Japanese policymakers have often promoted certain multilateral frameworks in quiet opposition to those preferred by China, in particular the EAS which includes the USA, Australia and India, against the more East Asian-exclusive framework of the APT favoured by China (Yahuda 2014: 82–96). In recent years Japan has invested increasingly in supporting the TPP framework, which is in essence US-led and -designed, in order to establish a set of liberal economic values that differ from the most state-centred model of Chinese development. In this way, multilateralism may not always deliver absolute gains but actually become a vehicle for pursuing more neo-realist-oriented relative gains.

Japan's commitment to forms of regional frameworks that diverge from those supported by China may militate against cooperation, and domestic institutions may also encumber the search for better ties. Japanese domestic political regimes, whether led by the LDP or the DPJ, have been under extreme stress in recent years to attempt to demonstrate their competence and thus legitimacy to govern in the face of economic stagnation and the 3/11 disaster. Japan remains fundamentally democratic, but the fluidity of its political direction, with frequent changes of administration, and now the return to the political mainstream of 'revisionist' conservative politicians such as Abe, have posed questions about how this will impact on regional cooperation (Samuels 2007). Japan's conservative politicians have felt emboldened to attempt to revise interpretations of colonial history, symbolized by their highly controversial visit to the Yasukuni Shrine, and such actions have clearly sparked concerns in China, South Korea, and other East Asian countries of possible Japanese revanchism (Hughes 2008). Hence, there are concerns that although Japan may be democratic now, it is drifting towards a return to nationalism and even militarism.

Meanwhile, Japan's emphasis on its democratic status may actually be a source of contention in the region if it becomes part of an effort to promote certain values that do not yet match the ambitions of other states. Prime Minister Abe's self-proclaimed 'values-oriented' diplomacy, and attempts to encourage collaboration among other regional states on the basis of democracy, human rights, liberal market economy and the rule of law, appears to clash with Chinese values, and thus is seen as a tool to encircle China (Hughes 2009a). In this instance, Japan's wish to emphasize its democratic status as an antidote to its declining economic influence actually becomes a source of potential conflict with China which has yet to even accept domestic pluralism as a basis for international relationships. The lesson, therefore, is that even if Japan portrays itself as a liberal power, it is engaging with a power that is predominantly non-liberal in nature politically, and 'liberal peace theory' would not necessarily view this relationship as one that is bound to be cooperative.

Japanese decline and 'normative constructivism'

Much of the dominant theorizing about Japan's international relations in recent years has focused on constructivist accounts of the strong traction of certain norms on its tendencies towards conflict or cooperation. In particular, Japan's international outlook is thought to have been deeply influenced by norms of anti-militarism derived from defeat in the Pacific

War, the atomic bombings of Hiroshima and Nagasaki, and Article 9 of the Constitution that rejects military power as an efficacious means of achieving national interests in favour of diplomatic and military means (Berger 1993; Katzenstein and Okawara 1993). In certain instances, Japan's normative stance appears to veer towards a stance of outright pacifisim.

Japan's inherently anti-militaristic normative stance should, then, function to avert a conflictual relationship with its neighbours, and continue to function due to the deep-rooted internalization of these norms even as Japan declines and faces potential security issues. Indeed, given that certain analysis has described Japan's security policy as an 'immovable object' even in the face of rising regional security tensions including those from China, it would seem that Japan would always tend towards non-military and peaceful solutions to resolve power struggles in the region (Friman *et al.* 2006). Certainly, many analysts point to the fact that Japan has not reacted in the same way or to the same degree as other powers might to security provocations through active military balancing or even retaliation. Japan's responses, for instance, to North Korean missile tests over Japanese airspace, and to increased Chinese naval activity within its maritime territory, have been highly restrained and appeared to do all possible to avoid military confrontation.

Nevertheless, even as constructivism argues for a Japan that due to anti-militaristic norms will seek to avoid confrontation, and instead seek non-conflictual or actively cooperative means to avert disputes resulting from relative decline, its logic may also indicate the possibility of a more conflictual response to decline. Constructivist theorizing about Japan has indeed tended to see norms as immovable and to focus on a very narrow definition of the norms that matter. The focus has been on 'liberal' or 'positive' norms such as anti-militarism that portray Japan in a cooperative light. However, these norms are not immutable and are capable of being eroded or challenged by others. Anti-militarism remains strong in Japan, but it might be also argued that it is being strongly challenged by norms of historical revisionism and nationalism that should be allowed for in the normative constructivist framework (Berger 2012: 214–229). Surveys of Japanese policymakers' and popular opinion demonstrate growing support for Japan to be more assertive on national defence issues, to enhance security cooperation with the USA, and a strongly declining lack of affinity with China as a regional neighbour (Hughes 2009b). This type of dynamic reformulation of normative attitudes indicates that the default position of constructivism that assumes that Japan will react peacefully to its declining economic status and ongoing security challenges needs constantly to be reassessed.

Conclusion: aggregating neo-realism, neo-liberalism and constructivism and the outlook for Japan's role in regional stability

The prognosis for the quality of Japan's international relations in East Asia remains more open than at any time in the post-war period due to its relative decline in the region. The story for most of this period was of a rising Japan, safely encompassed within strong US hegemony, and a relatively stable balance of power. Japan's predisposition towards a low-profile military and cooperative stance was reinforced by anti-miltiaristic norms, and the beginnings of increased economic interdependency with the region.

During the post-Cold War period the strategic landscape has become far more fluid. In neo-realist terms, the distribution of capabilities is highly uncertain. The USA's need to 'rebalance' is suggestive of relative decline vis-à-vis China, and Japan's own relative economic decline versus China is clear. Japan may be able to compensate for these declines by closer alliance relations with the USA to restore stability, and by strengthening its own defence posture. Geography and defensive weaponry are possibly other factors still on Japan's side to mitigate security tensions resulting from the shifting balance of power. However, at the very least it can be said that in this decade, for the first time in the post-war period, the prospect of military competition, and even conflict, between Japan and China can be talked about as serious possibilities.

Likewise, the evolving international system, in keeping with neo-liberal assumptions, has provided opportunities for cooperation through Japan's role in greater economic interdependence and new multilateral cooperation, which is reinforced by its democratic status. On the other hand, there is evidence in the Sino–Japanese relationship that economic interdependence has not led simply to the generation of absolute gains, but to concerns over relative gains, and this creates problems that are not dissimilar to neo-realist scenarios. Many regional multilateral institutions with which Japan is involved appear to produce only as yet 'stunted regionalism', and Japan's own democratic nature is equally capable of producing more assertive nationalist governments that are inherently set in opposition to the non-democratic regime in China (Rozman 2004). Finally, while normative constructivism might be correct to see Japan holding on to a stubborn anti-militarist or liberal stance in international relations, the challenge from the 'negative' norms of revisionism, nationalism, and even renewed militarism, is not inconsiderable.

Overall, therefore, there are strong grounds for recognizing that Japan's decline is currently compounding the problem of instability in the East Asia region. Conversely, though, it can be argued that there are avenues that Japan can continue to explore in order to avert the possibility of this decline generating any form of conflict. These include making extremely careful adjustments to the US–Japan alliance and national security capabilities so as not to fuel further security dilemmas but rather to create a more meaningful equilibrium in the regional balance of power; continued efforts to foster symmetrical economic interdependency, to restore Japan's economic vitality, and to make regional institutions function better; preventing Japan's changing domestic norms from spiralling into regional conflict; and improving cooperation dynamics.

Bibliography

Akaha, Tsuneo, 'Japan's Security Policy after U.S. Hegemony', in Kathleen Newland (ed.), *The International Relations of Japan*, Basingstoke: Palgrave Macmillan, 1990.

Berger, Thomas U., 'From Sword to Chrysanthemum: Japan's Culture of Anti-militarism', *International Security*, Vol. 17, No. 4, 1993.

Berger, Thomas U., *War Guilt and World Politics After World War II*, Cambridge: Cambridge University Press, 2012.

Bush, Richard C., *The Perils of Proximity: China-Japan Security Relations*, Washington, DC: Brookings Institution, 2010.

Friman, Richard H., Peter J.Katzenstein, DavidLeheny and Nobuo Okawara, 'Immovable Object? Japan's Security Policy in East Asia', in Peter J. Katzenstein and Takashi Shiraishi (eds), *Beyond Japan: The Dynamics of East Asian Regionalism*, Ithaca, NY: Cornell University Press, 2006.

Hook, Glenn D., Julie Gilson, Christopher W. Hughes and Hugo Dobson, *Japan's International Relations: Politics, Economics and Security*, London: Routledge, 2012.

Hughes, Christopher W., 'Japan's Policy Towards China: Domestic Structural Change, Globalization, History and Nationalism', in Christopher M. Dent (ed.), *China, Japan and Regional Leadership in East Asia*, Cheltenham: Edward Elgar, 2008.

Hughes, Christopher W., 'Japan's Response to China's Rise: Regional Engagement, Global Containment, Dangers of Collision', *International Affairs*, Vol. 85, No. 4, July 2009a.

Hughes, Christopher W., *Japan's Remilitarisation*, London: Routledge, 2009b.

Hughes, Christopher W., 'China's Military Modernization: U.S. Partners in Northeast Asia', in Ashley Tellis and Travis Tanner (eds), *Strategic Asia 2012–13: China's Military Challenge*, Seattle, WA: National Bureau of Asian Research, 2012a.

Hughes, Christopher W., 'The Democratic Party of Japan's New (But Failing) Grand Strategy: from Reluctant Realism to Resentful Realism?', *Journal of Japanese Studies*, Vol. 38, No. 1, 2012b.

Ishihara, Shintaro, *The Japan That Can Say No*, New York: Simon & Schuster, 1991.

Katzenstein, Peter J. and Nobuo Okawara, 'Japan's National Security: Structures, Norms, and Policies', *International Security*, Vol. 17, No. 4, 1993.

Keohane, Robert and Joseph Nye, *Power and Interdependence: World Politics in Transition*, Boston, MA: Little, Brown and Co, 1977.

Koshiro, Yukiko, *Imperial Eclipse: Japan's Strategic Thinking About Continental Asia Before August 1945*, Ithaca, NY: Cornell University Press, 2013.

Levy, Jack S., 'Declining Power and the Preventive Motivation for War', *World Politics*, Vol. 40, No. 1, 1987.

Maull, Hans W. 'Japan and Germany: the New Civilian Power', *Foreign Affairs*, Vol. 69, No. 5, 1990–91.

Mearsheimer, John J., *The Tragedy of Great Power Politics*, New York: W. W. Norton and Company, 2001.

Midford, Paul, *Rethinking Japanese Public Opinion and Security: From Pacifism to Realism?*, Stanford, CA: Stanford University Press, 2011.

Ministry of Defense, 'Heisei 26nen Ikō ni Kakawaru Bōei Keikaku no Taikō ni tsuite', 17 December 2013, www.mod.go.jp/j/approach/agenda/guideline/2014/pdf/20131217.pd.

Ministry of Foreign Affairs, *Japan's Official Development Assistance White Paper 2011*, Tokyo, 2011, www.mofa.go.jp/policy/oda/white/2011/pdfs/29_oda_wp_2011_1.pdf.

Rozman, Gilbert, *Northeast Asia's Stunted Regionalism: Bilateral Distrust in the Shadow of Globalizaton*, Cambridge: Cambridge University Press, 2004.

Samuels, Richard J., *Securing Japan: Tokyo's Grand Strategy and the Future of East Asia*, Ithaca, NY: Cornell University Press, 2007.

Samuels, Richard J., *3.11: Disaster and Change in Japan*, Ithaca, NY: Cornell University Press, 2013.

Soeya, Yoshihide, 'A "Normal" Middle Power: Interpreting Changes in Japanese Security Policy in the 1990s and after', in Soeya Yoshihide,Tadokoro Masayuki and David A. Welch (eds) *Japan as a Normal Country: A Nation in Search of its Place in the World*, Toronto: University of Toronto Press, 2011.

Väyrynen, Raimo, 'Economic Cycles, Power Transitions, Political Management and Wars Between Major Powers', *International Studies Quarterly*, Vol. 27, No. 4, 1983.

Vogel, Ezra, *Japan as Number One: Lessons for America*, New York: Harper & Row, 1979.

Wan, Ming, *Sino–Japanese Relations: Interaction, Logic and Transformation*, Stanford, CA: Stanford University Press, 2006.

Welfield, John, *An Empire in Eclipse: Japan in the Postwar American Alliance System*, London: Athlone, 1988.

Yahuda, Michael, *Sino–Japanese Relations After the Cold War: Two Tigers Sharing a Mountain*, London: Routlege, 2014.

14
Nationalism and revisionism
Hijacking Japan's security and defence policy agenda?

Axel Berkofsky

Introduction

Since Shinzo Abe came to power in Japan in December 2012 Japanese nationalists' and revisionists' (arguably very awkward and more often than not historically questionable and factually incorrect) views and interpretations of Japanese Second World War militarism have made impressive comebacks in the country's serious and not-so-serious academic and policy-oriented discourses. Indeed, Japanese policymakers and scholars who seek to whitewash Japan's World War militarism have been on a roll since Abe's Liberal Democratic Party (LDP) was returned to governing power, openly and self-confidently presenting views, which until then very rarely made it into the open and beyond meetings, pseudo-scientific conferences and round tables among like-minded stick-in-the-mud revisionists. Arguments that Japanese Second World War militarism and colonialism should be referred to as a 'war of liberation' liberating Asia from Western colonial powers and (at times noisy) calls to replace the country's US-imposed post-war Constitution with a 'truly' Japanese constitution without a war-renouncing clause[1] have – to a certain degree – become socially acceptable in Japan. In the same vein, Japanese revisionists are planning to reinstall the Japanese Emperor as head of state,[2] complaining (again, often noisily) that Japan has been supressed and 'kept down' ever since it accepted the judgements of the International Military Tribunal for the Far East, known as the Tokyo Trials (K. Takahashi 2014). Constitutional revision and getting rid of the US-imposed Constitution is – at least as far as Japan's revisionists are concerned – therefore necessary to restore Japan's full independence and sovereignty (Tisdal 2013). To be sure, (much) more often than not, Japanese revisionists' views and arguments are almost completely nonsensical and therefore normally should not have a prominent place in serious academic and policy-oriented publications and discourses. Nonetheless, in defiance of good sense and lessons that should have been learned from history, historical revisionism Japanese-style and calls to restore Japan's 'dignity' by revising Tokyo's post-war Constitution arguably sound less absurd to a smaller number among Japan's electorate and public than before December 2012 (Berkofsky 2012).

Given that Japan's Prime Minister believes in and advocates historical revision, does that also mean that Abe is about to throw the rest of Japan's US-imposed pacifism overboard and transform Tokyo's so-called defence-oriented defence policies from defensive to offensive? Neither the former nor the latter is taking place and contrary to what (overly) concerned policymakers and scholars in China and South Korea claim,[3] Tokyo's plans to adopt a legal framework that will allow the Japanese military to execute the right to collective self-defence when defending Japanese territory (see below) is not confirmation that Abe's nationalism and revisionism have had an impact on the country's actual security and defence policies. Nor do such plans plant the seeds for Japanese aggressive, regional go-it-alone policies. In fact, as will be shown below, the opposite is the case: Tokyo is currently expanding its bilateral and multilateral regional security and defence links seeking to counterbalance what is perceived as increasingly aggressive Chinese territorial expansionism in disputed Asian territorial waters. Indeed, Beijing's policies related to territorial claims in the East China Sea are clearly 'helping' the Prime Minister to adopt policies, which would have been harder to explain and justify without an arguably not-so-peacefully rising China. In other words: without regular Chinese intrusions into Japanese-controlled territorial waters in the East China Sea it would have been more difficult for Japan's government to justify why the budget for Japan's Self-Defence Forces and coastguard must – albeit very moderately – be increased better to equip the country's military to deal with and repel Chinese vessels in the East China Sea. Chinese policymakers insisting that the country has every right and indeed the obligation to protect what Beijing refers to as Chinese 'sovereign Chinese territory' in the East China Sea do their best to convince the Japanese public not to stand idly by watching Chinese vessels seeking to establish what Beijing refers to as 'dual control' over the disputed Senkaku/Diaoyu Islands in the East China Sea.

To be sure, government-sponsored nationalism at home accompanied by very assertive and at times aggressive policies related to territorial claims are part of China's and not Japan's regional security behaviour. Beijing's announcement in November 2013 of the establishment of an air defence identification zone (ADIZ[4]) overlapping that of Japan's and covering the disputed island in the East China Sea is but one example that Chinese policymakers have very few problems with changing Asia's territorial status, with or without other countries' blessings (International Crisis Group 2014). The ADIZ requires all aircraft entering the zone to identify themselves by submitting flight plans, maintaining radio and transponder communications and marking nationalities (Szecheny et al. 2013).

Abe: a diehard nationalist

Judging by his political track record[5] Abe is without much (if any) doubt a diehard nationalist and revisionist belonging to or leading a number of groups and committees, which have charged themselves with the ill-fated mission to reinterpret Japanese Second World War history (Katz 2014; T. Takahashi 2014). When Abe came to power in December 2012,[6] he made it clear that nationalism and historical revisionism would be on the agenda and indeed the 'entry ticket' into his cabinet. Fourteen members of his cabinet belong to the so-called League for Going to Worship Together at Yasukuni Shrine. Thirteen of those ministers are members of the Nippon Kaigi,[7] a nationalist think tank, which among other things urges policymakers and the Japanese people to reject what it (and Prime Minister Abe) call Japan's 'apology diplomacy' for its wartime policies. A further nine members of the Abe cabinet belong to a parliamentary association that seeks to revise the teaching of history in schools so that Japanese Second World War militarism and imperialism appear (far) less aggressive and (within certain limits) even acceptable and necessary in view of Japan's economic and geopolitical situation before and during the war (*The Economist* 2013). However, the nationalism and revisionism of these groups and associations do not represent or advocate what the majority of Japan's public considers to be accurate accounts of Japanese Second World War history and policies.

Wasting time and energy

When he took office in December 2012 Abe seemed determined to complete his grandfather's mission (Nobusuke Kishi was Prime Minister of Japan in the late 1950s[8]) to revise the Japanese Constitution, which arguably and a priori limits the extent to which any serving Japanese Prime Minister can be perceived as a 'serious' policymaker interested in pursuing his country's interests rather than his own. In other words, if Abe wished to make it his personal mission to bring to fruition his grandfather's goal of revising the US-imposed war-renouncing Constitution as opposed to concentrating on what is politically reasonable and sensible for the country's foreign and security policies then from a sober and non-revisionist perspective, he will enjoy very limited foreign policy credibilty. Indeed, the fact that constitutional revision remains under the current circumstances and political constellations next to impossible in Japan, further diminishes the credibility of the Prime Minister's policy agenda. Furthermore, policymakers such as Abe, who continue to invest resources and political capital for the purpose of revising and changing something that is virtually impossible to revise, are arguably wasting time that could usefully be invested elsewhere. The procedural and political obstacles for constitutional revision, a two-thirds' majority in both chambers of the Japanese parliament followed by a national referendum, will continue to remain in place and Abe's plans to lower the barriers for constitutional revision have (so far) got nowhere.

Furthermore, in defiance of rational policy choices that serve Japan's regional security interests, Japan's revisionists' obsession with rewriting sections of Japanese Second World War history arguably makes the country less secure. The more revisionists reinterpret (for which read falsify) Japanese Second World War militarism, the more Beijing's policymakers have an excuse to refer to Japan as aggressive, explaining to a domestic and international audience that Japan's Prime Minister is a 'trouble-maker',[9] which in turn 'obliges' China[10] to take countermeasures (in the form of 'defending' alleged Chinese territories in the East China Sea by making incursions into Japanese-controlled territorial waters). Put differently: the more Japan's revisionists deny that Japan's Imperial Army raped and killed hundreds of thousands of Chinese civilians in Nanjing in 1937,[11] the less Beijing policymakers will remain inclined to terminate intrusions into Japanese-controlled territorial waters in the East China Sea (regardless of the fact that the two issues are completely unrelated). While China's intrusions in Japanese-controlled territorial waters and regular 'encounters' between Chinese vessels and the Japanese coastguard continue to bear the risk of Japan and China militarily clashing in disputed waters in the East China Sea, they also make sure that a return to Japanese-Sino talks on the possible exploitation of natural resources (gas and oil) around the disputed islands continue to remain everything but completely off the Japanese-Sino agenda.[12] Japanese historical revisionism also stands in the way of bilateral Japanese-South Korean talks and cooperation on regional security as well as trilateral Japanese-US-South Korean talks on the same topic. Given the current political climate and the state of relations between Seoul and Tokyo, it is fair to conclude that nothing short of a complete reversal of Abe's thinking and rhetoric on Japan's Second World War policies will be acceptable to South Korea (Narusawa 2014).

Still sorry, again

Real world politics and security, however, seemed already (at least partially) to have caught up with the Prime Minister. While Abe had planned to revisit Japan's official and unambiguous apology for the country's wartime aggression made by former Japanese Prime Minister Tomiichi Murayama in 1993, in March 2014 he changed his mind and confirmed that Japan would stick to that apology which unambiguously referred to Japan as an 'aggressor' during the Second World War. In that month Abe also acknowledged the suffering of South Korean women who were forced to prostitute themselves for Japan's Imperial Army during Japan's occupation of the Korean peninsula. While Abe continued to refer to those women as 'comfort women', he (somehow) explicitly confirmed his understanding that Korean women were forced into prostitution (as opposed to having voluntarily chosen to 'work' in brothels established by the Japanese occupiers as Abe had previously suggested) (Sieg 2014). Some optimists even believe that Abe could also resurrect the Asian Women's Fund, a compensation fund promoted by Murayama[13] for former South Korean sex slaves (Yi 2014). That, however, is probably overly optimistic or indeed very unrealistic in view of Abe's claims made in 2013 that there is no scientific evidence to prove that Korean women were forced into prostitution.[14]

Indeed, Abe's willingness to keep his revisionist instincts in check cannot be counted on sustainably, as his visit in December 2013 to the controversial Yasukuni Shrine, the last resting-place of several convicted Japanese class-A criminals of war, demonstrated.[15] Abe decided to visit the shrine when Japanese policymakers were working on attempts to get Tokyo, Beijing and Seoul to talk to each other in order to address and ease tensions. Throughout 2013 Japan's Ministry of Foreign Affairs in particular was engaged in seeking to set up a trilateral encounter with China and South Korea. It transpired that these efforts were in vain when Abe decided to visit the Shinto shrine (Makino 2014).

Defence policy: (more or less) business as usual

While policymakers in Beijing beg to differ (very) strongly, recent and ongoing changes and developments on Tokyo's security and defence policy agenda do not provide any evidence that Japanese nationalist and revisionist thinking and rhetoric is about to translate into aggressive and revisionist Japanese foreign and security policies. First, as part of Abe's stated agenda of 'advancing Japan's diplomacy through a panoramic perspective of the world map', he visited much of South-East Asia in 2013, among other things increasing assistance to South-East Asian countries to build up their maritime capacity and enhance defence cooperation with Japan. Japan's support for the Philippines is particularly noteworthy as Tokyo is scheduled to provide Manila with 10 coastguard patrol vessels from Japan with a US $180m. loan. Furthermore, in June 2013 both countries agreed to enhance cooperation on the defence of remote islands, the defence of territorial seas as well as protection of maritime interests.

Tokyo pursues what it refers to as a 'collective response' to the perceived Chinese territorial expansionism, reacting to Beijing's increasingly aggressive territorial claims in the East China Sea and South China Sea. These policies, it is agreed over most of in Asia (with the exception of China), are in violation of international rules and norms, which were at the centre of Abe's speech at the May 2014 Shangri-La dialogue in Singapore, when Abe stated that 'rule of law should be the common language', a concept he based on three principles: making claims based on international law, not using force or coercion to advance claims, and settling disputes peacefully (IISS 2014). While this is arguably not the rhetoric of a Prime

Minister on the verge of fundamentally changing the nature of Japanese security and defence policies, at times there remains a (big) gap between Abe's nationalist rhetoric and his actual current position on security. His views on what Japan did to whom in the past are irrational, provocative and bereft of good sense, whereas advocating a Japanese leadership in Asia's multilateral regional security architecture makes a lot of sense given the country's capabilities, resources and Japan's decade-long track record as the promoter and financer of economic and political development in South-East Asia.

The upcoming revision of the US–Japan Guidelines for Defence Cooperation (last revised in 1997) provide further evidence that changes on Japan's defence policy agenda will continue to take place within the existing structures of Tokyo's security policies. The guidelines' revision will result in an expansion of the Japanese role and competencies in the context of US–Japanese military cooperation in the case of a military conflict in or beyond the region – above all an expansion of Japanese so-called rear area support for the US military in the case of a military contingency. The guidelines' revision underlines the centrality of the bilateral security alliance for Japanese regional and indeed global security policies. Indeed, strengthening defence ties with the USA is arguably the very opposite of aggressive Japanese 'go-it-alone' policies (Green and Hornung 2014).

Defending collectively ...

On 1 July 2014 the Abe cabinet announced its intention to reinterpret Japan's war-renouncing Article 9 of the Constitution to allow the Japanese Self-Defence Forces to execute their right to collective self-defence when defending Japanese territory. Contrary to what many (alarmist) Chinese policymakers and scholars suggest, such a reinterpretation of the Constitution's war-renouncing Article 9 is not the synonym for the re-emergence of Japanese militarism but instead evidence that Tokyo's defence policies will remain strictly defence-oriented. Up until now Article 9 – which strictly speaking does not even allow Japan to have armed forces in the first place (this being the reason why Japan's military is called the Self-Defence Forces) – seemed also to deny Japan the right to collective self-defence as stipulated in Chapter VII of the UN Charter, namely the right militarily to defend other countries' soldiers in bilateral or multilateral military operations.

The reinterpretation of Article 9 will neither lead to Japan acquiring the ability to strike overseas military bases nor will it permit Tokyo to develop expeditionary capabilities, enabling the country's armed forces to engage in high-intensity combat in East Asia and beyond. Indeed, 'under the new conditions for defence mobilization the Japanese Self-Defence Forces will only be dispatched to support allies under attack on the condition that the attack poses a clear danger to Japan. "True" collective self-defence, though, is a right which allows a nation to deem an attack on an ally or partner that presents no danger to itself as equivalent to an attack on itself and respond with the use of force' (Wallace 2014). Unless Tokyo decides to adopt a legal framework to allow Japanese soldiers the right to collective self-defence while defending soldiers from other countries with military force other than for the defence of Japanese territory, Japan's Self-Defence Forces will also in the future not be allowed to fight when deployed abroad for peacekeeping or humanitarian missions. Instead, when deployed abroad for UN peacekeeping operations, Japan's military might have to ask as in the past for military protection by other countries' armed forces. In 2004 and 2005, for example, the Japanese military camp in southern Iraq had to be guarded by Australian and Dutch contingents in view of the (very) tight restrictions on the use of military force by Japanese soldiers away from home.

While constitutional reinterpretation and indeed revision have been on top of Abe's policy agenda ever since he came to power in December 2012, the issue of collective self-defence has been on Japan's policy agenda for the last 20 years. Increasingly, regular Chinese intrusions into Japanese-controlled territorial waters in the East China Sea since then have provided the government with enough case studies plausibly to explain to the public why it is necessary to allow Japanese soldiers to do what their colleagues in most other 'normal' countries do at home and abroad – these are security and defence policies which turn Japan from a 'passive pacifist' to a 'proactive pacifist' country as Abe has explained on several occasions.

Certainly, Abe and his fellow revisionists wanted more than mere constitutional reinterpretation but were nevertheless obliged to settle for reinterpretation as opposed to the kind of constitutional revision (in essence the revision of war-renouncing Article 9) which the country's defence hawks had in mind. Indeed, even Japan's hardcore nationalists and revisionist policymakers had to come to terms with the fact that constitutional revision is not – due to the reason explained above – going to take place today, tomorrow or any time soon for that matter.

Fears in Beijing and Seoul that reinterpreting Article 9 stands for the remilitarization of Japanese defence policies might score some cheap political points at home but realistically has nothing to do with how Tokyo's defence organization will change in the years ahead. Indeed, 'recent changes in Japanese defence policy bind Japan in to its allies and partner countries, and further reduce any possibility of an aggressive military posture', concludes Simon Chelton, former British defence attaché in Tokyo (Scanlon 2014).

... but fighting at or close to home only

Meanwhile, Chinese concerns about Japanese collective self-defence apply much closer to home. If the legal framework accompanying the constitutional reinterpretation will provide for it, and equipped with an annual budget of close to US $50,000m. (arguably a lot for an officially pacifist country) Japan's Self-Defence Forces and the country's coastguard could be authorized to defend US soldiers when jointly defending Japanese-controlled territories in the East China Sea. Certainly, such bilateral cooperation would most probably have taken place anyway in the case of a Japanese–Chinese military clash in the East China Sea – with or without constitutional re-interpretation.[16] The official confirmation, however, that Japanese and US soldiers would defend each other in the case of jointly repelling a Chinese attempt to conquer the Japanese-controlled Senkaku Islands in the East China Sea has set off alarm bells in Beijing. However, this is not because Tokyo is about to fly the Japanese flag and declare formal sovereignty over the Senkaku Islands, but rather because Tokyo's ability to make an active contribution to defending Japanese-controlled territories away from home could stand in the way of Beijing's policy to attempt to establish the above-mentioned 'dual control' over the disputed islands through incursions into Japanese-controlled territorial waters surrounding the islands.

After the DPJ government bought three of the disputed islands in the East China Sea from their private Japanese owner in September 2012, Abe neither declared formal sovereignty over the islands nor did he go through with his earlier (bad) idea to send Japanese officials to the disputed islands and lift the ban on Japanese citizens visiting them (Berkofsky 2013). That said, however, the Abe government – in common with previous Japanese governments – refuses to admit that the Senkaku Islands in the East China Sea are disputed in the first place (as they belong to Japan de facto since 1895 and the Chinese defeat in the Japanese–Sino war of 1894/95) and instead established a cabinet secretariat to improve 'communications on Japan's territorial stances, mainly about Senkaku, both to international and domestic audiences' as the government explained. The government has furthermore revised teaching manuals for junior and senior high schools so that the islands are described as 'integral parts of Japanese territory' (*Japan Times* 2014). While it is debatable whether it is politically wise or constructive not to acknowledge that there is a territorial dispute with China in the East China Sea, insisting that none exists does not represent a departure from previous official Japanese positions on the ownership of the Senkaku Islands.

Exporting firepower

While allowing Japanese soldiers to execute the right to collective self-defence might not make the kind of security and defence impact that Japan's defence hawks had hoped for, constitutional reinterpretation has nonetheless helped to in the implementation of further changes to Tokyo's defence policy agenda adopted in early 2014. Indeed, Tokyo already has more freedom of action since the abolition (on 1 April 2014) of the country's veto on the exportation of weapons and weapons technology. Back then, the cabinet decided to scrap Japan's decade-old ban on the export of weapons and weapons technology. Originally, the embargo prevented Japan from selling weapons to communist countries, countries involved in conflicts, and countries subject to UN weapons embargoes. The ban was already partially abolished in 2011, thus allowing Japanese defence contractors to cooperate with their US counterparts on joint weapons development and production. In April 2014 the original ban was replaced with one on arms exports to countries in conflict. Scrapping the export ban was naturally greeted with enthusiasm by Japan's defence industry, which for years has been complaining that the weapons and weapons technology sectors account for less than 1 per cent of Japan's total industrial production. Very shortly after lifting the arms embargo, Tokyo proposed to set up and host a regional maintenance hub for Japanese, US, Australian and South Korean F-35 jet fighters and on 8 July 2014 Japan and Australia signed a bilateral agreement on the transfer of defence technology. Tokyo is planning to sign similar agreements with Vietnam and the Philippines in the years ahead.

And there is more ...

Abe's plans to expand regional security cooperation under Tokyo's leadership and without China do not stop here. The government also wants to revise Japan's official development assistance charter, assigning parts of the annual US $10,000m. budget to train foreign armed forces. While large parts of the budget will continue to be assigned to global infrastructure development and poverty reduction, some Japanese funds could in the years ahead be used to assist and finance non-combat operations, such as military-led disaster relief operations in South-East Asia. If the Prime Minister has his way —which is likely in view of the majorities held by his coalition government's in both chambers of the Japanese parliament – Tokyo could also provide training and ships for regional coastguard forces engaged in territorial disputes with China. When adopted, the Charter's revision could create the instrumental basis for a Japanese leadership role in regional so-called 'low-intensity' security cooperation.

In December 2013 the Japanese cabinet adopted the country's first National Security Strategy and updated the National Defence Program Guidelines (NDPG), outlining the country's armed forces structure and organization for the next ten years. In order to do that, Tokyo adopted the so-called Mid-term Defence Plan (MTDP), defining defence policy and capabilities to 2018 (Berkofsky 2013). All of that, however, is business as usual in terms of Japanese security and defence policies and will not be accompanied by anything resembling a noteworthy increase in Japan's defence budget. In 2014 Japan's defence spending amounted to US $47,000m. a 2 per cent increase compared to 2013 and the first increase in 11 years. China's defence spending on the other hand continues to grow at a double-digit rate and in 2014 amounted to $132,000m., a 12 per cent increase compared to 2013.

So what?

The above-mentioned changes currently taking place on the country's security policy agenda such as the government's initiative to reinterpret Japan's Constitution to allow Japanese soldiers to execute the right to collective self-defence are issues that have been on the country's foreign and security policy agenda for years and indeed decades. Put differently: sooner or later – with or without Abe-style nationalism – Tokyo would have proposed to allow Japanese soldiers to execute the right to collective self-defence in the context of a military operation for the defence of Japanese national territory. Not least as Washington has been urging its Japanese 'junior alliance' partner for years to acknowledge the right to collective self-defence in order to increase Japanese responsibilities and competencies within the framework of the US–Japan bilateral security alliance. There is no doubt that allowing the Japanese military to execute the right to collective self-defence is – in view of Article 9 of Japan's Constitution – legally and politically very controversial, but then again so has been the issue of the legality and constitutionality of Japan's armed forces ever since they were established in 1954.

What is more, the Japanese cabinet's decision to allow Japanese soldiers to execute the right to collective self-defence does not mean that Japan's military can execute that right tomorrow or any time (very) soon. In order to be able to reinterpret the Constitution, the government must adopt at least 10 amendments to existing laws. This law-making process could take years and will be prone to disagreements between Abe's LDP and his coalition partner, the Komeito Party. Komeito, originally a pacifist party with an aversion to attempts to investigate, let alone revise, Japan's war-renouncing Article 9 insists that the reinterpretation of the war-renouncing clause must be strictly limited to military scenarios that unambiguously constitute a direct attack on Japanese territory. Allowing Japan's armed forces to intercept North Korean missiles flying over Japanese territory on their way to California or fighting alongside US military in Afghanistan, Iraq or elsewhere will continue to remain off limits for Komeito.

Certainly, with or without the Komeito's blessing, there is already more on Abe's personal security policy agenda. He and like-minded members of his cabinet seek to adopt laws that allow Japan's navy and coastguard to defend allied warships in waters around Japan during a regional contingency that could lead to a direct attack on Japan. Currently, Japanese vessels are only allowed to defend US warships on the high seas when defending Japanese territory. Minesweeping in Japan's sea lanes without a formal cessation of conflict, further drawing Japan into region-wide US-led ballistic missile defence networks and allowing Japan's air forces to provide mid-air refuelling of US fighter jets during a regional contingency are also on the Prime Minister's agenda. Finally, Abe wants Japan's navy to contribute to the UN-sanctioned international minesweeping operations in the Strait of Hormuz[17] collective security framework (Fatton 2014).

For now, however, there is still significant public opposition against the cabinet's decision to allow Japan's military to execute the right to collective self-defence and Japan's pacifist electorate will make itself heard should the reinterpretation of Article 9 go beyond what the LDP agreed with the Komeito in July 2014 (*The Economist* 2014b).

Conclusion

The Prime Minister's current popularity can be explained by his (until now) successful economic policies much more than by his foreign policy assertiveness or plans to revise Japan's Constitution. Indeed, recent opinion polls on the Prime Minister's popularity and the approval ratings for his policies indicate that the Japanese electorate was (much) more satisfied with the Prime Minister and his policies in early 2014 than mid-2014 (*The Economist* 2014a). If the Japanese electorate and the public were as interested in constitutional revision and as concerned about a threat from China to Japan's national security as the country's nationalists and defence hawks are trying to make believe, Abe's decision to allow Japanese military to execute the right to collectiveself-defence should have boosted Abe's popularity. That this was not the case arguably demonstrates that the Japanese public is probably more interested in bread-and-butter issues such as the economic and structural reforms the Abe-led government promised to undertake when it took office in 2012.

What is more, the majority of the Japanese people are strong supporters of Japan's postwar pacifism and are much less interested in constitutional revision than the Japanese Prime Minister and his like-minded (or even more radical) colleagues (*Financial Times* 2014). Claims by Japanese nationalists and newspapers and magazines publishing and propagating their views that the majority of the Japanese public supports their views on constitutional revision and history are simply not supported by empirical evidence. Opinion polls regularly conducted by Japan's leading newspapers (*Yomiuri Shimbun, Asahi Shimbun, Mainichi Shimbun, Nikkei Shimbun*) typically indicate that most of the Japanese electorate is in favour of reinterpreting or even revising Article 9 of the Japanese Constitution if such a reinterpretation or revision would perhaps result in more active Japanese contributions to non-combat operations (e.g. humanitarian missions) in the context of UN-sanctioned peacekeeping operations. However, when asked whether constitutional reinterpretation or revision should also result in authorizing Japanese armed forces to contribute to international (UN-sanctioned or otherwise) combat missions requiring the execution of military force, opinion polls continue to show that a strong majority of the Japanese electorate is opposed to constitutional reinterpretation or revision.

When propagating the above-mentioned historical revisionism, Abe is in essence – at least for now – 'preaching to the converted'; in other words he is talking to those who already support his nationalist and revisionist views and policies. While such Japanese policymakers and scholars have without a doubt become more vocal during 2013–14, they still represent only a small minority among the Japanese public and electorate. Consequently, insisting on attempts to whitewash Japanese Second World War militarism and colonialism is not only a waste of resources and political energy (see above) but arguably also undemocratic because such views and policies interest only a small proportion of the Japanese public and electorate.

The above-mentioned (very) moderate increase in Japanese defence spending will contribute to equipping the country's armed forces and the coastguard with the means and capabilities to better deal with Chinese intrusions into Japanese-controlled territorial waters – something that would not be considered aggressive but instead 'normal' and legitimate in other countries. Concluding on a (at least partially) positive note, while Japanese security and defence policy 'normality' will certainly continue to be observed with a fair degree of suspicion in Beijing and Seoul, fears that day-dreaming Japanese diehard revisionists are on the verge of putting Japanese clocks back by 70 years are misplaced too (at least one hopes).

Notes

1. See Article 9 of the Japanese Constitution.
2. The Emperor became a 'symbol' of state with no political powers when Japan was de facto obliged to adopt its US-drafted post-war Constitution in 1946.
3. Many of these policymakers and scholars certainly know better and are aware that the current changes in Japan's security and defence policy agenda are in no way about to turn the country into an aggressive, regional, military bully.
4. These regulations are a departure from common international practice, which led the USA, Japan and also South Korea not to comply with them and indeed to ignore the ADIZ.
5. In 1993 Abe joined the LDP's History and Deliberation Committee, which in 1995 published a book in which it called Japan's participation in the Second World War a war of 'self-defence', and denied that Japan committed war crimes such as the Nanking Massacre and the forced recruitment of Korean so-called comfort women. In February 1997 Abe formed the Group of Young Diet Members for Consideration of Japan's Future and History Education with like-minded revisionists, and became its executive director. Before being appointed President of the LDP in 2012, Abe endorsed an advertisement in a New Jersey newspaper denying that Japan's military forced Asian women to 'work' as prostitutes for the Imperial Army during the Second World War. After coming to office in December 2012, Abe appointed Hakubun Shimomura as Minister for Education, who in 2012 urged Abe to declare that the 1937 Nanking Massacre did not take place and to deny the existence of the 'comfort women' issue. In his 2006 book *Towards a Beautiful Nation* Abe complains about what he calls post-war 'victor's justice', stating that the convictions of Japanese citizens as war criminals by the Tokyo International War Crimes Tribunal were unlawful as those convicted were not war criminals under Japanese law at the time. Currently, Abe heads Japan Rebirth (Sousei Nippon), a cross-party revisionist group of Japanese lawmakers.
6. Abe came to power for the second time after a very unsuccessful tenure as Prime Minister in 2006/07.
7. Nippon Kaigi means Japanese conference.
8. Nobusuke Kishi was a very controversial Prime Minister due to his role as Tokyo's representative overseeing the economic development policies in Japanese-occupied Manchuria throughout the 1930s.
9. The term is typically used in Beijing to describe Abe and his regional security policies.
10. At least from a Chinese perspective.
11. The invasion and six-week-long occupation of the Chinese city of Nanjing by Japan's Imperial Army in 1937.
12. In 2008 Tokyo and Beijing signed a memorandum of understanding on such possible exploitation and agreed to pursue what is referred to as 'functional cooperation' while agreeing to sideline litigations on the sovereignty over the islands.
13. A fund, however, that was not directly run by the Japanese government but instead by a government-financed non-governmental organization. This led South Korea at the time to argue that Japan sought to avoid official responsibility for financially compensating South Korean sex slaves.
14. Abe never explicitly and unambiguously acknowledged that Korean women were forced into prostitution. Instead, he spoke of the forced prostitution in very vague terms, which was never perceived as an honest and straightforward apology in Korea.
15. The shrine is – at least according to China, South Korea and (many) other Asian nations – a symbol of Japanese Second World War militarism.
16. As Article 5 of the US–Japan Security Treaty de facto obliges Washington to defend Japanese-controlled territory and territorial waters. Washington has confirmed just that several times officially and unambiguously over the last 18 months.
17. Eighty per cent of the oil tankers supplying Japan with crude oil sail through the Strait of Hormuz.

Bibliography

Berkofsky, Axel, *A Pacifist Constitution for An Armed Empire: Past and Present of Japanese, Defence and Security Policies*, Milan: Franco Angeli, 2012.

Berkofsky, Axel, *Japan and China: Bitter Rivals and Close Partners*, Asia Policy Brief 2013/3, Gütersloh: Bertelsmann Stiftung, 2013.

Berkofsky, Axel, 'Japan: (More or Less) Normal Military Power', in Andrew T. H. Tan (ed.), *East and South-East Asia-International Relations and Security Perspectives*, London: Routledge, 2013.

Fatton, Lionel Pierre, 'Japan's New Defense Posture', *The Diplomat*, 10 July 2014, http://thediplomat.com/2014/07/japans-new-defense-posture/.

Financial Times, 'Abe's Nationalism Takes a Worrying Turn', 9 February 2014, www.ft.com/intl/cms/s/0/90d24388-8ffc-11e3-8029-00144feab7de.html#axzz36t2BMopA.

International Crisis Group, 'Old Scores and New Grudges: Evolving Japanese–Chinese Tensions', Asia Report No. 258, July 2014, www.crisisgroup.org/~/media/Files/asia/north-east-asia/258-old-scores-and-grudges-evolving-sino-japanese-tensions.pdf?utm_source=china-japan-report&utm_medium=3&utm_campaign=mremail.

Green, Michael J. and Jeffrey W. Hornung, 'Ten Myths about Japan's Collective Self-Defense Change', *The Diplomat*, 10 July 2014, http://thediplomat.com/2014/07/ten-myths-about-japans-collective-self-defense-change/.

International Institute for Strategic Studies (IISS), Shinzo Abe's Keynote Address at the 13th IISS Asian Security Summit, the Shangri-La Dialogue, Singapore, 30 May 2014, www.iiss.org.

Japan Times, 'Isle Disputes to Make Schoolbooks', 4 April 2014.

Katz, Richard, 'Abe, Not Placating the Right; He Is the Right', *East Asia Forum*, 13 January 2014, www.eastasiaforum.org/2014/01/13/abe-not-placating-the-right-he-is-the-right/.

Makino, Yoshihiro, 'Insight: Abe's Shrine Visit Blew Japan-S. Korea Efforts for Summit Sky-High', *Asahi Shimbun*, 28 January 2014.

Narusawa, Muneo, 'Abe Shinzo, A Far-Right Denier of History', *Asia-Pacific Journal*, Japan Focus, Vol. 11, Issue 1, 13 January 2014, www.japanfocus.org.

Scanlon, Charles, 'Is Shinzo Abe Fanning Nationalist Flames?' *BBC News*, 23 April 2014, www.bbc.com/news/world-asia-26542992.

Sieg, Linda, 'Japan's Abe Says Won't Alter 1993 Apology on "Comfort Women"', *Reuters*, 13 March 2014, www.reuters.com/article/2014/03/14/us-japan-korea-idUSBREA2D04R20140314.

Szecheny, Nicholas, Victor Cha, Bonnie S. Glaser, Michael J.Green and Christopher K. Johnson, *China's Air Defense Identification Zone: Impact on Regional Security*, Washington, DC: Centre for Strategic and International Studies, 26 November 2013.

Takahashi, Kosuke, 'Shinzo Abe's Nationalist Strategy', *The Diplomat*, 13 February 2014, http://thediplomat.com/2014/02/shinzo-abes-nationalist-strategy/.

Takahashi, Toshiya, 'Abe's Yasukuni Visit: The View from Japan', *East Asia Forum*, 24 January 2014, www.eastasiaforum.org/2014/01/24/abes-yasukuni-visit-the-view-from-japan/.

The Economist, 'Back to the Future', 5 January 2013, www.economist.com/news/asia/21569046-shinzo-abes-appointment-scarily-right-wing-cabinet-bodes-ill-region-back-future.

The Economist, 'Not Quite so Invincible', 19 July 2014a.

The Economist, 'Clear and Present Dangers', 5 July 2014b.

Tisdal, Simon, 'Is Shinzo Abe's "New Nationalism" a Throwback to Japanese Imperialism?', *The Guardian*, 27 November 2013, www.theguardian.com/world/2013/nov/27/japan-new-nationalism-imperialism-shinzo-abe.

Wallace, Corey, 'Evolution, Not Revolution, for Japan's Military Posture', *East Asia Forum*, 7 July 2014, www.eastasiaforum.org/2014/07/07/evolution-not-revolution-for-japans-military-posture/.

Yi, Joseph, 'Understanding Shinzo Abe and Japanese Nationalism', *Foreign Policy Journal*, 26 May 2014, www.foreignpolicyjournal.com/2014/05/26/understanding-shinzo-abe-and-japanese-nationalism/.

15
Japan's defence
Challenges and future directions

Brad Williams

Introduction

In December 2012 the Liberal Democratic Party (LDP) emerged victorious in lower house elections, giving party leader, Shinzo Abe, a second tilt at the premiership. The election result was very much a protest vote against three years of highly anticipated yet immensely disappointing Democratic Party (DPJ) rule. Recognizing that the vote was far from a clear affirmation of support for the LDP and perhaps mindful of an unsuccessful first term in office when he seemed preoccupied with nationalist politics, Abe initially sought to reaffirm his pragmatist credentials by rolling out a much-needed three-pronged economic strategy of monetary easing, fiscal stimulation and all-important structural reform, dubbed 'Abenomics'. Japan's moribund economy soon responded, boosting Abe's public support, which translated into a further victory for the LDP-New Kōmeitō coalition government in upper house elections in mid-2013, ending the political stalemate of a 'twisted Diet' (*nejiri kokkai*). The Abe administration has utilized this domestic support to usher in sweeping reforms to Japan's defence policy, which, coupled with the Prime Minister's re-emerging nationalist impulses, has raised regional tensions, especially with an increasingly assertive China.

This chapter begins with an overview of Japan's major security changes since Abe's political resurrection, focusing in particular on the defence of the Sakishima Islands in the Ryukyu Archipelago. The boost in military spending and capabilities is indicative of a renewed emphasis on internal balancing, which is designed to supplement a strategy of continued external balancing manifested as enhanced security cooperation with the USA. The chapter then looks at the causes of Japan's balancing behaviour. It argues that while rising nationalist sentiments have created a propitious environment for conservative political actors to pursue a more assertive defence posture, China's burgeoning military power and Japanese perceptions of its mounting aggressiveness in the East China Sea and adjacent waters are directly contributing to these changes. The chapter then concludes by briefly highlighting the major security challenges facing Japan in the coming decades.

Japan's 'renewed' balancing

Military modernization

While the military alliance with the USA has long been the cornerstone of post-war Japanese foreign and defence policies and has been consolidated since the bilateral tensions of the early to mid-1990s, significant changes have also taken place within Japan's domestic security landscape. The reforms enacted in the brief period since Abe's political resurrection do not necessarily represent a radical departure but rather a robust reaffirmation of the general direction laid out by previous administrations, as well as an attempt to move beyond 'situational responses and superficial adjustments to the pursuit of a structural transformation in the security policy making process' (Bōei Kenkyūjō 2014: 35). An important institutional change has been the establishment in November 2013 of a National Security Council (NSC). Designed to serve as a 'command post' (*shireitō*), the NSC is centred on a quadrilateral assembly of the Prime Minister, the ministers of foreign affairs and of defence and the chief cabinet secretary who meet fortnightly to discuss basic security strategy and share ideas on important foreign and defence policies. The NSC is supported by a permanent secretariat, the National Security Bureau, and its functions can be supplemented by two broader ministerial bodies that convene as the need arises (Sunohara 2014: 3–4).

In addition to institutional reforms, the government has placed renewed emphasis on the building up of Japan's military capabilities, which have been facilitated by a 5 per cent boost in spending between 2014 and 2019, following a decade-long decline in defence outlays. This funding is earmarked for a broad range of military hardware that will be deployed as part of a strategic shift in the focus of the Japanese Self-Defence Forces (SDF) away from the north and the former Soviet threat to the south-west in defence of Japan's offshore islands. This focus beyond Japan's home islands, in fact, first appeared in the 2010 National Defence Program Guidelines (NDPG) drafted under the previous DPJ administration. The shift was reiterated in the most recent NDPG – revised an unusually brief three years after the last such document (the first was issued in 1976 and subsequently revised in 1995, 2004 and 2010) – which was released in conjunction with Japan's first National Security Strategy. The 2010 and 2013 NDPGs highlighted the need for a 'dynamic defence' that is proactive, flexible and highly mobile, with the latter version establishing 'proactive pacifism' as its philosophical basis.

Under the current Mid-term Defence Program, the five-year procurement and budget plan the Ministry of Defence (MoD) prepares 'to bring SDF capabilities and structure into line with the priorities set forth in the NDPG' (Grønning 2014: 4), defence of Japan's offshore islands will be bolstered in five main areas (Bōeishō 2014: 6–13):

1. Establishing a permanent reconnaissance system, which includes the deployment of a coastal surveillance unit on Yonaguni Island and an E-2C squadron in Naha. These patrol aircraft were previously based at Misawa in northern Japan and deployed to Naha temporarily when the need arose, as it has done frequently in recent times, necessitating a permanent deployment.
2. Achieving and maintaining air superiority through the acquisition of four F-35A fighter jets, three rescue helicopters and a medium-range surface-to-air missile battery, upgrades to the existing squadrons of F-15s and F-2s, as well as deployment of an additional F-15 fighter wing to Naha.

3   Achieving and maintaining naval superiority through the acquisition of P-1 patrol aircraft, SH-60K helicopters, submarines, search-and-rescue vessels, minesweepers and upgraded surface-to-sea missile systems, and extending the service life of P-3C patrol aircraft, SH-60J helicopters, destroyers and submarines.
4   Improving rapid response capabilities by examining the feasibility of introducing tilt rotator aircraft such as the controversial V-22 Osprey, upgrades to CH-47J transport helicopters and C-1 aircraft, military exercises, establishing an amphibious assault unit, upgrades to the three Ōsumi-class amphibious transport vessels, strengthening the command functions of the Izumo-class helicopter destroyer – with a length of approximately 250 m and displacement of 9,500 metric tonnes, the largest naval vessel Japan has built since the Second World War – the purchase of amphibious assault vehicles and bolstering SDF capabilities on the south-west islands through the acquisition of surface-to-air missiles and laser guided joint direct attack munitions systems.
5   Improvements to command and control systems and communications.

This boost in SDF capabilities is intended to respond at least partly to a new type of contingency outlined in the NDPG: 'grey zone' disputes. The term conveys a certain ambiguity, falling between peacetime (white) and emergency (black) situations. The former might manifest itself as a foreign vessel intruding into Japanese territorial waters and/or foreigners landing on an island, which law enforcement agencies such as the police or coastguard would be empowered to deal with. This type of scenario has played out on a number of occasions in the past involving Chinese and Taiwanese fishing vessels operating near the Senkaku Islands and activists from China, Hong Kong and Taiwan attempting to land on the disputed islands (successfully in 1996, 2004 and 2012). The latter would entail a military invasion during which the Japanese government would be able to order a defensive mobilization, thus triggering Article Five of the US–Japan Security Treaty and enabling both countries to respond jointly. Under a 'grey zone' scenario, a situation falling short of a full-scale armed attack, when for instance, a foreign armed group disguised as fishers clandestinely land on and occupy an island, presenting a fait accompli, the Japanese government would be unable to order a defensive mobilization, making the bilateral security treaty inapplicable. Beijing's apparent encouragement of the Chinese fishing fleet's operations in disputed waters for both commercial and geopolitical reasons has left Japanese defence planners scrambling to adopt countermeasures, which could bring about a revision of the SDF Law during a special session of the Diet as early as Autumn 2014 (Ryall 2014: A6; *South China Morning Post* 29 July 2014: A4; *Yomiuri Shinbun* 27 April 2014:1).

Militarizing the south-west islands

While maintaining sovereignty over thousands of islands, it is the Ryukyu Archipelago in the south-west, especially the disputed Senkaku Islands, where Japan feels most vulnerable. The Senkaku Islands are under the jurisdiction of Ishigaki, which along with Miyako and Yonaguni comprise the Sakishima Islands, stretching south-west from Okinawa Main Island. Unlike the heavily militarized Okinawa Main Island, nearly 20 per cent of whose land area is occupied by US bases – helping it to fulfil the role of American 'keystone of the Pacific' – the Sakishima Islands (apart from a small radar detachment on Miyako taken over by the Air Self-Defence Force (ASDF) post-reversion) hosted no permanent military installations. The only military involvement on these islands came in the form of the occasional Maritime Self-Defence Force (MSDF) port visit and the temporary deployment of a SDF Patriot PAC-3 missile battery during North Korea's ultimately failed rocket launch in April 2012 (*Ryūkyū Shinpō* 2 March 2011, 31 March 2012, 15 April 2012). The Sakishima Islands thus constituted a 'gap' in Japan's defences between Okinawa Main Island and Taiwan. By the late 2000s US and Japanese defence planners had begun to recognize the importance of addressing this deficiency and focused initial efforts on Yonaguni, Japan's westernmost point.

The first sign of Yonaguni's impending militarization came in June 2007 when two US anti-mining vessels docked in the island's Sonai port. This was believed to be 'the first [US] military visit to an Okinawan civilian port since reversion in 1972' (McCormack 2012), although two MSDF minesweepers had, in fact, docked in Yonaguni the previous month, raising speculation the two port calls were coordinated (*Ryūkyū Shinpō* 14 June 2007). While the ostensible reason for the US port visit was crew rest and relaxation, it also allegedly served as 'a covert mission to collect intelligence' on the island's potential role as a forward operating base 'in the event of a contingency in the Taiwan Strait' – a point revealed in a leaked secret despatch from a senior US government official (McCormack 2012). Located approximately 110 km from Taiwan's east coast, which is visible on a clear day, the propinquity of Yonaguni to a potential cross-Strait crisis must have been painfully evident to local fishers who were forced to suspend operations temporarily when missiles launched during China's intimidatory military exercises in 1996 landed in nearby waters (Chan 2005; Yamazaki 2010: 2).

At around the same time, the ground was being prepared in Yonaguni for a more permanent military presence. After some prompting from Japan's newly upgraded MoD, a Yonaguni branch of the Defence Association (*Bōei Kyōkai*) – 'a national organization closely connected to the [MoD] and incorporating former SDF members and associates' – was established in 2007, which soon began to lobby for a SDF facility on the island (McCormack 2012). At this point in time, the only 'armed' presence on Yonaguni was two police officers responsible for maintaining law and order among the island's 1,500 inhabitants. In 2008 the local assembly passed a supporting resolution and the following June the island's authorities under the soon-to-be re-elected Mayor Hokama Shukichi – a convert to the base proposal – made a formal approach to Tokyo (ibid.). While the MoD under the DPJ government set aside funding for the base, differences between the government and island authorities over the size of the subsidy for land appropriation prolonged negotiations. Following a narrow victory by the pro-base faction, led by Hokama, in mayoral elections in August 2013, Yonaguni authorities lowered their demands, paving the way for both sides to sign a land rental agreement in March 2014. In a sign of remarkable alacrity, construction work began the following month on what will be the first new SDF facility in Okinawa since reversion. Yonaguni, which is expected to be completed in 2015, will host a 150-strong coastal surveillance unit operating two radar sites (at Kubura in the west and Sonai in the east) with the ability to monitor both aircraft and ships, especially those in the vicinity of the Senkaku Islands, only 150 km away.

Unsurprisingly, the new SDF facility has divided opinions on Yonaguni. Proponents, driven by the familiar logic of 'compensation politics', perceive base construction and other forms of infrastructure spending as a panacea for the island's socioeconomic woes. Military spending does not necessarily stimulate sustainable growth, as Okinawa and more pertinently in this instance Tsushima demonstrates; the latter experiencing a decline in population following the establishment of a SDF base (*Ryūkyū Shinpō* 1 July 2009). Opponents, about 70 of whom protested at the April groundbreaking ceremony, have been critical of the decision making modalities, especially the lack of consultation, the sudden start of construction and the use of 'steamroller tactics' to complete the project as quickly as possible (*Ryūkyū Shinpō*

20 April 2014; *Okinawa Taimusu* 20 April 2014). More importantly, critics fear the base is the first step in Yonaguni's eventual transformation from a peaceful settlement to a military fortress or 'SDF island', which will only raise regional tensions and heighten the risk of the island becoming a target in the event of a contingency (*Reuters* 19 April 2014; *Yaeyama Mainichi Shimbun* 8 December 2010, 13 August 2013). With its small and declining population, concerns have also been voiced that the unit's deployment and subsequent arrival of the soldiers' dependants is likely to make the SDF an influential force in the island's politics, facilitating a further remilitarization should central authorities in distant Tokyo so decide (*Ryūkyū Shinpō* 21 June 2013).

Indeed, fears about the south-west islands' incremental militarization would seem to be justified. While the Yonaguni detachment's main task is intelligence, surveillance and reconnaissance, there have been calls from within the SDF to deploy an actual fighting force on the two largest population centres in the Sakishima Islands, Ishigaki and Miyako, for deterrence purposes (*Yaeyama Mainichi Shimbun* 12 February 2014). If the docking of MSDF and US Navy vessels in Yonaguni in 2007 presaged a permanent troop deployment on that frontier island, MSDF port visits to Ishigaki in recent years may have served a similar purpose, with mounting speculation that the island, along with Miyako and Amami Ōshima (located between Kyushu and Okinawa), have each been earmarked to host a 350–400 strong Ground Self-Defence Force (GSDF) early response battalion by 2018. Their missions will be to respond to attempted landings on outlying islands by armed groups and the politically less controversial disaster relief (*Ryūkyū Shinpō* 20 May 2014; *Okinawa Taimusu* 20 May 2014). Demilitarized during the Cold War and beyond and hitherto unknown to most of the outside world, these once peripheral islands are slowly being transformed into militarized outposts in the defence of Japan.

Consolidating alliance relations

The military alliance with the USA has long been the cornerstone of Tokyo's foreign and defence policies and bilateral security ties have been strengthened further in recent years. As efforts at alliance consolidation have been well documented elsewhere (Grønning 2014: 6–9), this section will focus on developments in two areas of Japanese defence policy under Abe that have profound implications for relations with Washington and regional security: collective self-defence and US force realignment in Okinawa.

As a United Nations member state, Japan possesses the right to collective self-defence: the ability to counter an armed attack on an ally, even if Japan itself is not targeted. However, since coming to the aid of an ally under attack is deemed to be beyond the 'minimum necessary' use of force permitted by the prevailing interpretation of the pacifist Constitution, Japan has been unable to exercise this right. Japanese conservatives have long chaffed at this restriction but have been impotent because of the high barriers to constitutional revision. The USA has sought a greater degree of defence burden sharing from Japan and has been repeatedly frustrated by the inability and unwillingness of successive Japanese governments to remove this legal obstacle, leading to periodic tensions in bilateral relations. Regional instabilities, slowly shifting power balances, as well as rapid advances and associated rising costs in weapons and defence systems, have resulted in a convergence of bilateral interests around this issue. The *Yomiuri Shinbun* (23 April 2014) opined that the Abe government's desire to exercise the right to collective self-defence stems from concerns about a possible decline in US deterrence capabilities following cuts in Pentagon spending, which has prompted Tokyo to seek assurances of a US commitment to the defence of Japan. Japan's declared participation in collective defence is the price Tokyo feels it needs to pay to ensure this commitment. The USA, on the other hand, clearly feels the need for unambiguous Japanese military assistance in dealing with potential regional contingencies, which prompted President Obama to voice his support for Abe's efforts at removing obstacles to exercising this right during a state visit to Japan in April 2014. Obama offered an additional verbal sweetener during the visit when he publicly declared Washington's recognition of Japan's administration of the Senkaku Islands and the subsequent applicability of Article Five of the US–Japan Security Treaty to these territories. While senior US government officials had issued statements to this effect in recent years, Obama became the first US president to confirm publicly the extension of the bilateral security treaty to the Senkaku Islands.

Cognizant of the domestic difficulties of enacting constitutional reform, Abe has instead simply sought to change the government's interpretation of Article 9 of the Constitution as a means of legalizing the use of collective self-defence. Discussions among the ruling parties on removing this self-imposed ban followed the release of a report from a hand-picked advisory panel that represented a significant departure from the government's traditional view. The report contended 'that there are some cases in which Japan's use of collective self-defence to protect an ally would fall within the range of the "minimum necessary" use of force for protecting lives and property' (Mie and Yoshida 2014). The issue is controversial in Japan since it strikes at the heart of post-war pacifism and generates fears among critics that a constitutional reinterpretation could open the floodgates to a substantial expansion of the SDF's overseas operations – plausible given Abe's reputation as a nationalist hawk, as well as comments to this end by LDP Secretary-General, Ishiba Shigeru. Seeking to allay public concerns, the report stipulated a limited range of scenarios permitting the exercise of collective self-defence, including 'using the right only when a country under attack specifically requests Japan's support; only with Diet approval; and limits the [SDF] from entering foreign countries unless they have permission' (ibid.). After persuading coalition partner, New Kōmeitō, which evinced a preference for political power over principle, to accept the proposals, the Cabinet approved reinterpretation of the Constitution on 1 July 2014. While no serious observer believes this change will lead the country into another 'dark valley' (*kurai tanima*) – the 15-year period 'of militarism and repression that preceded Japan's surrender in 1945' (Dower 1993: 9), Abe's unwillingness to put this monumental issue to a referendum does undermine democracy and constitutionalism. Irrespective of this, a major 'slicing of Japan's pacifist loaf' (see Samuels 2007: 38, 89, 91) has certainly been undertaken.

Another area in the bilateral defence relationship that has seen 'progress' since Abe's return to the Prime Minister's office is the US force realignment in Okinawa. The US military presence in Okinawa is regarded by both Washington and Tokyo as indispensable to the security of Japan and regional stability but from the perspective of many Okinawans who have to deal with the negative spillover effects of the bases, it is a major irritant. In an attempt to ameliorate local concerns, the US and Japanese governments agreed in 1996 to relocate the controversial Futenma Marine Corps Air Station, located in the middle of the densely populated community of Ginowan and famously described by former US Defence Secretary as the 'world's most dangerous base', to an existing facility at Henoko on the environmentally sensitive north-east coast of the main island. The plan had stalled since the initial agreement was reached due primarily to widespread opposition among Okinawans who felt the base transfer represented a reshaping rather than a reduction of the US military footprint on the island (see McCormack and Norimatsu 2012). Continuing a long-standing Japanese government position of prioritizing US interests over Okinawan concerns, Abe has sought to advance the stalled relocation plan, resorting to the familiar practice of compensation politics, which is part of a broader package of US force realignment that will see half the Marine presence (9,000 troops) shifted to Guam and the return of some bases on the southern main island to Japan.

Factors behind Japan's balancing

Nationalism

Japan has been swept by a rising tide of nationalism since the early 1990s. The salience of nationalist sentiments and the generally more assertive national mood are attributable domestically in large part to Japan's prolonged socioeconomic slump, which has made people more insecure and sensitive to perceived sovereignty violations. The demise of the political left, which during the Cold War was able to keep a check on conservatives' revisionist tendencies, and the passing of the older generation who experienced at first hand the horrors of war, have also contributed to the creation of a more encouraging environment for nationalism. It should be no surprise that a politician with Abe's nationalist credentials would thrive in this milieu. Indeed, one astute observer asserted that the current Abe administration is the culmination of a movement of conservative lawmakers opposed to historical repentance in pursuit of 'a right-leaning agenda' (Yamaguchi 2014).

However, it must be noted that Abe and the LDP were voted back into office in 2012 not because of any overt appeals to nationalism but because of the profound public disappointment at the performance of the much-anticipated DPJ government, especially its lack of leadership and inability to right the listing economic ship. Initially, Abe the pragmatist seemed to have learnt from the mistakes of his brief, first term in office when, soon after regaining power, he unveiled his 'Abenomics' reform policy, which breathed life into the moribund economy and boosted his popularity. Abe demonstrated that his nationalist impulses were always lurking in the shallows when he unwisely visited the controversial Yasukuni Shrine in December 2013 and attempted to reopen the 'comfort women' issue. This nationalist posturing has provoked domestic and international criticism, especially from Japan's neighbours, with China mounting a high profile international campaign against Tokyo and essentially declaring the Prime Minister *persona non grata*. China's harsh response has only served to galvanize the Japanese, even non-supporters of Abe, who are suffering from 'apology fatigue', and feel that China is ungrateful for Tokyo's substantial economic assistance and unnecessarily interfering in Japan's domestic affairs. These mutual recriminations have triggered a vicious cycle of nationalism in both countries. It is therefore understandable to conflate Abe's personal convictions and the bubbling wellspring of nationalism from which he seeks to draw with Japan's recent military build-up (Berkshire Millar 2014: 2). However, while nationalism has provided the necessary backdrop, it is China's rising power and aggressiveness within the region that has served as a direct justification in the minds of policymakers for Japan's more robust defence posture. It is difficult to imagine the degree of Japan's balancing behaviour without China's regional assertiveness.

The China factor

China is now perceived in Japan as representing the most pressing threat to national security. The Japanese mass media's often sensationalist reporting has certainly contributed to heightened fears among the public regarding the possible danger to the nation's security emanating from China. These fears have unsurprisingly contributed to growing negative images of

China. A large majority of Okinawans, who have close historical and cultural ties to China, also share this perception, although it should be noted that most seek a peaceful resolution to the Senkaku Islands issue, including taking the case to the International Court of Justice (*Ryūkyū Shinpō* 17 April 2014), a sign of moderation not evident in either national capital.

Nevertheless, perceptions of a threat posed by China have a certain material basis. Chinese People's Liberation Army Navy (PLAN) vessels have passed through waters close to Japanese territory en route to the Pacific Ocean for military exercises with increasing regularity in recent years. In the period between November 2008 and May 2013 Chinese navy vessels passed through the narrow Tsugaru Strait between northern Honshu and Hokkaido and between Okinawa Main Island and Miyako on 11 separate occasions (Bōeishō 2013). In May 2013 two Chinese frigates passed between Yonaguni and Iriomote, the third time PLAN vessels had entered Yonaguni's contiguous zone in seven months (*Ryūkyū Shinpō* 7 May 2013). While not a violation of international maritime law, the periodic PLAN presence in these waters has a relatively brief history and is regarded in Japan as a sign of mounting Chinese pressure. Even more disconcerting for the Japanese is China's significant expansion of maritime patrols in or near Japan's 12-nautical-mile border around the Senkaku Islands, becoming almost a daily occurrence, following the DPJ government's nationalization of three of the eight islands in September 2012. In a clear display of aggression, Chinese warships locked their fire-control radar on a Japanese helicopter and destroyer near the 'disputed' islands on two occasions in January 2013. Previous Chinese intrusions into the Senkaku Islands' contiguous zone were mostly non-military, involving fishing and the occasional activists' vessels.

China's increasing assertiveness can also be seen in the skies. According to Japan's MoD, Japanese fighters had to scramble 415 times against Chinese intrusions into Japan's airspace in 2013, an increase of 109 from the previous year (cited in *Ryūkyū Shinpō* 9 April 2014). Tensions in the skies have also escalated following China's announcement of a new air defence identification zone (ADIZ) over waters in the East China Sea claimed by both Japan and South Korea in late 2013. While Japan, South Korea, Taiwan and the USA have all declared ADIZs, China's establishment of such a buffer zone has nevertheless exacerbated fears within the region of Beijing's long-term intentions. One such concern, expressed by Michael Green (2013: 2), a former senior official in the Bush administration, 'is that the new ADIZ is part of a longer-term attempt by Beijing to chip away at the regional status quo and assert greater control over the East and South China Seas'. In a clear demonstration of non-compliance, Japan, whose own ADIZ overlaps with China's, flew military sorties through the zone, along with the USA and South Korea. Since China's and Japan's ADIZs overlap and are transited by aircraft travelling at high speed, the chances of a collision cannot be dismissed, as was clearly evident when Chinese fighter jets flew dangerously close (50 m and 30 m) to two Japanese reconnaissance planes in May 2014. Since the Japanese planes were monitoring Sino-Russian military exercises in the East China Sea, the Chinese response was perhaps not completely unexpected, although it did revive memories of a collision involving US and Chinese aircraft near Hainan Island in 2001.

China's regional assertiveness vis-à-vis Japan is driven by a mix of nationalism, geoeconomics and geopolitics. Since the Chinese Communist Party lacks political legitimacy, it has had to search for alternative bases for authority, settling on a blend of developmentalism and nationalism. Without diminishing the terrible suffering of Chinese victims, Beijing's aggressive posturing towards a Japan that is perceived to lack remorse over wartime atrocities serves as a convenient diversion away from serious domestic problems and is an attempt to assert its own sovereignty over what it refers to as the Diaoyu Islands (or Senkaku Islands) or in the very least a means of forcing Tokyo to admit the existence of a territorial dispute. The waters around the Senkaku Islands are also believed to be rich in the energy resources needed to fuel China's continued growth. Japan's south-western islands also form the northern sector of a First Island Chain, stretching from the Korean peninsula, the Okinawan Islands, Taiwan, the Philippines and Borneo. Japan's establishment of military bases on the Sakishima Islands would not only help it better to respond to attempted landings on the Senkaku Islands but could also enable it to encumber Chinese naval access into the Western Pacific in the event of hostilities.

Conclusion: future challenges

Japan's security architecture has undergone sweeping changes since the end of the Cold War, which have been deepened and accelerated since the return to power of Shinzo Abe and the LDP in late 2012. The shift to a more robust defence posture has entailed both a renewed emphasis on the strengthening of Japan's military capabilities while continuing to consolidate alliance relations with the USA – internal and external balancing, respectively. Perhaps nowhere in Japan will these changes be more keenly felt than in the south-western Sakishima Islands, which have been earmarked to host, for the first time, permanent military installations. The more assertive national mood has certainly provided a propitious environment for Japan's enhanced balancing behaviour. However, Japan's military build-up and tightening embrace of its superpower ally is driven primarily by fears of China's rising military power and growing assertiveness in the East China Sea and adjacent waters.

Japan will find it difficult, as Toshi Yoshihara (2014: 26) notes, to keep pace with China's military modernization unless the government can successfully turn around the nation's fiscal fortunes. While the monetary and fiscal arrows of 'Abenomics' have hit their mark, leading to a short-term economic boost, sustainable growth is dependent upon all-important structural reform, which vested interests are determined to block. Japan's economic woes have been compounded by the dual problem of a shrinking and greying population, the magnitude of which is unprecedented in peacetime. If Japan's demographic crisis remains unabated, a gradually diminishing working population will be forced to support a ballooning number of retirees. Social security and labour costs will rise – the latter possibly contributing to a further 'hollowing out' of industry and adversely impacting on food security and public safety. Savings and investment could decline, undermining further long-term growth (Williams 2013). The demographic crisis could not only undermine human security but also adversely impact traditional security in terms of problematizing recruitment for the SDF, constraining defence budgets and diminishing Japan's strategic importance in the Asia-Pacific region. Perhaps Japan's one solace is that China is likely to face a similar demographic dilemma, albeit in several decades' time.

Bibliography

Berkshire Millar, J., 'Battle-Ready Japan?' *Foreign Affairs*, 10 January 2014.
Bōei Kenkyūjō, *Higashi Ajia Senryaku Gaikan*, National Institute for Defense Studies, East Asian Strategic Review, 2014.
Bōeishō, *Bōei Hakusho*, Ministry of Defense, Defense of Japan (Annual White Paper), 2013, www.mod.go.jp/j/publication/wp/wp2013/pc/2013/figindex.html.
Bōeishō, *Bōei Hakusho, Waga Kuni no Bōei to Yosan*, Ministry of Defense, Defense Programs and Budget of Japan, 2014, www.mod.go.jp/j/yosan/2014/gaisan.pdf.

Chan Zuichan, 'Unmei Izon no Shimajima: Taiwan to Ryūkyū Rettō', *AJW Fōramu*, 14 February 2005.
Dower, John W., *Japan in War and Peace: Selected Essays*, New York: New Press, 1993.
Green, Michael J., 'Safeguarding the Seas', *Foreign Affairs*, 2 December 2013.
Grønning, Bjørn Elias Mikalsen, 'Japan's Shifting Military Priorities: Counterbalancing China's Rise', *Asian Security*, Vol. 10, No. 1, 2014.
McCormack, Gavan, 'Yonaguni: Dilemmas of a Frontier Island in the East China Sea', *Asia-Pacific Journal*, Vol. 10, Issue 40, No. 1, October 2012.
McCormack, Gavan and Satoko Oka Norimatsu, *Resistant Islands: Okinawa Confronts Japan and the United States*, Lanham, MD: Rowman & Littlefield, 2012).
Mie, Ayako and Yoshida Reiji, 'Panel Lists Steps for Bypassing Article 9', *Japan Times*, 15 May 2014, www.japantimes.co.jp/news/2014/05/15/national/politics-diplomacy/panel-lists-steps-bypassing-article-9/.
Okinawa Times, 'Yonaguni Rikuji Kikōshiki: Kokkyō no Shima, Mapputatsu', 20 April 2014, www.okinawatimes.co.jp/article.php?id=67246.
Okinawa Times, 'Amami ni Rikuji Keibi Butai, Miyako, Ishigaki mo Kentō', 20 May 2014, www.okinawatimes.co.jp/article.php?id=70039.
Reuters, 'Yonagunijima ni Jieitai Rēdā Kichi, Chūgoku Nirami Sora to Umi no Kanshi Kyōka', 19 April 2014, http://jp.reuters.com/articlePrint?articleId=JPTYEA3101520140419.
Ryall, Julian, 'Tokyo Pressures U.S. Over Islands', *South China Morning Post*, 15 July 2014: A6.
Ryūkyū Shinpō, 'Kaiji Sōkaitei ga Sengetsu Nyūkō, Yonaguni', 14 June 2007, http://ryukyushimpo.jp/news/storyid-24604-storytopic-3.html.
Ryūkyū Shinpō, 'Jieitai Yūchi, "Gun" de Shima wa Kasseika shinai', 1 July 2009, http://ryukyushimpo.jp/news/storyid-146519-storytopic-3.html.
Ryūkyū Shinpō, 'Ishigaki ni Kaiji Ījisukan Asu Kikō, Iriomote, Yonaguni ni wa Sōkaitei', 2 March 2011, http://ryukyushimpo.jp/news/storyid-174124-storytopic-3.html.
Ryūkyū Shinpō, 'PAC3 Haibi Ishigakishi wa Shinkō Chiku Jieitai Yonaguni 30-nin, Miyako 90-nin', 31 March 2012, http://ryukyushimpo.jp/news/storyid-189343-storytopic-3.html.
Ryūkyū Shinpō, 'Jieitai ga Tesshū "Hakai Sochi Meirei" Bōeishō ga Kaijo', 15 April 2012, http://ryukyushimpo.jp/news/storyid-189992-storytopic-3.html.
Ryūkyū Shinpō, 'Chūgoku Kantei, Yonagunioki o Kōkō', 7 May 2013, http://ryukyushimpo.jp/news/storyid-206287-storytopic-3.html.
Ryūkyū Shinpō, 'Yonaguni Jieitai Haibi, Kokkyō Kōryū koso Shinka subeki da', 21 June 2013, http://ryukyushimpo.jp/news/storyid-208289-storytopic-3.html.
Ryūkyū Shinpō, 'TaiChūgoku no Kinkyū Hasshin ga Kako Saikō 13-nendo, 415kai', 9 April 2014, http://ryukyushimpo.jp/news/storyid-223209-storytopic-3.html.
Ryūkyū Shinpō, 'Nicchū Kankei Ishiki Chōsa, Jūsōteki Kōryū koso Yokushiryoku ni', 17 April 2014, http://ryukyushimpo.jp/news/storyid-223727-storytopic-3.html.
Ryūkyū Shinpō, 'Rijuji Haibei e Yonaguni de Kikōshiki, Hantai Nezuyoku', 20 April 2014, http://ryukyushimpo.jp/news/storyid-223926-storytopic-3.html.
Ryūkyū Shinpō, 'Rikuji Butai, Ishigaki, Miyako, Amami Haibi e', 20 May 2014, http://ryukyushimpo.jp/news/storyid-225635-storytopic-3.html.
Samuels, Richard, *Securing Japan: Tokyo's Grand Strategy and the Future of East Asia*, Ithaca, NY: Cornell University Press, 2007.
Sunohara, Tsuyoshi, *Nihonban NSC to wa Nanika*, Tokyo: Shinchōsha, 2014.
Yaeyama Mainichi Shimbun, 'Heiwana Shima o Kyōi ni Makikomuna', 8 December 2010, www.y-mainichi.co.jp/news/17312/.
Yaeyama Mainichi Shimbun, 'Wazuka 47-hyōsa de Min'i Eta to Ieru noka', 13 August 2013, www.y-mainichi.co.jp/news/23054/.
Yaeyama Mainichi Shimbun, 'Nishi no Yokushi Taisei o Kyōka, Bōei Kyōkai wa Ishigakijima Yōbō', 2 February 2014, www.y-mainichi.co.jp/news/24338/.

Yamaguchi, Jiro, 'Abe's Pace on Two Right Legs', *Japan Times*, 27 March 2014, www.japantimes.co.jp/opinion/2014/03/27/commentary/japan-commentary/abes-pace-on-two-right-legs/.

Yamazaki, Shōhei, 'Comparative Study of International Policies on Border Towns of Japan: From a Periphery to a Frontier', 2010, www.trip.t.u-tokyo.ac.jp/triponline/2010/docs/yamazaki.pdf.

Yomiuri Shimbun, 'Shūdan Jieiken Giron ni Hazumi', 23 April 2014: 4.

Yomiuri Shimbun, 'Ritō Senkyo ni "Taikō Sochi"', 27 April 2014: 1.

Yoshida, Reiji, 'Pacifism at a Crossroads Following Panel's Verdict', *Japan Times*, 15 May 2014, www.japantimes.co.jp/news/2014/05/15/national/politics-diplomacy/pacifism-crossroads-following-panels-verdict/.

Yoshihara, Toshi, 'Troubled Waters: China and Japan Face Off at Sea', *World Affairs*, January/February 2014.

Williams, Brad, 'Japan's Demographic Crisis: Security Implications and Obstacles to Resolving an Issue Symptomatic of National Decline', in Andrew H. Tan (ed.), *East and Southeast Asia: International Relations and Security Perspectives*, London: Routledge, 2013.

16
Prospects of conflict in Korea
The threat of North Korea's continuing WMD programme and unreformed economy

Nolan Theisen

Introduction

Since the collapse of the 1994 Agreed Framework the ability of North Korea to continue successfully to develop its nuclear and missile programmes is a testament to years of failed US policy and lack of initiative that has left the White House largely sidelined amid defunct bilateral talks and a stalled six-party format that is unlikely to be revived. China, like the USA, is opposed to a nuclear North Korea not only because of the direct threat it would pose but also due to the potential for greater regional instability. This is something that the President of South Korea, Park Guen-hye, has referred to publicly in order to remind the Chinese leadership of the serious implications of an expected fourth nuclear test, hoping that Xi Jingping will more vigorously try to pressurize Pyongyang not to carry it out. However, in Beijing's policy calculus a negotiated end to the weapons of mass destruction (WMD) programme is not given quite the same priority as it is in Washington. China is wary of pushing North Korea too far, and the long-standing economic support it has provided is a testament to its inherent value as a stable, pro-China/anti-USA buffer state. While frustrated by North Korea's refusal genuinely to attempt a transposition of Chinese-style economic reform, Beijing has tolerated the mercurial antics of the North Korean leadership and is unlikely to abandon the regime until a more secure strategic option presents itself.

Even though both powers are officially opposed to accepting a nuclear North Korea, China has been unwilling to impose penalties for non-compliance and North Korea is empowered with the knowledge that China will not let it fail. Chinese policymakers have been forced tacitly to support North Korea's nuclear programme while insisting publicly on further dialogue within the Six-Party framework and privately encouraging North Korea to pursue reforms. The USA and China appear to share the same aim of denying North Korea its nuclear status but priorities and process remain entirely divergent.

The policy of condoning financial transactions that circumvent international sanctions and enable North Korea's leadership to pursue a nuclear programme could reach a turning point if Beijing interprets advancement as a threat to the current status quo. Yet this threshold remains only a distant possibility given the overwhelming economic leverage that Beijing has over North Korea. For now, Kim Jong-un and his confidants are far from being able completely to shun Chinese overtures due to this dependency, but the young leader's legitimacy – a demonstration of firm control over the leadership hierarchy and society – remains his source of power in bilateral relations. Without internal economic reform any politically motivated restrictions imposed on Chinese exports and foreign direct investment would cripple the regime and threaten its survival. Thus, China maintains a tenuous balance on its north-east border, propping up the North Korean regime but unable to gain its full compliance.

Meanwhile, Kim Jong-un has to manage his own balancing act between external and domestic policy in the knowledge that Beijing might eventually try to limit the development of the nuclear programme that has been identified as the lynchpin of regime survival by the Kim family. During 2014 efforts were underway to diversify away from China, with Pyongyang courting Moscow and agreeing to an ambitious bilateral trade target for 2020 (Vorontsov 2014). At the same time, renewed efforts led personally by Kim Jong-un were being made to broach and resolve the abductee issue with Japan[1] in the hope of economic normalization, although given Japan's concerns about the nuclear programme it is difficult to predict what reconciliation will achieve (Smith 2014). It will certainly be challenging for North Korea to truly diversify away from its powerful neighbour, which supports some 90 per cent of its trade balance.

In the absence of any creative US policy towards North Korea, Kim Jong-un's power consolidation continues to incubate and guide the maturing nuclear programme that he inherited from his father. Any hope for reform and opening up to the international community under the new leader was dashed following the April 2011 missile launch. According to Chun Yung-woo, who served as South Korea's national security advisor until 2013, 'I'm now convinced North Korea would prefer to collapse with nuclear weapons than try to survive without nuclear weapons' (Sanger 2014). If this is the case and the regime continues to resist overtures to concede its nuclear programme while resisting economic reform, the Chinese may be forced to reassess their policy and consider the possibility of unification.

Kim Jong-un's consolidation of power

Many North Korea watchers thought that Kim Jong-un would be more open to deviating from his father's failed economic policies and would possibly resume denuclearization negotiations with the USA. Instead, he has adhered to the existing conservative ideology while consolidating power, replacing old cadres linked to his father with younger, unknown figures who are loyal to him.

He has certainly demonstrated hard-line tendencies so far, playing to both domestic and external audiences with missile launches, a nuclear test and the unusually public banishment of Jang Song-thaek. It is difficult to predict exactly what the implications of these manoeuvres are beyond the seemingly natural progression of dynastic power consolidation under the backdrop of ideological rhetoric. With this in mind, it not surprising that amid a smooth and evolving internal leadership transition the country's external relations remain hostile to any type of negotiation with Chinese and US interlocutors who continue to insist on prompting change in Pyongyang.

On the one hand, if Kim Jong-un has determined that risky changes will be needed to restructure and open up the economy in order to secure his rule, it is unlikely that he will take any action until he has replaced regents with hand-picked and inexperienced loyalists who will not question his decision making. In this sense it is too early to establish the strategies that he will pursue until his power structure is comfortably in place. On the other hand, achieving absolute power at such a young age without any vocal opposition can perpetuate a hubris and belief that he can improve upon his father's legacy by continuing the same policies through new figureheads, and aiming towards the achievement of nuclear recognition under an autarkic economy. While consolidation can ensure greater stability, the process is also inherently unstable particularly when high-ranking officials such as Jang Song-thaek are suddenly removed from power. These cadres typically have their own network of loyalists and associates whose affiliation and subsequent guilt are determined according to subjective assessments, thus creating a deeper fog of uncertainty in the leadership that could be difficult to manage neatly.

Kim Jong-un's recent inclinations might change once he is comfortably in control, perhaps establishing his own doctrine in recognition of the dangerously dysfunctional economy, but external experts can only speculate. North Korea watchers tend to attribute meaning to movement within the upper party and military ranks based on their perceived reputations regarding foreign policy, the nuclear programme and the economy as being hard line, moderate or unknown. Therefore, the purge of high-ranking officials such as Jang Song-thaek comes under greater scrutiny because it can foreshadow potentially significant policy shifts. At the same time, not much is known about these individuals, their true sentiments, and the broader implications of any secretive power plays that they are involved in.

It is important to track these movements but equally it is difficult to infer policy implications. There has been excessive conjecture and over-analysis concerning the leadership carousel, and optimism about interpretations that the regime will shift to more liberal policies under Kim Jong-un seem naïve. Speculation tends to underestimate not only the indoctrination of the subordinate population but also the loyalty within the party and the strong desire to uphold the rent-producing status quo. In North Korea moderates, reformists and hardliners are defined differently, and there is not much to discriminate between them. Those individuals who might seek to effect reform would be likely do so within the system, while newly replaced officials can be expected to maintain continuity rather than initiate any changes – which is why they were selected in the first instance.

At present it is particularly difficult to determine who influences the decisions of Kim Jong-un but increasingly he is surrounding himself with loyal subordinates with no perceived entitlement or autonomy at the expense of incumbents who served under his father. Jang Song-thaek was Kim Jong-il's most influential advisers, particularly with regard to North Korea's external economic policy and through his personal relationship with China's political establishment (Babson 2014). The idea that he was some kind of latent reformer has been mostly dispelled by experts who correctly recognize that he was a victim of his own success and a threat to Kim Jong-un's power. The clear signal is that Kim Jong-un is becoming more powerful with each cabinet reorganization.

Prospects for North Korea's economy

China's vision: status quo and the soft push for economic reform

Overall, China favours a non-nuclear Korean peninsula, but it is still unwilling to apply any substantial pressure on the regime that would endanger its survival. This gives North Korea a high degree of latitude in its relations with the USA and South Korea. In effect, Chinese complicity makes it impossible for the USA to lead an effective international sanctions regime. Nonetheless, most experts believe that Beijing is increasingly pragmatic in its approach to North Korea, only providing assistance out of self-interest. Thus, Beijing would prefer Pyongyang eventually to agree to a long-term framework that would arrest the WMD programme as well as achieving a path to normalization with the USA because this would significantly reduce tension. North Korea's rulers have determined that the nuclear programme represents the best chance for long-term survival and they have the freedom to make this choice without consequence owing to China's unconditional patronage. The patience of the Chinese leadership reflects a sustained confidence in the current 'least' worst option as opposed to any shift that would accelerate unification and weaken influence over its immediate periphery.

As diplomatic solutions seem more distant than ever, China continues to feel the brunt of pressure from the USA over its handling of North Korea while it attempts to steer the regime towards economic reform. Secretary of State John Kerry reiterated a two-track strategic approach of pressure and inducements in a February 2014 meeting in Seoul. He also emphasized the importance of China's influence over North Korea and the need to enlist its cooperation to achieve denuclearization. He stressed that China should be using its economic leverage over North Korea more aggressively in this regard. US policymakers have been communicating this message to their Chinese counterparts for years, hoping that China can be convinced that the threat of a nuclear North Korea should be enough to shift its policy. For China to be comfortable with the notion of applying pressure to North Korea, the USA will need to make concessions over its presence on the peninsula and military alliance with South Korea if not direct security guarantees, which will be a complex process fraught with credibility challenges. At this point China's strategic outlook with respect to the Korean peninsula dovetails with its ambitious rise to a global power, and cooperation with the USA is seen within this context.

Internal economy

Since taking office Kim Jong-un's profligate expenditure on entertainment and construction follows publicly stated promises to the citizens of North Korea that living standards will improve (Frank 2014). In such a poorly performing economy that lacks reforms and without the possibility of borrowing on the global market, the sustainability of this funding is certainly in question. Ultimately, this could force an imminent decision among the top echelons of the leadership with regard to the path of the economy. If the economy stagnates and fails to deliver the necessary services, Kim Jong-un may succumb to social pressure and be forced to adopt limited reforms. Of course, he could just as easily opt to maintain state monopoly over all sectors of the economy to avoid anything that would jeopardize his ability to control the flow of the limited resources available.

Any type of transition comes at a cost in this respect, from the moment reforms are enacted and parts of the economy move outside the direct control of the party, the hierarchical system of patronage will also be weakened as rent seekers have the option of turning to the market rather than the party. Thus far, the choice to keep things as they are has been too convenient for Kim Jong-un as it was for his father before him, although many experts do not expect it to remain this way – particularly if the lavish social spending continues.

Special economic zones

Pyongyang has shown an interest in the potential of special economic zones (SEZs), but there are a number of reasons why they will not work in North Korea under current conditions.

Beyond the oversight and discretion of Kim Jong-un, there are fundamental institutional problems that will continue to dissuade investors. The lack of transparency and information regarding the business environment is prohibitive to any long-term financial commitment, and North Korea has one of the worst economic policies in the world, according to World Bank indicators (Noland 2013). It also has poor infrastructure, particularly in power generation, and industrial enterprises will demand reliable supplies of energy. Finally, North Korea's reputation has suffered through its handling of the Kaesong Industrial Complex (KIC). Its closure and the reported exit of some South Korean firms have demonstrated that Pyongyang is unwilling or capable of managing an SEZ independently of political motivations. Unfortunately for North Korea it must compete with other host countries that offer cheap pools of labour along with superior investment conditions. This all occurs under the macro-climate of parallel nuclear and economic development, the latter ensuring ever tightening international sanctions and astronomical insurance risk premiums for investors. Considering all of these factors, the idea of obtaining risk insurance in an open market for any major investment seems unfathomable outside of a politically motivated government.

Success will largely be dependent on the underlying intentions of the North Korean leadership; if the zones are treated as nothing more than isolated pockets of foreign revenue for use by the government they will have limited or no linkages with the broader economy and will not generate significant interest from prospective investors. This is important to decipher since historically well-designed SEZs bring about change in the broader economy through spillover and policy effects (Farole 2011). In most instances this is the motivation behind a host country's decision to endorse SEZs, in essence attracting foreign investment in an otherwise risky investment climate to spawn a ripple effect of economic liberalization – like China in the 1980s. With North Korea, the leadership might continue to resist any reform of the real economy and try to limit rather than encourage the 'trickle' effect of these areas.

Diversification

Options to open trade and attract investment outside of China are very limited for North Korea, but Kim Jong-un will pursue opportunities to procure hard currency and diversify away from China's economic linkage.

Russia

In the short term, expanding trade with Russia makes sense for both countries. During 2014 North Korea made overtures that culminated in a late April visit from a high-ranking Russian government official to the country for the first time in 30 years. For Russia, which is facing sanctions from the USA over its intrusion into Ukraine, economic cooperation also offers a chance to undermine Washington's efforts in the region while reaping potentially significant financial gains and accomplishing a modicum of stability.

Similarly to China, Russia has a vested interest in regional stability and an aversion to North Korea's WMD programme but would prefer to bolster its economic integration in order to avoid a disorderly collapse. For Moscow, this involves three major trilateral infrastructure projects including connecting the railroads in North and South Korea with the Transiberian Railway, and constructing gas pipelines and power lines from Primorye to South Korea via North Korea. Of course, such ventures depend on the regime reforming its economy and meeting international financial standards to provide investment security which, given the recent difficulties experienced by the KIC that forced its temporary closure in

2013, will be a challenging endeavour requiring massive confidence-building measures. Somehow, Pyongyang will need to demonstrate that long-term returns to investors will not be held hostage to political interference or blackmail.

At the same time, Russia also realizes that it has a window of opportunity to negotiate commercial contracts without competition from major international companies in Japan, South Korea, the European Union and even the USA, who are limited by their governments' strict economic sanctions (Voronstsov 2014). There has been some preliminary success with the development of the port in Rajin, which is planned to be transformed into a major transshipment hub similar to that in Rotterdam, Netherlands. Business representatives from South Korean industry – Hyundai, Posco and Korail – have expressed keen interest in the Russia–North Korea joint venture in Rajin and participated in the Conference of General Directors under the auspices of the Organisation for Cooperation between Railways held in Pyongyang in April 2014.

This is the most logical way for North Korea to achieve some degree of economic independence from China, although it is likely that the Chinese would be involved in most major infrastructure projects as part of a consortium. It is also in the economic interests of regional governments that would have to support and essentially underwrite such investments, as did the South Korean government in support of the KIC. This would effectively be the price of stability as defined and sought after by China and Russia. Of course, China would gain significantly from the ability to make transshipments across North Korea, but other international companies would also take advantage of more efficient trade routes out of eastern China. This would provide alternative revenue for North Korea and reduce its overall dependence on China's steadfast trade and investment. Even though this is not acceptable for Washington as an end game, and in fact could be considered directly counterproductive to US-led international sanctions that seek to reverse the nuclear programme, there is not much it could do to stop it.

Japan

Japan could conceivably be a significant source of investment if the abductee issue is resolved, but it is also concerned about North Korea's nuclear programme and does not want indirectly to facilitate its advancement. However, given the deteriorating relations between Seoul and Tokyo, fostering an economic relationship could undermine North Korea's economic relations with South Korea and thus send a message.

South Korea

Arguably, economic interdependence can ultimately lead to the political will for negotiation and/or harmonization between states, but this does not necessarily apply in the case of North and South Korea (Lu et al. 2013). By comparison, this has certainly been evident in cross-Strait relations between Beijing and Taipei, where economics can be linked to favourable political and societal interactions and peaceful relations, but one could argue that this has not changed China's long-term strategy with respect to Taiwan that the USA has forestalled for the time being. In fact, drawing Taipei closer to its economic orbit makes Taiwan more dependent on China for trade and investment, which reflects China's strategy in South-East Asia.

Economic interactions between North and South Korea are perhaps the most important and pertinent factors that will affect future political reconciliation, if this ever occurs at all. If it does, it is likely that it will be a result of growing economic interdependence leading to political compromise. However, to date this has not been the case. International Relations theory can be applied differently to various bilateral relations, and on the Korea peninsula realism rather than rapprochement and constructivism has been evident. What can be deduced from the failure of South Korea's 'Sunshine Policy' under President Kim and President Roh is that the principle of 'politics first, economics later' does not work. Rather, it seems that strong economic and social ties will need to be established in order to achieve sustainable peace. With North Korea's consistent refusal to reciprocate in agreements, relations between the two countries have become stagnant and the risk of conflict continues to linger as has been the case for the past decade.

The USA: running out of patience and ideas

The most important relationship influencing peace and stability along the Korean peninsula is between North Korea and the USA, and unfortunately the two have never been at a greater impasse. In fact, it is unlikely that trust between the USA and North Korea can ever be established given the latter's use of ideological manipulation and need to portray the USA as a great evil that the masses should rally against. Washington refuses to abandon its preconditions for good reasons – the regime has shown no inclination to surrender its nuclear programme – but the clock is ticking. A recent US State Department communiqué reveals an implicit recognition of the impotency of recent policy, stating that, 'we are embarked in an effort to translate denuclearization from a noun to a verb' and calling on China to recognize the severity of a nuclear North Korea (US Department of State 2014).

The utility of Washington's diplomatic quest to convince Beijing to end its support of the regime and compel North Korea to capitulate and negotiate under duress is questionable, but the alternatives would require an entire rethinking of its strategic position in the Korean peninsula and the Asia-Pacific. For a grand bargain that would allow South Korea to absorb North Korea, the issue of US troops and military doctrine will have to be addressed, but for now the lack of mutual trust between the superpowers could be more detrimental to a solution than that between the USA and North Korea.

Conclusion: China's choices

Eventually, provocative nuclear and missile tests might force a re-evaluation of China's strategic position, when North Korea is finally deemed more of a liability and obstacle to stability. While stability is the key operative word, so is control. Although tensions remain as a result of past nuclear tests leading to what is expected to be a fourth, China is the only country to exercise a degree of 'control' over North Korean actions. It is better characterized as influence or respected input that Kim Jong-un must at least process owing to the country's economic vulnerability. As long as North Korea depends so comprehensively on its patron, with no economic reforms and the inability to diversify, China will be in a position to dictate the regime's fate and disrupt the status quo. Ultimately, North Korea's aggressive pursuit of nuclear weapons could actually prove to be its undoing by changing the risk calculus in Beijing that eventually leads to an understanding with Washington and Seoul, but this would involve far broader regional implications that are beyond the scope of this chapter.

Although officials in Beijing have publicly admonished North Korean for carrying out highly destabilizing nuclear tests, China will continue to be cautious and push for the opening of a dialogue which it believes is better than no communication at all. Given China's pragmatic policy over the buffer zone is difficult to imagine what North Korea might be able to do that could convince the Chinese to relinquish their position, short of a proven deliverable nuclear capability. It would take a serious commitment from the USA to realign its military relationship with South Korea to entertain any other type of policy.

In as much as China's international reputation has suffered as a result of its disregard of United Nations Security Council resolutions over North Korea, it ensures a commanding position over North Korea relative to its other security and commercial interests. This allows Beijing to continue to buy time in the hope that it can persuade the North Korean regime to embrace economic reform and China hopes to oversee this process. Fundamentally, undermining US-led international sanctions is also valuable in the bilateral context of its contentious relationship with the USA over other geopolitical flashpoints.

Note

1 The abductee issue refers to the period from 1977 to 1983 when Japanese citizens were abducted from their home country by agents of the North Korean government.

Bibliography

Babson, Bradley, 'The Demise of Jang Song Thaek and the Future of North Korea's Financial System', *38 North*, February 2014.

Farole, Thomas, 'Special Economic Zones: What Have We Learned?' *Economic Premise*, Washington, DC: World Bank, September 2011.

Frank, Ruediger, 'A Guide to Kim Jong Un's 2014 New Years Speech', *38 North*, January 2014.

Haggard, Stephen, *SEZ Update, North Korea: Witness to Transformation*, Washington, DC: Peterson Institute for International Economics, 28 May 2014, http://blogs.piie.com/nk/?p=13175.

Lu, Yeh-chung, Park Byuang Kwang, Tsai Tung-chieh, 'East Asia at the Crossroads: A Comparative Study on Taiwan and Korea's Reconciliation with Adversaries', *Korea Economic Institute of America*, July 2013.

Noland, Marcus, 'Build It and They Will Come', *North Korea: Witness to Transformation*, Washington, DC: Peterson Institute for International Economics, November 2013.

Noland, Marcus, 'Conversations in China', *North Korea: Witness to Transformation*, Washington, DC: Peterson Institute for International Economics, May 2014.

Redfield, Garret, 'Interview: North Korean Expert Evans J. R. Revere', *Penn State International Affairs Review*, April 2013.

Sanger, David, 'U.S. Confronts Consequences of Underestimating North Korean Leader', *The New York Times*, April 2014.

Smith, Sheila A., 'Pyongyang's New Overtures and Abe's Diplomacy', *38 North*, May 2014.

US Department of State, Background Briefing on Secretary Kerry's Trip to Republic of Korea, China and Indonesia', February 2014, www.state.gov/r/pa/prs/ps/2014/02/221631.htm

Vorontsov, Alexander, 'Is Russia-North Korea Cooperation at a New Stage', *38 North*, May 2014.

17
The paradoxes of vulnerability
Managing North Korea's threat to regional security

Andrew O'Neil

Introduction

The Democratic People's Republic of Korea (North Korea) is an oddity in contemporary international relations. Ruled by a brutal, yet highly idiosyncratic, regime whose authority derives from a fusion of personality cult and dynastic succession, North Korea is in many respects a failed state. It may be the world's newest nuclear power, but ordinary North Koreans confront basic hardships in their everyday lives that have more in common with poverty-stricken parts of Africa than with anything experienced by citizens across the rest of Asia. Acutely dependent on external aid for its economic survival, North Korea is ruled by a regime that has pariah status in the international system. North Korea has no allies to speak of, possesses the dubious record of broken commitments to a host of international agreements, and the treatment of its own citizens is probably the worst of any country on the globe. The profound human rights abuses perpetrated by the Pyongyang regime have most recently been documented in painstaking detail in a landmark 2014 report by the United Nations (UN) Human Rights Council, which concluded that 'systematic, widespread and gross human rights abuses have been, and are being, committed by North Korea, its institutions and officials. In many instances, the violations of human rights entail crimes against humanity' (UNHRC 2014: 23).

Yet North Korea is also a case study in how weak states can sometimes achieve stunningly counter-intuitive outcomes. Indeed, it is hard to think of any state that has achieved so much with so little despite the predictions from so many. North Korea experienced a series of triple shocks during the 1990s that led observers to foretell the imminent collapse of the regime in Pyongyang (Armstrong 2013: 282–283). In 1990 the country's primary benefactor, the Soviet Union, ceased to exist. This had an immediate and profound economic impact on North Korea, with the country having to absorb the loss of its largest preferential trading partner. Between 1990 and 1991 North Korea's total trade nearly halved, and South Korean estimates put the decline of North Korea's overall gross domestic product at between 2 per cent to 5 per cent (Cumings 2005: 436). Politically, the loss of the country's key ally accentuated North Korea's deepening sense of isolation. The death in 1994 of 'the Great Leader', Kim il-Sung, threw into stark relief just how durable North Korea's leadership had been since the partitioning of the country in 1948 and how challenging it would be to ensure a stable succession. Following a decisive purge of elements of the Korean People's Army (KPA), by 1998 Kim Jong-il had succeeded his father as only the second North Korean leader in half a century (see Kim 2012: Chapter 2). Around the same time, in the mid 1990s, North Korea experienced a humanitarian catastrophe with the advent of major famine. Triggered by once-in-a-generation flooding and the subsequent destruction of food yields, the famine had its origins in years of economic mismanagement and corruption. It is estimated that anywhere from between half a million to two and a half million North Koreans perished as a result of the famine, with many more being permanently impacted by the debilitating effects of malnutrition (see Natsios 2001).

At the same time, however, the regime tightened its grip further over North Korean society, skilfully bargained the Agreed Framework with Washington effectively to preserve its nuclear programme, and crafted an increasingly close bilateral relationship with China to offset the cost of losing the support of the Soviet Union. Throughout the 1990s the prevailing orthodoxy in the policy and academic worlds was that North Korea's situation was untenable and that the country's collapse was only a matter of time. When *Foreign Affairs* published Marcus Noland's 1997 article, 'Why North Korea Will Muddle Through', it finally signalled a shift in thinking about North Korea's future prospects (Noland 1997). Against extraordinary odds, the Pyongyang regime had staved off collapse by demonstrating a degree of resilience that few external observers anticipated. Yet at the same time no country or group of countries seriously wanted to see North Korea collapse. It seemed that, for as long as the North Korean regime desired survival more than others desired its termination, North Korea would endure, if not necessarily prosper.

By mid-2014 North Korea's economic situation appeared to be improving; the country has navigated only its second leadership transition (to Kim Jong-un in 2011), and it has acquired nuclear weapons. For a state said to be teetering on the edge of collapse for much of the 1990s, this is quite an achievement. More generally, it highlights the failure of international relations scholarship to predict how North Korea's fortunes would develop and the regime's capacity to achieve preferred outcomes against materially stronger adversaries. Above all, it illustrates how resilient small states in the face of huge external and domestic pressures can achieve their goals against tremendous odds. In recent years, the story of North Korea has been a classic reflection of the principles of asymmetric warfare where more determined entities that are relatively weak still achieve victory against richer, more advanced adversaries because they have greater interests at stake in the outcome (Mack 1975). This leaves little room for standard international relations theories that frequently overlook the agency of small and middle powers and which tend to assume the dominance of materially stronger states.

This chapter delves further into the North Korean case by evaluating the nature of the contemporary threat posed by North Korea; what key factors motivate the regime in Pyongyang; and how regional powers seek to manage North Korea.

What is the nature of the North Korean threat?

The threat from North Korea to regional security exists both at the domestic and international level. Domestically, a key consideration is the stability and coherence of the regime in Pyongyang. While predictions about North Korea's collapse have yet to come to pass, this outcome remains plausible. There are several scenarios in which serious internal instability could trigger the dislocation of central state control in North Korea, that in turn might lead to the gradual disintegration of North Korea. A military coup against the Kim regime has been canvassed given the status of the KPA as the dominant (and most organized) institution in the North Korean polity, even more so than the Korean Worker's Party, which has increased its influence under Kim Jong-un (Radio Free Asia 2013). Despite the totalitarian nature of the regime, there is some evidence that its hold on power remains contingent on the continuing support of the KPA; so much so that some have argued that the early brinkmanship on the part of Kim Jong-un was designed to demonstrate his leadership credentials to senior echelons of the military (International Crisis Group 2013). Another scenario is external intervention to remove the regime from power. The most likely context for this occurring would be full-scale war in which US and South Korean forces moved to overthrow the regime in the later stages of a conflict. Short of full-scale conflict, it is possible that an external power could intervene to 'stabilize' North Korea in the event that central control had evaporated. A core aim would be to secure North Korea's weapons of mass destruction (WMD) and missile strike forces. Some reports indicate that China already has top-secret plans on the drawing board for this very scenario (McCurry and Branigan 2014).

The consequences of regime collapse in North Korea are hard to envisage, but would in all likelihood involve the massive internal displacement of North Koreans, many of whom would probably be looking to flee the country as quickly as possible. Apart from South Korea, this would pose particular problems for China, which shares a 1,400-km border with North Korea. Beijing's current insistence on repatriating North Korean refugees – consigning many to certain death – may provide a worrying sign of things to come in the event of a mass exodus of North Koreans.

Internationally, North Korea's nuclear weapons programme has introduced a destabilizing variable into its relations with other states. North Korea's nuclear programme has been characterized by persistence, long-term strategic vision and constant evasion (for background, see Pollack 2011). From the decision of the Kim il-Sung regime to initiate a dedicated weapons programme in the 1960s, up until the 2012 insertion of a clause into the North Korean Constitution that embeds in law the country's status as a nuclear power, North Korea has worked assiduously to acquire and project a credible nuclear strike force. Possessing a dual track plutonium and highly enriched uranium programme, Pyongyang has developed the key to increasing the number of its nuclear warheads over time: stocks of fissile material for use in bombs. This is worrying from the perspective of North Korea becoming a major nuclear weapons state in its own right, but it is also disquieting because it is not known whether the current regime will try to export fissile material to other states with nuclear aspirations and deep pockets. The willingness of North Korea to export just about any military capability to customers with the ability to pay does not bode well for nuclear security in North-East Asia.

It is clear that the regime regards its possession of nuclear weapons as non-negotiable, and there is virtually no prospect that Pyongyang will voluntarily divest itself of nuclear arms. Decades of negotiating with North Korea have yielded nothing in the way of disarmament, and the country is today not subjected to any formal arms control commitments. Past bilateral negotiations with Washington as part of the Agreed Framework and discussions within the framework of the China-led Six-Party Talks produced little more than delays in North Korea's weapons programme. For Japan and South Korea in particular, coping with a neighbour that is both unpredictable and nuclear-armed will be a major challenge. US extended deterrence will be important in reassuring policymakers in Tokyo and Seoul, but any hint that Washington is not fully committed to responding forcefully to attempted coercion from Pyongyang during crises may have the effect of encouraging elites in Japan and South Korea to explore their own nuclear weapons options. Indeed, conservative elements in both countries have already signalled their sympathy for the latter course, and given the history of proliferation pressures in South Korea and Japan, it is something that cannot be ruled out.

Compounding the anxiety surrounding North Korea's nuclear programme is the rapid development of its long-range missile strike force; indeed, the two programmes have gone hand-in-hand. Pyongyang demonstrated its ability to develop an intercontinental ballistic missile by successfully launching a satellite payload in late 2012 just before its third nuclear test the following year, and many believe it is only a matter of time before Pyongyang will be able credibly to strike the west coast of the USA. If and when this happens, it could completely change the dynamics of crisis management on the Korean peninsula by deterring a future US administration from pushing back against North Korean attempts at coercion. Knowing that North Korea possesses the capacity to strike continental USA with nuclear weapons would be a major game changer strategically and would test the depth of the extended deterrence commitment Washington has to its East Asian allies. The risk is that policymakers in Seoul and Tokyo may choose to avoid this altogether by acquiring their own indigenous nuclear capability in the spirit of Charles de Gaulle's scepticism over whether any US president would seriously put at risk an American city for those of its allies.

While it is true that there are real risks attached to North Korea's nuclear and missile programmes, we should be wary of not exaggerating the dangers. After all, there is little evidence that North Korea regards US extended deterrence as lacking credibility or that its WMD serve any purpose other than to deter Washington and raise North Korea's status. The real risk may have more to do with accidental nuclear use occurring as a consequence of underdeveloped command and control systems than with any deliberate premeditated decision to push the button. There is no reason to believe that North Korea will behave any differently than any other new nuclear weapons states in underinvesting on software to coordinate nuclear forces in favour of concentrating on the hardware of missiles and warheads (see O'Neil 2014).

Explaining North Korean behaviour

What do North Korea's leaders want? This question in many respects encapsulates the essential puzzle of North Korea. No member of the North Korean regime has ever penned their memoirs, surveying the views of serving North Korean elites is off limits, and Pyongyang's public statements are laden with hyperbole that renders a proper interpretation of the regime's intentions problematic. Another challenge is that, while North Korea is undoubtedly a totalitarian state, there are numerous actors with various interests that shape its approach to the outside world. Kim Jong-un as supreme leader exercises control over state and society in a manner that is characteristic of totalitarianism (Friedrich and Brzezinski 1956), but the extent to which he exercises *complete* control over every institution, particularly the powerful military, is less clear. This has implications for interpreting North Korea's actions and by consideration of possible motives. As Robert Jervis observes, 'a state's behaviour is usually seen as centrally controlled rather than as the independent actions of actors trying to further their own interests and their partial and biased conceptions of the national interest' (Jervis 1976: 324).

Gauging what North Korean leaders want is closely linked to explaining motives. Traditionally, the most common explanation has been that Pyongyang is motivated by the straightforward goal of survival. This explanation gained traction in the wake of the triple shocks of the 1990s referred to earlier, and the idea that North Korea is driven purely by defensive intent still has appeal among analysts (see Armstrong 2011). As with all governments everywhere, in its foreign relations, the actions of the North Korean regime are undoubtedly motivated by the protection of its interests, the preservation of territorial integrity, and the defence of the state from external threats. In North Korea's strategic culture, the calamitous impact of the Korean War looms large and the visceral sense of injustice from the preceding period of Japanese colonial rule permeates Pyongyang's statements in relation to security (Cumings 2004: Chapter 1). As argued by Adrian Buzo, North Korea's national ideology dwells on past wrongs and focuses on future retribution (Buzo 1999). A deep sense of postcolonial anxiety accentuated by a shrill Hobbesian view of international relations as nasty and brutish (and short without robust military capabilities) underpins North Korea's engagement with the outside world. In such a world, where meaningful alliances do not exist, and autarky through *Songun* (military first) and *Juche* (which roughly translates as self reliance) are idealized, defensive measures are at a premium.

However, the regime in Pyongyang is not driven solely by defensive motives. Keeping adversaries off balance and divided is a proactive strategy that owes much to the guerrilla experiences of North Korea's founding leader, Kim il-Sung. This approach has been embraced and pursued by his son and now grandson. Reneging on agreements reached with other states and escalating crises before initiating tactical retreats after extracting concessions is integral to this strategy. This is not merely driven by defensive considerations. Indeed, on a number of occasions in the past, the USA, South Korea and others have offered Pyongyang security assurances only to be rebuffed (see Cha 2013: Chapter 7). Moreover, as North Korea's nuclear and missile programmes have evolved, Pyongyang seems to have become more confident that issuing direct nuclear threats of its own can change the behaviour of its adversaries – in other words, that coercion can work.

This was especially evident during high-level tensions on the Korean peninsula in April–May 2013, which witnessed particularly aggressive rhetoric from Pyongyang. This was in response to the UN Security Council's reaction to North Korea's third nuclear test in March and coincided with the commencement of the annual US–South Korea military exercise, Key Resolve. The 2013 crisis was significant because it marked the first occasion that North Korea issued explicit nuclear threats against other countries. These statements moved beyond an exclusively retaliatory justification to strongly hint at a pre-emptive rationale for first use, directly contradicting North Korea's stated no-first-use commitment issued shortly before its first nuclear test in 2006 (KCNA 2013). These 2013 statements were accompanied by several high-profile flights by the USA over South Korean territory of nuclear-capable B-52 and B-2 platforms, which constituted the most direct extended deterrence warning from Washington since the 1993–94 nuclear crisis (Reuters 2013).

What do North Korea's leaders hope to achieve from their attempts at coercion? As Thomas Schelling argues, coercion can have a variety of motives. For North Korea, it is likely that defensive and offensive motives coexist (Schelling 1966: Chapter 1). Defensively, coercion can be perceived as reinforcing deterrence, and North Korean elites probably surmise that the acquisition of nuclear weapons confers greater authority on the issuing of threats, whether these are conventional or nuclear. Offensively, North Korean elites may perceive a window of opportunity to wield more influence in North Korea's interactions with the USA and its regional allies with a long-term view to dominating North-East Asia's strategic landscape. Given the history of North Korea as an expansionist power on the Korean peninsula, the possibility cannot be ruled out that Pyongyang still harbours visions of conquering South Korea. In distinct comparison from the invasion in 1950, next time around it may be domination through the threat of military action. Much will depend on the perception of US extended deterrence credibility.

Regional powers and North Korea

Historically, Korea has been acutely vulnerable to external domination. This was a major feature of the 20th century when the peninsula was occupied and colonized by Japan (1910–45) and the division between North and South was manufactured geopolitically by the superpowers (Oberdorfer 1997). Koreans perceive themselves as being at risk of subjugation by external great powers and vigilance against this threat is a constant theme permeating Korean nationalism. It is an especially powerful theme underlying North Korea's worldview, which emphasizes relentless threats from a variety of foreign sources determined upon weakening the country's sovereignty. For Pyongyang, the authorities in Seoul are mere 'puppets' of foreign (mainly US) agents and North Korea is portrayed as the only genuine representative of Korean interests. Even North Korea's closest foreign interlocutor, China, is treated somewhat coolly in public statements, despite Beijing's large-scale economic support and its willingness to protect North Korea from any meaningful punishment meted out by the UN Security Council. In sum, North Korea is profoundly distrustful of all foreign countries.

For North Korea's neighbours, Pyongyang's distrust of the outside world, coupled with the regime's highly capricious nature, makes serious engagement difficult. This has certainly been the case at the multilateral level, with the Six-Party Talks revealing just how challenging it is to extract meaningful commitments from North Korea. The Six-Party Talks were initiated by China with strong backing from Washington following North Korea's withdrawal from the Non-Proliferation Treaty and the collapse of the Agreed Framework in 2002. Held from 2003 until the most recent meeting in 2008, the talks were designed to freeze North Korea's nuclear weapons programme and build on this through a series of agreed steps towards denuclearization in exchange for security assurances from the USA, including a non-aggression pact (for the timeline, see ACA 2012). During the six years of the Six-Party Talks, negotiations yielded a major joint declaration (in 2005) that outlined a process of disarmament on the Korean peninsula, but in 2006 North Korea carried out its first nuclear test, which sounded the death-knell for the negotiations. While further agreements were reached in 2007 and 2008 for phased disarmament measures, it was clear that Pyongyang regarded the talks as a means of buying time to build up its weapons programme and as a way to mollify Chinese concerns in relation to pressure from the USA.

With the Six-Party Talks now defunct, how are North Korea's neighbours attempting to manage it? The approaches of North Korea's neighbours are predominantly bilateral in scope and each has its own interests that in several senses are incompatible. Since the 1970s China's approach to North Korea has been focused on preserving the status quo on the Korean peninsula, which in practice has meant minimizing the potential for regime collapse while preserving the security of China's sprawling land border with North Korea. Yet it is apparent that Beijing is becoming increasingly ambivalent about North Korea. Pyongyang's erratic behaviour, its ambitious WMD programme, and the regime's stubborn refusal to pursue serious economic reform have caused major headaches for Beijing (BBC 2010). Moreover, in recent years it has become increasingly problematic for Beijing to protect the regime in Pyongyang while at same time improving the bilateral relationship with South Korea, China's third largest trading partner after the USA and Japan (North Korea is ranked 82nd). And while for some in China it may still be attractive to have North Korea as a strategic foil in North-East Asia for the USA and Japan, Pyongyang's decision to ignore Chinese entreaties to exercise restraint with its WMD programme and embark on economic reform raises serious questions about how much net value Beijing extracts from its relationship with North Korea.

South Korea's attempts to engage North Korea have resulted in fairly mixed outcomes since the landmark inter-Korean summit of 2000. The 'Sunshine Policy' period under the Kim Dae-jung and Roh Moo-hyun governments (1998–2008) yielded few concessions from Pyongyang, while the more hard-line period under President Lee Myung-bak (2008–12) saw little progress in the bilateral relationship (Moon 2012). The new 'Trustpolitik' approach of President Park Guen-hye seeks to synthesize harder and softer edges of previous approaches to Pyongyang, but so far the response from North Korea has been largely negative. It is difficult to escape the conclusion that North Korea has consistently acted in bad faith when dealing with South Korean governments from both the left and right of the political spectrum. Put simply, Pyongyang has taken advantage of the magnanimity of the Sunshine Policy to maximize economic aid inflows from Seoul while avoiding any binding commitments itself, and has used more hard-line policies from Seoul as a pretext not to engage in meaningful dialogue or restraint. Seoul has little choice but to continue its attempts to engage North Korea on a bilateral level, but it also regards US extended deterrence as more important than ever in providing formal reassurance that Washington will act militarily in the event that North Korea uses force against South Korea. The US nuclear umbrella has become increasingly salient in the thinking of South Korea and Japan as North Korea has acquired an operational nuclear force, something Beijing is no doubt conscious of (see O'Neil 2013: Chapters 4 and 5).

One sensitive area in which regional countries may have to develop multilateral cooperation mechanisms over time is in relation to a possible stabilization intervention in North Korea in the event of regime collapse in Pyongyang. As Bruce Bennett and Jennifer Lind have noted, there is no evidence of any consultation among regional governments regarding possible scenarios in which cooperation could take place (Bennett and Lind 2011). This becomes especially vexing when one considers the question of who is in control of North Korea's WMD assets during any internal dislocation and how the security of these assets might be guaranteed by external powers. The risk is not only that these assets could be commandeered by rogue elements of the military – a major concern in itself. Another challenge will be to ensure that conflict between external powers is not triggered as a result of separate US-led and Chinese interventions to seize nuclear, chemical, missile and possibly biological weapons assets. Unless a series of understandings are reached on areas of responsibility for intervening states prior to any collapse, the potential for confrontation and conflict remains very much in prospect.

Conclusion

Of all the challenges in contemporary international relations, managing the threat from North Korea must rank as one of the toughest. The nuclear-armed regime in Pyongyang remains deeply distrustful of the outside world and has consistently resisted repeated attempts to integrate North Korea into the international and regional community of nations. Multilateral mechanisms have proven inadequate as a means for promoting restraint in Pyongyang, and the North Korean regime has been highly adept at resisting bilateral pressure to engage in meaningful domestic reform and craft a constructive foreign policy consistent with internationally accepted norms and rules of behaviour. The paradox of North Korea is that it is one of the world's weakest and strongest countries. Ostensibly, North Korea's morally bankrupt system of governance, its egregious human rights record, and its largely broken economy make it something of a failed state in international relations. Yet the regime's resilience has been tested time and time again by adversity and not only does it survive, it also seems to thrive. To say North Korea is unique tells us little about the complex reasons why it endures despite its profound shortcomings. A capricious nuclear-armed state in a neighbourhood fraught with territorial contests and tensions based on deep historical fault lines hardly seems like a recipe for stability, but one of the other paradoxes of North Korea is that it lacks a real appetite for armed conflict, despite its frequent sabre rattling. The challenge for its regional neighbours will be how to prolong this lack of appetite through a mixture of engagement and deterrence in the years ahead.

Bibliography

Arms Control Association (ACA), 'The Six Party Talks at a Glance', 2012 www.armscontrol.org/factsheets/6partytalks.

Armstrong, Charles, 'Trends in the Study of North Korea', *Journal of Asian Studies*, Vol. 70, No. 2, 2011.

Armstrong, Charles, *Tyranny of the Weak: North Korea and the World, 1950–1992*, Ithaca, NY: Cornell University Press, 2013.

Bennett, Bruce and Jennifer Lind, 'The Collapse of North Korea: Military Missions and Requirements', *International Security*, Vol. 36, No. 2, 2011.

British Broadcasting Corporation (BBC), 'WikiLeaks Cables: China "Frustrated" by North Korea', *BBC News*, 30 November 2010, www.bbc.co.uk/news/world-us-canada-11871641

Buzo, Adrian, *The Guerilla Dynasty: Politics and Leadership in North Korea*, Sydney: Allen & Unwin, 1999.

Cha, Victor, *The Impossible State: North Korea, Past Present and Future*, London: Random House, 2013.

Cumings, Bruce, *North Korea: Another Country*, New York: The New Press, 2004.

Cumings, Bruce, *Korea's Place in the Sun: A Modern History*, New York: W. W. Norton and Company, 2005.

Friedrich, Carl and Zbigniew Brzezinski, *Totalitarian Dictatorship and Autocracy*, Cambridge, MA: Harvard University Press, 1956.

International Crisis Group, 'North Korean Succession and the Risks of Instability', *Asia Report*, No. 230, 2013, www.crisisgroup.org/en/regions/asia/north-east-asia/north-korea/230-north-korean-succession-and-the-risks-of-instability.aspx.

Jervis, Robert, *Perception and Misperception in International Politics*, Princeton, NJ: Princeton University Press, 1976.

Kim, Sung Chull, *North Korea Under Kim Jong-il: From Consolidation to Systemic Dissonance*, New York: SUNY Press, 2012.

Korean Central News Agency (KCNA), 'U.S. Should Ponder over Grave Situation: Statement issued by a spokesman for the General Staff of the Korean People's Army (KPA)', 4 April 2013, www.kcna.co.jp/index-e.htm.

McCurry, Justin and Tania Branigan, 'China Denies Making Preparations for Collapse of North Korean Regime', *The Guardian*, 6 May 2014.

Mack, Andrew, 'Why Big Nations Lose Small Wars: The Politics of Asymmetric Conflict', *World Politics*, Vol. 27, No. 2, 1975.

Moon, Chung-In, *The Sunshine Policy: In Defense of Engagement as a Path to Peace in Korea*, Seoul: Yonsei University Press, 2012.

Natsios, Andrew, *The Great North Korean Famine*, Washington, DC: US Institute of Peace Press, 2001.

Noland, Marcus, 'Why North Korea Will Muddle Through', *Foreign Affairs*, Vol. 76, No. 4, 1997.

O'Neil, Andrew, *Asia, the US and Extended Nuclear Deterrence: Atomic Umbrellas in the Twenty-First Century*, London and New York: Routledge, 2013.

O'Neil, Andrew, 'Command without Control? Nuclear Crisis Instability on the Korean Peninsula', *North Korean Review*, Vol. 10, No.1, 2014.

Oberdorfer, Don, *The Two Koreas: A Contemporary History*, London: Addison-Wesley, 1997.

Pollack, Jonathan, *No Exit: North Korea, Nuclear Weapons and International Security*, London: Routledge and the International Institute for Strategic Studies, 2011.

Radio Free Asia, 'North Korea's Workers' Party Takes Economic Control', 12 July 2013, www.rfa.org/english/news/korea/economy-07122013154816.html.

Reuters, 'North Korea Readies Rockets After US Show of Force', 29 March 2013, www.reuters.com/article/2013/03/29/us-korea-north-idUSBRE92R13R20130329.

Schelling, Thomas, *Arms and Influence*, New Haven, CT: Yale University Press, 1966.

United Nations Human Rights Council (UNHRC), *Report of the Commission of Inquiry on Human Rights in the Democratic People's Republic of Korea*, 7 February 2014, New York: United Nations.

18
Park Geun-hye, foreign policy innovation and risk on the Korean peninsula

John Swenson-Wright

A new president and a new approach to inter-Korean relations

As South Korea's first female President, Park Geun-hye was confronted by a number of critical challenges after assuming office in February 2013. Operating in a domestic political environment that is both fractious and chauvinistic, and facing a challenge from the country's northern neighbour, under the leadership of Kim Jong-un, a youthful, bellicose and seemingly erratic leader, Park has had to show resolve and determination in managing her country's foreign policy and particularly relations with the Democratic People's Republic of Korea (DPRK or North Korea). That she has been able to do this is perhaps not entirely surprising. As the daughter of South Korea's former authoritarian leader, Park Chung-hee, who dominated the politics of the Republic of Korea (ROK or South Korea) from the early 1960s when he seized power in a military coup, until his assassination in 1979, Park has lived a life steeped in political history and the challenges of executive office. Having grown up in the Blue House, the country's presidential residence, Park can claim to have witnessed major political change and to have had the opportunity to acquire first-hand political experience from an early age.

Following the assassination of her mother at the hands of an ethnic Korean Japanese national in 1974, while still in her early twenties Park effectively became the country's de facto first lady, assuming the formal role of accompanying her father to official events. This close engagement with political life, as well as the tragic experience of having lost both parents in violent circumstances within the space of five years, appears to have left the President with a profound sense of commitment to national service. Indeed, as a candidate for the presidency in 2012, Park spoke of healing the long-standing and often bitter political divisions between left and right in South Korean society by serving as a President for all Koreans (Kim and Yoon 2012). Whether she will deliver on this promise remains to be seen, and there is little doubt that her popularity has been significantly dented in the wake of national disaster in the form of the sinking in April 2014 of the *Sewol*, a passenger ferry that capsized with the loss of 304 lives, the majority of them high school pupils (Fiefield 2014).

The following analysis provides an initial and cautious assessment of President Park's foreign policy overtures in her first year or so in office, focusing in particular on her policy towards North Korea. It is perhaps too early at this stage to pass a definitive judgement on the President's approach, but it is useful to consider how effective she has been in translating principle into practice when dealing with North Korea, and how much strategic vision she has shown in developing her foreign policy priorities in the face of a number of distinctive and urgent foreign policy challenges. From this, it may be possible to reach a tentative assessment on the prospects for improved relations with North Korea and consider some of the options for policy innovation on the part of the South Korean government.

Trust and constancy in policy towards North Korea

Perhaps the most striking element of Park's policy towards North Korea has been her attempt to walk a middle path between the pro-engagement forces of the left in Korea, associated with the late President Kim Dae-jung and President Roh Moo-hyun and the more hawkish approach of conservative leaders such as Lee Myung-bak, her immediate presidential predecessor. This is not a surprising gambit. New presidents typically wish to distinguish themselves from their predecessors and where North Korea is concerned coming up with something original and distinctive has often proven difficult given the long history of seemingly intractable enmity dating back to the onset of the Korean War in 1950. Cleverly, Park has chosen not simply to split the difference between the two opposing sides of the political spectrum, but instead has sought to place a new variable – 'trust' – at the heart of her diplomacy towards the DPRK.

In the September/October 2011 issue of *Foreign Affairs* Park argued for an approach that stresses the importance of constancy and a long-term approach towards inter-Korean relations (Park 2011). North Korea must be encouraged to keep its promises to the international community, and a new international framework should be constructed in the form of a new Northeast Asia Peace and Cooperation Initiative (as well as a possible peace park on the Korean peninsula) – one which harmonizes South Korea's own approach with the efforts of the international community towards North Korea. Park, despite the constraints imposed by a fixed, single five-year term as President, appears to have her eyes firmly fixed on the long term – a move that has the merit of allowing her to appear decisive and clear in her interactions with North Korea but which runs the risk of limiting her options for manoeuvre and flexibility in a changing political and international landscape.

Park's article in *Foreign Affairs* attempts to situate her approach in a historical context, one which acknowledges the important achievements of past bilateral diplomatic breakthroughs such as the Middle Israel-Egypt peace process of 1979 under President Carter, or the Sino–US rapprochement that occurred during the Nixon Administration in 1971–72. Prior to becoming President, Park visited Pyongyang in 2001 and met with the then leader, Kim Jong-il, the father of the current incumbent. In doing so, she has shown herself to be an individual willing to take risks and to avoid bearing grudges – an extraordinary characteristic given North Korea's attempts in the past to assassinate senior members of the South Korean government, including her own father. As she noted on one occasion when asked to reflect on her visit to North Korea, 'We must look to the future with hope, not with bitterness' (Gregg 2013). It may well be the case that her conservative credentials as leader of the governing Saenuri Dang (New Frontier Party) provide her with political 'cover' and credibility to advance a policy of greater accommodation with North Korea, much in the same way as a Republican President Nixon was able to bury the hatchet with communist China. However, to date her overtures have yielded at best limited progress in the face of a North Korean leadership that has blown hot and cold in its attitudes to South Korea, sometimes engaging in quite vicious, personalized attacks on Park herself, while at other moments seeming to adopt a more accommodating positive posture towards South Korea (Branigan 2014).

Dresden and the dangers of aid asymmetry

'Trustpolitik' embodies both sticks and carrots: sticks in the form of a strengthened South Korean deterrence posture and reiteration of the basic point that North Korea will face real consequences for any actions that are perceived to threaten peace on the peninsula; carrots in the form of a willingness to offer substantial forms of economic cooperation and humanitarian assistance, perhaps including help in constructing a trans-Korean railway. The latter represents an ambitious and positive agenda for closer engagement and integration with North Korea. Park fleshed out much of the substance of this idea in a high-profile public speech she gave in the (former East) German city of Dresden, on 28 March 2014 (Park 2014).

Her speech was distinctive in stressing identity politics and her willingness to focus on the commonalities between the two Koreas. As she noted, 'What we need is not one-off promotional events, but the kind of interaction and cooperation that enables ordinary South Koreans and North Koreans to recover a common sense of national identity as they help each other out'. Yet while much of the speech focused on the benefits that South Korea could bring to its northern neighbour, whether in the form of infrastructure construction, educational exchange, and economic management, there was precious little reference to the benefits that North Korea might bring to South Korea, other than the supply of natural resources.

The danger of this one-sided focus on what South Korea can do to transform North Korea, is that it allows no space for the DPRK to promote its own achievements (modest as these might be) and as such, the proposal is psychologically unimaginative and unempathetic. A more nuanced approach might have sought to highlight the positive contribution that North Korea might make to any joint initiative – an important observation given that since coming to power in December 2011 Kim Jong-un has been keen to portray himself as a leader capable of delivering real economic benefits to his people (Hamisevicz 2013). Military modernization plus economic prosperity is a tough proposition to achieve for cash-poor North Korea, and one wonders whether Kim has made himself a hostage to fortune and how public opinion in the DPRK will respond if he fails to deliver on his ambitious promise.

For all the talk of a new approach to North Korea, it's worth stressing that there have been some important similarities that link Park's approach to that of her predecessors, of whichever political persuasion. Like Roh Moo-hyun, the ill-fated successor to Kim Dae-jung, who sought a pro-engagement approach that continued Kim's 'Sunshine Policy' intended to offer unconditional dialogue with North Korea, Park has cited the importance of learning lessons from Europe in thinking about new institutional approaches for dealing with North Korea. Specifically, Park has shown some receptivity to the idea of borrowing from the experience of the Organization for Security and Cooperation in Europe (OSCE).

The OSCE's multilateral and multi-basket approach for engaging with the former Soviet Union at the height of the Cold War offers a model for promoting a comprehensive peace dialogue in North-East Asia that would allow progress in some areas, such as economic and energy cooperation, even when discussions about denuclearization or human rights remain relatively intractable.

Similarly, Park has also aligned herself with the tough security posture of her predecessor, Lee Myung-bak, in making it clear both publicly and privately that she will brook no military aggression from North Korea and will be firm in responding strongly and unambiguously to any form of armed provocation or intimidation from the DPRK. In doing so, Park has shown significant political courage by, in particular, devolving the initiative for any security response to her uniformed military commanders – a bold decision in a polity where in the past the willingness of the military to intervene in politics and foreign policy has often proved controversial and of dubious constitutional legitimacy.

Following a series of rocket and missile launches from North Korea, in July 2014 Park spoke to a group of South Korean military leaders and said that the North Korean government was so unpredictable that it was impossible to foresee its behaviour 'even an inch ahead'. She said, 'If they launch a provocation, I ask you, commanding officers of the military, to retaliate with a strong initial countermeasure' (Choe 2014).

In other respects, Park has been very different from her predecessors. There is no prospect of South Korea offering unconditional aid to North Korea as a means of encouraging positive change from the DPRK – an approach that Roh favoured; likewise, Park has largely steered clear of prioritizing human rights or offering a grand bargain to North Korea in the manner supported by Lee.

North Korea's provocations

Notwithstanding Park's attempt to forge a new approach towards inter-Korean relations, the challenge has been an uphill one, not least because North Korea has proved to be persistently provocative. Prior to President-elect Park assuming office, Pyongyang heightened tensions on the peninsula by launching a satellite on 12 December 2012, which many observers argued was cover for developing its medium-range ballistic missile capabilities. It followed this with a dramatic third nuclear test on 12 February 2013 and then proceeded throughout March and April to engage in a series of provocations that contributed to a marked deterioration in relations between the two Koreas (Kim and Negishi 2012).

In part, North Korea's approach has been more rhetorical than substantive, including warning that it was prepared to launch a pre-emptive strike against South Korea and its neighbours, as well as potentially launching a nuclear strike against the continental USA. Pyongyang was also quick to announce its abrogation of past agreements with South Korea, such as the 1991 North-South accord, as well as its refusal to accept the terms of the 1953 Armistice, and its decision to suspend a number of critical military and civilian hotlines with South Korea (*The Guardian* 2013).

More dramatically, in April 2013 North Korea unilaterally suspended access to the Kaesong Industrial Complex, just north of the Demilitarized Zone (DMZ) – a key facility for promoting economic interaction between the two Koreas, employing some 53,000 North Koreans and providing valuable income and health care to a further 200,000 or so North Korean family dependents. Pyongyang was eventually forced to retract this short-sighted, and ultimately self-defeating gesture in September 2013, after a painstaking set of negotiations with Seoul in which the Park administration was able to extract from North Korea a commitment both to avoid any future unilateral closures and an agreement to open the area to greater internationalization and access to foreign companies (Williamson 2014).

How should we make sense of North Korea's belligerence in the face of a South Korean president who seems intent on finding a working compromise to improve bilateral relations? A number of possible explanations come to mind.

The North Korean leadership, and especially the young, inexperienced new leader, may have been intentionally generating a sense of crisis with South Korea in an effort to shore up Kim's legitimacy at home. It remains almost a truism of political theatre in the DPRK that leaders will seek to present themselves as united-in-arms guardians of the nation, leading the country in a perennial struggle with the outside world as a means of fostering national unity and resolve (Kwon and Chung 2012; Swenson-Wright 2014). In this sense, crisis is synthetic and needs to be manufactured in order to distract public opinion at home from more pressing day-to-day issues, including economic hardships. In this sense, Kim Jong-un differs little from his father and grandfather, although it is arguable that his limited experience as leader, his relative youth (he was born in 1983), and his short time in office has intensified the importance of this type of dynamic.

A second explanation may be more diplomatic rather than political, in a domestic sense. Provoking a crisis with South Korea may be motivated by a desire to generate dissension between the USA and one of its key regional allies. It may also have been shaped by the desire to test the resolve of President Park early on during her time in office. If this were indeed the motivation it seems to have failed as a strategy on both counts. Park has herself remained resolute and consistent in her posture towards North Korea, and Washington and Seoul have remained lock-step in tune with one another throughout the crisis during the spring of 2014. If anything, ties have deepened between the two countries over the course of the year. Clear evidence of this has been the deliberate and very public efforts by the two countries to reinforce the message of deterrence they have sought to send to North Korea, underpinned by such actions as the deployment of B-52 bombers and B-1 stealth bombers and F-22 stealth fighters in the vicinity of the Korean peninsula, as well as the early deployment to the region by the USA of terminal high-altitude area (THAAD) defence radar and missile defence systems (Chance and Stewart 2013).

A third factor may have been a desire to play for time. By provoking a new crisis, North Korea may have felt it could improve its practical leverage in a number of ways. The risk of imminent conflict may at one level be perceived as a means of extracting economic and diplomatic concessions from the international community (which has been particularly ineffective); it may also (and here the evidence suggests that North Korea has been relatively more successful) have helped to delay any prospect of the immediate resumption of negotiations over North Korea's nuclear capabilities. This has enabled Pyongyang, in its eyes, legitimately to suspend or abrogate past agreements, and to continue to engage in illegitimate actions, for example the open and covert reactivation of its plutonium and uranium reprocessing activities at its nuclear power plant at Yongbyon.

Finally, and notwithstanding North Korea's desire to play for time, it may have been hoping to use the spectre of hostilities on the peninsula to force the Obama administration to agree to direct talks, less explicitly on the nuclear issue, but more on issues such as talks to discuss a formal peace treaty to end the Korean War, political accommodation via diplomatic recognition from the USA, and the provision by Washington of formal economic assistance and trade and investment opportunities. Once again, North Korea's gambit does not appear to have paid off. President Obama has continued his de facto policy of 'strategic patience' and in a White House preoccupied with competing crises in the Ukraine and Syria there has been very little appetite for active contact with the DPRK (Sigal 2014).

John Swenson-Wright

Options for the Park administration

Looking ahead to the future, what lessons can the Park government draw from the recent crisis and what are the notable achievements of the administration to date? Park's approach has been broadly calm and measured. Her rhetoric when discussing the situation on the Korean peninsula has been careful to avoid demonizing North Korea and she has shrewdly avoided the sort of ad hominem attacks that Pyongyang has used when describing her administration. Additionally, she has displayed consistency and remarkable patience in seeking to maintain open channels for dialogue with Pyongyang, an approach which has sometimes, but not always, elicited a positive response from the North Korean leadership, which has swung from positive to negative extremes in its interaction with South Korea (Yonhap 2014).

Maintaining deterrence by bolstering relations with the Obama administration, by giving maximum tactical and strategic discretion to the ROK military, and by skilfully deploying media imagery at home to present herself as a tough and resourceful leader has allowed Park to avoid any appearance of negotiating weakness that might be exploited by North Korea. At the same time, she has been careful to avoid getting swept along by a tide of rising anti-North Korea populism at home. For example, Park has wisely resisted growing public calls to promote plans for South Korea's own independent nuclear weapons capacity in the face of North Korea's de facto nuclear programme. While some 66 per cent of the South Korean public were reported in a February 2013 poll as favouring a South Korean nuclear weapons programme, there has been no suggestion that the Blue House is willing to contemplate pursuing such an option (Asian Institute for Policy Studies 2014). While it would no doubt be technically feasible, the damage it would do to relations with the USA, which strongly backs an anti-proliferation agenda, and the impetus it would give to a nuclear arms race in the region, all militate against such an approach.

Sticking closely to the USA's anti-nuclear agenda does not necessarily mean that Seoul and Washington are firmly on the same page on all issues. For example, military and political planners in Seoul appear less inclined to accept the more pessimistic projections of the US Defence Intelligence Agency estimates suggesting that North Korea will, within three to five years, be able to place a miniaturized nuclear warhead on one of its medium-range ballistic missiles (Shanker et al. 2013). Similarly, Seoul has retreated from earlier plans to transfer operational command from US to ROK military forces by 2015. Sentiment among military officials in Seoul is now to maintain existing arrangements with the USA to avoid any hint of a weakening of alliance resolve in the face of North Korea's more aggressive and potentially more unpredictable military posture.

Perhaps most notable of all divergences from Washington has been the Park administration's new-found policy of diplomatic closeness with Beijing, symbolized by two high-profile and diplomatically successful visits by the two leaders to their respective countries in the course of this year – first Park's visit to Beijing in June 2013, and just over a year later the follow-up visit by Xi Jinping to Seoul (Cha and Kim 2014).

Of course, in so many ways China is the key to resolving tensions with North Korea. As its only ally, and as a provider of substantial amounts of food and energy assistance to the DPRK, China is theoretically in a position to influence the Kim regime. Moreover, as public opinion in China has become increasingly exercised by concerns that the nuclearization of North Korea may increase the risk of radiation exposure in Northern China, and as elite Chinese opinion becomes more irritated by the DPRK's diplomatic brinksmanship, it is logical that Xi Jinping and other Chinese leaders might be minded to put pressure on their junior partner. Paradoxically, however, North Korea's very weakness and vulnerability gives it added leverage. China wishes to avoid regime collapse, a mass exodus to China of millions of North Korean refugees, and the attendant power vacuum that might emerge in North Korea only to be filled by US and ROK forces if the security crisis were to escalate. Consequently, Pyongyang, conscious of these fears, skilfully exploits Chinese concerns to test the limits of independent decision-making.

It would be a mistake, however, to view the burgeoning Sino-South Korean relationship as unambiguous proof of deft diplomacy on the part of Seoul. Elsewhere, the fraught relationship between South Korea and Japan is powerful proof of some serious shortcomings in Park's approach to foreign policy. To the Obama administration, the sharp deterioration in bilateral ties between Park and the more assertive (some might argue nationalistic) Abe administration in Japan is a source of acute frustration, if not despair. The USA's two most critical Asian allies appear to be incapable of working constructively together, bogged down as they are in long-standing disputes over territory (the Dokdo-Takeshima controversy) and bitter disagreements about pre-war and wartime responsibilities, in particular the status of South Korea's so-called comfort women – a dwindling group of elderly female survivors of the policy of enforced sexual servitude dating from Japan's colonial domination of the peninsula in the first half of the 20th century (Uchiyama and Nakayama 2014).

Tensions with Japan beg the question of how adept Park's handling of diplomacy truly is. Many of the tensions between Seoul and Tokyo seem to be rooted in personal differences between Park and Abe (not merely political calculations as some have suggested). If South Korea is to capitalize on its advantages vis-à-vis North Korea, both in terms of the new, closer relationship with China, or its relative economic and strategic strength, surely it needs to develop a more sophisticated approach. South Korea must bury the hatchet with Japan, especially in light of the Abe administration's recently improved dialogue with North Korea on the long-stalled abduction issue; it also needs to add substance to its own high-profile Northeast Asian Peace and Cooperation Initiative and plans for the creation of a DMZ peace park – two diplomatic initiatives that are getting nowhere. It would be wrong, of course, to assume that the limitations in South Korea's diplomacy are exclusively its own responsibility. The purge of Kim Jong-un's close adviser and senior confidant, Jang Song-thaek, in December 2013, vividly demonstrated the precarious nature of North Korea's reform agenda. Jang was widely perceived as being both sympathetic to economic reform and close to China. His purge and execution took outside opinion by surprise and has strengthened the view that political consolidation at home and shoring up the authority of the new young, North Korean leadership are more important than substantive reform (Swenson-Wright 2013).

Ultimately, this is an unpromising (some might argue depressing) scenario for any South Korean leader to confront. It offers few immediate political or strategic options for improving bilateral ties. However, there are a few, limited positive opportunities on the horizon. One area for improved bilateral dialogue might be education. North Koreans, like their South Korean counterparts, have an inexhaustible thirst for knowledge. Foreign countries (Sweden, Australia, India, Vietnam, Canada, the UK, even the USA, to name but a few) have proven track records of training North Korean visitors and students at graduate and post-doctoral level. A concerted, internationally funded effort to enable North Korean students to study abroad, across a wide range of disciplines, might be a very positive first step. This could take the form of truly international, collective commitment – a Marshall Plan for Education in North-East Asia, one might say – with the principal focus in the short term on both offering opportunities for young North Koreans to study overseas, as well as allowing foreign academics and students to visit the DPRK. The precedent here might be the sort of educational opening up that China experienced during the 1970s – a form of internationalization that did not threaten the foundations of the Chinese state, and therefore could be regarded as politically safe by Pyongyang if transposed to a North Korean context.

For now, however, the sobering conclusion is that trust, while important in fostering improved relations, takes time and mutual effort to establish securely. Whether President Park has the time and the opportunity to realize this in the three years left in her term of office remains to be seen.

Bibliography

Asian Institute for Policy Studies, 'The Fallout: South Korean Public Opinion Following North Korea's Third Nuclear Test', 24 February 2014, http://en.asaninst.org/contents/issue-brief-no-46-the-fallout-south-korean-public-opinion-following-north-koreas-third-nuclear-test/.

Branigan, Tania, 'North Korea Labels South's President as "Crafty Prostitute" After Obama Visit', *The Guardian*, 27 April 2014, www.theguardian.com/world/2014/apr/27/north-korea-attacks-south-president-park-geun-hye-obama.

Cha, Victor and Ellen Kim, 'President Xi Jinping's State Visit to the Republic of Korea', *CSIS Online*, 3 July 2014, http://csis.org/publication/president-xi-jinpings-state-visit-republic-korea.

Chance, David and Phil Stewart, 'North Korea Readies Missiles After U.S. Stealth Bombers Fly Over South', *Reuters*, 29 March 2013, http://uk.reuters.com/article/2013/03/29/uk-korea-north-idUKBRE92R13Q20130329.

Choe, Sang-hun, 'South Korea Begins Naval Drills with the U.S.', *New York Times*, 16 July 2014, www.nytimes.com/2014/07/17/world/asia/south-korea-begins-naval-drills-with-the-us.html?_r=0.

Fiefield, Anna, 'Grieving Families of Sewol Ferry Victims Want Independent South Korean Probe', *Washington Post*, 5 August 2014, www.washingtonpost.com/world/asia_pacific/south-koreas-grieving-sewol-families-want-independent-investigation/2014/08/05/3e7e3afd-88ae-4daf-bc81-8a1b2dd9d909_story.html.

Gregg, Donald, 'Reaching Out to North Korea', *Los Angeles Times*, 1 April 2013, http://articles.latimes.com/2013/apr/01/opinion/la-oe-gregg-why-obama-should-engage-with-north-kor-20130401.

Hamisevicz, Nicolas, 'No Illusions for North Korea: What Recent Provocations tell us about Kim Jong-un', National Bureau of Asian Research, 12 February 2013, www.nbr.org/research/activity.aspx?id=308.

Kim, Cynthia and Sangwoon Yoon, 'Dictator Daughter Elected Korean Leader Vowing to Heal Scars', *Bloomberg*, 20 December 2012, www.bloomberg.com/news/2012-12-19/dictator-s-daughter-takes-korean-presidency-vowing-to-heal-scars.html.

Kim, Jack and Mayumi Negishi, 'North Korea Rocket Launch Raises Nuclear Stakes', *Reuters*, 12 December 2012, www.reuters.com/article/2012/12/12/us-korea-north-rocket-idUSBRE8BB02K20121212.

Kwon, Heonik and Byung-Ho Chung, *North Korea: Beyond Charismatic Politics*, Lanham, MD: Rowman & Littlefield, 2012.

Park, Geun-hye, 'A New Kind of Korea. Building Trust between Seoul and Pyongyang', *Foreign Affairs*, September/October 2011.

Park, Geun-hye, 'Full Text of Park's Speech on N. Korea', *Yonhap*, 28 March 2014, http://english.yonhapnews.co.kr/full/2014/03/28/40/1200000000AEN20140328008000315F.html.

Shanker, Thom, David Sanger and Eric Schmitt, 'Pentagon Finds Nuclear Strides by North Korea', *New York Times*, 11 April 2013, www.nytimes.com/2013/04/12/world/asia/north-korea-may-have-nuclear-missile-capability-us-agency-says.html?pagewanted=all.

Sigal, Leon, 'A Nuclear North Korea vs. a Strategically Patient U.S.: Who Wins?' *National Interest*, 24 April 2014, http://nationalinterest.org/feature/nuclear-north-korea-vs-strategically-patient-us-who-wins-10301.

Swenson-Wright, John, 'North Korea Purge: Brutal But Risky Move', *BBC Online*, 13 December 2013, www.bbc.com/news/world-asia-25361473.

Swenson-Wright, John, 'North Korea's Artful Long Game', *Prospect*, 5 April 2014, www.prospectmagazine.co.uk/author/john-swenson-wright.

The Guardian, 'North Korea Ends Armistice with South Amid War Games on Both Sides of Border', 11 March 2013, www.theguardian.com/world/2013/mar/11/north-korea-declares-end-armistice.

Uchiyama, Kiyoyuki and Shin Nakayama, 'Time Hasn't Closed Tokyo-Seoul Gap Over "Comfort Women"; Can Abe and Park?' *Nikkei Asian Review*, 25 June 2014, http://asia.nikkei.com/Politics-Economy/International-Relations/Time-hasn-t-closed-Tokyo-Seoul-gap-over-comfort-women-can-Abe-and-Park.

Williamson, Lucy, 'Koreas Restart Operations at Kaesong Industrial Zone', *BBC Online*, 16 September 2014, www.bbc.com/news/world-asia-24104774.

Yonhap, 'Park Calls for N. Korea's Positive Response to Her Overture', 19 August 2014, http://english.yonhapnews.co.kr/northkorea/2014/08/19/76/0401000000AEN20140819005251315F.html.

19
North Korea endgame

Terence Roehrig

(The views expressed in this report are the author's alone and do not represent the official position of the US Department of the Navy, the US Department of Defense, or the US government.)

Introduction

Since the end of the Cold War, many have been predicting the demise of North Korea followed by the reunification of the Korean peninsula. The 1997 National Intelligence Council report entitled *Global Trends 2010*, predicted that 'the next 15 years will witness the *transformation of North Korea and resulting elimination of military tensions on the peninsula*' (National Intelligence Council 1997: 10, emphasis in the original). Yet despite a crumbling economy, appalling human rights record (UNHRC 2014), and increasing international isolation, the Democratic People's Republic of Korea (DPRK or North Korea) continues to muddle along (Noland 1997).

For the next 20 to 30 years there is likely to be no North Korea endgame. Despite its economic problems, the DPRK and the Kim family regime will remain in power, and barring any unexpected health issues, Kim Jong-un will rule into his sixties and possibly longer. Most importantly, China will continue to support the regime to keep its neighbour afloat and maintain access to North Korea's natural resources. Thus, policymakers should act on the assumption that North Korea will have considerable longevity and will not disappear anytime soon.

Although the DPRK is predicted to continue for the next two or three decades, there are three wild cards that could possibly bring about significant change to the regime or signal its end: information leakage into North Korea that erodes the leadership's ability to control the national narrative; pressures from below that prompt some level of economic reform; and a North Korean response such as a military action when Pyongyang is unable to control the escalation spiral. These three wild cards are not necessarily discreet and could happen in tandem, in stages, or all at the same time. In many respects, North Korea has already begun to change and predicting its future is a risky undertaking. Most of those who have tried before have been off the mark. This chapter is a further attempt at tackling this difficult task but admittedly the timeline may be long, and unexpected events may occur that prove everyone wrong.

Continuity – the most likely North Korean endgame

The most probable future for the DPRK is its continued survival. Indeed, over the past three decades, North Korea has faced several political and economic challenges that many thought would bring down the regime (Kim *et al.* 2011: 28–43). Yet despite the challenges and the popular predictions, North Korea endured.

Political continuity

Politically, some of the most challenging times have coincided with the deaths of North Korean leaders and the subsequent transitions to power. On 8 July 1994 long-serving leader Kim Il-sung passed away, whereupon power shifted to his then 53-year-old son, Kim Jong-il. In 1980 Kim Jong-il had been publicly proclaimed heir apparent, 14 years before the death of his father. These intervening years provided Kim Jong-il with the time to establish his power base, serve in lower level positions that prepared him for the job, and learn how to lead the North Korean state, the Korean Workers Party (KWP), and Korean People's Army (KPA). Yet when his father died many people wondered whether the power transition would be smooth. Would Kim Jong-il, who possessed few of his father's credentials and had never served in the military be able to consolidate his power and keep the DPRK afloat?

Despite these concerns, Kim Jong-il ruled North Korea for the next 17 years upholding his father's guiding *juche* ideology of self-reliance, and adding his own ideological contribution of *songun* or 'military first' politics. When Kim Jong-il succeeded his father, the economy was already starting its slide and the party became less and less effective in achieving the state's political and economic goals. As McEachern (2010: 85) notes, 'By the time Kim Jong-il came to power, the party was a fish out of water. Aging officials from a previous era continued to trumpet the importance of applying revolutionary principles to specific policies, but the calls rang increasingly hollow.' While Kim Il-sung ruled through the KWP, Kim Jong-il turned to the military as the lead institution. Moreover, Kim Jong-il needed to control and co-opt the military to ensure it supported his succession. KWP failings were particularly evident during the famine years, and while the state and party struggled, the KPA was portrayed to the public as the institution best equipped to endure these hard times. Kim Jong-il also set up the National Defense Commission as the chief political institution and ruled North Korea largely as chairman of that body.

Throughout his time in office and despite continued predictions of the regime's demise, Kim Jong-il maintained his grip on power. The regime was tested severely during the 1990s and yet persevered (Cha and Anderson 2012). Kim Jong-il was able to survive largely because the regime had put in place several measures that helped to 'coup-proof' his rule (Byman and Lind 2010). To prevent an overthrow from below, the regime made it nearly impossible for opposition to coalesce. First, the DPRK has put in place numerous policies that restrict free speech and the ability to organize any type of collective action against the state. Second, from an early age the populace is indoctrinated with regime ideology – *juche* and *songun* – that preaches nationalism and loyalty with all of this buttressed by the cult of personality and the ubiquitous reminders of the leaders' importance through illustrations and monuments throughout North Korea. Finally, the regime maintains a heavy coercive arm to ensure that the populace maintains its loyalty to the regime (Gause 2012). The DPRK has multiple state security organs that are purposely divided and pitted against each other with all reporting directly to the leadership. McEachern (2010: 45) notes that 'the complex web of security relationships demonstrates the top leadership's concerns about violent overthrow from within and concerted efforts to spy on the spies'. The country maintains an *inminban* (neighbourhood watch) system that reports any activity that could be deemed subversive or anti-regime, making any organization from below very difficult (Lankov 2013: 38–41). If an individual is caught carrying out any form of anti-state activity, three generations of that individual's family may be sent to one of the many labour camps in North Korea (Harden 2013).

Cha and Anderson (2012) also argue that any hope for a 'North Korean Spring' similar to the uprising from the populace that occurred in the Middle East is largely wishful thinking. Several of the key variables in the Middle East are not present in the same way in North Korea. Most of North Korea is poor so there is no development gap to spark a revolt; most people are far too concerned with survival to contemplate an uprising. Furthermore, the DPRK does not have the problem of a youth bulge comprising disaffected, educated but unemployed young men who vent their unhappiness by criticizing the government. Most men spend up to 10 years in the military which provides employment and the opportunity further to indoctrinate this segment of the population. Finally, given the lack of social media and modern communications, any type of contagion effect is unlikely. Thus, while North Korea's leaders may fear an overthrow, the likelihood of an uprising from below is small.

The regime has also taken several other measures to insulate itself from an overthrow from above by elites (Byman and Lind 2010). First, the regime has worked hard to co-opt elites in the party, military, and government bureaucracies by buying them off with higher salaries, access to subsidized luxury goods, and an overall better quality of life than most North Koreans. The elite comprises just 1 per cent of the population who often reside in Pyongyang, for which special permission is required and comes with perks such as access to the best schools and medical care, for example. Military leaders have been especial beneficiaries of the Kim family's largesse with the 'military first' policy giving the KPA priority to many of North Korea's scarce resources. Indeed, North Korea's pursuit of nuclear weapons in part helps to placate hardliners in the military and the party.

Second, North Korea has also been adept at squeezing aid from foreign governments to prop up the regime and demonstrating the fact that the collapse of the DPRK is a problem that no one wants (Byman and Lind 2010: 64–66). Finally, as noted above, the regime has created parallel and competing security institutions and installed family members in key posts to help to 'coup-proof' institutions that could be hubs for opposition towards the Kim family.

As the years passed and Kim Jong-il grew older, speculation turned to his possible successor, yet there was little indication that a selection process had begun. However, in late 2008 the world learned that Kim Jong-il had suffered a stroke and had been incapacitated for several months. Suddenly, succession became an urgent matter. For a variety of reasons, Kim Jong-il did not believe his first and second sons were fit to rule and chose instead his youngest, Kim Jong-un who was believed to be in his late twenties at the time. Kim Jong-un had only a few years of preparation for office before his father died on 17 December 2011.

Once again, speculation was rife for the likelihood of a stable power transition to the young Kim. In the years since the death of Kim Jong-il, the regime has worked to resuscitate the power of the KWP and for Kim Jong-un to rule through it rather than the military, a process that had already begun before his father's demise. To cement his control of the military, Kim Jong-un has purged over 40 military officers including to the surprise of many, Ri Yong Ho, a Kim family loyalist and head of the KPA at the time. In December 2013, Kim went to even greater lengths with the purge and execution of his uncle, Jang Song-thaek who was married to Kim Jong-il's sister and believed to be the regent behind Kim Jong-un's rule. Jang's demise raised many questions about the stability of the regime and while Kim Jong-un continues to consolidate his power, there are no visible signs of opposition and continuity appears likely.

Economic continuity

Many of the predictions of North Korea's end have involved economic collapse where the failing economy implodes generating revolt from below or a coup from above. Once again, these predictions have been around for years and despite numerous economic factors that indicate North Korea cannot last, it continues to plod along.

During the early years of the division of Korea after the Second World War, North Korea's economy outpaced that of South Korea's, but by the end of the 1960s this started to change. South Korea's economy took off after Park Chung-hee seized power in 1961 and implemented major reforms that turned the country into an economic power house (Heo and Roehrig 2010: 78–103). In turn, North Korea's economy began a slow descent as a result of the inefficiencies of a command economy and poor economic decision making. Despite Pyongyang's ideological foundation in *juche*, North Korea's economic dependence on aid and subsidized trade with the Soviet Union and China increased (Cha 2012).

With the ending of the Cold War, several factors came together to jolt the DPRK. First, Moscow was no longer able to provide assistance to prop up the economy as it had done in the past. The post-Soviet economy could not take care of its own people, much less support North Korea. In addition, assistance from China decreased significantly as Beijing altered the terms of its economic ties with Pyongyang. To make matters worse, both Russia and China established diplomatic relations with Seoul. Despite North Korea's objections, South Korea offered too many economic opportunities for either DPRK patron to ignore any longer but Pyongyang felt betrayed nonetheless. Second, the accumulated effects of central control and mismanagement were taking their toll, and the economy was already struggling before the country was hit by the great famine. During most of the 1990s the country was affected by a series of floods and droughts that decimated the agriculture sector. In what North Korean leadership dubbed the 'arduous march', the resulting famine destroyed the state's ability to provide for the population's basic needs through the public distribution system (PDS). Estimates of those who perished range from 600,000 to 1m., or approximately 3 per cent to 5 per cent of the population (Haggard and Noland 2007).

The country slowly recovered with the help of international food aid and other assistance but overall the North Korean economy remains in difficulties and experiences chronic food shortages. Data on North Korea are hard to come by but sources have been able to provide estimates. With a population of 24.7m., the 2012 gross domestic product (GDP) was estimated at US $40,000m. when measured on a purchasing-power parity (PPP) basis. Measured at current exchange rates, GDP drops to approximately $28,000m. Using the PPP measure, North Korea's GDP per head is estimated to be $1,800, and the economy grew by 1.3 per cent in 2012 (CIA 2014).

The North Korean economy remains heavily dependent on China. Beijing is the DPRK's leading trade partner accounting for 76.6 per cent of total trade in 2012. The next closest trade partner was India at 5.6 per cent (European Commission 2014). North Korea depends on China for 90 per cent of its energy and a large proportion of its consumer goods and food imports. Much of this trade is subsidized by Beijing since Pyongyang has relatively little hard currency or the ability to borrow in order to finance its trade deficit with China.

Chinese support is critical to North Korea's survival, and Pyongyang is nervous about the degree of leverage this dependency creates for the country. Indeed, some reports for the first quarter of 2014 indicated China may have cut off oil supplies to North Korea to show its displeasure at the execution of Jang Song-thaek but others maintain that the oil has continued to flow as aid and assistance rather than as part of Chinese trade statistics. Although China has been concerned about some of Pyongyang's provocative actions, particularly its nuclear weapons tests, there are limits to what China is willing to do to coerce North Korea. Many Chinese fear that significant pressure on North Korea risks bringing about the DPRK's collapse, creating an unstable mess on their border along with the loss of a buffer state. As a result, China continues to have important strategic interests in maintaining the North Korean regime, and its support will keep the Kim family afloat through its economic struggles, another reason for the probable continuity of the regime.

Military continuity

The final element favouring North Korea's continuity is the country's military establishment and state security apparatus. The KPA is a large, powerful force that remains a threat to security on the Korean peninsula while providing an effective deterrent to actions taken against the DPRK (Roehrig 2005). North Korea devotes approximately 25 per cent of its GDP to defence fielding an active duty military of close to 1.2m. personnel supported by a reserve force of 600,000 and paramilitary units comprising 5.7m. troops (IISS 2014: 254). These numbers help to make the DPRK one of the most militarized countries in the world.

The army is the largest branch of the KPA fielding over 4,000 tanks of various types and over 8,500 self-propelled and towed artillery pieces, along with 5,100 multiple rocket launchers (MRLs). Though the tank numbers are impressive, many are old Soviet models like the T-34, T-54/55, and T-62 as well as Chinese light tanks. North Korea has built a more modern tank, the Pokpung-ho, or 'Storm Tiger' but it is unclear how many of these newer models Pyongyang has been able to manufacture given the state of its economy. The artillery and MRL systems are a particular concern since many of these weapons have sufficient range to reach Seoul. North Korea also has large, well-trained special operations forces estimated to number from 88,000 to 180,000 personnel (Harden 2009; IISS 2014: 255). Approximately 70 per cent of North Korea's military assets are deployed within 100 miles of the demilitarized zone, and although a serious concern for South Korean and US defence planners, a Korean War-style invasion or other type of large-scale military operation by the KPA is highly unlikely.

North Korea has a small surface navy comprising only three frigates supplemented by 382 patrol and coastal vessels (IISS 2014: 255). Reports indicated that the Korean People's Navy has constructed two new helicopter carrying frigates that would improve its ability to protect fisheries in the West (Yellow) Sea and counter South Korea's growing submarine fleet by increasing North Korea's anti-submarine warfare capability (Bermudez Jr 2014). Of particular concern following the sinking of the South Korean corvette *Cheonan* is North Korea's submarine fleet. Submarines have been used to deliver special operations forces and have the capability to disrupt ROK shipping, a serious concern since South Korea generates over 50 per cent of its GDP through exports.

The Korean People's Air Force (KPAF) has 603 combat aircraft, a fairly large number though only 52 are the more advanced Soviet model MiG-29 and Su-25. The majority of its airframes are older Soviet and Chinese models that would fare badly against South Korean and US fighters. In addition, the KPAF lacks fuel and spare parts to maintain the aircraft and according to the IISS (2014: 256), pilots train for an average of only 20 hours per year in their planes raising serious concerns about the readiness of the force.

In addition to its conventional assets, North Korea also possesses a robust ballistic missile programme, chemical weapons, and a nuclear weapons programme. For many years, North Korea has worked to grow its ballistic missile capabilities, beginning in the 1980s when Pyongyang acquired a Scud B missile from Egypt and reverse engineered the system to produce its own short-range ballistic missiles. North Korea is believed to have approximately 200 Scud missiles that can cover most of the Korean peninsula and 150 medium-range Nodong missiles that can target most of Japan (Thielman 2013: 5). Pyongyang continues to develop longer-range systems such as the Musudan and KN-08, both mobile missiles, and the Taepodong missile. The Musudan and KN-08 have not been flight tested, but the systems have been deployed and are displayed during parades. The KN-08 and Taepodong missiles are designed to have the capability of reaching the continental USA.

North Korea's chemical weapons programme has long been a concern for defence planners. Estimates maintain that North Korea has 2,500 to 5,000 metric tons of various types of chemical munitions including mustard gas, sarin, phosgene, and V-agents (Jane's Sentinel Security Assessment 2011). These weapons are indigenously manufactured and are deliverable by artillery, ballistic missiles and rockets. There are also concerns that North Korea possesses biological weapons but the extent of this programme remains uncertain.

Finally, North Korea is continuing to develop nuclear weapons. North Korea has conducted three nuclear tests and is believed to have between four and 10 nuclear devices based on the amount of spent fuel it has available from its reactor at Yongbyon. Reports indicate that North Korea has restarted the reactor (turned off in 2007 in exchange for foreign aid) and if successful, could produce one additional nuclear weapon per year. North Korea also has embarked on a parallel programme using uranium enrichment to produce weapons grade uranium but even less is known about this programme (Roehrig 2012; Thielmann 2013).

Two key obstacles remain: North Korea's ability to weaponize a warhead, perhaps on the medium-range Nodong missile, and the development of a longer-range ballistic missile equipped with a warhead capable of reaching the continental USA. There are many other technological challenges to develop an effective and reliable nuclear deterrent that can be launched when needed, land on the intended target, and detonate when expected. As Struckman (2013) notes, North Korea will continue to improve its capabilities 'but it won't be easy ... or cheap'.

North Korean military capabilities protect the Kim family, the party and the state by providing a deterrent to prevent an invasion and regime change by South Korea and the USA. A military operation to remove the current regime would be a costly endeavour. Moreover, North Korea does not need nuclear weapons to constitute a reliable deterrent as its chemical weapons and the ability to lob artillery shells and rockets on Seoul are more than sufficient for this purpose. In addition, continued high levels of military spending accompanied by the rhetoric of 'military first' politics and the purges of high-ranking officers ensure that Kim Jong-un is in control of the military that helps to maintain the continued existence of the regime.

Three wildcards for North Korea's future

The continuation of North Korea for the next two to three decades appears fairly certain at the moment. However, there are three wild cards that could possibly change this outcome, depending on how they evolve.

Loss of information control

For years, North Korea has been able to maintain control of its people by restricting the flow of information into the country. As a result, the regime has been able to craft its own narrative of the DPRK with little competition from outside sources. Grounded in *juche* ideology, the regime portrayed capitalism and foreign ideas as 'spiritual pollution' and a threat to the purity and sanctity of the regime. As Oh and Hassig (2000: 143) note, 'the lack of information from foreign sources prevents people from judging the validity of the Kim regime's negative propaganda about the outside world'.

During the famine of the 1990s North Korea's ability to control the information flow into the country began to wane. With the breakdown of the PDS people were forced to survive by their own efforts, and increasing numbers of North Koreans crossed the border to China in pursuit of markets or things to buy. The cross-border traffic was tolerated as a safety valve – border guards and security personnel could be bribed and the state was too weak to enforce existing restrictions against such activities. This illegal commerce generated a new inflow of outside information in the form of various types of media crossing the border, and despite periodic government efforts to crack down, the leakage of information continues.

A study published by InterMedia in 2012 based on interviews with North Korean defectors, refugees and travellers concluded that many North Korean inhabitants have watched South Korean or Chinese movies and television dramas on smuggled DVDs or thumb drives. Those living close to the Chinese or South Korean border were also likely to have viewed television programing from either of the two countries. As a result, 'North Koreans today are learning more about the outside world than at any time since the founding of the country. As the information environment opens, the North Korean government no longer maintains a total monopoly over the information available to the population and, as a result, North Koreans' understanding of the world is changing' (Kretchun and Kim 2012: 1). Moreover, the report concludes that North Korean citizens are very willing to share this newfound knowledge with those they trust, thus facilitating further spreading of awareness about the outside world. All of these activities are illegal but corruption and bribery has allowed gaping holes to appear in the state's ability to control the information flow. As North Koreans have more and more access to what is happening outside their borders and continue to see the inaccuracies of the regime's narrative, pressure could eventually build for some type of political or economic change.

Economic reform and pressure from below

For years, China has sought to convince North Korea that it could embark on Chinese-style economic reform without jeopardizing the regime. Yet North Korea has been reluctant to undertake such measures. As the argument goes, the regime would face difficulties in squaring its ideological foundations with extensive reform measures. More importantly, North Korean leaders probably fear that widespread economic reform could unleash similar internal forces similar to those that toppled the Soviet and Romanian regimes rather than imitate Beijing's economic success story (Lankov 2013: 109–114).

While there is a clear survival logic behind Pyongyang's reluctance to introduce economic reform, in many respects, some of this reform has already begun with a plethora of market activity in North Korea along with the increasing importance of money in the DPRK. North Korean society has already started to change via 'bottom-up marketization' that began during the famine years and continues to grow despite periodic government efforts to rein it in (Cha and Anderson 2012). As this pressure from below builds and as the Kim regime consolidates its power, leaders may become convinced that it can increase the extent of economic reform that not only changes the country's trajectory but also pushes it to moderate its behaviour for the sake of its economic interests. Indeed, in April 2013 North Korea unveiled the '*byungjin* line' that prioritized the simultaneous goals of developing nuclear weapons and growing the economy, and some small-scale reforms of the agricultural sector have already begun. Though we have heard the story of possible reform before and had hopes dashed when North Korea retreated on economic liberalization plans, this could just be a future wild card, especially if the leadership feels sufficiently confident it can implement and control reform measures.

DPRK miscalculation

A final possible wild card concerns North Korea's penchant for brinkmanship and provocative behaviour. Since the division of the peninsula, on numerous occasions Pyongyang has taken actions to destabilize South Korea, generate tension in the region to obtain political and economic benefits, or improve its military capabilities through the testing of various weapons systems, especially nuclear weapons. In the past, South Korea and the USA have been willing to tolerate Pyongyang's behaviour for fear of escalation should they retaliate. Following the sinking of the *Cheonan* and the shelling of Yeonpyeong island, the South Korean government made it very clear that next time, there would be a response. In addition, it was announced in March 2013 that South Korea and the USA had signed the Combined Counter-Provocation Plan to guarantee a joint response to a limited use of force by North Korea.

Pyongyang appears to have got the message and has refrained from challenging this enhanced ROK-US deterrence posture. Yet there is always the danger that North Korean leaders could miscalculate, particularly in a crisis, and conduct a small-scale military operation if they believe escalation could be controlled. Given the very determined positions taken in Seoul and Washington to respond, there is a strong likelihood that matters would escalate and if the response spiral continues, could lead to a major military conflict that North Korea would lose and thus bring about the end of the DPRK. Although North Korea's leaders might not intentionally go down this path, history is littered with occasions when leaders believed they could control an outcome only to discover that they had miscalculated.

Conclusion

North Korea and the Kim family are likely to continue to exist for the next two to three decades. Despite a number of indicators to the contrary, the DPRK has shown a penchant for survival, and perhaps most importantly, will continue to enjoy the Chinese economic and political support that props up the regime, especially if Pyongyang moderates its behaviour. North Korea will face significant challenges, particularly if it continues a pattern of brinkmanship and nuclear weapons tests, and the Arab Spring that spread across the Middle East in early 2011 demonstrated that unexpected events in international relations are possible. There are signs of social and economic change in North Korea, and the DPRK we know today may be very different by 2034, but it is likely to exist nonetheless. Moreover, even if the Kim regime were to collapse for some reason, it is not certain that this would result in reunification and the demise of North Korea. There is a strong possibility the KPA would step in and rule by itself, or after restoring order, rule jointly with the KWP. In either case, North Korea would endure.

For policymakers, the message seems clear. If US policy is to be based on the future collapse and elimination of the North Korean regime, it may be a long time coming. North Korea remains a difficult and dangerous policy problem that requires careful attention and a robust defence commitment to South Korea, but it is not going away anytime soon. As a result, it must be recognized that a policy for North Korea cannot be based on the hope that this is a waiting game where the problem will disappear. The cost of a policy grounded on this assumption is too high and is unlikely to succeed.

Bibliography

Bermudez Jr, Joseph, 'New North Korean Helicopter Frigates Spotted', *38 North*, 15 May 2014, http://38north.org/2014/05/jbermudez051514/.

Byman, Daniel and Jennifer Lind, 'Pyongyang's Survival Strategy: Tools of Authoritarian Control in North Korea', *International Security*, Summer 2010.

Central Intelligence Agency (CIA), *The World Factbook*, Washington, DC: CIA, 2014.

Cha, Victor, *The Impossible State: North Korea, Past and Future*, London: Bodley Head, 2012.

Cha, Victor and Nicholas Anderson, 'A North Korean Spring?' *Washington Quarterly*, Winter, 2012.

European Commission, 'European Union, Trade with North Korea', 6 April 2014, http://trade.ec.europa.eu/doclib/docs/2006/september/tradoc_113428.pdf.

Gause, Ken, 'Coercion, Control, Surveillance, and Punishment', Committee for Human Rights in North Korea, 2012, www.hrnk.org/uploads/pdfs/HRNK_Ken-Gause_Web.pdf.

Haggard, Stephan and Marcus Noland, *Famine in North Korea: Markets, Aid, and Reform*, New York: Columbia University Press, 2007.

Harden, Blaine, 'North Korea Massively Increases Its Special Forces', *Washington Post*, 8 October 2009, www.washingtonpost.com/wp-dyn/content/article/2009/10/08/AR2009100804018.html.

Harden, Blaine, *Escape from Camp 14: One Man's Remarkable Odyssey from North Korea to Freedom in the West*, London: Penguin Books, 2013.

Heo, Uk and Terence Roehrig, *South Korea since 1980*, Cambridge: Cambridge University Press, 2010.

International Institute of Strategic Studies (IISS), *The Military Balance, 2014*, London: IISS, 2014.

Jane's Sentinel Security Assessment, 'Strategic Weapons Systems: North Korea', London: Jane's Information Group, 20 January 2011.

Kim, Suk Hi, Terence Roehrig and Bernhard Seliger, *The Survival of North Korea*, Jefferson, NC: McFarland Press, 2011.

Kretchun, Nat and Jane Kim, 'A Quiet Opening: North Koreans in a Changing Media Environment', *InterMedia*, 2012, http://audiencescapes.org/sites/default/files/A_Quiet_Opening_FINAL_InterMedia.pdf.

Lankov, Andrei, *The Real North Korea: Life and Politics in the Failed Stalinist Utopia*, Oxford: Oxford University Press, 2013.

McEachern, Patrick, *Inside the Red Box: North Korea's Post-totalitarian Politics*, New York: Columbia University Press, 2010.

National Intelligence Council, 'Global Trends 2010', Washington, DC: Office of the Director of National Intelligence, November 1997.

Noland, Marcus, 'Why North Korea Will Muddle Through', *Foreign Affairs*, July/August 1997.

Oh, Kong Dan and Ralph Hassig, *North Korea: Through the Looking Glass*, Washington, DC: Brookings Institution, 2000.

Roehrig, Terence, 'Restraining the Hegemon: North Korea, the United States and Asymmetrical Deterrence', *Pacific Focus*, September 2005.

Roehrig, Terence, 'North Korea's Nuclear Weapons Program: Motivations, Strategy, and Doctrine', in Toshi Yoshihara and James Holmes (eds), *Strategy in the Second Nuclear Age: Power, Ambition, and the Ultimate Weapon*, Washington, DC: Georgetown University Press, 2012.

Struckman, Dana and Terence Roehrig, 'Not So Fast: Pyongyang's Nuclear Weapons Ambitions', *Georgetown Journal of International Affairs*, 20 February 2013, http://journal.georgetown.edu/2013/02/20/not-so-fast-pyongyangs-nuclear-weapons-ambitions-by-dana-struckman-and-terence-roehrig/.

Thielmann, Greg, 'Sorting Out the Nuclear and Missile Threats From North Korea', Arms Control Association, 21 May 2013, www.armscontrol.org/files/TAB_Sorting_Out_North_Korea_2013.pdf.

United Nations Human Rights Council (UNHRC), *Report of the Commission of Inquiry on Human Rights in the Democratic People's Republic of Korea*, 2014, www.ohchr.org/EN/HRBodies/HRC/CoIDPRK/Pages/ReportoftheCommissionofInquiryDPRK.aspx.

Part 4
Conclusions

20
China's future role in East Asia

Richard Weixing Hu

As China rises rapidly, its growing economic, military and diplomatic power is reshaping the balance of power and strategic landscape in East Asia. Yet how and to what extent China will reshape future international relations in East Asia is still uncertain. Leaders in Beijing have yet to formulate a clear grand strategy on East Asia, and regional countries grapple to understand China's future role in East Asia.

China's rising and East Asian international relations are mutually transformative. As China rises, East Asian countries all feel the heat. They respond by taking either a balancing strategy or an accommodating policy, or both of them, towards China. For Beijing, rising Chinese power does not make the regional environment more favourable; instead, it makes it more challenging for China. With rising tensions over maritime and territorial disputes in the East and South China Seas, there is an increased probability of limited conflicts in East Asia. Since the 1990s China's good neighbourhood policy has run into difficulties. As the Obama administration develops its 'rebalancing to Asia' strategy, more and more Chinese people feel that Washington is organizing a de facto regional coalition to contain China's rise in East Asia. In the next 10 to 20 years, the Chinese leadership will face some fundamental questions about its East Asian policy, and the answers to these questions will determine the future role of China in East Asian international relations. These questions include: How will China develop relations with its East Asian neighbours as tensions over maritime and territorial disputes rise? How will Beijing manage its relations with the USA as Washington's rebalancing to Asia strategy increases pressure on China? What measures will Beijing take to dampen the impact of the security dilemma in East Asia as it continues to develop its military power? How will Beijing reassure neighbouring countries about its intention to achieve a peaceful rise? In connection with these foreign policy challenges, how will Beijing manage rising popular nationalism at home?

This chapter will analyse China's future role in East Asia by focusing on three issues: (1) How does Beijing perceive and assess changes in East Asian international relations? (2) Given the changing regional environment, how will Beijing manage future relations with its Asian neighbours over the maritime and territorial disputes? (3) Since the Sino–US relationship is a pivotal factor in China's relations with other Asian countries, how will Beijing manage and build a new model of major power relations with the USA?

Richard Weixing Hu

Rising China and changing East Asia

Chinese President Xi Jinping is facing a much tougher regional environment in comparison to his predecessor Hu Jintao. During Hu's time in office (2002–12) the international environment for China was relatively favourable. Following the attacks on the US mainland on 11 September 2001, the George W. Bush Administration reversed its hard-edged policy of treating China as a strategic competitor, with the US 'war on terror' helping to forge a more constructive Sino–US relationship. During Hu Jintao's tenure, Beijing pursued an active diplomacy in hosting the Six-Party Talks and managing the Korean nuclear crisis, nurtured a good neighbourly partnership with ASEAN (Association of Southeast Asian Nations) members and with Japan and South Korea within the framework of ASEAN+3, improved relations with Russia and India, and established the Shanghai Cooperation Organization with the Central Asian states. China's economy surpassed Japan's in 2011 to become the second largest in the world. The 2008 global financial crisis further consolidated China's position in the global economy. Chinese influence has increased in international peacekeeping, climate change negotiations, and global governance bodies such as the G20. According to former President Hu Jintao, China wishes to reassure other countries that it will rise peacefully in a 'harmonious world'.

For Xi Jinping, however, the regional environment in East Asia has now turned out to be tougher than he had expected. Although Xi wants to continue to focus on economic growth and domestic reforms, he is facing much more complicated foreign policy challenges. Economic ties with neighbours are still subject to rising tensions involving contested maritime and territorial boundaries in the East and South China Seas. President Obama's rebalancing to Asia strategy further complicates China's regional environment. There is even evidence of 'hard balancing' of East Asian countries targeting China as indicated by the formation of exclusive alliances or competitive armament races. China's neighbours appear to be hedging, and Sino–US relations continue to be characterized by collaboration and contention. Domestically, nationalist sentiments in China – as well as elsewhere – often hamper foreign compromises and accommodation.

China's deteriorating security environment is partially due to its own rapid rise. As one leading Chinese security studies scholar has argued, China's changing regional environment in East Asia has been the result of three factors: external pressures; China's rapid rise; and its interactions with neighbours (Shen 2011). China's rapid growth naturally creates pressures for other countries. Its increasing military capabilities cause anxieties on the part of others, and raise questions about trust. John Mearsheimer, an offensive realist, argues that as China continues its rise as a great power, military conflicts in East Asia are likely, if not inevitable (Mearsheimer 2003). He bases his future predictions on historic precedents as well as offensive realist assumptions. According to his realist logic, no country can be sure of other countries' intentions and must therefore maximize its relative power in order to achieve security. China's rise will therefore not be peaceful and it will end up going to war with others, as it follows in the footsteps of other great powers. When China's power rises rapidly, why should other Asian countries trust China when ongoing power shifts will make China stronger tomorrow? This problem of trust is ubiquitous in international relations (Fearon 1995) and is not unique to China, except that the speed and magnitude of its rise makes credible reassurance even more imperative in the eyes of its neighbours. As a country becomes stronger and even dominant, it tends to trust others less because it can now take matters into its own hands without relying on others' promises or goodwill (Kydd 2000), while others demand more convincing promises from it that it will not wantonly use its newly acquired capabilities. Not surprisingly, not wanting to rely on the promises of either China or the USA, East Asian countries are increasingly engaging in multilateral diplomacy. A further implication follows from this discussion. Mistrust feeds on mistrust, so that a country's professed views and actual behaviour influence others' perceptions and conduct, thus possibly causing a chain reaction of escalating recriminations and suspicions.

Since the early 1990s the underlying theme of Chinese foreign policy has been reassurance, namely to reassure others that China's rise is peaceful. However, winning the trust of others has proved difficult. Until Xi Jinping took office in 2012, the Chinese leadership from Jiang Zemin to Hu Jintao conducted foreign policy under a framework of guiding principles laid down by Deng Xiaoping after the 4 June 1989 Tiananmen incident. The two most important principles are *Tao Guang Yang Hui* (which literally means to bide time and build up capabilities) for economic development, and to prioritize Sino–US relations in Chinese foreign policy.[1] Deng Xiaoping's maxims, as guiding principles, have influenced Chinese foreign policy during the last two decades. During Jiang Zemin and Hu Jintao's periods in office Beijing was able to be vague about territorial disputes and focus on reassuring its neighbours that China's rise in East Asia was peaceful. However, this relatively peaceful approach is no longer possible for Xi Jinping (Chen and Wang 2011).

Rising nationalism is another factor for Xi Jinping's foreign policy change. Believing in its rising national power, the Chinese public has become more nationalistic and is demanding that claims over territorial issues should be asserted more forcefully. This has prompted the Chinese leadership to find new ways to rally domestic support for its foreign policy while not putting itself in a politically vulnerable position. As China increasingly becomes a pluralistic society, its foreign policymaking is becoming more complex, with social actors and public opinion playing a greater role in this process. Beijing sometimes finds itself in the predicament of being criticized at home for being too 'soft' in handling China's foreign relations, while its conduct abroad is censored for being too 'assertive'. Increasing criticism from Chinese netizens has placed a powerful constraint on the government's dealings with foreign countries, particularly with Japan and the USA (Wang 2010).

Although Xi Jinping wants to continue economic development and stability at home, he feels increasing pressure from rising popular nationalism to be more straightforward in defending China's national interests. He cannot be seen to allow Chinese interests overseas to be violated or eroded by other countries. From the beginning of his tenure in office he has made it clear that China wants to maintain good relations with its neighbours but that this should not be at the expense of China's national interests. China's tough stance on maritime and territorial disputes since 2012 has thus signalled a more confrontational policy with the Philippines and Vietnam in the South China Sea and with Japan in the East China Sea. Xi is not shy in drawing red lines for neighbouring countries as he perceives the old policy to be no longer effective. Beijing has since been successful in using a law enforcement force in asserting its claims and control over contested territory in the East and South China Seas. It has established a pattern of employing force short of military means to pressurize the other parties in its territorial and maritime disputes. The hardening of China's posture has serious implications for China's neighbours and other concerned powers, such as the USA.

Xi Jinping's policy shift is compelled by both China's rising power and Beijing's changing perception of the regional environment (Johnson *et al.* 2014). While Chinese national power is becoming much stronger than before, the regional environment is also becoming more complicated and less favourable to China's long-term policy goals. China's new toughness on maritime disputes is also driven by rising patriotic and nationalist sentiments within the Chinese elite and public opinion. With growing capabilities in China's military, coastguard, fisheries, and oil exploration, the Chinese elites and public tend to support greater willingness to use coercion in seeking advances over territorial and maritime disputes. Nationalist sentiment remains a volatile and potentially very disruptive force in the Chinese society. In the 21st century Xi no longer has the power of Mao Zedong or Deng Xiaoping to play down or compromise on foreign policy disputes in order to focus on other priorities. He must find a more nuanced line to rally the public behind him on foreign policy. Xi's policy change also signals a shift in his foreign policy outlook. As articulated by Chinese foreign policy scholars, Xi is redirecting foreign policy debate in China and quietly replacing Deng Xiaoping's maxim of *Tao Guang Yang Hui* with a new approach called *Fen Fa You Wei* (literally, to strive for achievement).[2]

Beijing's new emphasis on maritime power, sovereign rights and sustained military build-up is also a strategic response to Washington's 'pivot' to Asia. During the Hu Jintao era, China gave the impression of trying to avoid confrontation at all costs and that it would never oppose Washington in international conflicts to which China was not a party. In order to maintain a constructive relationship with the USA, Beijing even tried hard to find a way to defuse tensions over sovereignty disputes with Japan and other South-East Asian nations, and to manage ties with North Korea. Yet in the last two years Beijing frequently has reported breakthroughs in China's military build-up, advanced weaponry technology, and the increasing capability of the People's Liberation Army's combat readiness. By declaring an air defence identification zone in the East China Sea in February 2014 Beijing took a major step in intensifying its confrontation with Japan over the Diaoyu/Senkaku Islands dispute. This step also signifies the calculated expansion of China's 'strategic space' in East Asia, especially over the maritime space beyond China's offshore water and traditional defence boundary. This signals a clear and conscious intention to challenge US dominance in the West Pacific.

In order to implement his policy, President Xi Jinping is also consolidating his foreign policy power by reorganizing and centralizing the decision-making process within the party and government apparatus. In November 2013 the Chinese Communist Party decided to establish a US-style National Security Committee (NSC). The Chinese NSC aims for more smoothly integrated decision making on domestic and foreign security issues. The Committee conflates domestic security challenges with foreign threats and gives Xi comprehensive authority to make decisions on all security related issues. In addition, Xi also chairs the central groups on cyber security and national financial policy. Xi thus has obtained all the political capital and authority necessary for addressing foreign and security threats.

Managing relations with neighbours in East Asia

Territorial disputes in the East and South China Seas are becoming more complicated and multilateralized, whether Beijing likes it or not. Although it is in everyone's interest to maintain the status quo, there is no guarantee that military conflict will not break out in these disputes. As tension develops, small-scale skirmishes and clashes are probably not avoidable. All parties concerned now have more patrol boats as well as warships deployed in these regions, and one cannot be sure that they will not confront each other. China, for example, now has more fishing, ocean surveillance, and coastguard patrol boats on duty in the East and South China Seas, and the scope of its maritime operations is much greater than 20 years ago. After a decade of tranquility, tension is rising again over territorial and resources disputes between China and its Asian neighbours. Yet at the same time, and as mentioned above, these conflicts have to be seen in the context that China has actually settled most of its land border disputes with its neighbours. Land quarrels tend historically to be more likely to cause wars than maritime disputes. Moreover, there is much evidence suggesting that conflicts between a major power and a minor power are likely to be limited unless there is intervention by another major power (Vasquez 2009). Thus, alternative future developments hinge to a significant extent on the role and policies of the USA.

The South China Sea is rich in natural resources such as oil and natural gas. Oil deposits have been discovered and it is estimated that there are about 7,500m. barrels of proven oil reserves, compared to 15,400m. to 29,000m. barrels in the Caspian Sea, 2,700m. barrels in the Gulf of Mexico, and 16,800m. barrels in the North Sea. The offshore oil disputes have great implications for the region as well as for the global economy (Daly 2011). East Asia is an energy-hungry region given that its rate of economic growth has been among the highest in the world over the last three decades. East Asia's high economic growth has led to an increasing demand for energy. Over the next 20 years oil consumption among developing Asian countries is expected to rise rapidly.

China's claim over the South China Sea is best expressed by the famous u-shaped 'nine-dash line'. This encompassing line gives the impression that China claims sovereignty over almost the entire South China Sea (including the Spratly and Paracel Islands), which is also claimed in whole or in part by Vietnam, the Philippines, Taiwan, Malaysia, and Brunei. Beijing's current awkward position has a lot to do with its ambiguous position on what it means by the nine-dash line. This ambiguity, however, may not be accidental. It gives Chinese officials scope for negotiation and also deflects domestic criticism over possible concession making. It appears that for China and the other claimants, biding their time is the dominant strategy. While China declines to submit these disputes to international arbitration, the other contestants are also understandably reluctant to be forced into negotiating individually with Beijing. As a result recurrent clashes and confrontations are likely; however, it does not necessarily mean that they will necessarily escalate into something more serious. The incentives for such escalation appear to be limited on all sides even though all countries, especially China, have at their disposal increasing capabilities to make an assertive move. Therefore, the most likely scenario for the near future is a continuation of the status quo, with all sides seemingly preferring not to resolve their disputes rather than to conclude them. Putting such matters in context, there were long-running disputes about the demarcation of borders between the USA and British Canada and territorial contests between the USA and Mexico in the 19th century. Recently, Canada also detained Spaniards for fishing illegally in its waters. Letting time take its course seems to be part of traditional Chinese thinking on strategic matters. As Taylor Fravel (2011: 292) argues, 'since the mid-1990s, China has pursued a strategy of delaying the resolution of the dispute. The goal of this strategy is to consolidate China's claims, especially to maritime rights or jurisdiction over these waters, and to deter other states from strengthening their own claims at China's expense, including resource development projects that exclude China'. If China has waited over 60 years to resolve the status of Taiwan, it can wait that long again to settle the island dispute in the South China Sea. Naturally, this long-term perspective is not unrelated to Beijing's calculation on whether unfolding trends will strengthen, or weaken, its bargaining power over time.

In the meantime, Beijing is likely to continue its existing dual strategy. On the one hand, it employs a 'charm offensive' and economic diplomacy to attract the ASEAN states, seeking in particular to cultivate some of them (such as Cambodia and Myanmar) as its close associates. On the other hand, it is building up its military capabilities in the region. The new Chinese leadership will likely continue to rely on exchanges of high-level visits and economic assistance to stabilize relations with the South-East Asian states and to prevent the formation of an anti-China united front within ASEAN. At the same time, it is likely to engage in occasional military displays and demonstrations in order to deter what it perceives to be other claimant states' encroachment. This dual strategy is merely a variation of the same theme that Beijing has adopted towards Taiwan – that of trying simultaneously to be 'softer' and 'harder'.

The recent Sino–Japanese standoff over the Diaoyu/Senkaku Islands, triggered by Tokyo Governor Ishihara's proposal to purchase the islands from their private owners in April 2012, has turned into an ugly confrontation between the two East Asian powers. China believes that Japan has violated the two countries' implicit agreement of maintaining the status quo, a compromise reached 40 years ago when they entered into a full diplomatic relationship. Under pressure to assert its sovereignty claim from both domestic and foreign sources, Beijing saw no room to retreat and decided to retaliate strongly. Since then China has instigated regular patrols around the islands to assert its territorial claims. On the Japanese side, Tokyo has also boxed itself into a corner by insisting that there is no territorial dispute over the contested islands, which it claims are Japan's 'inherent territories'. Of greater concern is the Abe administration's use of the dispute to rally public support and strengthen Japanese military power with a view to reclaiming the country's past power status. The clash of nationalism between the two countries seems, once again, to have put them on a collision course.

China's future role also hinges on how it manages relations with ASEAN and other allies in Asia. Taking China's three close associates (North Korea, Myanmar, and Pakistan) for example, there are signs of ambivalence in describing Beijing's role. China has sought to discourage Pyongyang from carrying out nuclear and missile tests, while at the same time opposing US policies that may bring about that regime's downfall. It sees continued value in having North Korea as a buffer state but is also wary of the danger of entrapment that can involve it involuntarily in a conflict with the USA (or South Korea) over Pyongyang's reckless policies of brinksmanship. Delicate balancing of competing objectives also characterizes Beijing's approach to dealing with Myanmar. While encouraging that country's leaders to initiate economic reform (as it has tried to persuade the North Koreans), it also refrains from pushing too hard lest it loses its influence in Myanmar. This predicament is repeated in Islamabad. Although hailed as a steady friend, Beijing is acutely aware of the problems afflicting Pakistan's government, and has tried to avoid being played off against either Washington or New Delhi in multilateral manoeuvres. It has rebuffed Pakistan's overtures to establish a formal alliance in the wake of the US raid which resulted in the killing of Osama bin Laden, the founder and leader of the militant Islamist group al-Qa'ida, and popular opposition in Pakistan against drone attacks by the USA.

Building a new model for major power relations with the USA

China and the USA are two great powers bound together by deep political, economic, security, cultural and social ties. How the Sino–US relationship evolves in the future is another key variable for assessing China's role in East Asia. China–US relations are characterized by economic interdependence as well as security interdependence. On one hand, this interdependent relationship requires cooperation, but on the other hand the relationship also demonstrates strong elements of competition. This competitive cooperation is increasingly dysfunctional in recent years (e.g. Shambaugh 2012). Building a stable and cooperative relationship between a rising power and a dominant power is a major challenge as the two countries search for a new type of strategic relationship. The lack of mutual strategic trust is a major obstacle for building stable and cooperative relations. This said, the long process of building such a relationship – whereby rivals become friends – requires both favourable conditions and conducive policies as shown by Charles Kupchan's (2010) comparative case studies, including the evolution of Anglo-American relations.

As discussed above, China's rising power status has created a new dynamic of strategic anxieties in East Asia. Prominent Chinese and American scholars have commented on strategic distrust in Sino–US relations (Lieberthal and Wang 2012). As China rises, it will continue to invest in building a regional defence buffer and expanding the strategic space on its periphery. However, this move is viewed by Washington as intended to constrain the USA or even to drive it out of East Asia. The strategic suspicions resulting from this anticipated geopolitical rivalry exist not just between the USA and China, but also between China and other Asian powers. Elizabeth Economy observes that any trust-based relationship requires that the parties have a certain willingness to give before receiving in the process of building friendly ties over the long term (Economy 2012). This observation is surely true, but it is also conditional on extensive and repeated interactions. Trust is gained through continuous exchanges of views, so that countries learn over time that the other side will not exploit their goodwill but will return cooperation with cooperation. This understanding and the trust developing from it will bring about a successful outcome if the prospective rewards of future interactions are greater than any momentary gain to be made from opportunistic behaviour at the present (Axelrod 1984).

Building strategic mutual trust between China and the USA must be from a long-term process so that both sides learn that the other will eschew opportunism at its expense even when such defection or self-serving behaviour may be rewarding (Kydd 2005). It is established only after a long series of experiences when each side has deliberately and consistently demonstrated its trustworthiness by foreswearing egoistic actions. China, for instance, refrained from devaluing its currency when other Asian countries adopted this policy during the financial crises in the late 1990s, and this action communicated reassurance and helped to build trust. A country can also make concessions in order to demonstrate its trustworthiness. Thus, the Anti-Ballistic Missile Treaty signed between the USA and the Soviet Union ensured that the two countries would leave all but one of their urban centres unprotected against a possible nuclear attack by the other side, thereby building confidence that neither of them had any intention of launching a pre-emptive strike. In the same way, the large amount of US debt held by China is a form of reassurance because if their relations were to deteriorate, both would suffer enormous economic and financial losses (Chan 2012).

Obama's 'pivot to Asia' strategy is a key factor affecting future Sino–US relations in East Asia.[3] According to the US State Department, America's 'rebalancing' to Asia is targeted at revitalizing bilateral security alliances; renewing relationships with rising powers; re-engaging with regional multilateral institutions; and reinforcing economic and military strategic partnerships (but not at the expense of democracy or human rights).[4] How Washington actually executes its plan and how Beijing perceives and responds to it are obviously important variables for Asia's future strategic configuration. Although one can expect Beijing to complain about this US plan as a strategic encirclement of China, it is not evident that it will necessarily respond in kind by ramping up its military expenditures and get into an arms race with the USA as the USSR did during the Cold War. Such a response would undermine China's overriding priority of sustaining its domestic economic development, and this is also a contest that it is unlikely to win.

It is China's intention to forge a more stable and positive Sino–US relationship. After taking office in 2012, President Xi Jinping introduced a new formula and commitment to build a 'new model of major power relations' with the USA. For the Chinese, this new relationship means 'to deepen dialogues, seek win-win cooperation, properly manage frictions, and share global responsibilities' (Cui and Pang 2012). In the past, Washington has urged Beijing to advance a comprehensive vision of the two nations' respective regional and global roles in the era of interdependence and growing Chinese strength, and China has largely ignored this call. This Chinese proposal for a new model of major power relations is thus welcomed by Washington, as it is a vision for future cooperative relations.

To date, however, the proposal for a new relationship predictably has focused more on what each side wants the other to do, rather than on what China and the USA must do (Lampton 2013). From the Chinese perspective, President Xi made it clear at the 2013 Sunnylands Summit, held in California, USA, that he had no intention of backing away from Chinese interests in the South China and East China Seas. Meanwhile, Washington does not want to give the impression that the US acceptance of the concept means that it will prioritize the US–China relationship above all its other commitments in Asia. Washington recognizes that if it did so its Asian allies would be less likely to cooperate with it and instead would seek alternative strategies to ensure their security, thereby undermining the USA's leadership role in Asia.

The USA could accept China's future leading position in such areas as its gross domestic product, volume of foreign trade, and diplomatic/economic impact in Asia, and to a lesser degree, the mutual strategic deterrence between the two countries, along with the peaceful co-existence of two great powers. However, Washington would never accept a future Chinese military advantage over the USA. China's relatively marginal military advantage against the USA in the West Pacific could provide it with a sizable strategic space in East Asia, which means the off-shore waters along the South China Sea, the Taiwan Strait, and up to the Korean peninsula (beyond what is the first island chain). The dominant role of the USA in East Asia has been built on Washington's overall military superiority in the West Pacific, east of Okinawa and Guam, under the so-called San Francisco System after 1945, which consolidated its position in Asia.

China's future role in East Asia and the power distribution between China and the USA will also be contingent on the two countries' respective strengths in functional areas as well as their respective contributions to regional governance. There is a tendency for bifurcation in East Asian international relations. Regional countries turn to China for economic benefits while seeking security protection from the USA. This situation creates possibilities for power-sharing, close consultation and selective collaboration between Beijing and Washington (Lampton 2013). In economic and financial affairs, the USA needs China to play a more positive role in East Asia. Although Sino–US relations have been frequently affected by problems in regional and third country affairs, situational frictions and competition, it is not impossible to achieve a more positive and cooperative China–US relationship. In such a scenario, the USA would accept a peaceful and constructive China as a world power, and China, in turn, would respect the essential interests and rightful international concerns of the USA as a world dominant power.

Current Sino–US relations are quite different from Soviet-US relations during the Cold War. Whatever may be said about the China threat, Beijing is not propagating a competing ideology as Moscow did (as Washington currently does when it promotes regime change in countries that it dislikes), or organizing an anti-US international coalition such as the Warsaw Pact. Nor is it engaging in competitive strategic armament as Moscow did in attempting to match the USA militarily, and it is not deploying troops and establishing bases abroad. In this respect, China has refrained from infringing on Washington's core national interests. Moreover, unlike the Soviet-US relationship during the Cold War there are vibrant and extensive commercial exchanges between China and the USA today – surely an indication of strong mutual interests. US investments in China and Chinese holdings of dollar-denominated loans, in addition to the enormous amount of bilateral trade, differentiate the Sino–US relationship from the Soviet–US relationship during the Cold War. This does not deny the presence of friction and distrust in the former relationship, but suggests that it is also qualitatively different from the latter one, suggesting the possibility of building a new type of great power relations between the USA and China.

Conclusion

As a result of China's rapid rise Beijing must try harder to reassure its neighbours as well as the USA about its peaceful intentions. Although it now commands greater capabilities and enjoys arguably a more secure environment than at any time since 1949, some of the challenging issues confronting its leaders are not easy to resolve and will require skill, vision and time to address. China's new leadership must realize that China possesses both strengths and weaknesses as its national power continues to rise in the coming years. Regional perceptions and reactions to China's rise are not always positive. The leadership needs to resist the temptation to use military power to solve territorial disputes with China's neighbours. Reassuring regional countries about its peaceful intentions and nurturing a good neighbourly relationship will be imperative for China to sustain an open and stable international environment that has thus far made its economic growth and rising international stature possible.

The Chinese leadership should continue to follow Deng Xiaoping's diplomatic strategy and not overreact to international and regional developments. The new leaders need to bring hawkish nationalist sentiments under control, as it is clear that assertive behaviour will lead to more negative reactions from the international community. Significantly, Sino–US relations will continue to be pivotal to Beijing's foreign relations in general and, in many ways, will hold the key to managing China's core interests as well as other issues that are of secondary importance in East Asia. Importantly, China's relations with Taiwan, North and South Korea, the ASEAN states, and even Japan are derivative of and are invariably dependent upon Sino–US relations. How Sino–US relations evolve in the future will depend on leaders on both sides as well as on the evolving policy environment that they will have to contend with. Rising international stature and relative power gains have stimulated the emerging Chinese nationalism and popular assertiveness. Economic difficulties and foreign policy setbacks, however, can also arouse nationalist feelings, popular disaffection, and a tendency to blame foreign scapegoats (e.g. the strident US partisan rhetoric about 'Chinese cheating' in efforts to mobilize voters in recent US presidential campaigns). For its part, Chinese leaders need to have a clear vision of what China's role in East Asia should be, and how to be a responsible great power in the region as well as in world affairs.

Notes

1 There are different translations of the term *Tao Guang Yang Hui*. Others translate it as 'to hide brightness and cherish obscurity'. See Elizabeth Economy, 'The Game Changer: Coping with China's Foreign Policy Evolution', *Foreign Affairs*, November/December 2010: 142.
2 In contrast to Deng's *Tao Guang Yang Hui*, this term emphasizes a more proactive posture in foreign policy and takes initiative to shape the external environment. For further discussion, see Shi Yinghong, 'China's New Leadership: Balancing Tensions in Foreign Policy', *China and U.S. Focus*, 19 March 2014, www.chinausfocus.com/foreign-policy/chinas-new-leadership-balancing-tensions-in-

foreign-policy/. Shi Yinhong, a Professor of International Relations at Renmin University of China, is a leading scholar on Chinese foreign policy.
3 The Obama administration has changed the term 'pivot to Asia' to 'rebalancing' strategy in Asia, to avoid the misconception that it has neglected other strategic regions to focus solely on Asia.
4 For a longer version of policy articulation, see State Department, 'The East Asia-Pacific Rebalance: Expanding U.S. Engagement', 16 December 2013, www.state.gov/r/pa/pl/2013/218776.htm

Bibliography

Axelrod, Robert, *The Evolution of Cooperation*, New York: Basic Books, 1984.
Chan, Steve, 'Money Talks: International Credit/Debt as Credible Commitment', *Journal of East Asian Affairs*, Vol. 26, No. 1, 2012.
Chen, Dingding and Jianwei Wang, 'Lying Low No More?: China's New Thinking on the Tao Guang Yang Hui Strategy', *China: An International Journal*, Vol. 9, No. 2, September 2011.
Cui, Tiankai and Pang Hanzhao, 'China–U.S. Relations in China's Overall Diplomacy in the New Era: On China and U.S. Working Together to Build a New-Type Relationship between Major Countries', Ministry of Foreign Affairs of the People's Republic of China, 20 July 2012, www.fmprc.gov.cn/eng/zxxx/t953682.htm.
Daly, John, 'Offshore Oil Dispute in South China Sea Has Enormous Global Implications', *Oil Price*, 3 June 2011, http://oilprice.com/Energy/Crude-Oil/Offshore-Oil-Dispute-in-South-China-Sea-Has-Enormous-Global-Implications.html.
Economy, Elizabeth, 'Xi's Visit Won't Fix US–China "Trust Deficit"', *Foreign Affairs*, 15 February 2012, www.foreignaffairs.com/articles/137236/elizabeth-economy/xis-tour-wont-fix-the-us-chinese-trust-deficit.
Fearon, James D., 'Rationalist Explanations for War', *International Organization*, Vol. 49, No. 3, 1995.
Fravel, Taylor M., *Strong Border, Secure Nation: Cooperation and Order in China's Territorial Disputes*, Princeton, NJ: Princeton University Press, 2008.
Fravel, Taylor M., 'China's Strategy in the South China Sea', *Contemporary Southeast Asia*, Vol. 33, No. 3, 2011.
Friedberg, Aaron, *A Contest for Supremacy: China, America and the Struggle for Mastery in Asia*, New York: W. W. Norton and Company, 2011.
Johnson, Christopher, Ernest Z. Bower, Victor D. Cha, Michael J. Green and Matthew P. Goodman, *Decoding China's Emerging 'Great Power' Strategy in Asia*, Washington, DC: Center for Strategic and International Studies, 2014.
Kupchan, Charles, *How Enemies Become Friends: The Sources of Stable Peace*, Princeton, NJ: Princeton University Press, 2010.
Kydd, Andrew H., 'Trust, Reassurance, and Cooperation', *International Organization*, Vol. 54, No. 2, 2000.
Kydd, Andrew H., *Trust and Mistrust in International Relations*, Princeton, NJ: Princeton University Press, 2005.
Lampton, David M., 'A New Type of Major-Power Relationship: Seeking a Durable Foundation for U.S.-China Ties', *Asia Policy*, No. 16, July 2013, www.nbr.org/publications/element.aspx?id=650.
Lieberthal, Kenneth and Wang Jisi, *Addressing U.S.–China Strategic Distrust*, Washington, DC: Brookings Institution, 2012.
Mearsheimer, John J., *The Tragedy of Great Power Politics*, New York: W. W. Norton and Company, 2003.
Shambaugh, David (ed.), *Tangled Titans: The United States and China*, Lanham, MD: Rowman & Littlefield, 2012.
Shen, Dingli, 'A Chinese Assessment of China's External Security Environment', *China Brief*, Vol. 11, No. 5, 25 March 2011.
Swaine, Michael D., 'Perceptions of an Assertive China', *China Leadership Monitor*, No. 32, 2010, http://media.hoover.org/sites/default/files/documents/CLM32MS.pdf.

US State Department, 'The East Asia-Pacific Rebalance: Expanding U.S. Engagement', 16 December 2013, www.state.gov/r/pa/pl/2013/218776.htm.

Vasquez, John A., *The War Puzzle Revisited*, New York: Cambridge University Press, 2009.

Wang, Jun, 'Online Nationalism, Civil Society and Chinese Diplomacy', *World Economy and Politics*, Vol. 10, 2010.

21
The future role of the USA in East Asia

Paul J. Smith

Introduction

In January 2012 the US Department of Defense announced a major adjustment in its strategic focus vis-à-vis the Asia-Pacific region. According to the new plan, the US military, while continuing to contribute to security globally, would 'of necessity rebalance toward the Asia-Pacific region'. The Pentagon further stated that US 'relationships with Asian allies and key partners are critical to the future stability and growth of the region' (US Department of Defense 2012: 2). Overall, the new 'rebalance strategy', sometimes referred to as the 'pivot', reflected a strong desire by the administration of President Barack Obama to transition US power from conflicts in the Middle East and South Asia towards East Asia, a region widely viewed as increasingly central to the global economy.

From a military perspective, the rebalance heralded critical shifts in the US military presence and deployments in East Asia. First and perhaps most importantly, the US would give greater priority to maritime (specifically naval) power by calling for 'continued production of a broad range of naval ship types, including relatively "high-end" Aegis radar-equipped destroyers' (Manyin et al. 2012: 13). A new US presence would be established in Darwin, Australia. Four littoral combat ships would be stationed in Singapore. In the Philippines, US officials affirmed that joint US-Philippine military exercises would increase in frequency. In addition, the USA stressed economic aspects of the rebalance by pursuing new trade relationships, by joining the East Asia Summit and by encouraging negotiations for the establishment of the Trans-Pacific Partnership free trade area.

In the years following the announcement of the rebalance, reactions from the region have been varied and predictable; some East Asian countries – particularly those that consider themselves allies of the USA – have responded positively or enthusiastically, while other countries have been more cautious or reserved. For its part, the People's Republic of China has viewed the US posture shift as an unsettling if not alarming trend. A number of Chinese media reports have emphasized the theme that China is the target of the US rebalance, a narrative that American officials have assiduously attempted to downplay or counter.

A related factor underlying the rebalance is the bifurcated economic and political environment that the USA confronts in East Asia. On the economic front, interstate investment and trade relations are productive, interdependent and generally positive. In sharp contrast, certain political and military relationships, for example, China and Japan, or China and Vietnam, appear to be growing more tense (Roehrig 2008). Military spending has increased rapidly in a number of East Asian countries, which in turn has stimulated more assertive behaviours. For example, China, buoyed by its growing military and economic confidence, has announced more ambitious territorial claims in the East and South China Seas. North Korea, meanwhile, adds to regional insecurity by developing and (potentially) deploying nuclear weapons in defiance of the United Nations and regional powers which have sought to prevent such eventualities.

Amid these various trends, the USA remains a central geopolitical and military actor. This is primarily a legacy of the end of the Second World War, when the USA became East Asia's primary underwriter of security, a pattern that has persisted for more than six decades. As Chairman of the Joint Chiefs of Staff, Martin Dempsey recently explained: 'The US has more alliances in this region than anywhere else in the world', including those with Japan, South Korea, Philippines, Thailand and Australia. These alliances, according to Dempsey, 'underpin a growing network of increasingly important trilateral and multilateral relationships and forums', which in aggregate means that 'when you ally with the United States, you ally with the region' (Dempsey 2013).

The question that the USA must confront – and indeed regional countries must consider – is how sustainable the US security guarantee is likely to be, particularly in light of growing budgetary pressures building in Washington. The corollary to that question is whether East Asia can build a security architecture that can keep the peace in a future era in which American involvement may be less robust. Moreover, assuming that such a structure could be created, what threat, whether state-based or non-state based, would it be aligned against? These are uncomfortable questions, but the long-term trajectory of geopolitical transitions and competition in East Asia suggests that they must be confronted eventually, preferably sooner rather than later.

The central role of China in past and future US strategy in East Asia

The US–China relationship is the central factor in any American calculations about its future presence or activities in East Asia. Defense Secretary Chuck Hagel stated that 'the China–US relationship is important for stability and security in the Asia-Pacific and achieving security and prosperity for our two nations in the 21st century' (Hagel 2013). However, even though US officials hesitate to admit it, the American strategic rebalance is widely viewed (both in the USA and in East Asia) as a reaction to growing Chinese power and thus has inevitably contributed to some deterioration in the US–China relationship.

For its part, China views the rebalance policy as yet another attempt by the USA to contain its political and economic ascendancy, which Beijing views as reflecting prior US containment efforts directed against China in the 1950s and 1960s. Indeed, US–China relations can be analysed in three distinct phases. First, the containment phase lasted from roughly 1950 to 1969. Following the diplomatic breakthrough orchestrated by Chairman Mao Zedong and President Richard Nixon in the early 1970s, US–China relations progressed to the rapprochement and pseudo-alliance phase, which lasted roughly to about 1989. This warm diplomatic period was largely the product of a delicate balancing game in which Washington and Beijing joined forces to balance against the Soviet Union. On 1 January 1979 formal diplomatic relations were initiated, which ushered in an even deeper relationship in the 1980s, and this can be attributed partially to the Soviet Union's invasion of Afghanistan that same year.

The great Chinese–US entente of the 1970s and 1980s declined precipitously in 1989 with the Tiananmen Square massacre, followed by the dismantling of the Berlin Wall, which signified the end of the Cold War and, ultimately, the dissolution of the Soviet Union two years later. This ushered in the third – post-entente – phase in the US–China relationship. Without an exogenous common enemy, Beijing and Washington searched for an elusive framework to engage one another. On the US side, the policy choice adopted by both Republican and Democratic presidents was to maintain engagement as a means of shaping Chinese behaviour. During the 1990s the Clinton administration adopted a strategy of 'comprehensive engagement' in which it was presumed that US national interests would be best served 'by developing and maintaining friendly relations with a China which is strong, stable, prosperous, and open' (Wiedemann 1995).

Second, the USA sought to guide or shape Chinese behaviour by encouraging Beijing to adopt norms – such as protecting human rights – consistent with Western liberal values. In the 1990s US officials cultivated a narrative that emphasized the importance of fostering a 'responsible' China: 'We want a China that freely accepts its full range of international responsibilities with respect to human rights, nuclear proliferation safeguards, and environmental protection', stated Admiral Charles Larson, Commander-in-Chief, US Pacific Command, to the Senate Armed Services Committee in 1994 (Larson 1994). This theme would be picked up later in subsequent administrations, including those of George W. Bush and Barack Obama.

However, as Chinese military power grew and US–China interests began to diverge, it was clear that there was no perfect 'label' that could capture or guide the USA and China. On the military front, China continued to focus on building its military, and particularly, its naval power. On this point, Jesse Karotkin of the Office of Naval Intelligence recently stated: 'Over the past 15 years the PLA(N) has carried out an ambitious modernization effort, resulting in a more technologically advanced and flexible force' (Karotkin 2014: 70). China's navy currently features more than 77 surface combatants, 60 submarines, 55 amphibious ships and 85 missile-equipped smaller combatants. Such capabilities underpin or enable China's push into maritime East and South-East Asia. In March 2014 China's Minister of Foreign Affairs, Wang Yi, emphasized China's strong position with regard to territorial disputes with Japan and several South-East Asian countries. In the dispute with Japan, Wang stated that 'there is no room for compromise' and with regard to disputes in the South China Sea, he noted that Beijing would 'never accept unreasonable demands from smaller countries' (*New York Times* 2014).

Thus, as Robert Sutter recently observed: 'Repeated efforts to create a new cooperative framework (e.g., "strategic partnership", "responsible stakeholder", "G=2") have failed in the face of strong and enduring differences between the world's largest powers which are disinclined to change and have the means to resist pressures to do so' (Sutter 2014). One answer may be for Washington and Beijing to focus on those core issues in which the two countries share common interests, such as nuclear non-proliferation, global terrorism, or stability on the Korean peninsula. This appears to be the underlying logic of China's proposed 'new model' of great power relations. 'The new model of relationship is based on the new realities of the world', explained Chinese Ambassador (to the USA) Cui Tiankai. Such new realities include interdependence and connectivity. Thus, as Cui asserts, the 'new model' provides a framework to 'build a 21st-century world order', which can transcend the competitive and destructive tendencies of the past. According to Cui, '19th-century solutions can no longer work to solve 21st-century problems. And indeed, many of them even failed in the 19th century' (Cui 2014).

However, the persistence of differences – including US reactions to China's expansion into its neighbouring maritime realm – must be managed in order for this strategy to become viable. The gravity of this challenge was illustrated in a tense news conference held on 8 April 2014 between US Secretary of Defense Chuck Hagel and Chinese Minister of Defence Chang Wanquan. Hagel warned of increased risks of miscalculation due to increasingly close proximity between US and Chinese forces 'as the PLA modernizes its capabilities and expands its presence in Asia and beyond' (Reuters 2014). Chang called on the USA to keep its ally Japan 'within bounds and not to be permissive and supportive' (ibid.). The challenge will be for both countries to work productively within a cooperative framework – whether it is the 'new model' or its progeny – that can prevent conflict and promote mutual trust.

The Taiwan issue: critical flashpoint in US–China relations

On 3 April 2014 the US Senate Foreign Relations Subcommittee on East Asian and Pacific Affairs, held a hearing on Taiwan in recognition of the 35th anniversary of the Taiwan Relations Act. In his opening statement, Senator Benjamin Cardin, the chairman of the Subcommittee, observed that 'Taiwan has been and remains one of our most important partners in Asia'. He went on to praise Taiwan's vibrant democracy, its values which are shared by the American people, its economic prowess and its role as a 'strong security partner and leader in the region' (Cardin 2014). What Senator Cardin did not emphasize was Taiwan's role as a visceral flashpoint in the US–China relationship. Nor did he mention the fact that China views reunification with Taiwan as a core interest over which it would be willing, under certain circumstances, to go to war.

Taiwan's flashpoint status dates back to the early 1950s when the USA, as a matter of policy, decided to protect Taiwan (the Republic of China) from aggressive military actions from neighbouring China. When the Korean War started in 1950, President Harry Truman deployed the 7th Fleet in the Taiwan Strait to prevent Mao Zedong from launching a military attack on the island, among other reasons. Subsequent years would witness additional Taiwan Strait 'crises', including the first major one in 1954–55 which caused the USA to enter into a Mutual Defense Treaty with Taiwan. Another crisis occurred in 1958 following China's decision to launch artillery attacks on Jinmen (Quemoy) and Matsu. A third crisis occurred in 1962; that year President John F. Kennedy stated that the USA 'would defend Quemoy and Matsu if there were an attack which was part of an attack on Formosa and the Pescadores' (Chai 1999: 66).

In more recent years the most serious Taiwan Strait crises occurred in 1995 and 1996. In March 1995 the USA granted the President of Taiwan, Lee Teng Hui, permission to visit his alma mater, Cornell University. China responded by launching a live-fire ammunition drill near Taiwan. In July 1995 China fired six missiles in an area roughly 80 miles north of Taiwan. The following year, China continued its muscle-flexing campaign against Taiwan in an effort to influence the March 1996 presidential elections. The USA responded by deploying two aircraft carrier strike groups to the region. Nine years later, China would pass an Anti-Secession Law which formalized the option to use force in the event that Taiwan attempted to declare independence.

In dramatic contrast to previous decades, relations between Taiwan and China have now become much more benign and tranquil. In February 2014 Taiwan and China held their first direct meeting since 1949. One of the key factors behind the warming relationship has been the creation in 2010 of the Economic Cooperation Framework Agreement. Since that time, cross-Strait investment has grown considerably; cross-Strait trade exceeded US $197,000m. in 2013. Currently, Taiwan operates 118 flights per day that connect with 54 cities in China, carrying tourists, businesspeople and students (*Los Angeles Times* 2014: 1). However, growing economic interdependence does not negate the fundamental problem of Taiwan's ambiguous political status, which most Taiwanese would prefer to maintain and which the Chinese government would prefer to change.

Some believe that Taiwan's days as a de facto independent country may be numbered, particularly as the military power asymmetry between Taiwan and China continues to widen. Consequently, US policies towards Taiwan may become more schizophrenic in the future, depending on which political party controls the executive and legislative branches. Thus, Taiwan is likely to remain a flashpoint and potential cause for US–China military conflict in the years and decades ahead, notwithstanding favourable trends in recent years. In short, the 'Taiwan problem' has not faded away; it persists in a state of geopolitical hibernation.

The US–Japan alliance: lynchpin of the US regional architecture

In his April 2014 visit to Japan, President Barack Obama characterized the US–Japan alliance as the 'foundation for not only our security in the Asia-Pacific region but also for the region as a whole (*Washington Post* 2014). Similar descriptions have been proffered by other US officials, including Vice President Joe Biden who described the US–Japan security alliance as the 'cornerstone of stability and security in East Asia' (The White House 2013). These statements echo past ones by previous US presidents and other US officials that emphasize a common theme: the US–Japan alliance is the heart of the US East Asian security architecture.

The alliance is the by-product of an American effort, begun in earnest following the 1951 San Francisco peace treaty, to build Japan into a bulwark against the expansion of communism, from both the Soviet Union and China. A secondary purpose of the alliance was to balance against North Korea. Since the 1995–96 Taiwan Strait missile crises, China gradually emerged as a primary concern for the alliance, although initially this reorientation was downplayed. US Assistant Secretary of Defense Joseph Nye, for example, told a Congressional panel in 1995 that 'China must realize that the US–Japan security dialogue is not an effort to constrain or ostracize China'. He further stated that the 'the US and Japan must engage China constructively to assure it is integrated into the regional security system' (Nye 1995).

Nevertheless, China, North Korea and, increasingly, Russia continue to be key concerns for the alliance, particularly in recent years. Yet such exogenous geopolitical pressures cannot conceal the occasional tensions and disagreements between Tokyo and Washington. First, Japan has been continually unhappy about US 'neutrality' concerning the question of sovereignty over the Senkaku/Diaoyu Islands in the East China Sea, a US policy established in the early 1970s when control of Okinawa reverted from the USA to Japan. However, the USA does recognize Japan's administrative rights over the islands. On this basis, President Obama sought to assuage Tokyo's concerns by directly declaring in April 2014 that Article 5 of the US–Japan defence treaty would apply to those islands.

Second, Japan is unhappy with US criticism of its leaders' actions, such as Prime Minister Shinzo Abe's visit to the Yasukuni Shrine in 2013. The USA expression of 'disappointment' with Abe's visit generated some consternation among Japan's official elite. Similarly, President Obama raised the 'comfort women' issue in his 2014 visit to South Korea, which he described as a 'terrible and egregious violation of human rights' (*Japan Times* 2014). Third, some

Japanese perceive that US influence and power are waning in Asia – if not globally – and that a post-US security architecture is needed. One Japanese lawmaker has even proposed an Asian analogue of the North Atlantic Treaty Organization (NATO): 'It will become necessary for us to have an Asian version of NATO', stated Shigeru Ishiba, Secretary-General of the Liberal Democratic Party. 'We will likely see a continued rise in China's defence budget, and US influence waning', he added. 'So we need balance here in the region with China' (Deutsche Presse Agentur 2014).

The Korean peninsula and the US–South Korea alliance

In January 2014 the USA and South Korea agreed a five-year Special Measures Agreement, under which South Korea promised to raise its contribution by 6 per cent (bringing the total to US $867m. in 2014) for hosting US forces in its country. Four months later President Barack Obama, during a visit with South Korean President Park Geun-hye in Seoul, agreed to re-examine the issue of operational control of the South Korean military – the so-called OPCON (Operational Control during Wartime) issue – and possibly delay its actualization beyond the previously agreed date of 2015. During that same visit President Obama characterized the US–South Korean relationship as a 'linchpin of security in Asia' and that US commitment to the north-east Asian nation 'will never waver' (Obama 2014a).

The US commitment to – and sustained presence in – South Korea is a legacy of the devastating Korean War, which lasted from 1950 to 1953. Clearly, North Korea's persistent threat to South Korea has served as the *raison d'être* for the US presence in South Korea for more than six decades. More recently, US policy vis-a-vis North Korea has centred on two specific goals: denuclearization and deterrence (Seiler 2014). However, it appears – to date – that only the second goal has been reasonably obtained. The USA has pursued a policy of 'strategic patience', but it appears that this strategy is increasingly making Pyongyang impatient. US officials have gradually conceded that denuclearization is a nearly unobtainable goal in North Korea, particularly without China's assistance. For this reason, the USA has sought to leverage China's influence in pursuit of the denuclearization goal, but as one senior US official stated: 'It's no secret that the United States and China do not have perfectly congruent sets of interests when it comes to North Korea' (Federal News Service 2014).

With regard to the US–South Korea military alliance, there are growing signs that continued adjustment and evolution lies in the future. In recent years the US and South Korean governments have looked for ways to restructure and improve their alliance. Beginning in 2009 the two sides initiated steps designed to transform the alliance in hope of 'broadening it from its primary purpose of defending against a North Korean attack to [expanding it to] a regional and even global partnership' (Manyin *et al.* 2014:12). However, regardless of whether OPCON occurs sooner or later, it is clear that changes in the relationship are imminent; nevertheless, the US commitment to South Korea's security will probably remain for the foreseeable future.

The USA in South-East Asia

In April 2014 the USA and the Philippines announced the signing of the Enhanced Defense Cooperation Agreement. The pact, which gives US military forces better access to facilities as well as training privileges in the Philippines, would be the first between the two countries since US military bases were closed in 1992. President Barack Obama asserted that the purpose of the agreement was 'to build Philippine capacity, to engage in training, [and] to engage in coordination' (Obama 2014b) More importantly, the agreement was designed to reinforce treaty commitment that the USA had maintained since 1951. 'For more than 60 years, the United States and the Philippines have been bound by a mutual defense treaty', Obama stated. He further maintained that US commitment to defend the Philippines is 'ironclad'.

Such affirmations from US officials could not have come at a better time, as the Philippines is engaged in a territorial dispute with China over islands in the South China Sea. The new defence agreement, according to Philippine officials, may put Washington in a position of being required to defend the Philippines' island claims. During Obama's visit, Philippine Secretary of Foreign Affairs Albert del Rosario confidently told journalists that the USA would 'come to the assistance of the Philippines if [its] metropolitan territory is attacked' or if Philippine 'armed forces are attacked in the Pacific area' (*Philippines Daily Inquirer* 2014). According to del Rosario, the South China Sea would be considered part of the 'Pacific area'; nevertheless, US officials have been far more publicly taciturn regarding their own interpretations of the agreement.

The US commitment to Philippine security reflects a long-standing orientation towards South-East Asia, which, similar to other parts of East Asia, finds its origins in the aftermath of the Second World War. The consistent theme, at least until the end of the Cold War, centred on preventing the spread of communism in the region. In a 1952 assessment the US Security Council stated that 'the loss of any of the countries of Southeast Asia to communist control as a consequence of overt or covert Chinese Communist aggression would have critical psychological, political and economic consequences' (Foreign Relations of the United States 1952: 127–128). This was the basis of the creation of the Southeast Asia Treaty Organization (SEATO) in 1954, which was headquartered in Bangkok, Thailand. However, the organization was structurally flawed in that it was largely perceived to be a Western-dominated group with inadequate participation by regional states, many of which preferred to maintain their neutrality as the USA became increasingly mired in the conflict in Vietnam. Eventually, in 1977 the organization was dissolved, thus ending hopes that South-East Asia would have its own region-based security architecture.

A more hopeful development occurred in 1967 when five regional nations founded the Association of Southeast Asian Nations (ASEAN). The US response to this was – and still remains – generally positive, notwithstanding the expression of occasional frustration regarding the organization's limited or protracted progress in addressing regional security challenges. In general, US officials view ASEAN as providing numerous partnership opportunities for the USA. For example, Admiral Robert Locklear, head of the US Pacific Command, recently stated that 'USPACOM [US Pacific Command] will continue to explore ways to support the ASEAN Defense Minister's Meeting (ADMM) and ASEAN Regional Forum for addressing common security challenges' (Locklear 2014). What ASEAN and its subsidiary organizations (particularly the ASEAN Regional Forum) provide for South-East Asia is an institutional embryo in which a more robust region-centred security architecture could emerge, which would supplement – if not ultimately supplant – security guarantees provided by the USA.

US–Australian relations and the US rebalance to East Asia

Australia and New Zealand have been consistent US allies in the American Pacific perimeter strategy dating back to the end of the Second World War. This posture was formalized with the signing of the ANZUS (Australia–New Zealand–USA) treaty on 1 September 1951. Following US–New Zealand disagreements over nuclear-powered vessels in the 1980s, the

New Zealand arm of the triangle atrophied, which then shifted the greatest emphasis of the former ANZUS triumvirate onto the US–Australian security relationship. The traditional view in Australia is that the long-standing alliance with the USA is something that should be sustained, if not expanded. 'Our alliance with Washington is overwhelmingly in our national interest', stated Lowy Institute Executive Director Michael Fullilove recently to the National Press Club of Australia. 'Any argument that we should downgrade the alliance in order to please China is wrong-headed. Unsolicited gifts to rising powers are not reciprocated, they are pocketed' (Fullilove 2014).

At the same time, there are growing worries within the Australian political elite about the country being torn in different directions in the wake of a rising US–China rivalry. Australia's 2013 White Paper on Defence addressed this issue directly, but suggested that Australia need not be forced into an awkward position of having to choose: 'The [Australian] Government does not believe that Australia must choose between its long-standing Alliance with the United States and its expanding relationship with China; nor do the United States and China believe that we must make such a choice' (Australian Government Department of Defence 2013: 11). However, some observers are less optimistic about Australia's ability to maintain this balancing act. Professor Hugh White argues, in essence, that pressure from both Beijing and Washington may make it more difficult for Canberra to compartmentalize its relationship with both countries because 'both the United States and China now see their political and strategic relationship with Australia primarily in terms of their own rivalry' (White 2013). Not having to choose would be the ideal scenario for Australia, but the possibility of such outcome will depend on East Asia's future power dynamics combined with Canberra's evolving calculations regarding its national interests.

Conclusion

An overall assessment of the future role of the USA in East Asia leads to three broad conclusions. First, the US rebalance to Asia has more continuity than many may realize. It is a reaffirmation of a security architecture that has existed, to a greater or lesser degree, since the end of the Second World War. Or put another way: the USA has rebalanced to East Asia on multiple occasions on both large and small scales, including during the Korean War, the 1954, 1958 and 1962 Taiwan Strait Crises, the Vietnam War, rapprochement with communist China in the 1970s, the 1995–96 Taiwan Strait Crises, the 'war on terror' and on numerous other less well-known occasions.

Second, the current US rebalance has provided assurance to key allies, such as Japan, South Korea, the Philippines, Thailand and Australia. More negatively, however, the rebalance has perhaps reduced incentives or motives for regional countries to create a truly indigenous security architecture. The ASEAN Regional Forum represents a trend in this direction, but it cannot be considered a substitute for the security guarantees that the USA has provided for more than six decades. This issue is important because current fiscal pressures and public sentiments inside the USA may constrain Washington's ability continuously to underwrite security in East Asia in the decades ahead.

Third, the most dangerous aspect of the rebalance is the widespread perception that it is directed at China, notwithstanding various statements by US officials attempting to downplay this angle. This means, potentially, that security dilemma dynamics have been triggered, perhaps encouraging China to rapidly accelerate its military build-up on a scale beyond which might have occurred otherwise. Some view the purpose of the USA in East Asia as primarily focused on balancing China. However, balancing behaviour among states undergoing power transitions can be fraught with danger and miscalculation. This is the challenge that the USA – and indeed the region – faces in the years and decades ahead.

Bibliography

Australian Government, Department of Defence, Defence White Paper, 2013, www.defence.gov.au/WhitePaper2013/docs/WP_2013_web.pdf.

Cardin, Benjamin, Transcript before the Hearing of the East Asian and Pacific Affairs Subcommittee of the Senate Foreign Relations Committee, Subject: 'Evaluating United States Policy on Taiwan on the 35th Anniversary of the Taiwan Relations Act', *Federal News Service*, 3 April 2014.

Chai, Winberg, 'Relations between the Chinese Mainland and Taiwan: Overview and Chronology', *Asian Affairs*, Vol. 26, No. 2, Summer 1999.

Cui, Tankai (Transcript of Remarks), Discussion at the United States Institute of Peace, Subject: "US–China Cooperation in Peace and Security', *Federal News Service*, 10 April 2014.

Dempsey, Martin, Remarks at the National Institute for Defense Studies, Tokyo, Japan, *Federal News Service*, 26 April 2013.

Deutsche Presse Agentur, 'Asia Needs NATO-like Alliance Against China, Japan Lawmaker Says', 6 March 2014.

Federal News Service, Senior US Administration Official [unidentified], Background Briefing, Subject: Secretary Kerry's Trip to Republic of Korea, China and Indonesia, 12 February 2014.

Foreign Relations of the United States, Report to the National Security Council by the Executive Secretary (Lay), United States Objectives and Courses of Action with Respect to Southeast Asia, NSC 124/2, Washington, 25 June 1952, 1952–1954, Vol. 12.

Fullilove, Michael, Transcript of Address to the National Press Club: 'A Larger Australia', 12 March 2014, www.lowyinstitute.org/publications/speech-larger-australia.

Hagel, Charles and Chang Wanquan, Minister of National Defense General Chang Wanquan, Location: Pentagon Briefing Room, *Federal News Service*, 19 August 2013.

Haig, Alexander, US State Department, Secretary [Alexander] Haig's Visit to the Far East-ASEAN Conference, June 1981, Digital National Security Archive, Document PH01943, p. 34.

Intelligence Memorandum No. 197, Subject: Implications for US Security Developments in Asia, 25 July 1949, p. 2 (quoting findings from prior CIA estimate ORE 17–49) [CB disc 7].

Japan Times, 'In Seoul, Obama Urges Japan to Settle "Terrible" Sex Slave Issue', 25 April 2014, www.japantimes.co.jp/news/2014/04/25/national/politics-diplomacy/in-seoul-obama-urges-japan-to-settle-terrible-sex-slave-issue/.

Karotkin, Jesse L., 'Trends in China's Naval Modernization, U.S.-China Economic and Security Review' Commission Testimony, 30 January 2014, as reported in Appendix A in Ronald O'Rourke, *China Naval Modernization: Implications for U.S. Navy Capabilities – Background and Issues for Congress*, Washington, DC: Congressional Research Service, 28 February 2014.

Larson, Charles R., US Navy Commander in Chief, United States Pacific Command, Transcript of Remarks before the Senate Armed Services Committee Posture Hearing, Federal News Service, 2 March 1994.

Locklear, Samuel, Transcript of Testimony, Congressional Documents and Publications, 26 March 2014.

Los Angeles Times, 'Taiwan's Ties to China Falter', 5 April 2014.

Manyin, Mark E., Emma Chanlett-Avery, Ian E. Rinehart, Mary Beth Nikitin and William H. Cooper, *Pivot to the Pacific? The Obama Administration's 'Rebalancing' Toward Asia*, Washington, DC: Congressional Research Service, 28 March 2012.

Manyin, Mark E., Emma Chanlett-Avery, Ian E. Rinehart, Mary Beth Nikitin and William H. Cooper, *U.S.-South Korea Relations*, Washington DC: Congressional Research Service, 12 February 2014.

National Security Council (NSC) U.S. Policy Towards Formosa and the Government of the Republic of China, NSC 5503 (Document 12), National Security Council Report, Washington, DC, 15 January 1955, Foreign Relations of the United States, 1955–1957, Vol. 2, pp. 30–32.

New York Times, 'China's Hard Line: "No Room for Compromise"', 9 March 2014.

Nye, Joseph, Prepared Statement Before the House Committee on Asia and the Pacific, *Federal News Service*, 25 October 1995.

Obama, Barack, News Conference with South Korean President Park Guen-hye, *CQ Transcriptions*, 25 April 2014a.

Obama, Barack. Joint Press Conference with President Benigno Aquino, *CQ Transcriptions*, 28 April 2014b.

Philippines Daily Inquirer, 'US Will Defend PH if Attacked: DFA Chief', 30 April 2014.

Reuters, 'U.S. Defense Chief Gets Earful as China Visit Exposes Tensions', 8 April 2014, www.reuters.com/article/2014/04/08/us-china-usa-idUSBREA370N020140408.

Roehrig, Terence, *A Changing Paradigm of U.S.–East Asian Relations: Strategic and Economic Perspectives*, Newport, RI: Naval War College, April 2008.

Seiler, Sydney A., Transcript of Remarks at the Institute for Corean-American Studies (ICAS) Winter Symposium, Subject: 'The Korean Peninsula Issues and United States National Security', *Federal News Service*, 14 February 2014.

Sutter, Robert, Professor of Practice of International Affairs, Elliott School of International Affairs, George Washington University, Testimony before the U.S.-China Economic and Security Review Commission, 'China's Grand Strategy in Asia', 13 March 2014, www.uscc.gov/sites/default/files/SUTTER_Testimony.pdf.

Sydney Morning Herald, 'U.S. Navy Commander Warns of Naval Standoff Over Chinese Aggression', 9 April 2014.

The White House, 'Remarks to the Press by Vice President Joe Biden and Prime Minister Shinzo Abe of Japan', 3 December 2013, www.whitehouse.gov/the-press-office/2013/12/03/remarks-press-vice-president-joe-biden-and-prime-minister-shinzo-abe-jap.

US Congress, *Sino-American Relations: From the Shanghai Communique to the Present*, Report Prepared for the Subcommittee on Asian and Pacific Affairs, of the Committee on Foreign Relations, US House of Representatives, July 1980, p. 4.

US Department of Defense, *Sustaining U.S. Global Leadership: Priorities for 21st Century Defense*, Washington, DC: US Department of Defense, January 2012.

US State Department, Talking Paper, 'Guidelines for U.S. Policy and Operations in the Far East', 17 August 1961, Declassified Documents Reference System, Farmington Hills, MI: Gale, 2013.

Washington Post, 'Obama Reassures Japan as He Begins Asia Visit', *Washington Post*, 24 April 2014.

White, Hugh, 'Australia's Choice: Will the Land Down Under Pick the United States or China?' *Foreign Affairs*, 4 September 2013, www.foreignaffairs.com/articles/139902/hugh-white/australias-choice.

Wiedemann, Kent, Deputy Assistant Secretary of State, East Asian and Pacific Affairs, Testimony Before the House Ways and Means Committee, Subcommittee on Trade, *Federal News Service*, 23 May 1995.

22
Preventing the next war in East Asia

Andrew T. H. Tan

East Asia and the next war

The rise of Asia, particularly East Asia, is due largely to its sustained high economic growth. According to the World Bank, East Asia recorded gross domestic product (GDP) growth rates of 8.3 per cent in 2011, 7.5 per cent in 2012 and an estimated 7.9 per cent in 2013. By comparison, the eurozone, still gripped by the Euro crisis, grew by 1.5 per cent in 2011, and shrank by 0.4 per cent in 2012, with an estimated decrease in GDP of 0.1 per cent in 2013. The comparative figures for the USA, still recovering from the Global Financial Crisis (GFC) of 2008, were 1.8 per cent for 2011, 2.2 per cent for 2012 and an estimated 1.9 per cent for 2013 (World Bank 2013a). Increasingly, the centre of the global economy no longer resides in Europe or North America but in Asia, in particular, East Asia.

Asia's importance has been acknowledged by US President Barack Obama, who stated in his seminal 'Asia Pivot' speech to the Australian Parliament in 2011 that it is in the Asia-Pacific that the USA saw the future, as it is the world's fastest growing region and is home to more than half of the global economy. Thus, Obama declared that the USA would 'make our presence and missions in the Asia Pacific a top priority', and that 'as we plan and budget for the future, we will allocate the resources necessary to maintain our strong military presence in this region' (*The Australian* 2011).

However, the evidently high tensions in East Asia in 2013, the highest since the end of the Second World War, have led to fears over the outbreak of open warfare involving the key state actors in the region. This could come about due to uncontrolled nationalism, brinkmanship and sheer miscalculation. Indeed, the USA, China and Japan are the three largest economies in the world, with South Korea ranked 15th in global terms (World Bank 2013b). More seriously, any conflict could quickly escalate into a nuclear war, as some of the key players involved, namely China, North Korea and the USA, possess nuclear weapons. East Asia is also becoming the epicentre of the increasingly tense and competitive relationship between the USA and its emerging global peer competitor, China. The strategic, political and economic impact of a regional conflict in East Asia will therefore be global, with a devastating impact on the global economy as well as uncertain consequences for the international system.

The next major conflict, sparked by miscalculation, could thus begin in East Asia, with global repercussions. This essay, which concludes this volume, argues that the two key regional and global players, namely China and the USA, must finally begin the process of accommodation with each other through a serious and broad-ranging dialogue to manage not just their relations but also regional security issues.

Key areas of conflict

The overarching context is the increasingly tense strategic competition between China and the USA. The economic rise of China, accompanied by its rapid military modernization, has enabled China to challenge the dominant position of the USA both in Asia as well as globally. However, as Steve Chan warned, 'the danger of a war among the great powers is greatest when a newcomer dissatisfied with the status quo overtakes a once-dominant state' (Chan 2005: 688). As a key player in Asia, and particularly in East Asia where the bulk of its regional military forces are based (in Japan and South Korea), the USA is not about to relinquish voluntarily its dominant position in the region to a rising peer challenger, namely China, despite the current parlous state of its finances and economy.

Since the end of the Cold War in 1989, tensions between the USA and China have been steadily on the rise. The Tiananmen Square massacre of pro-independence student and worker activists in Beijing in 1989 led to a deterioration of relations with the USA, and the public was shocked by the violent crackdown viewed on live television broadcasts around the world. In 1996, in response to China's missile tests near Taiwan, designed to prevent any declaration of independence by the then pro-independence Taiwanese government of Chen Shui-bian, the USA stepped in to deter China by deploying a naval task force with two aircraft carriers near Taiwanese waters (Ding 2003: 379–381). This, however, only served to confirm to many Chinese people the notion that the USA has been preventing the reunification of Taiwan with China.

The attacks on the USA on 11 September 2001 pushed the emerging US–China strategic rivalry into the background as the USA declared a global 'war on terror' and proceeded to invade Afghanistan and Iraq. However, the gradual ending of those conflicts inevitably reignited the issue of strategic competition between the two countries. This was exacerbated by the severe long-term economic difficulties experienced by the USA following the 'sub-prime' mortgage crisis, which led to the GFC in 2008, and the burgeoning deficits and massive debt, which exceeded US $16,500,000m. by the end 2013 (US Department of the Treasury 2013). On the other hand, China grew through the GFC and the subsequent Euro crisis which afflicted Europe, by helping to sustain the global economy. Perceiving that the strategic environment was moving in its favour, China began to behave in a bold and even aggressive manner to assert its territorial claims in the South and East China Seas. This was epitomized by a serious confrontation in March 2009, when Chinese ships surrounded a US Navy surveillance vessel, the *Impeccable*, in the South China Sea, which China claims but which the US regards as international waters (US Department of State 2012).

China's assertiveness has coincided with rising anti-China sentiments in the USA, spurred by the apprehension over China's rising challenge to the USA. James Kraska, a former policy advisor to the US Department of Defense, wrote a speculative scenario in 2010, in which 'years of strategic missteps in oceans policy, naval strategy and a force structure in decline set the stage for US defeat at sea in 2015', the defeat in question being a surprise attack by China which destroys the US nuclear-powered aircraft carrier USS *George Washington*, forward deployed in Japan, with the loss of some 4,000 lives (Kraska 2010). A Pearl Harbour moment, it conjures images of an aggressive, war-hungry and expansionist state akin to Japan before the Second World War. Similarly, in 2012 James Dobbin, a former US Assistant Secretary of State, using Cold War analogy and language to speculate about possible war with China, asserted that 'if it chose, China could ... become a more capable opponent than either the Soviet Union or Nazi Germany at their peak, neither of which ever approached America's economic might' (Dobbins 2012: 7).

The USA has thus taken steps to strengthen its alliances in the Asia-Pacific, particularly with India, Australia, Japan and South Korea, while reaching out to others concerned about China's rise, such as Vietnam and the Philippines, both of which are engaged in territorial disputes with China in the South China Sea. Following President Obama's 'Asia Pivot' speech in Australia in 2011, the USA stationed troops in Australia's Northern Territory (*Daily Telegraph* 2012). It also deployed its newest warships, namely the littoral combat ships, in Singapore, with the first vessel, the USS *Freedom*, arriving in Singapore in April 2013 (*Straits Times* 2013). The USA is also developing a joint war-fighting doctrine, Air-Sea Battle, which echoes the Air-Land Battle doctrine developed to counter Soviet and Warsaw Pact forces in Europe during the Cold War.

The development of Air-Sea Battle reflects concern about China's anti-access capabilities, such as its long-range cruise missiles, should regional conflict break out over Taiwan, Japan or the Korean peninsula. The US navy and its vaunted aircraft carrier battle groups would have to stay out of range, thus substantially reducing their effectiveness, and thus enabling China's air force and navy to conduct military or coercive operations in East Asia. Air-Sea Battle is designed to overcome this (Von Tol *et al.* 2010: 95). However, its assumption that any conflict would remain conventional is dangerous, since it involves attacking China's surveillance, intelligence and command systems. Such actions are likely to be interpreted by China as attempts to disarm its nuclear strike capability and could thus lead to a quick and unwanted escalation into a nuclear conflict (Schreer 2013).

It is within this overall strategic context of increasingly tense relations between the two major powers, namely China and the USA, that the dangers of conflict over Korea, the friction between China and Japan, and the still problematic issue of Taiwan have to be understood. By early 2013 tensions on the Korean peninsula had deteriorated to their worst level since the end of the Korean War in 1953, sparking fears of miscalculation and accidental war as a result of North Korea's brinkmanship (ICG 2013a). Any open conflict could escalate rapidly, drawing in China, the USA, Japan, and possibly other US allies from further afield.

Over the years North Korea has frequently used brinkmanship as part of its foreign policy. Its aggressive behaviour can be explained by its internal fragility and perceived threats from abroad, which have heightened North Korea's sense of vulnerability. Assertions made by President George W. Bush in the wake of the 9/11 attacks on the USA that North Korea, Iraq and Iran formed part of an 'axis of evil' rogue states, followed by the swift conventional victory of US-led forces in Iraq, heightened North Korea's fears for its own survival (*Washington Post* 2002). North Korea thus concluded that it needed to acquire nuclear weapons to deter the USA. Internally, the North Korean regime has been challenged by its failed economy, which resulted in economic collapse in the 1990s and a famine that led to the deaths of up to 1m. people (Smith 2013: 127–129). More recently, the leadership succession from Kim Jong-il (who died in December 2011) to his young and inexperienced son, Kim Jong-un, has led the regime to exaggerate external threats and crises as a means of shoring up its legitimacy, particularly given the evidence of internal power struggles within North Korea. Ultimately, these led to the dismissal and deaths of its minister of defence and Kim Jong-un's powerful uncle, Jang Song-thaek (CNN 2013b).

These factors explain North Korea's recent unprecedented and aggressive behaviour. In 2010 a South Korean naval corvette, the *Choenan*, was sunk by a torpedo fired from a North Korean midget submarine, killing 46 sailors (CNN 2010a). This was followed in the same month by the artillery shelling of Yeonpyeong, a South Korean island located close to North Korea's maritime border (Reuters 2010). In early 2013 North Korea carried out its third nuclear test, and in response to a fresh round of UN sanctions against it, unilaterally abrogated the armistice that had ended the Korean War in 1953, thus returning the Korean peninsula to a state of war (Bloomberg 2013). North Korea also openly threatened to attack the USA (*The Telegraph* 2013). In April of that year North Korea threatened to destroy Tokyo in a nuclear attack (*Express* 2013). The International Crisis Group warned in March 2013 that the risk of open conflict on the Korean peninsula had risen dramatically, due to the possibility of miscalculation leading to an inadvertent escalation (ICG 2013).

At about the same time as the Korean crisis, relations between Japan and China also deteriorated to the extent that Christopher Hughes described them as 'the most serious for Sino–Japanese relations in the post-war period in terms of the risk of militarised conflict' (BBC 2013). The high tensions between the two countries revolve around the dispute over the Diaoyu/Senkaku Islands. In recent years there have been a number of increasingly serious incidents concerning the islands. In September 2010, for instance, collisions between a Chinese fishing vessel and two Japanese coastguard vessels near the Diaoyu/Senkaku Islands led to the detention of the crew of the fishing vessel by Japan. Under pressure from China, the crew and the captain were released (BBC 2010). In September 2012 the Japanese government purchased the disputed islands from their private Japanese owners to pre-empt a plan by the right-wing Governor of Tokyo, Ishihara Shintaro, from purchasing them and then removing the prohibition imposed by the government on landings by right-wing activists, which would be provocative to China. However, this move was interpreted differently in China, which perceived it as a move permanently to claim the territory as part of Japan. This led to a wave of emotive anti-Japanese protests in China (ABC News 2012). Indeed, China's rising nationalism has been strongly tinged with anti-Japanese sentiment, the result of historical memories of Japan's invasion of China prior to 1945 and the government's determination to sustain popular memory of those events. Reflecting a common perception in China, Liu Xiaoming, China's ambassador to Japan, thus opined in an article in the *Financial Times* in November 2012 that 'unlike Germany, Japan has never seriously reflected on its behaviour during the second world war', citing the fact that 'war criminals are still worshiped at the Yasukuni shrine in Tokyo (and) senior Japanese officials often pay tribute there'. Liu also asserted that 'Japan's leaders have occasionally offered grudging apologies but these have never convinced its neighbours' (*IHT Rendezvous* 2013).

Japan has thus become a useful bogeyman, particularly in bolstering nationalism and the legitimacy of the ruling Chinese Communist Party (CCP). However, the danger, as the International Crisis Group has warned, is that 'while in the past it could more easily dial up or down nationalism through control of state-run media, the rapid rise of Internet use has eroded that control and begun to shape the context of policymaking … the government must now satisfy increasingly outspoken and critical citizens' (ICG 2013b). For its part, Japan has also not been blameless in stoking tensions with its neighbours, with right-wing politicians guilty of a series of controversial statements attempting to whitewash Japan's role in the Second World War, which only appear to confirm to China and South Korea that Japan has never really been contrite about past events (CNN 2013a).

Tensions came to a head in January 2013, when Chinese warships locked their fire-control radars onto a Japanese destroyer, a provocative act that could have led to open war had the

Japanese destroyer responded by firing first (*Japan Times* 2013). In late 2013 China unilaterally declared an air defence identification zone around the Diaoyu/Senkaku Islands, prompting the USA to warn China that such actions increased the danger of military conflict and that the US–Japan Mutual Defense Treaty applied to the islands (Gertz 2013). The USA also flew B-52 bombers over the island to challenge this. As at mid-2014 tensions in East Asia between China and Japan remained at their highest levels since the end of the Second World War.

Finally, there is another serious issue which has been deceptively quiet amid the tensions over Korea, and between China and Japan. The Taiwan problem, the legacy of China's civil war after 1945 and the subsequent Cold War, has not gone away. The Kuomintang (KMT), which lost the civil war, fled to Taiwan in 1949, while the victorious CCP established the People's Republic of China. The onset of the Cold War and fears of a monolithic communist plan to take over Asia led to the USA intervening to prevent the reunification of Taiwan with China when it signed the mutual security treaty with Taiwan in 1954. Although the USA later normalized relations with China in 1979 and accepted the 'One China' principle, it also passed the Taiwan Relations Act, under which the USA reserved the right to sell defensive weapons to Taiwan, and further stated that any use of force to resolve the Taiwan issue would be treated with 'grave concern' by it (Taiwan Relations Act 1979). For China, however, Taiwan is an emotive nationalist cause, as it is regarded as territory which was 'lost' due to foreign imperialism, and China purports that it is the USA that is preventing the reunification of Taiwan with the motherland.

Tensions in the Taiwan Strait abated following the electoral victory of the KMT over the pro-independence Democratic Progressive Party in 2008. The improvement in cross-Strait relations is epitomized by the signing of the free trade agreement in 2010 which further consolidated the strong economic ties between China and Taiwan (CNN 2010b). Indeed, in 2011 some 86 per cent of Taiwan's outward investment went to China, which has become a low-cost manufacturing base for Taiwanese products. In the same year 40 per cent of Taiwan's exports went to China (Chiang 2012: 73). China's strategy has been to offer economic incentives to convince the Taiwanese of the merits of reunification with China. As China's objective is clearly focused on reunification, it expects that this would pave the way for Taiwan to reunify with China. China has repeatedly made clear it will use force if necessary as reunification is considered non-negotiable. However, most Taiwanese are not enthusiastic about reunification with China. A recent poll in 2012 found that only 9 per cent favoured reunification, while 61 per cent wanted to maintain the status quo (*DefenseNews* 2012). Most Taiwanese have difficulty identifying with China and also expect, since they have a functioning democracy, that only the people of Taiwan should decide the country's future.

However, maintaining the status quo is akin to accepting a situation of de facto independence, which China will not tolerate indefinitely. The current status quo, while outwardly appearing to be stable, is therefore not sustainable. The Taiwan problem in fact remains very much alive and can be described as akin to the proverbial ticking time bomb, since its resolution will have to occur at some future point. The problem is that its ultimate resolution could involve conflict, given China's growing nationalism and military might.

Preventing the next conflict in Asia

The absence of effective regional institutions, regimes, norms and laws that could regulate tensions and conflicts between states has meant that the geostrategic environment in East Asia is reminiscent of that in Europe before the world wars, characterized by changing power balances and the outbreak of serious inter-state crises. A regional war in East Asia would have devastating global consequences. Three of the key players, namely the USA, China and Japan, are, in that order, the three largest economies in the world. More seriously, any conflict could escalate rapidly into nuclear war, as the conventional war capabilities of the USA could compel North Korea and China to resort to weapons of mass destruction, such as nuclear missiles and biological and chemical weapons. By 2013 the possibility of open warfare in East Asia had been taken seriously, with widespread warnings that tensions between China and Japan, for instance, had reached the highest levels since the end of the Second World War. Due to the possibility of misperception and miscalculation, accidental war could break out – however implausible from a rational perspective that might sound.

What can be done to prevent possible conflict in East Asia? One of the key lessons of the previous two world wars is the need for strong international institutions, regimes, norms and laws which could better manage the inevitable conflicts of interests between states. Another important lesson, taken from the Cold War in Europe, has been the need for a long process of confidence and security building measures – such as the Conventional Forces in Europe process – which would improve transparency and build trust, to accompany the parallel processes of deep dialogue, engagement and cooperation. This could eventually lead to more intrusive forms of regionalism which could reduce tensions, resolve or manage disputes without resort to violence, and more generally keep the peace among the main regional powers.

While the imperative to take regionalism seriously is there, it remains to be seen whether there is far-sighted leadership among the key state actors in East Asia to do so, even when the terrible consequences of a regional conflict are obvious and no one actually wants such a conflict to occur. Much depends on the two key players in East Asia, namely the USA and China. While the USA faces serious economic and financial difficulties, and its long-term decline is evident, it remains a key player in the region. China must thus realize that unless it arrives at an accommodation with the USA as well as its allies in managing regional security, it cannot hope to maintain regional stability in the long term, which it needs for its economic modernization and development. While it believes that the balance of power is shifting in its favour, it has to understand that effective regional influence ultimately has to be earned, not imposed. Similarly, the reality of China's rise means that Washington must learn to accommodate it – the alternative being a dangerous and destabilizing arms race that would bankrupt the USA and lead to unpalatable outcomes, such as a general conflict. Learning to live with a peer competitor requires leadership, engagement and dialogue, rather than instinctively reaching out for a Cold War containment strategy.

The two countries must therefore begin a broad-ranging dialogue to manage not just their relations but also regional security, as they are key players in ensuring stability in the region. In this respect, a glimmer of hope can be discerned from China's unusual silence and lack of open support for its traditional ally, North Korea, even as it carried out its unprecedented brinkmanship since the young Kim took power. China has also openly criticized North Korea for its nuclear tests and has supported United Nations sanctions, and there are clear signs of disarray in China's traditional policy of uncritical support for North Korea, as its behaviour could lead to unpalatable outcomes for China, such as an unwanted war on the Korean peninsula, or the acquisition of nuclear arms by Japan and South Korea. In April 2013, for instance, President Xi Jinping obliquely criticized North Korea, stating that 'no one should be allowed to throw a region and even the whole world into chaos for selfish gains … while pursuing its own interests, a country should accommodate the legitimate interests of others' (*Washington Post* 2013). Media reports also indicate a flurry of visits by US officials to Beijing in early 2013 to discuss the situation in North Korea (*New York Times* 2013a). The surprise purge and execution in late 2013 of Kim Jong-un's powerful uncle, Jang Song-thaek, who had been the key interlocutor in China's relations with North Korea, has also demonstrated that China is not in control of events in North Korea (*New York Times* 2013b). Thus, there is the possibility that China and the USA could in fact cooperate in managing regional security, such as over the Korean peninsula.

The high tensions and historical animosities between China and Japan are more difficult to resolve, but these require strong and capable foreign policy leadership on the part of both countries, which appear to be lacking at this time. China, in particular, needs to understand that the long-term consequences of its promotion of nationalism by arousing anti-Japanese sentiments domestically would lead to an unstable regional neighbourhood and ultimately conflict with Japan, surely an undesirable outcome given that the two countries are each other's major trading partners with much to gain from joint cooperation. On Japan's part, the failure by its leaders, particularly conservative right-wing politicians, to come to terms with its role in the Second World War has led to various controversial statements which have only played to anti-Japanese nationalism in China and South Korea. As CNN noted in an opinion piece in May 2013, 'nearly 68 years after surrender, some Japanese conservatives are engaged in counterproductive battles over history that make Japan appear weak and undignified, unable to take the measure of its history' (CNN 2013a). As an analyst noted regarding Shinzo Abe's performance as Prime Minister, Abe has in fact undermined Japan's interest by 'preserving redundant renderings of Japan in the 21st century, negating the positive and responsible record of Japan as a post-war nation-state' (Kersten 2013: 50). The high tensions in 2013–14 between the two countries, which are both now on a quasi-war footing, points to the urgent need for conflict and crisis management mechanisms to be immediately implemented to hold tensions in check. Ultimately, both governments would need to stop fuelling nationalist sentiments, and instead focus on maintaining stability as well as preserving the benefits arising from the deep economic interdependence between the two countries.

The long-term decline of the USA's influence in the region, despite the fact that it has pledged to maintain or even increase its military presence in East Asia, is probably unavoidable. However, an effective US presence and role in the region remains essential. Through deterrence as well as engagement as an equal power, China could be persuaded to take part in dialogue about the management of regional security instead of making unilateral military moves which raise tensions and might spark conflict. This requires other states in the region to help to shore up regional stability by becoming more effective security partners, first by investing in their own military capabilities, and second by providing more effective regional security cooperation. The reason for this is not, however, to contain China, given that much greater efforts will have to be made to engage it, but to ensure the maintenance of a regional balance of power that would channel foreign policy choices towards more peaceful means of resolving disputes. Ultimately, however, China and the USA will have to find the strategic wisdom and political will to work out some form of *entente cordiale* in East Asia if conflict in the region is to be avoided.

Bibliography

ABC News, 'Anti-Japan Protests Spread Across China', 19 September 2012, www.abc.net.au/news/2012-09-18/anti-japan-protests-spread-across-china/4268494.
British Broadcasting Corporation (BBC), 'Japan Frees Chinese Boat Captain Amid Diplomatic Row', *BBC News*, 24 September 2010, www.bbc.co.uk/news/world-11403241.

British Broadcasting Corporation (BBC), 'Viewpoints: How Serious Are China–Japan Tensions?' *BBC News*, 8 February 2013, www.bbc.co.uk/news/world-asia-21290349.

Bloomberg, 'North Korea Fuels Regional Tensions by Quitting Armistice', 9 March 2013, www.bloomberg.com/news/2013-03-08/north-korea-fuels-region-s-tensions-by-quitting-armistice.html.

Chan, Steve, 'Is There a Power Transition Between the US and China? The Different Faces of National Power', *Asian Survey*, Vol. 45, No. 5, September/October 2005.

Chiang, Min-hua, 'Taiwan's Economy: Slower Growth and Dependence on China', *East Asian Policy*, Vol. 4, No. 68, 2012.

CNN, 'U.S. Official: N. Korea Torpedo Likely Sunk S. Korean Warship', 26 April 2010a, http://news.blogs.cnn.com/2010/04/26/u-s-official-n-korea-torpedo-likely-sunk-s-korean-warship/.

CNN, 'Taiwan, China Sign Historic Trade Deal', 29 June 2010b, http://articles.cnn.com/2010-06-29/world/china.taiwan.deal_1_taiwan-strait-china-and-taiwan-chen-yunlin?_s=PM:WORLD.

CNN, 'Opinion: Japanese Politicians Still Struggle with Wartime Past', 16 May 2013a, http://edition.cnn.com/2013/05/16/opinion/japan-wartime-past-nationalism-kingston/index.html?hpt=hp_c1.

CNN, 'How Kim Jong Un Got Rid of His Uncle', 13 December 2013b, http://edition.cnn.com/2013/12/10/opinion/ghitis-purge-north-korea/.

Daily Telegraph, 'US to Station Troops in Northern Australia as Fears of China's Pacific Presence Grow', 2 February 2012, www.telegraph.co.uk/news/worldnews/australiaandthepacific/8883558/US-to-station-troops-in-northern-Australia-as-fears-of-Chinas-Pacific-presence-grow.html.

DefenseNews, 'China Tries to Expand Control as Taiwan Resists: Report', 28 August 2012, www.defensenews.com/article/20120828/DEFREG03/308280011/China-Tries-Expand-Control-Taiwan-Resists-Report.

Ding, Arthur S., 'The Lessons of the 1995–1996 Taiwan Straits Crisis: Developing a New Strategy Toward the USA and Taiwan', in Laurie Burkitt, Andrew Scobell and Larry M. Wortzel (eds), *The Lessons of History: The Chinese People's Liberation Army at 75*, Carlisle, PA: Strategic Studies Institute, U.S. Army War College, July 2003.

Dobbins, James, 'War With China', *Survival*, Vol. 54, No. 4, August/September 2012.

Express, 'North Korea States "Nuclear War is Unavoidable", as It Declares First Target Will Be Japan', 12 April 2013, www.express.co.uk/news/world/391376/North-Korea-states-nuclear-war-is-unavoidable-as-it-declares-first-target-will-be-Japan.

Gertz, Bill, 'U.S. Warns China Over East China Sea Maritime Grab', *Washington Free Beacon*, 25 November 2013, http://freebeacon.com/national-security/u-s-warns-china-over-east-china-sea-maritime-grab/.

IHT Rendezvous (International Herald Tribune), 'Despite Tensions, U.S. and Japan Begin a New Set of War Games', 4 November 2013, http://rendezvous.blogs.nytimes.com/2012/11/04/despite-tensions-u-s-and-japan-begin-a-new-set-of-war-games/.

International Crisis Group (ICG), 'The Korean Peninsula: Flirting With Conflict', 13 March 2013a, www.crisisgroup.org/en/publication-type/alerts/2013/north-korea-the-korean-peninsula-flirting-with-conflict.aspx.

International Crisis Group (ICG), 'Dangerous Waters: China–Japan Relations on the Rocks', *Asia Report* No. 245, 8 April 2013b, www.crisisgroup.org/en/regions/asia/north-east-asia/china/245-dangerous-waters-china-japan-relations-on-the-rocks.aspx.

Japan Times, 'Chinese Target-Locked MSDF Ship, Chopper', 6 February 2013, www.japantimes.co.jp/news/2013/02/06/national/japan-says-chinese-warships-locked-weapons-radar-on-msdf/#.UZHAw9evPIU.

Kersten, Rikki, 'Japan's Strategic Dilemmas: Navigating the U.S. "Rebalance" and the Rise of China', *AIIA Policy Commentary*, No. 15, November 2013.

Kraska, James, 'How the USA Lost the Naval War of 2015', *Orbis*, Winter 2010.

New York Times, 'Playing Chinese Chess', 10 May 2013a, www.nytimes.com/2013/05/11/opinion/global/The-Chinese–US-North-Korea-Japan-Diplomatic-Rectangle.html?_r=0.

New York Times, 'Public Ouster in North Korea Unsettles China', 9 December 2013b, www.nytimes.com/2013/12/10/world/asia/a-gamble-for-north-korea-leader-kim-jong-un.html?_r=0.

Reuters, 'North Korea Shells South in Fiercest Attack in Decades', 23 November 2010, www.reuters.com/article/2010/11/23/us-korea-north-artillery-idUSTRE6AM0YS20101123.

Schreer, Benjamin, *Planning the Unthinkable War: AirSea Battle and Its Implications for Australia*, Canberra: Australian Security Policy Institute, 2013, www.aspi.org.au/htmlver/ASPI_planning_the_unthinkable_war/index.html.

Smith, Hazel, 'North Korea's Security Perspectives', in Andrew T. H. Tan (ed.), *East and Southeast Asia: International Relations and Security Perspectives*, London: Routledge, 2013.

Straits Times, 'First U.S. Navy Littoral Combat Ship, USS Freedom, Arrives in Singapore', 18 April 2013, www.straitstimes.com/breaking-news/singapore/story/first-us-littoral-combat-ship-uss-freedom-arrives-singapore-20130418.

Taiwan Relations Act, 10 April 1979, www.taiwandocuments.org/tra01.htm (accessed 15 May 2013).

The Australian, 'U.S. President Barack Obama's Speech to Parliament', 17 November 2011, www.theaustralian.com.au/national-affairs/obama-in-australia/obamas-speech-to-parliament/story-fnb0o39u-1226197973237.

The Telegraph, 'North Korea Defeats U.S. Troops in New Video', 9 May 2013, www.telegraph.co.uk/news/worldnews/asia/northkorea/9947489/North-Korea-defeats-US-troops-in-new-video.html.

US Department of State, 'South China Sea', Press Statement, 3 August 2012, www.state.gov/r/pa/prs/ps/2012/08/196022.htm.

US Department of the Treasury, Gross External Debt Position, 31 December 2013, www.treasury.gov/ticdata/Publish/debta2013q4.htm.

Von Tol, Jan, Mark Gunzinger, Andrew F Krepinevich and Jim Thomas, *AirSea Battle: A Point-of-Departure Operational Concept*, Washington, DC: Centre for Strategic and Budgetary Assessment, 2010.

Washington Post, 'President Bush's 2002 State of the Union Address', 29 January 2002, www.washingtonpost.com/wp-srv/onpolitics/transcripts/sou012902.htm.

Washington Post, 'President Xi Jinping Expresses Concern Over North Korea's Rhetoric', 7 April 2013, http://articles.washingtonpost.com/2013-04-07/world/38354043_1_south-china-sea-schumer-united-nations.

World Bank, 'The Global Economic Outlook in Summary, 2011–2015', *Global Economic Prospects 2013*, Washington, DC: The World Bank, 2013a, http://web.worldbank.org/WBSITE/EXTERNAL/EXTDEC/EXTDECPROSPECTS/EXTGBLPROSPECTS/0,contentMDK:23327491~menuPK:612510~pagePK:2904583~piPK:2904598~theSitePK:612501,00.htm (accessed 7 May 2013).

World Bank, *GDP Data (Current US$)*, Washington, DC, The World Bank, 2013b, http://data.worldbank.org/indicator/NY.GDP.MKTP.CD?order=wbapi_data_value_2011+wbapi_data_value+wbapi_data_value-last&sort=asc (accessed 6 May 2013).

Index

ABC News 9, 26, 227
Abe Shinzo 9, 24, 25, 56, 86, 136, 138, 142–50, 151n5, 151n6, 151n9, 151n14, 153, 154, 158, 159, 161, 218, 230; 'Abenomics' reform policy 153, 159, 161; government of 25, 55, 86, 157, 187
Academy of Military Science and CCP Central Documents Studies Office (AMS-CDSO) 37
Acharya, Amitav 51
active electronically scanned array (AESA) radar 27
Aegis combat system 29, 30, 113, 214
African trade of China, importance of 63
Agence France Presse (AFP) 29, 54
aid asymmetry, dangers of 183–4
air defence identification zone (ADIZ) 56–7, 143, 151n4, 160
Air-Land Battle (ALB) war-fighting 75, 226
Air-Sea Battle (ASB) 74–6; regional responses to 76–7, 78–9; strategy of 3, 6, 73, 226; US pivot policy in Asia and 74–6, 76–7
Air Self-Defence Forces of Japan 55
Airborne Early Warning and Control (AEW&C) 27, 28, 30, 45
aircraft carriers 6, 28–9, 30, 38, 42–3, 45–8, 74–6, 105, 113, 135, 217, 225, 226
Airforce-Technology.com 27, 29
Akaha, Tsuneo 133
Angell, Normal 21
Anti-Access/Area Denial (A2/AD) strategy 75–6, 111, 112–3, 117, 121–2, 128; Taiwan and 125–7
anti-Japanese nationalism in China 9, 25, 57, 81, 230
anti-ship cruise missiles (ASCMs) 46, 47, 126
anti-submarine warfare (ASW) capability 6, 29, 41, 46, 47, 48, 125, 194
Aquino, Benigno (and administration of) 53
armoured personnel carriers 6, 10, 11, 28
Arms Control Association (ACA) 177
arms race in East Asia 24–5; implications of 31
Armstrong, Charles 172, 176
Army Construction Institute of NDU in China 37
Asahi Shimbun 150

Asia: Asian Institute for Policy Studies 186; communist movement in, Chinese claims for leadership of 18–19; concert of democracies in 5; conflict within, prevention of 228–30; future dynamics of 66–9; determinants of 66–7; hedging with US, power relations and 65; non-government US engagement with 65; rebalance to Asia by US 5–6; effects of 221–2; regional trade arrangements, US exclusion from 61; regionalism of, Chinese promotion of trade expansion and 85; US as security guarantor for 65; US government engagement with 65
Asia-Pacific Economic Cooperation summit in Bali (2013) 116
Asia-Pacific region: Chinese strengths and influence in 63–4, 66; trade and investment in 63
Asia Sentinel 95
Associated Press (AP) 55
Association of Southeast Asian Nations (ASEAN) 92, 94, 137, 204, 207–8, 211, 220, 221; ASEAN-China Cooperation Partnership 97; ASEAN Plus Three (APT) 137, 204; China, Treaty of Amity and Cooperation with 38, 99; China–ASEAN Cooperation Partnership (2014) 97; 'creeping assertiveness' of China and members of 92; cultivation of ties between China and 98–9; Declaration of Code of Conduct with regarding South China Sea 38, 51–2, 96–7; East Asia Summit (EAS) 137; Hainan Provincial People's Congress offshore border defence and security management law, concerns about 96; Japan–ASEAN Summit (2013) 56; Malacca Strait and China, concerns for 104, 106; Maritime Cooperation Fund, China and 96–7; Ministerial Meeting (AMM) in Phnom Penh (2012) 52–3; Regional Forum in Hanoi (2010) 52
asymmetric defence 6, 7–8, 27, 30, 125, 126, 127–8
asymmetric warfare 127, 173
Australia 17; ANZUS (Australia–New Zealand–USA) Treaty (1951) 220–21; Australian–US relations and rebalance to East Asia 220–21;

233

Index

Defence Department 221; International Relations (IR) Theory in 67
The Australian 6, 25, 224
Axelrod, Robert 209

Babson, Bradley 166
Bader, Jeffrey A. 52
balance of power 9, 11, 66, 68, 134, 135–6, 139, 140, 203, 229, 230
Ball, Desmond 24, 27, 29, 113, 114
Bateman, Sam 24
BBC (British Broadcasting Corporation) 7, 8, 57, 94, 105, 177, 227
Bennett, B. and Lind, J. 178
Benvenuti, Andrea x, 15–23
Berger, Thomas U. 139
Berkofsky, Axel x, 142–52
Berkshire Millar, J. 159
Bermudez Jr, Joseph 198
Best, A., Hanhimäki, J.M., Maiolo, J.A. and Schulze, K.E. 21
Biden, Joe 218
bilateral trade: Japan and China 137; North Korea and China 165; Taiwan and China 114, 115; United States and East Asia 210–11; *see also* trade
Bitzinger, R.A. and Raska, M. 77
Bitzinger, Richard A. xi, 71–80
Black Island Youth Alliance 115
Blanchard, B. and Mogato, M. 96
Blanchard, B. and Ruwitch, J. 97
Bland, Ben 53
Bloomberg 4, 7, 26, 29, 227
Bōei Kenkyūjō, 154
Bower, Ernest 73
Branigan, T. and Farrell, P. 107
Branigan, Tania 183
brinkmanship 3, 7, 11, 24–5, 26, 31, 174, 197, 224, 226, 229; *see also* North Korea
Brunei 51, 73, 74, 91, 207
Bush, George W. (and administration of) 68, 74, 160, 204, 216, 226
Bush, Richard C. 64, 65, 84, 85, 133
Buszynski, Leszek 92
Buzo, Adrian 176
Byman, D. and Lind, J. 191, 192

cable-cutting events, destabilizing effects of 94–5
Cairo Declaration (1943) 83
Cambodia 5, 52–3, 57n1, 207
Cardin, Benjamin 217
Carter, Ashton B. 5
Carter, Jimmy 182
Castro, De E. and Ng, R. 95
Central Documents Study Office (CDSO) 37
Central Intelligence Agency (CIA) 193
Central People's Government (China) 111, 114
Cha, V. and Anderson, N. 191, 192, 197

Cha, V. and Kim, E. 186
Cha, Victor 176, 193
Chai, Winberg 217
Chalk, Peter 103
Chan, Minnie 94
Chan, Steve 209, 225
Chan Zuichan 156
Chance, D. and Stewart, P. 185
Chang, R. and Wang, C. 115
Chang Wanquan 217
Chao Chien-Min 114
Chase, Michael S. 125
Chelton, Simon 147
Chen, D. and Wang, J. 205
Chen, Dean P. 111, 115, 116, 117
Chen, Ian T.Y. and Yang, A.H. 104
Chen Jian 16, 17, 18, 19
Chen Shaofeng 102, 106
Chen Shui-bian 10
Cheonan incident 7, 8, 26, 194, 197
Chiang Kai-shek 83
Chiang Min-hua 115, 228
China, People's Republic of (PRC): A2/AD focus, US concerns about 5, 75–6; Academy of Military Science and Chinese Communist Party Central Documents Studies Office (AMS–CDSO) 37; air defence identification zone (ADIZ) 56–7, 143, 151n4, 160; amelioration of strategic concerns about Malacca Strait 105–7, 109; anti-Japanese nationalism in 9, 25, 57, 81, 230; Army Construction Institute of NDU 37; ASEAN–China Cooperation Partnership (2014) 97; Asia-Pacific region, strengths and influence in 63–4, 66; assertiveness of, constraints on 62–5; balance of power In East Asia, shift towards 9; bilateral relations with Japan, territorial disputes and changes in 84–7; Central Documents Study Office (CDSO) 37; Central People's Government 111, 114; China–Japan–South Korea Trilateral Cooperation Dialogue 137; China Maritime Surveillance and China Fishery Law Enforcement Command 40; combat aircraft development 27–8; Commerce Ministry 114; communist movement in Asia, claims for leadership of 18–19; cultivation of ties between ASEAN and 98–9; Cultural Revolution in 18, 19; Declaration of Code of Conduct with regarding South China Sea with ASEAN 38, 51–2, 96–7; destabilizing potential 15–16; Diaoyu/Senkaku Islands, Sino–Japanese relations and dispute over 55–6, 81–9; domestic constraints on recognition of Taiwan sovereignty 116–17; domestic preoccupations 63; East Asia policy since 2009 of 51–7; economic and security policies, US in hyperbolic attacks on 61; economic integration

with world trade 38; economic rise of 5; e-passport map (and diplomacy concerning) 96; externalization of threats to 98; far seas capabilities 45–7; *Fen Fa You Wei,* approach of 206; fenqing (angry young people), rise of 97–8; Five Joint Implementation Regulations, Tiawan and 114–15; fluid assertiveness of, growth of 92–7, 99; Foreign Affairs Ministry 56, 83, 91, 94, 96, 216; future Asian dynamics and 66–9; future role in East Asia 203–11; General Political Department (GPD) 39; geopolitical concerns of, Taiwan and 111; Germany, pre-1945 power trajectory and, parallels between 15, 21–2; Hainan Provincial People's Congress offshore border defence and security management law 96; impact on Asian security of naval modernizations of 48–9; Indian Ocean, requirement for naval bases in 40–41; information-based system of systems operations (ISSSO) 41–3, 44, 45–6, 48; international affairs, place and role in 15–16; International Relations (IR) Theory in 67; Japan and, Cold War normalization of relations between 19–20; Japan and, tensions between 8–10, 11; Korean War involvement 17, 18; 'leapfrogging development,' notion of 37; Malacca Strait and 102–9; Malaysian Airlines MH370, Malacca Strait and search for 107–8, 109; Marine Surveillance fleet 55; maritime claims, assertiveness over 111–12; maritime interests of, emergence of 39; Maritime Silk Road, proposal for 97; Maritime Surveillance and China Fishery Law Enforcement Command 40; military balance between Taiwan and 112–14, 117–18; military developments in, quality and quantity of 30; military modernization 37; military power of 5, 6; Ministry of National Defense 112, 113, 114, 121, 124, 125–6, 128; mutual interdependence with US 63; National Defense White Paper (NDWP) 39–40; National Offshore Oil Corporation (CNOOC) 95; National People's Congress 112, 119; National Security Committee (NSC), setting up of 206; nationalism in 5, 31, 93; naval capability, evolution of 45–8, 48–9; naval modernization 6, 37–49; naval strategy, evolution of 38–45; naval strategy, Hu Jintao's contributions to 38–9, 48; near seas capabilities 47–8; near seas missions, prioritization of 40–41; North Korea, continuing support for 190; North Korea, policy choices on 170–71; North Korea, pragmatic approach to 166–7; North Korea nuclear issue for 53–4, 57; Obama government policy and competition with 61–2; pivot back to Asia for, Sino–US relations and 71–9, 88; PLAAF (PLA Air Force) 38, 122; PLAN (PLA Navy) assets 122; PLAN (PLA Navy) capabilities, new developments in 46–7; PLAN (PLA Navy) missions in near and far seas 38, 39–40, 41, 48–9, 160; PLAN (PLA Navy) operations, conduct of 41–5; PLAN (PLA Navy) operations, RoCN capabilities against 126; policy on South China Sea, conceptualization of 91–2, 98–9; position in Asia-Pacific, insecurity of 63–4; power relations with US, building new model for 208–11; preferential economic agreements, Taiwan and 114–16, 118; problem of Taiwan for 10–11, 26, 38–9; 'reactive assertiveness,' policy of 92, 93–4, 95; regime survival, CCP objective of 111; regional territorial disputes, policy shift on 62; relations with neighbours in East Asia, management of 206–8, 211; relationships with, measurement of 64–5; restructuring initiatives 98; reunification with Taiwan, aim of 10, 11, 26, 38, 40, 114, 123, 217, 225, 228; Review News Agency (CRNA) 41; rise in power of, change in East Asia and 204–6, 211; rise of, power relations and 65, 86–7; shipbuilding in 47–8; Sino–Japanese relations 8, 25–6, 51, 54–7, 81, 84–5, 86, 140, 227; Sino-Japanese Treaty of Peace and Friendship (1978) 83; Sino–Japanese two-way trade, growth of 84–5; Sino–Japanese Wars 25, 82; Sino–Soviet tensions 19; Sino–US relations 16, 19, 61, 77–8, 203, 204, 205, 208–9, 210–11; South China Sea, assertion of claims to 4, 91–9; South China Sea activities of, domestic rationale for 97–8, 99; South China Sea dispute, fluid assertiveness in 91–9; South China Sea issue for 51–3, 57; South Korea–China trade volume 63; State Council Information Office 76; strategic importance of Malacca Strait to 103–5, 108–9; systems operations, information-based system of (ISSSO) 41–3, 44, 45–6, 48; Taiwan, strategy towards 111–18; Taiwan–China, imbalance of military capabilities between 11, 111–13, 117–18, 121, 122–3, 128; *Tao Guang Yang Hui,* principles of 205, 206, 211n1; territorial disputes, non-yielding stance on 86–7; traditional active defence strategy (TADS) 41, 43–5; Treaty of Amity and Cooperation with ASEAN 38, 99; turning points in US–China relations 60; United States and, strategic rivalry between 4–6, 11, 60–69; US–China Economic and Security Review Commission 122; US geopolitical contest with 4–5; US leadership, in shadow of 65; US strategic rebalance, perspectives on 93–4

China Can Say No (Zhang, Z.Z. et al.) 5
China Defense 45
China Dream (Liu Mingfu) 5

Index

China factor, Japanese military rebalancing and 159–61
China Is Unhappy (Song, Q. et al.) 5
China.com.cn 45
Choe, S.-H. and Perlez, J. 54
Choe Sang-hun 184
Chongkittavon, Kavi 4
Chosun Ilbo 29
Chun Yung-woo 165
Cliff, R., Burles, M., Chase, M.S., Eaton, D. and Pollpeter, K.L. 123
Clinton, Bill (and administration of) 68
Clinton, Hillary 51, 87, 88
CNN 7, 10, 26, 226, 227, 228, 230
CNTV 94
Code for Unplanned Encounters at Sea 88
Cody, Edward 84
Cold War 21, 24, 26, 31, 60, 63, 78, 83, 85, 183, 190, 193, 216, 220, 225, 226, 228, 229; arms race in East Asia 24, 26, 31; conflict in East Asia, prospects for 5, 8, 9, 10; East Asia (1949–89) 16–20; East Asia and end of 20–21; Japan, defence challenges for 157, 159, 161; United States, future role in East Asia for 209, 210, 211
Cole, Michael J. 115, 117, 124
command, control, communications, computers, intelligence, surveillance and reconnaissance (C4ISR) capabilities 114, 126
Commerce Ministry in China 114
competitive action-reaction dynamic 26–30
conflict in East Asia, key areas of 225–8
Constitutional revisionism in Japan 144
constructive engagement with China, US policy of 61, 62
'counter-China' feature of US pivot policy 72–3, 78–9
(USS) *Cowpens* incident 49
Cross-Strait Services Trade Agreement (CSSTA) 115, 117, 228
Cui, T. and Pang, H. 210
Cui Tiankai 216, 217
Cultural Revolution in China 18, 19
Cumings, Bruce 172, 176

Daily Telegraph 5, 226
Daly, John 207
Dan, X. and Ning, J. 44
De Gaulle, Charles 175
Declaration on the Conduct of the Parties in the South China Sea (2002) 38, 51–2, 96–7
Defence Talk 6
Defense Authorization Act (US, 2013) 88
Defense News 6, 28, 123, 228
Defense Secretary in US, Office of 4–5, 75
Del Rosario, Albert 53, 220
Delisle, Jacques 51
Democratic Progressive Party (DPP) in Taiwan 10, 228
Dempsey, Martin 215
Deng, Shasha 116
Deng Xiaoping 19, 20, 37, 83, 91, 114, 205, 206, 211, 211n2
Dent, Christopher M. 114
Department of Defense in US 71, 72–3, 76–7, 112, 113, 122, 123, 190, 214, 225
DePillis, Lydia 73
destabilizing potential of China 15–16
destroyers 6, 11, 29, 30, 38, 46–7, 48, 127–8, 135, 155, 214
Deutsche Presse Agentur 219
Diaoyu/Senkaku Islands 8–9; bilateral diplomatic dialogue on, need for encouragement of 88–9; conflict over, US responses to 56; deadlock over, prospects for resolution of 88–9; dispute about, contentious issues underlying 82, 86; dispute over, Japan and 147–8; history of dispute over 82–4; Sino–Japanese relations and dispute over 55–6, 81–9; sovereignty over, historic claims of 82–3; stalemate in confrontation over 85; United States and, role in dispute over 87–8
Dillon, Dana R. 91
Ding, Arthur S. 225
Disraeli, Benjamin 15
Dittmer, Lowell 116
Dobbins, James 226
Dokdo-Takeshima controversy 26, 187
Donilon, Tom 73
Dower, John W. 158
Du, Juan 107
Dua, Nusa 116

East Asia: armaments, rapid rise in quality and quality of 30–31; arms race in 24–5; implications of 31; Asian conflict, prevention of 228–30; China's future role in 203–11; Chinese policy on (since 2009) 51–7; Cold War in (1949–89) 16–20; competitive action-reaction dynamic 26–30; conflict and cooperation in, decline of Japan and consequences for 133–40; conflict in, key areas of 225–8; defence spending in 24–5; East China Sea and future role of China in 203, 204, 205, 206, 210; end of Cold War and 20–21; future dynamics in Asia, determinants of 66–7; impact of regional conflict in 3–4; inter-state antagonisms 25–6; inter-state investment and trade relations in 214–15; international relations of, historical perspective on 15–22; major weapons systems in (2013) 28; naval arms race in 29–30; next war in, prospects for 224–5; political dynamics post-Cold War in 20–21; prevention of war in 224–30; regional institutions, weaknesses of

31; security of, impact of Chinese naval modernizations of 48–9; South China Sea and future role of China in 203, 204, 205, 206–7, 210; strategic and economic importance of 6; tensions in, nature of 3–4, 11; threat from North Korea to 7–8, 11, 173–5, 178–9; US future role in 214–22; US response to China in 71–9; US strategy in, role of China in 215–17

East China Sea 21, 24–5, 31, 55–6, 61–2, 71, 76, 78, 98, 104, 133, 143–4, 145, 147–8, 153, 160, 161, 215, 218, 225; future role of China in East Asia and 203, 204, 205, 206, 210; Malacca Strait, China and 8–10, 81, 82, 83, 84–5, 88; oil and gas resources in 8, 83, 114; Taiwan, China and 111, 113, 116–17, 118; tensions in 8–10, 81, 82, 83, 84–5, 88; *see also* Diaoyu/Senkaku Islands

Easton, Ian 111
Economic Cooperation Framework Agreement (ECFA) between China and Taiwan 114–15
economic interdependence, power of 21–2
economic prospects for North Korea 166–70, 190, 196–7
economic rise of China 4, 5, 21, 86–7, 116, 133–4, 225
The Economist 9, 52, 115, 144, 150
Efimova, Larisa 16
Eisenhower, Dwighyt D. (and administration of) 17
Election Study Center in Taiwan 116–17
electronic warfare (EW) 27, 28, 46, 125
Emmers, Ralf 105
Enav, Peter 124
e-passport map (and diplomacy concerning) 96
Era Survey Research Center in Taiwan 117
Erickson Andrew S. 111
European Commission 193
exclusive economic zones (EEZs) 39, 40, 52, 83, 84, 91, 95

Farole, Thomas 168
fast attack aircraft (FACs) 47, 48
Fatton, Lionel Pierre 152
Fearon, James D. 204
Federal News Service 219
Fedorova, Maria 84
Feng, L., Zichuan, G. and Tingzhi, D. 40
Feng, Liang 47
fenqing (angry young people), rise in China of 97–8
Fenton, Damien 17
Fiefield, Anna 181
finance and trade, interdependent nature of 21
Financial Times 4, 11, 150, 227
Fingar, Thomas 22
Fisher, R.D. and O'Connor, S. 127
fishing in South China Sea, China's unilateral ban on 94

Five Joint Implementation Regulations, Tiawan and China 114–15
Flightglobal 27, 29
Foreign Affairs 173, 182
Foreign Affairs Ministry of Japan 8, 135, 145
Foreign Relations of the United States 220
Fox News 8, 96
Frank, Ruediger 167
Fravel, Taylor M. 83, 92, 96, 207
free trade, Chinese support for 66, 68
French Revolution 15
Friedberg, Aaron L. 4, 62, 66, 81
Friedrich, C. and Brzezinski, Z. 175
frigates 6, 29, 40, 46–7, 48, 56, 126, 127, 160, 194
Friman, R.H., Katzenstein, P.J., Leheny, D. and Okawara, N. 139
Fu Ying 54
Fullilove, Michael 221

Gao Jianjun 82
Garver, John 63
Gause, Ken 191
Gayduk, Ilya V. 16, 17
Gendercide.org 25
General Political Department (GPD) in China 39
geopolitical concerns for Taiwan and China 111
Germany: assertive power (pre-1945) of 15; pre-1945 power trajectory and, parallels with China 21–2
Gertz, Bill 9, 228
Ghosh, Nirmal 52
Gienger, Viola 123
Glaser, Charles 123
global economy, Asian centrality within 3–4
Global Times 94, 98, 99
Global Trends 2010 (National Intelligence Council) 190
Glosserman, Brad 31
Gordon, Bernard 74
Gormley, D.M., Erickson, A.S. and Jingdong, Y. 122
Gray, Colin 25
The Great Illusion (Angell, N.) 21
Green, Michael 160
Green, M.J. and Hornung, J.W. 146
Gregg, Donald 182
Grønning, Bjørn Elias Mikalsen 86, 154, 157
Guancha.cn 45
The Guardian 7, 29, 57n4, 109, 184

Hagel, C. and Wanquan, C. 193
Hagel, Chuck 72, 215, 217
Haggard, S. and Noland, M. 193
Hagström, Linus 84
Hainan Provincial People's Congress offshore border defence and security management law 4, 96, 99, 106
Hakubun Shimomura 151

237

Index

Hamisevicz, Nicolas 183
Han Yong-sup 8
Hanhimäki, Jussi M. 19
Harden, Blaine 192, 194
Harlan, Chico 55
Harrison, Selig S. 84
Harry, R. Jade 82, 83
Hastings, Justin V. xi, 102–10
Hatton, Celia 54
He, K. and Fung, H. 86
He Yafei 54
He Yinan 85
helicopter carriers 28, 29, 30, 77
helicopter-carrying frigates 194
helicopters 10, 25, 26, 29, 45, 126, 154, 155; attack helicopters 106, 109, 126
Heo, Uk and Roehrig, T. 193
Herring, George C. 20
Hickey, Dennis V. 126
The Hindu 41
historical revision, Japanese advocacy for 142–3
Ho Chi Minh 16
Hokama Shukichi 156
Holmes, James R. 126
Holmes, J.R. and Yoshihara, T. 105, 122
Hong Kong, return to Chinese control of 112, 114, 116
Hong Lei 94, 96
Honolulu Star-Advertiser 6
Hook, G.D., Gilson, J., Hughes, C.W. and Dobson, H. 137
Hook, Glenn D. 86
Hookway, James 95
Horn of Africa, Chinese engagement with 105
Hornby, Lucy 56
Hsu, Kimberly 28
Hu, Richard Weixing xi, 203–13
Hu Jintao 37, 38, 39, 41, 48, 52, 57n1, 85, 111, 204, 205, 206
Huang Binbin 41
Huang Yukon 97
Huffington Post 6
Hughes, Christopher 3, 8
Hughes, Christopher W. xi–xii, 133–41
Huo, Y. and Cui, X. 94
'hyper-power,' US emergence as 20

IHT Rendezvous 9, 227
India 5, 64, 66, 71, 105, 138, 187, 193, 204, 226; International Relations (IR) Theory in 67
Indian Ocean, Chinese requirement for naval bases in 40–41
Indochina, US involvement in 18–19
Indonesia 19, 66, 67, 96, 104; Foreign Affairs Ministry 106; International Relations (IR) Theory in 67; littoral state of Malacca Strait 103; Natuna Islands 91, 103, 106

information-based system of systems operations (ISSSO) 41–3, 44, 45–6, 48
Inquirer 95
inter-Korean relations, Park Geun-hye and new approach to: South Korea 181–2
inter-state antagonisms in East Asia 25–6
InterAksyon 97
InterMedia 196
international affairs, Chinese place and role in 15–16
International Crisis Group (ICG) 3, 7, 9, 10, 52, 84, 88, 92, 143, 174, 226, 227
International Institute of Strategic Studies (IISS) 6, 8, 11, 24, 27, 28, 29, 84, 112, 113, 126, 145, 194
International Military Tribunal for the Far East 142
international relations, historical perspective on 15–22
International Relations (IR) Theory 67
Ishiba Shigeru 158, 219
Ishihara Shintaro 133, 208, 227
Itsunori Onodera 55

Jacobson, Linda 64
Jacques, Martin 25
Jane's Sentinel Security Assessment 195
Jang Song-thaek 54, 165, 166, 187, 192, 194, 226, 230
Japan 62; Air Self-Defence Forces 55; alliance relations, consolidation of 157–9; Allied Air-Sea Battle (ASB) concept for 77; apologies for wartime aggression (again) 145; ASEAN–Japan Summit (2013) 56; bilateral relations with China, territorial disputes and changes in 84–7; China and, Cold War normalization of relations between 19–20; China and, tensions between 8–10, 11; China factor, military rebalancing and 159–61; China–Japan–South Korea Trilateral Cooperation Dialogue 137; collective amnesia concerning Second World War 25–6, 86; 'collective response,' pursuit of policy of 145–6, 146–7; collective self-defence, rights to 149–50; colonial mentality, accusation of 55; Constitutional revisionism 144; decline of, consequences for conflict and cooperation in East Asia 133–40; 'declinist' theses of, interest in 133–4; defence of, future challenges for 161; defence policy 145–6, 153–61; Democratic Party of Japan (DPJ) 136, 138, 147–8, 153, 154, 156, 159, 160; Diaoyu/Senkaku Islands, Sino–Japanese relations and dispute over 55–6, 81–9; Diaoyu/Senkaku Islands dispute, defence cooperation and 147–8; export of firepower from 148; Foreign Affairs Ministry 8, 135, 145; foreign direct investment (FDI) from 137, 138; Fukushima Daiichi nuclear power plant 135; Futenma Marine Corps Air Station 158;

government-sponsored nationalism 143–4; historical revision, advocacy for 142–3; International Relations (IR) Theory in 67; Japanese Self-Defence Forces (JSDF) 136–7, 146, 147; Joint Dynamic Defence Force (JDDF) 136; Kōmeitō Party 149–50, 153; Liberal Democratic Party (LDP) 136, 138, 142, 149, 150, 151n5, 153, 158, 159, 161; Maritime Self-Defence Force (MSDF) 155–6; Meiji Restoration (1868) 25, 82; Mid-term Defence Plan (MTDP) 148–9, 154–5; militarism of Second World War, whitewashing of 142, 144; military developments in, quality and quantity of 30; military modernization 154–5; Ministry of Defence 136; Mutual Security Treaty with US (1961) 8, 9, 87–8, 155, 158, 228; Nanking Massacre (1937) 85, 144, 151n5; National Defence Programme Guidelines (NDPG) 136, 148, 154, 155; National Security Council (NSC) 154; nationalism, military rebalancing and 159; nationalism and revisionism in 142–50; neo-liberal institutionalism in, logic of 137–8; neo-liberal perspective and decline of 140; neo-realism and decline of 134–5, 135–6; Nippon Kaigi 143, 151n7; 'normative constructivism' and decline of 138–9, 140; North Korea, prospects for investment from 169; oil dependency of 83–4; pacifism of, support for 150; power transitions and decline of 134–7, 139–40; realism and decline of 134–7, 139–40; regional cooperation and conflict, ramifications of decline of Japan for 134; regional power, failure post-Cold War to consolidate as 20; regional power, failure to consolidate as 20; regional security cooperation, expansion plans for 148–9; regional stability, outlook for role in 139–40; Ryukyu Archipelago, militarization of 155–7; Sino–Japanese relations 8, 25–6, 51, 54–7, 81, 84–5, 86, 140, 227; Sino-Japanese Treaty of Peace and Friendship (1978) 83; Sino–Japanese two-way trade, growth of 84–5; Sino–Japanese Wars 25, 82; Sino–Japanese arms race 136; South Korea and, relations between 26; South Korean sex slaves 145; US forces in (2013) 6; US–Japan alliance, lynchpin of regional architecture 218–19; US–Japan Guidelines for Defence Cooperation 146
Japan Times 9, 148, 218, 228
Jervis, Robert 31, 175
Jiang Z. and Hu J. 39
Jiang Zemin 37, 38, 39, 41, 42, 205
Jinji Koga 87
Johnson, C., Bower, E.Z., Cha, V.D., Green, M.J. and Goodman, M.P. 205
Johnson, Lyndon B. (and administration of) 18

joint strike fighter (JSF) 27–8, 29, 30
Jones, D.M. and Khoo, N. 52
Jones, Matthew 17

Kaiman, Jonathan 98
Kan, Shirley A. 113, 122, 123, 125, 128
Kang, David 51
Karotkin, Jesse L. 216
Kasiviswanathan, Shanmugam 52
Katz, Richard 143
Katzenstein, P.J. and Okawara, N. 139
Kawashima Shin 82, 83
Kazakhstan 106–7
Kazuo Komada 55
Keck, Zachary 103, 106
Kelsey, Jane 74
Kennedy, John F. 217
Keohane, R. and Nye, J. 137
Kerry, John 167
Kersten, Rikki 230
Keyser, Don 61
Khoo, Nicholas xii, 31, 51–9
Khrushchev, Nikita 18
Kim, C. and Yoon, S. 181
Kim, J. and Negishi, M. 184
Kim, Jong Il 170
Kim, S.H., Roehrig, T. and Seliger, B. 191
Kim Dae-jung 178, 182, 183
Kim family (and regime) 165, 186, 192, 194, 195, 197
Kim Il-sung 173, 174, 176, 191
Kim Jong-il 26, 54, 173, 182, 191, 192, 226
Kim Jong-un 7, 26, 54, 165–70, 173–5, 181, 183, 185, 187, 190, 192, 193, 195, 226, 229, 230
Kissinger, Henry 15, 18, 19
Kleine-Ahlbrandt, Stephanie 92
Koo Min Gyo 85
Kopp, Carlo 27
Kor Kian Beng 107
Korea Times 7
Korean Central News Agency (KCNA) 176
Korean War (1950–53) 3, 7, 16–17, 26, 31, 176, 182, 185, 194, 217, 219, 221, 226, 227; Chinese involvement in 17, 18; 'game-changer' in East Asia for US 17
Koshiro Yukiko 133
Kraska, James 225
Kraus, C., Radchenko, S. and Kanda, Y. 85, 86
Krepinevich, Andrew F. 75
Kretchun, N. and Kim, J. 196
Kuomintang (KMT) in Taiwan 10, 26, 111–12, 115, 117, 228
Kupchan, Charles 209
Kwon, H. and Chung, B.-H. 185
Kydd, Andrew H. 204, 209
Kyodo Press 56

Index

Lampton, David M. 81, 88, 210
land attack cruise missiles (LACMs) 46, 75, 113, 122
Landing, R., Pilling, D. and Soble, J. 53
landing ships 11, 28
Lankov, Andrei 192, 196
Lanteigne, Marc 103
Larson, Charles R. 216
Lawrence, Susan 66
'leapfrogging development,' notion of 37
Lee, Peter 88
Lee, S. and Schreer, B. 113, 125
Lee, Sheryn xii, 111–20
Lee Kuan Yew 19
Lee Myung-bak 26, 178, 182, 184
Lee Teng Hui 217
Levy, Jack S. 134
Li, Mingjiang xii, 91–101
Li, N. and Weuve, C. 45
Li, Nan xii, 37–50
Li Badong 55
Li Jianwei 92, 94
Li Ming Jiang 99, 99n1
Li Yitan 111
Liberation Army Daily 46
Lieberthal, K. and Wang, J. 61, 209
Lim, B. and Rajagopalan, M. 98
Limaye, Satu 64
Lin Dong 41, 42
Liu, D.-N. and Shih, H.-T. 115
Liu Fang 37, 44
Liu Huaqing 38, 43
Liu Xiaoming 227
Locklear, Robert 220
Logevall, Frederik 16
Loh Ming Hui Dylan xii, 91–101
Long Tao 94
Los Angeles Times 218
Lovell, Julia 98
Lu, Y.-c., ParkByuang K. and Tsai, T.-c. 169
Luke, Leighton 105
Luo Xiangde 43

Ma Keqing 53
Ma Ying-jeou (and administration of) 10, 38, 39, 111, 115, 117, 123, 128
Macau, return to Chinese control of 112, 114, 116
McCormack, G. and Norimatsu, S.O. 158
McCormack, Gavan 156
McCurry, J. and Branigan, T. 173
McDevitt, Michael 78, 82, 83, 84
McEachern, Patrick 191
Mack, Andrew 173
McMahon, Robert J. 18
Macmillan, Margaret 15
Mainland Affairs Council in Taiwan 115
Makino Yoshihiro 145

Malacca Strait: amelioration by China of strategic concerns about 105–7, 109; China and 102–9; China and, concerns for ASEAN 104, 106; East China Sea and 8–10, 81, 82, 83, 84–5, 88; geostrategic liabilities posed by 106–7; important Chinese trade route 105–7, 109; military presence of US 104–5; South China Sea and 102, 103, 104–5, 106, 109; strategic importance to China 103–5, 108–9
Malaysia 4, 18, 19, 51, 73, 91, 104, 207; International Relations (IR) Theory in 67; littoral state of Malacca Strait 103; Malaysian Airlines flight MH370 49, 102, 103, 107–8, 109
Manchuria 81, 83, 151n8
Manyin, Mark E. 83, 87, 88
Manyin, M.E., Chanlett-Avery, E., Rinehart, I. E., Nikitin, M.B. and Cooper, W.H. 214, 219
Mao Zedong 17, 18, 60, 206, 215, 217
Marine Surveillance fleet 55
maritime claims, Chinese assertiveness over 111–12
Maritime Cooperation Fund, China and ASEAN 96
maritime interests of China, emergence of 39
Maritime Silk Road, Chinese proposal for 97
Martina, Michael 98
Maull, Hans W. 133
Mearsheimer, John J. 123, 134, 204
Medeiros, E. and Taylor, F. 51
Medeiros, Evan S. 71
medium-range ballistic missiles (MRBMs) 122, 184, 186, 195
Meidan, Michal 106
Meiji Restoration (1868) in Japan 25, 82
Midford, Paul 136
Mie, A. and Yoshida, R. 158
Military-Today 29
Miller, Robert 22n1
Ming Wan 57
Mingfu, Colonel Liu 5
Ministerial Meeting (AMM) in Phnom Penh (2012) 52–3
Ministry of Defence in Japan 136
Ministry of National Defense in China 112, 113, 114, 121, 124, 125–6, 128
Minnick, Wendell 126
Montgomery, Evan Braden 122
Moon Chung-In 178
Moore, Gregory 85
Moyar, Mark 18
Mukden Incident (1931) 81
multi-role combat aircraft 27, 76
Murphy, Ann Marie 91
Murray, William 123, 124, 125
Mutual Defence Treaty with US (Taiwan, 1954) 10, 217
Mutual Security Treaty with US (Japan, 1961) 8, 9, 87–8, 155, 158, 228
Myanmar 5, 106–7, 207, 208

Index

Nanking Massacre (1937) 85, 144, 151n5
Narusawa Muneo 144
Nasr, Alexander 9
Nathan, A.J. and Scobell, A. 112
Nathan, Andrew J. 62
The National 28
National Defense White Paper (NDWP) 39–40
National People's Congress in China 112, 119
nationalism 82, 85, 93, 224; anti-Japanese nationalism in China 9, 25, 57, 81, 230; Chinese nationalism 5, 9, 11, 21, 25, 31, 57, 93, 97, 112, 116, 118, 160, 203, 205, 211, 227, 228, 230; clash between China and Japan of 208; government-sponsored nationalism in Japan 143–4; Japanese military rebalancing and 138, 159; Korean nationalism 177, 191; revisionism in Japan and 9, 139, 142–50; Taiwanese nationalism 116, 118
Natsios, Natsios 173
Natuna Islands, Indonesia 91, 103, 106
Nau, H. and Ollapally, D. 67
naval arms race in East Asia 29–30
NBC News 9
neo-liberal perspective and decline of Japan 137–8, 140
Networked Integrated Attack-in-Depth strategy 75
New York Times 3, 26, 216, 229, 230
New Zealand 17, 73, 74, 104; ANZUS (Australia–New Zealand–USA) Treaty (1951) 220–21
News China 28
Nikkei Shimbun 150
Nippon Kaigi 143, 151n7
Niu Jun 16
Nixon, Richard M. (and administration of) 19, 60, 182, 215
Nobusuke Kishi 144, 151n8
Noda Yoshihiko (and government of) 85, 88
Noel, Pierre 106
Noland, Marcus 168, 173, 190
'normative constructivism' and decline of Japan 138–9, 140
North Atlantic Treaty Organization (NATO) 5, 219
North-East Asia 62, 174, 176, 177–8, 183, 187
North Korea: Agreed Framework with US 173, 174; behaviour of, explanation of 175–7; brinkmanship of 3, 7, 24–5, 26, 31, 174, 197, 226, 229; China, continuing support from 190; China, nuclear issue for 53–4, 57; China, policy choices on 170–71; China, pragmatic approach to 166–7; China, trade partnership with 193–4; demise of, predictions of 190; diversification from economic linkage to China 168; economic continuity, prospects for 193–4; economic prospects 166–70; economic reform and pressure from below, prospect of 190, 196–7; information control, impact of loss of 190, 196; inter-Korean relations 26, 181–2; internal economy 167; Japan, prospects for investment from 169; Korean People's Air Force (KPAF) 194–5; Korean People's Army (KPA) 173, 174, 191, 192, 194, 197; Korean Workers Party (KWP) 191, 192, 197; military continuity, prospects for 194–5; miscalculation by, prospect of 190, 197; National Defense Commission 191; 'North Korean Spring,' hopes for 192; nuclear weapons, development of 7, 8, 27, 30, 54, 165, 170, 173, 174–5, 176–7, 192, 194, 195, 197, 215, 226; paradox of 178–9; political continuity, prospects for 191–3, 197; power consolidation by Kim Jong-un in 165–6; provocation from, prospect of war with South Korea and 7–8; public distribution system (PDS) in 193, 196; regional powers and 177–8; regional security, management of threat from 172–9; resilience of 172–3, 179, 197–8; Russia, prospect for expansion of trade with 168–9; Russia, prospects of trade with 168–9; Sino–North Korean relations 54; South Korea, prospects for harmonization with 169–70; special economic zones (SEZs) 167–8; threat from 7–8, 11; threat from, nature of 173–5, 178–9; trust and constancy in policy of South Korea towards 182–3; United States and, impasse between 7, 170; weaknesses of 172; weapons of mass destruction (WMD) programme 164–5, 167, 168, 174, 175, 177–8; Yongbyon nuclear reactor 185, 195
nuclear weapons: deterrent use of, US consideration of 17; North Korea and development of 7, 8, 27, 30, 54, 165, 170, 173, 174–5, 176–7, 192, 194, 195, 197, 215, 226; powers in possession of 3, 31, 224; Six-Party talks on North Korea's programme for 31, 53–4, 164, 174, 177, 204; South Korea and options for 175, 186; Taiwan and acquisition of 112
Nye, Joseph 218

Obama, Barack (and administration of) 5, 7, 21, 53, 56, 60, 63, 65, 66, 68, 69, 72, 74, 88, 123, 126, 158, 185, 187, 204, 212n3, 214, 216, 218–20, 224, 226; policy and competition with China 61–2
Oberdorfer Don 177
Oh, K.D. and Hassig, R. 196
oil and gas resources: East China Sea 8, 83, 114; Japan, oil dependency of 83–4; South China Sea 4, 94
Okinawa Main Island 155–6, 160
Okinawa Prefecture 82, 136
Okinawa Reversion Treaty (1971) 83, 87
OkinawaTaimusu 157

241

Index

O'Neil, Andrew xii, 172–80
Ong, Graham Gerard 103
Operational Control during Wartime (OPCON) 219
Orendain, Simone 97
Organization for Security and Cooperation in Europe (OSCE) 183
Organski, A.F.K. 4
O'Rourke, Ronald 5, 113, 123
Osama bin Laden 208

Pacific Command, Hawaii 6, 216, 220
Pacific Ocean 74, 160
pacifism: of Japan, support for 143, 150, 158; 'proactive pacifism,' establishment of 154
Pakistan 208
Pan Zhongqi 82
Panetta, Leon 55
Paracel Islands 4, 52, 95, 96, 207
Park Chung-hee 181, 193
Park Geun-hye 7, 181–8, 219
Park Geun-hye's Dresden speech on relations with North Korea 183–4
Patalano, Alessio 85
Pechatnov, Vladimir O. 16
Pei, Minxin 116
People's Online Daily 10
Perlez, Jane 54, 56, 81, 97
Philippines 16, 19, 52–3, 62, 68, 72, 92, 93, 103, 106, 145, 148, 161, 205, 207, 226; China–Philippines dynamics 94–6; Enhanced Defence Cooperation Agreement with US 74; future role for US in East Asia and 214, 215, 219–20, 221; Scarborough standoff between China and 95; Second Thomas Shoal, China and disputes over 95–6, 98; typhoon destruction in 48
Philippines Daily Inquirer 220
Phipps, Gavin 113, 127
Ping, Z., Zeng, X. and Zhang, X. 42
Pingtan Comprehensive Experimental Zone 114–15
pivot back to Asia for, Sino–US relations and 71–9, 88
PLAAF (PLA Air Force) 38, 122
PLAN (PLA Navy): assets 122; capabilities, new developments in 46–7; missions in near and far seas 38, 39–40, 41, 48–9, 160; operations, conduct of 41–5; operations, RoCN capabilities against 126
political continuity, prospects for North Korea 191–3, 197
political dynamics post-Cold War in East Asia 20–21
Pollack, Jonathan 65, 174
power relations between China and US, building new model for 208–11
power transitions and decline of Japan 134–7, 139–40

preferential economic agreements, Taiwan and China 114–16, 118
Press TV 99
prevention of war in East Asia 224–30
Przystup, James 64
Pu Zhendong 64

Qiang Zhai 17, 18
Qin Jize 53
Qing Dynasty 82
Qu Jianwen 39
Quadrennial Defense Review (QDR) in Taiwan 121, 124, 125–6, 127–8
Quinjing Wanbao 95

Radio Free Asia 174
Raiwan: China-Taiwan free trade agreement (2010) 10
Rajca, Jennifer 108
Ratner, Ely 92
'reactive assertiveness,' policy 92, 93–4, 95
rebalance to Asia by US 5–6; effects of 221–2
Reed Bank incident (2011) 52
Regional Forum of ASEAN in Hanoi (2010) 52
regional power: China and power relations in East Asia 65, 86–7, 204–6, 211; Chinese relations with neighbours 64–5, 206–8, 211; cooperation and conflict, ramifications of decline of Japan for 134; engagement in East Asia, post-Cold War US failure to build on 20–21; Japan's failure post-Cold War to consolidate on 20; North Korea and 177–8; security and, management of threat from North Korea 172–9; security cooperation, Japanese expansion plans for 148–9; territorial disputes, Chinese policy shift on 62; US as security guarantor for Asia 65; weaknesses of regional institutions 31
Reilly, James 57
Ren Liansheng 39, 42
Republic of China Navy (RoCN) 122, 126, 127, 128
resilience of North Korea 172–3, 179, 197–8
reunification with Taiwan, Chinese aim of 10, 11, 26, 38, 40, 114, 123, 217, 225, 228
Reuters 6, 7, 26, 56, 157, 176, 217, 227
Ri Yong Ho 192
Rice, Susan 72, 74
Richardson, Michael 5
Ririhena, Y. and Santosa, N. 96
Roach, Stephen 63
Roehrig, Terence xiii, 190–99, 215
Rogers, William 87
Roh Moo-hyun 170, 178, 182, 183, 184
del Rosario, Albert 53, 220
Rosen, D.H. and Wang, Z. 115
Ross, Ed 126

Ross, Robert S. 78
Rozman, Gilbert 64, 67, 140
Ruane, Kevin 18
Rublee, Maria Rost 3
Rudolph, Josh 107
Russel, Daniel 57
Russia 38, 45, 82, 84, 193, 204, 218; International Relations (IR) Theory in 67; prospects of trade with North Korea 168–9
Ryall, Julian 155
Ryukyu Archipelago, militarization of 155–7
Ryūkyū Shinpō 156–7, 160

Sakishima Islands 153, 155–6, 157, 161
Salon 7
Samuels, Richard J. 135, 138, 158
San Francisco Peace Treaty (1951) 83
Sanger, David 54, 165
Sansha municipality 4, 52, 95
Santamaria, Carlos 96
Saunders, Phillip C. 62, 116, 126, 128
Savin, V. and Ouyang, C.-S. 107
Scanlon, Charles 147
Schelling, Thomas 176
Schreer, Benjamin xiii, 3, 77, 121–30, 226
Schwartz, Laura 84
Scobell, Andrew 97, 113
Seiler, Sydney A. 219
Sekiguchi Toko 86
Semple, K. and Schmittapril, E. 108
Senkaku Islands *see* Diaoyu/Senkaku Islands
Shambaugh, David 51, 60, 208
Shanker, T., Sanger, D. and Schmitt, E. 186
Shen Dingli 204
Shi Yinghong 211n2
Shimonoseki, Treaty of (1895) 25, 82
Shintaro Ishihara 81
shipbuilding in China 47–8
Shlapak, D.A., Orletsky, D.T., Reid, T.I., Tanner, M.S. and Wilson, B. 123
Shoal, James 4
short-range ballistic missiles (SRBMs) 122, 195
Shu Guan Zhang 18
Sieg, Linda 145
Siew, Vincent 116
Sigal, Leon 185
Singapore 5, 6, 19, 72, 73, 74, 77, 145, 214, 226; International Relations (IR) Theory in 67; littoral state of Malacca Strait 103–4
Sino–Japanese relations 8, 25–6, 51, 54–7, 81, 84–5, 86, 140, 227; dispute over Diaoyu/Senkaku Islands and 55–6, 81–9
Sino–Japanese Treaty of Peace and Friendship (1978) 83
Sino–Japanese two-way trade, growth of 84–5
Sino–Japanese Wars 25, 82
Sino–North Korean relations 54

Sino–Soviet tensions 19
Sino–US relations 16, 19, 61, 203, 204, 205, 208–9, 210–11; dangerous deterioration in 77–8
Six-Party talks on North Korea's programme for nuclear weapons 31, 53–4, 164, 174, 177, 204
Sky News 107
Smith, J. 226
Smith, Paul J. xiii, 214–23
Smith, Sheila A. 165
Snyder, Scott 64
Soeya Yoshihide 137
Song, Q., Huang, J., Song, X., Wang, X. and Liu, Y. 5
Soong, Grace 114
South China Morning Post 4, 155
South China Sea 5, 31, 61, 62, 64, 82, 87–8, 145, 160, 215, 216, 220, 225, 226; cable-cutting events in, destabilizing effects of 94–5; Chinese assertion of claims to 4, 91–9; Chinese policy on, conceptualization of 91–2, 98–9; dispute over, fluid assertiveness of China in 91–9; domestic rationale for activities of China in 97–8, 99; fishing in, China's unilateral ban on 94; and future role of China in East Asia 203, 204, 205, 206–7, 210; issue for China of 51–3, 57; Malacca Strait, China and 102, 103, 104–5, 106, 109; oil and gas deposits in 4, 94; Taiwan, China's strategy and 111, 113, 116–17, 118; United States pivot back to Asia and 71, 72–3, 74, 76, 78–9
South-East Asia 5, 6, 9, 16, 38, 64, 71, 77, 93, 94, 97, 145–6, 148, 169, 206, 207; economic integration with East Asia and Asia-Pacific 133–4; Malacca Strait, China and 102–4, 106, 108; North Korean nuclear issue, China and 53–4; South China Sea issue, China and 51–3; United States influence in 216, 219–20
South Korea: aid asymmetry, dangers of 183–4; China–Japan–South Korea Trilateral Cooperation Dialogue 137; Demilitarized Zone (DMZ) 184, 187; inter-Korean relations 26; Park Geun-hye and new approach to 181–2; International Relations (IR) Theory in 67; Japan and, relations between 26; Korean peninsula and US–South Korea alliance 219; military developments in, quality and quantity of 30; nuclear weapons, options for 175, 186; options for Park administration 186–8; Park Geun-hye's Dresden speech on relations with North Korea 183–4; prospects for harmonization with North Korea 169–70; provocation from North, prospect of war with 7–8, 184–5; provocations from North Korea for 184–5; Saenuri Dang (New Frontier Party) in 182–3; South Korea–China trade volume 63; trust and constancy in policy towards North Korea 182–3

243

Index

Southeast Asia Treaty Organization (SEATO) 220
Soviet Union 5, 8, 16, 17, 60, 85, 172–3, 193, 209, 215–16, 218, 226; post-Cold Wra weakness of 20; Sino–Soviet tensions 19
special economic zones (SEZs) in North Korea 167–8
Spratly Islands 38, 52, 95, 96, 207
Stalin, Josef 16
Starr, Robert 87
State Council Information Office in China 76
State Department in United States 4, 56–7, 87, 170, 209, 212n4, 225
stealth combat aircraft 6, 27, 29
Steinberg, Jonathan 15
Stokes, M. and Schriver, R. 124
Storey, Ian 51, 92
Straits Times 5, 226
Strategic Comments 5
Struckman, D. and Roehrig, T. 195
Su, J. and Low, Y.F. 123
submarines 5–6, 7, 8, 11, 26, 28, 29–30, 38, 41, 45–6, 74, 75, 76, 77, 84, 113, 122, 125–6, 135, 136, 155, 194, 216; midget submarines 7, 8, 27, 29, 227; submarine defence, Tiawan's problem of 127; *see also* anti-submarine capability
Sunohara, Tsuyoshi 154
surface combat vessels 29, 30, 76
surface-to-air missiles (SAMs) 46, 47, 154, 155
Sutter, R. and Huang, C.-H. 62
Sutter, Robert xiii–xiv, 31, 60–70, 216
Swaine, Michael D. 56, 57, 121, 124
Swenson-Wright, John xiv, 181–9
systems operations, information-based system of (ISSSO) 41–3, 44, 45–6, 48
Szecheny, N., Cha, V., Glaser, B.S., Green, M.J. and Johnson, C.K. 143

Tabuchi Hiroko 56
Taepodong missile 8, 195
Taiwan: Anti-Access/Area Denial (A2/AD) strategy for 125–7; asymmetric defence, joint efforts needed on 127–8; Black Island Youth Alliance 115; budget pressures, challenge to modernization of 123–4; China–Taiwan, imbalance of military capabilities between 11, 111–13, 117–18, 121, 122–3, 128; Chinese strategy towards 111–18; combat aircraft replacement, problem of 127; cross-Strait military balance 122–3; Cross-Strait Services Trade Agreement (CSSTA) 115, 117, 228; defence capabilities, erosion of 10–11; defence options of 121–8; defence spending, conceptual capability gap in 127; Democratic Progressive Party (DPP) in 10; demographic trends, challenge to modernization of 123–4; deterrent strategy, defence resources and 127–8; domestic challenges, military modernization and 123–4; domestic politics of, cross-Strait relations with China and 117, 118; East China Sea, China and 111, 113, 116–17, 118; Economic Cooperation Framework Agreement (ECFA) with China 114–15; Election Study Center 116–17; Era Survey Research Center 117; issue of, flashpoint in US–China relations 217–18; Kuomintang (KMT) in 10, 26, 111–12, 115, 117, 228; Mainland Affairs Council 115; military options for 124–5; Mutual Defence Treaty with US (1954) 10, 217; nuclear weapons, acquisition of 112; outlook for defence of 128; problem of 10–11, 26, 38–9; Quadrennial Defense Review (QDR) 121, 124, 125–6, 127–8; Republic of China Navy (RoCN) 122, 126, 127, 128; South China Sea, China and 111, 113, 116–17, 118; strategic challenges for 121–2; submarine defence, problem of 127; Taiwan Relations Act (US, TRA, 1979) 121
Takahashi, K. 142, 143
Takeuchi Hiroki 86
Tan, Andrew T.H. x, 3–14, 24–33, 224–31
Tang, F. and Wu, Y. 39
The Telegraph 9, 27, 227
terminal high-altitude area (THAAD) defence radar 185
Thailand 5, 18, 19, 103, 104, 215, 220, 221; littoral state of Malacca Strait 103
Thayer, Carl 74
Theisen, Nolan xiv, 164–71
Thielman, Greg 195
threat from North Korea to East Asia 7–8, 11, 173–5, 178–9
Tiankai Cui 52
Tiezzi, Shannon 74
Time 9
Tisdal, Simon 142
Tomiichi Murayama 145
Tow, William 5
trade: African trade of China, importance of 63; Asia-Pacific region, trade and investment in 63; Asian regional trade arrangements, US exclusion from 61; Asian regionalism, Chinese promotion of trade expansion and 85; bilateral trade between East Asia and US 210–11; bilateral trade between Japan and China 137; bilateral trade between North Korea and China 165; bilateral trade between Tiawan and China 114, 115; Cross-Strait Services Trade Agreement (CSSTA) 115, 117, 228; East Asia, interstate investment and trade relations in 214–15; economic interactions between North and South Korea, political reconciliation and 169–70; finance and, interdependent nature of

21; free trade, Chinese support for 66, 68; integration of Chinese economy with world trade 38; interdependent nature of Chinese trade in Asia 64; international trade of China, oil and raw materials imports and 87; Malacca Strait, important Chinese trade route 105–7, 109; North Korea and China, trade partnership between 193–4; North Korea and Russia, prospect for expansion of trade between 168–9; preferential economics and 114–16; regional affairs, trade and investment, China's role in 68; Sino–Japanese two-way trade, growth of 84–5; South Korea–China trade volume 63; Taiwan–China free trade agreement (2010) 10; Trans-Pacific Partnership (TPP) trade pact 61, 73–4, 135, 138, 214; United States, concerns about protectionism of 68; United States, intra-Asian trade and 65; United States trade in Asia, protection of 20–21; World Trade Organization (WTO) 115

traditional active defence strategy (TADS) of China 41, 43–5

Trans-Pacific Partnership (TPP) trade pact 61, 135, 138, 214; China and 73–4

Treasury Department of United States 225

Truman, Harry S. (and administration of) 17, 217

Uchiyama, K. and Nakayama, S. 187

United Nations (UN): Commission on the Limits of the Continental Shelf (UNCLCS) 52, 53; Economic Commission for Asia and the Far East (ECAFE) 83; Human Rights Council (UNHRC) 172, 190; Security Council (UNSC) Resolution 187454; Tribunal for the Law of the Sea 96

United States: Air-Sea Battle (ASB), China and 74–6; Air-Sea Battle (ASB), regional responses to 76–7, 78–9; ANZUS (Australia–New Zealand–USA) Treaty (1951) 220–21; Asian hedging with, power relations and 65; assertiveness of China towards, growth of 62; Australian–US relations and rebalance to East Asia 220–21; bilateral trade between East Asia and 210–11; China's A2/AD focus, concerns about 5, 75–6; Chinese economic and security policies, hyperbolic attacks on 61; concert of democracies in Asia idea 5; constructive engagement with China, policy of 61, 62; 'counter-China' feature of pivot policy 72–3, 78–9; Defense Authorization Act (2013) 88; Defense Secretary, Office of 4–5, 75; Department of Defense 71, 72–3, 76–7, 112, 113, 122, 123, 190, 214, 225; Diaoyu/Senkaku Islands conflict, responses to 56; Diaoyu/Senkaku Islands conflict, role in 87–8; essential economic partner for Asia 65; Foreign Relations of the 220; future Asian dynamics and 66–9; future role in East Asia 214–22; geopolitical contest with China 4–5; government engagement with Asia 65; 'hyperpower,' emergence as 20; Indochina, involvement in 18–19; International Relations (IR) Theory in 67; intra-Asian trade and 65; Japan, forces in (2013) 6; Japan–US alliance, lynchpin of regional architecture for 218–19; Japan–US Guidelines for Defence Cooperation 146; Korean peninsula and US–South Korea alliance 219; Korean War, 'game-changer' in East Asia for 17; leadership in shadow of China 65; Malacca Strait and military presence of 104–5; mutual interdependence with China 63; Networked Integrated Attack-in-Depth strategy 75; non-government engagement with Asia 65; North Korea and, impasse between 7, 170; Obama government policy and competition with China 61–2; Pacific Command, Hawaii 6, 216, 220; pivot back to Asia for, Sino–US relations and 71–9, 88; protectionism of, concerns about 68; rebalance to Asia 5–6; rebalance to Asia, effects of 221–2; regional engagement in East Asia, post-Cold War failure to build on 20–21; response to China in East Asia 71–9; security guarantor for Asia 65; Sino–US relations 16, 19, 61, 77–8, 203, 204, 205, 208–9, 210–11; Sino–US relations, dangerous deterioration in 77–8; South China Sea and pivot back to Asia 71, 72–3, 74, 76, 78–9; in South-East Asia 219–20; State Department 4, 56–7, 87, 170, 209, 212n4, 225; strategic rebalance, Chinese perspectives on 93–4; strategy in East Asia, role of China in 215–17; Taiwan issue, flashpoint in US–China relations 217–18; Taiwan Relations Act (TRA, 1979) 121; trade in Asia, protection of 20–21; Trans-Pacific Partnership (TPP) 61, 73–4, 135, 138, 214; Trans-Pacific Partnership (TPP), China and 73–4; Treasury Department 225; turning points in US–China relations 60; US–China Economic and Security Review Commission 122; US–China strategic rivalry in East Asia 4–6, 11, 60–69; White House 218

unmanned arial vehicles (UAVs) 25, 28–9

Valencia, Mark J. 83, 84

Van Tol, J., Gunzinger, M., Krepinevich, A.F. and Thomas, J. 6, 76, 226

Vasquez, John A. 207

Väyrynen, Raimo 134

Vedrine, Hubert 20

vertical launching systems (VLSs) 46

Vietnam 16, 17, 19, 51, 52, 92, 93, 103, 106, 148, 187, 205, 207, 226; China–Vietnam dynamics 94–6; future role in East Asia, US and 215, 220, 221; International Relations (IR)

245

Index

Theory in 67; North Vietnam 18; US pivot in Asia, rebalancing and 72, 73, 74; War in 24, 113, 221
Vietnam Breaking News 94
VOA News 26, 68
Vogel, Ezra 133
Vorontsov, Alexander 165, 169

Wallace, Corey 146
Wan Ming 86, 133
Wang, Chris 124
Wang Jin 47, 97
Wang Y.K. 111
Wang Yi 56, 99, 116, 216
Wang Zhang 86
WantChinaTimes 115
Warnock, Eleanor 56
Washington Post 4, 10, 218, 226, 229
weapons of mass destruction (WMD) programme in North Korea 164–5, 167, 168, 174, 175, 177–8
Welfield, John 133
Wen, Philip 108
Wen Jiabao 53, 55
Wertime, David 98
Westad, Odd Arne 16
Western Pacific Naval Symposium 88
Whaley, Floyd 53
White, Hugh 221
White House 218
Wiedemann, Kent 216
Wiegand, Krista E. 85
Wilhelm I, King of Prussia 15
Williams, Brad xiv, 153–63
Williams, Carol J. 53
Williamson, Lucy 184
Wong, Edward 52, 56, 113
World Bank 4, 103, 168, 224
World Trade Organization (WTO) 115
Wu Xinbo 112

Xi Jinping (and administration of) 54, 56, 63, 86, 98, 116, 117, 164, 186, 204, 205, 206, 209, 210, 229
Xinhua News Agency 52, 107
Xinhua newspaper 116
Xu Dai 5

Yaeyama Mainichi Shimbun 150, 157
Yahuda, Michael 16, 17, 19, 20, 21, 135, 138
Yamaguchi Jiro 159
Yamazaki Shōhei 156
Yan Xuetong 86
Yang Jiechi 52, 55
Yasukuni Shrine 56, 85, 138, 143, 154, 159, 218, 227
Yee, Andy 104
Yellow Sea 76, 194
Yeoh En-Lai 104
Yeonpyeong incident 7, 197, 227
Yi, Joseph 145
Yip, M. and Webber, C. 98
Yomiuri Shimbun 150, 155, 157
Yonaguni Island 154, 155–7, 160
Yongbyon nuclear reactor 185, 195
Yongxing (or Woody) Island 52
Yonhap 186
Yoshihara Toshi 161
You Ji 92
Yu Bin 64
Yuan, Jingdong xiv–xv, 81–90

Zha Daojiong 98
Zhang, H. and Yu, Z. 41
Zhang Jian 92
Zhang Z. Z., Tang Z., Song Q, Qiao B. and Gu Q. 5
Zhu Bangzao 10
Zhu Feng 54